P9-BYS-409

In Praise of
All You Need to Know About the Music Business

"Considered a [music] industry bible."
> —ROBERT HILBURN & CHUCK
> PHILIPS, *Los Angeles Times*

"There are a number of books like this . . . [but] Passman's is particularly accessible because it translates the whole minefield of legal terms into common English."
> —DAVID HINCKLEY, *New York
> Daily News*

"A lucid, detailed, and frequently entertaining compendium of knowledge that lives up to its title. Written with neophyte pro musicians in mind, it covers the waterfront from how to choose one's business associates to the various ways one may be screwed by one's seemingly beneficent record company. With the artist's interests forefront, but devoid of axe-grinding, most of these kernels of knowledge are not likely to date quickly, even in a biz as mercurial as pop music. If you want a thorough education in a hurry, this is the book."
> —MARK ROWLAND, *Musician*

"A must-read for aspiring rock stars, Donald S. Passman's *All You Need to Know About the Music Business* is a veritable how-to-bible. With his expert knowledge, Passman details how to negotiate record deals, calculate foreign-video royalties, and handle merchandise packages (you'll have to learn to write the hits yourself)."
> —*Details*

"An intriguing assemblage of advice and council . . . the book offers a wealth of information for young musicians, songwriters, and executives about record advances, royalty computations, cross collateralization, and other inscrutable record biz practices. . . . Not every artist has an attorney with Passman's clout, hence the value of his new book."
> —PATRICK GOLDSTEIN,
> *Los Angeles Times*

"This man is so knowledgeable that it's difficult negotiating with him. The book is terrific and a must-read if you want to know how the music business works."

—JOE SMITH, former President and CEO, Capital Records-EMI Music, Inc.

"At last, a practical musician's guide that covers *everything* an artist needs to know. . . . Before you get screwed, read Passman's primer."

—GARY CEE, *Circus*

"Essential and thorough. If only all music industry books were this instructive."

—KEVIN ZIMMERMAN, *Weekly Variety*

"There are many books available which give inside information on the music business, but few are as detailed or as enjoyable as attorney Donald Passman's *All You Need to Know About the Music Business*. This book is a vital resource of information for anyone, whether just starting out or already in the music business industry."

—SUE GOLD, *Music Paper*

"This book is an easy to understand overview of the complicated music business. Reads like Great Fiction. The great Russian novelists of the nineteenth century come to mind."

—RANDY NEWMAN

"Let it be known: Passman's [book] is the real McCoy."

—STANN FINDELLE, *Performance*

"Informative, definitive, easy to read and, as Randy Newman says, 'It reads like great fiction.' "

—JOAN TARSHIS, *Guitar for the Practicing Musician*

All You Need to Know About the Music Business

DONALD S. PASSMAN

Illustrations by Randy Glass

SIMON & SCHUSTER
New York   London   Toronto   Sydney   Tokyo   Singapore

SIMON & SCHUSTER
Rockefeller Center
1230 Avenue of the Americas
New York, New York 10020

Copyright © 1991, 1994, 1997 by Donald S. Passman
All rights reserved,
including the right of reproduction
in whole or in part in any form.

SIMON & SCHUSTER and colophon are registered trademarks
of Simon & Schuster Inc.

Manufactured in the United States of America

10 9 8 7 6 5 4 3 2

Library of Congress Cataloging-in-Publication Data

Passman, Donald S.
　　All you need to know about the music business / Donald S.
　　Passman; illustrations by Randy Glass. — [New rev., updated, and
　　expanded ed.]
　　　　p.　　cm.
　　Includes index.
　　1. Music trade—United States.　2. Music—Economic aspects—
United States.　3. Copyright—Music—United States.
4. Popular music—Writing and publishing.　I. Title.
ML3790.P35　1997
780′.23′73—dc21   96–6610
　　　　　　　　　　　　　　　　　　　　　　　　　　　　　CIP
　　　　　　　　　　　　　　　　　　　　　　　　　　　　　MN

ISBN 0-684-83600-9

Did You Know That . . .

- Most record deals don't require the record company even to make a record, much less to release it?

- The term *phonograph record* in recording contracts included home video devices at least ten years before these devices even existed?

- You don't have to register in Washington to get a copyright?

- If we write a song together, and you write only the lyrics and I write only the music, each of us owns a piece of the music and each of us owns a piece of the lyrics? And that neither of us can use just the music, or just the lyrics, without paying the other?

- Prior to 1972, the United States had no law prohibiting the unauthorized reproduction of records?

- Some film music composers can't even write music, much less create the arrangements for each instrument of an orchestra?

- MTV-type videos, which didn't become popular in the U.S. until close to 1981, have been around since the early 1960s in Europe?

- A brain surgeon and a rock star have something in common?

IMPORTANT

The materials in this book represent the opinions of the author and may not be applicable to all situations. Many circumstances appear similar, but differ in respects which may be legally significant. In addition, laws and customs change over time, and by necessity of the lapse in time between the writing and printing of this book, some aspects may be out of date even upon first publication. Accordingly, the author and publisher assume no responsibility for actions taken by readers based upon the advice offered in this book. Each reader should use caution in applying any material contained in this book to his or her specific circumstance, and should seek the advice of an appropriate professional. (Author's note: Use your common sense and be careful!)

To my precious Shana,
and our boys, Danny, David, Josh, and Jordan.

Acknowledgments

PLEASE READ MY THANK YOUS. I KNOW IT'S A BUNCH OF PEOPLE YOU'VE PROBABLY NEVER HEARD OF, BUT THINK HOW MUCH YOU'D WANT OTHER PEOPLE TO READ IT IF YOUR NAME WAS HERE.

No creative work is ever the product of one person alone (no matter how tempting it is to believe our own hype), and I want to acknowledge and thank all the following people for their inspiration and help:

Payson Wolff and Bruce Ramer, my mentors and spiritual brothers.

Dave Dunton, editor and musician extraordinaire, who kept me in focus.

Mike Ovitz and Bob Bookman, for their friendship and salesmanship.

Bea Shaw, my Mommy, who helped edit me, and who paid for my first soft-drink stand.

Snuff Garrett, for believing in me early on.

Mike Gorfaine, for his invaluable advice on film music.

Jeff Ayeroff and Jordan Harris, for their assistance with the section on record company/distribution structures.

Rob Light, for his help with the touring section.

Ed Ritvo, for the confidence to do all sorts of things.

Lisa Thomas, my right arm, for her help with publishing and marketing.

Hermione Brown, who helped lawyer my book deal so I didn't have to contradict my own advice and represent myself.

Alan Garner, for his extraordinary communication skills and advice on conversation, books, and salesmanship.

Steve Bigger, for his help with the section on protecting the rights in a group name.

Chris Castle, for his help with the classical music chapter.

Barbie York, who has typed this book more than six times—may Andy need every page of it.

Kim Mitchell and Linda Ross, who typed inserts so Barbie didn't have to type this book fourteen times.

Jules Levine and Corky, for having bulldogs.

But most especially to all the garage bands—you're the lifeblood of our business.

In addition, the following people (in alphabetical order) generously gave the benefit of their expertise: Paul Adler, David Altschul, Jill Berliner, Don Biederman, Todd Brabec, Kevin Breen, Nancy Chapman, David Cohen, Gary Cohen, Fern Cranston, Henry Droz, Bruce Eisenberg, Gary Ford, Dell Furano, Mark Goldstein, Lauren Gordon, Trudy Green, Peter Grosslight, Rand Hoffman, Zach Horowitz, Cathy Jacobson, Art Jaeger, Howard Kaufman, Chuck Kaye, Larry Kenswil, Paul Lenz, Jay Morgenstern, Jay Murray, Bob Philpot, Jon Pikus, Ken Powell, Peter Reichardt, Bruce Resnikoff, Jon Reynolds, Rick Riccobono, Larry Rosen, Tom Ross, Eva Saks, Joel Sill, Packy Smith, Patricia Smith, Sandy Tanaka, Joan Taylor, Lance Tendler, Ray Tisdale, Wayne Volat, Lenny Waronker, and Ron Wilcox.

Contents

PART IV
Group Issues

PART V
Touring

PART VI
Merchandising

PART VII
Classical Music

PART VIII
Music in Multi-Media, On-Line, and Other Adventures in Cyberspace

PART IX
Motion Picture Music

1

First Steps

OPEN UP AND SAY "AHHH"

For over ten years I've taught a class on the music business at the University of Southern California Law School's Advanced Professional Program. The class is for lawyers, accountants, record and film company executives, managers, agents, and bartenders who want to manage groups. Anyway, at the beginning of one of these courses a friend of mine came up to me. She was an executive at a major film studio and was taking the class to understand the music industry as it relates to films. She said, "I'm here to open up the top of my head and have you pour in the music business." I loved that mental picture (because there are many subjects I have wanted to absorb this same way), and it spurred me to develop a painless way of infusing you with the extensive materials in this book. So if you'll sit back, relax, and open up your mind, I'll pour in all you need to know about the music business (and a bit more for good measure).

HOW I GOT STARTED

I really love what I do. I've been practicing music law over twenty years, and I represent recording artists, record companies, film companies, songwriters, producers, music publishers, film music composers, industry executives, managers, agents, business managers, and virtually every other permutation of the music business you can imagine (plus some you can't).

I got into this business on purpose, because I've always been interested in creative arts. My first show-biz experience was in grade school, performing magic tricks for assemblies. I also started playing accordion in grade school. (I used to play a mean accordion; everyone applauded when I shook the bellows on "Lady of Spain.") By high school, I had graduated from accordion to guitar, and in college at the University of Texas I played lead guitar in a band called Oedipus and the Mothers.

While I was with Oedipus, we recorded a demo that I tried to sell to our family friend, Snuff Garrett (more about him later). Snuff, a powerful record producer, very kindly took the time to listen to the demo and meet with me. That meeting was a major turning point in my life. Snuff listened to the record, smiled, and said, "Don . . . go to law school."

So I took Snuff's advice, and went to Harvard Law School. In law school I continued to play lead guitar with a band called The Rhythm Method, but it was becoming apparent that my ability to be in the music business and eat regularly lay along the business path. So when I graduated, I began doing tax planning for entertainers. Tax law, like intricate puzzles, was a lot of fun, but when I discovered there was such a thing as music law, the electricity really turned on. In fact, I took the USC class that I now teach, and it got me so excited that I left tax practice for my current firm. Doing music law was so much fun that it wasn't even like working (I'm still not over that feeling); and I enjoyed it so much that I felt guilty getting paid (I got over that).

My first entertainment law experience was representing a gorgeous, six-foot model, referred to me by my dentist. (I promised him I would return the favor, because most of my clients had teeth.) The model was being pursued (I suspect in every way) by a manager who wanted a contract for 50% of her gross earnings for ten years. (You'll see how absurd this is when you get to chapter 3.) Even then I knew this wasn't right, and so I nervously called up the guy to negotiate. I said I thought his proposal was out of line with the standard in the industry, and I told him that most managers took only 15% (which was true). He retorted with, "Oh yeah? Who?" Well, he had me. I wasn't even sure what a manager did, much less who they were. So I learned my first lesson in the art of humility.

As I began to really understand how the music business worked, I found that my love of both creative arts and business allowed me to move smoothly between the two worlds and help them relate to each other. The marriage of art and commerce has always fascinated me, and the process of taking complex business concepts and cutting them into small, digestible chunks is a challenge I really love.

So now I channel my creative energies into innovative business deals, and my need to perform is satisfied by teaching, lecturing, writing, and playing guitar at my kids' campouts. (I do a great "Kum-Ba-Ya.") Just to be sure I don't get too straight, however, I've kept up my weird assortment of hobbies: magic, ham radio, weight-lifting, guitar, dog training, five-string banjo, karate, chess, and real estate investment.

BRAIN SURGERY

Speaking of marrying creativity and business, I've discovered that a rock star and a brain surgeon have something in common. It's not that either one would be particularly good at the other's craft (and I'm not sure which crossover would produce the more disastrous results), but rather that each one is capable of performing his craft brilliantly, and generating huge sums of money, without the need for any financial skills whatsoever. In most businesses, before you can start earning big bucks, you have to be pretty well schooled in how the business works, what the moving parts are, what makes the difference between a profit and a loss, etc. But in entertainment, as in surgery, creative people can soar to the heights and never develop even minimal expertise in the business end of their profession.

Making a living from a business you don't fully understand can be risky. Yet a large number of artists, including major ones, have never learned such basics as how record royalties are computed, what a copyright is, how music publishing works, and a number of other important factors that directly affect their lives. They don't know these things because (a) their time was better spent making music, (b) they weren't interested, (c) it sounded too complicated, and/or (d) it was too much like being in school to have to learn it. But without understanding these basics as a foundation, it is impossible for them to understand the intricacies of their professional lives. And as their success grows and their lives get more complex, they become even more lost.

While it's true that some artists refuse to even listen to business talk (I've watched them go into sensory shut-down if you so much as mention the topic), others take a keen interest in, and become quite sophisticated about, their business lives. The vast majority, however, are somewhere in the middle of these extremes. They don't really enjoy business, but they would like to understand it so they can participate intelligently in their career decisions. These artists are smart enough to know that *no one ever takes as good care of your business as you do.*

It was for my moderate-to-seriously interested clients that I developed a procedure of explaining the basics in simple, everyday language. With only a small investment of time, these clients found that the essential concepts were really easy to understand, and everyone enjoyed the process (including me). It also made an enormous difference in the artist's self-confidence about his or her business life and allowed him or her to make valuable contributions to the process.

Because the results of these brief learning sessions were so positive, a number of my clients asked if we could explore the subjects more deeply. Thus the conception of this book. It's designed to give you a general overview of the entire music industry as it currently exists. You can read it as casually or as intensely as suits your personal style, interest level, and attention span. It's not written for lawyers or technicians, so it doesn't include the jargon or minutia you'll find in a textbook for professionals. Instead, it gives a broad overview of each segment of the industry, and goes into enough detail for you to understand all the major issues you're likely to confront in your professional life.

JUNGLE MAPS

When I was in high school, I heard a policeman speak at an assembly, pushing police recruitment. He said that life as a crime fighter would be terrific for us, and that he was sure we all secretly wanted to be cops. While his lecture (obviously) didn't work on me, he did make a lasting impression.

The policeman showed us a film in which the camera merely moved down a street. It was black and white, only about thirty seconds long, and it consisted of a camera going along a sidewalk in front of a row of shops. When it was finished, the policeman asked if we'd seen anything unusual. No one had. Apart from a couple of people bouncing in and out of the doorways, it looked pretty much like pictures taken by a camera moving along the street. He then said that a "trained observer" (meaning a police officer) who watched the film could spot six crimes being committed—which none of us had seen. He then showed the film again, pointing out each of the incidents (there was a quiet exchange of drugs, a pickpocket, etc.). This time, the crimes were obvious. It was a fascinating experience.

Any time you learn a new skill, you go through a similar process. At first, things look either ordinary and deceptively simple or else like a bewildering blur of activity. But as you learn what to look for, you see a whole world you never knew was there. To work your way through the process, and become a "trained observer," you need a guide to the basics, so that you can have a framework within which to put the various bits and pieces. And that is the purpose of this book—to give you a map through the jungle and show you where the crimes are.

ANOTHER MOTIVE

There's a second motivation for this book. As a teacher, I've been asked repeatedly if there was a book that laid out the basics of the music business and could be used as a supplement for my course. My desire to fill that need was also an incentive to write this book.

DETAILS

There is no way one book (even one filling several volumes) could poke into every nook and cranny of a business as complicated as the music business. Accordingly, the purpose here is to give you the big picture, not all the details. (Besides, for some of those details, I charge serious money.) And, even if I tried to lay out all the little pieces, as fast as everything moves in this biz, it would be obsolete within a few months. Thus, this book is designed to give you a broad overview (which, while fluid, doesn't change nearly as quickly), so you'll have a bare tree on which to hang the leaves of your own experience. Oddly, it's easier to pick up details (from trade publications, gossip at cocktail parties, etc.) than it is to learn the structural overview, because few people have the time and patience to sit down and give it to you. In fact, giving you the overall view turned out to be a much bigger job than I thought when I started. But you're worth it.

EARLY RESULTS

Since this is the third edition, I now have feedback from experiments using the book on actual human beings. Of all the responses I got, I thought you'd enjoy hearing about two in particular. First, I received an irate call from a music lawyer, who was upset because he charged thousands of dollars to give clients the advice I had put in the book. Second, I received an equally irate call from a manager, who said that all the artists he'd approached lately had been pushing my book in his face.

Way to go! Keep shoving, and tell them I said "Nyaah."

STAPLE, SPINDLE, AND MUTILATE

When you go through this book, forget everything you learned as a kid about taking good care of books, treating them as sacred works of art, etc. Read this book with a pencil or highlighter in your hand. Circle or star passages you think you'll need, fold over pages, stick paper clips on them—whatever helps. This is an action book—a set of directions on how to jog through the music biz without getting mugged. So treat it like a comfortable pair of old shoes that you don't mind getting dirty. It doesn't matter what they look like, as long as they get you where you want to go.

CHOOSE YOUR OWN ADVENTURE

When my sons David, Josh, and Jordan were little, their favorite books were from a series entitled *Choose Your Own Adventure*. They work like this: You start reading the book on page 1 and, after a few pages, the author gives you a choice. For example, if you want Pinocchio to go down the alley, you turn to page 37, but if you want him to go to school, you turn to page 53. (My boys never picked school.) From there, every few pages you have more choices, and thus there are several different endings to the book. (The boys liked the ending where everyone gets killed, but that's another story.) These books are not meant to be read straight through; if you tried, because of their structure, you'd find yourself crashing into various endings, twists, and turns of different plots and stories. Instead, you're supposed to skip around, following your own path each time.

This concept gave me the idea of how to organize this book. As noted below, you have a choice of reading for a broad overview, or reading in depth. The book tells you where to skip ahead if you want to do this. However, unlike the *Choose Your Own Adventure* books, you can read straight through with little or no damage to the central nervous system.

Here's how it's organized (there's no particular magic to the order, except that you need some concepts before you can understand others):

> **Part I** deals with how to put together a team to guide your career, consisting of a personal manager, business manager, agent, and attorney.
> **Part II** looks at record deals, including the concepts of royalties, advances, and other major deals points.

Part III talks about songwriting and publishing, including copyrights and the structure of the publishing industry.

Part IV explores peculiarities you encounter if you're a group.

Part V deals with concerts and touring, including agreements for the appearances themselves, and the role of your various team members in the process.

Part VI, on merchandising, tells you how to profit from plastering your face on posters, T-shirts, and other assorted paraphernalia.

Parts VII through **IX** explore classical music, music in cyberspace, and motion pictures. They're the last sections because you need to understand all of the other concepts before we can tackle them.

You have four choices of how to go through this book:

1. **EXTREMELY FAST TRACK**
   If you *really* want a quick trip, then:
   (a) Read Part I (on how to pick a team of advisors)
   (b) Get people who know what they're doing
   (c) Let them do it
   (d) Put this book on your shelf to impress your friends; and
   (e) Say "Hi" to me backstage at one of your concerts.

2. **FAST TRACK**
   Short of this radical approach, if you want a broad-strokes overview of the business, without much detail, skip ahead each time you see the **FAST TRACK** directions.

3. **ADVANCED OVERVIEW**
   If you want a more in-depth overview, but less than the full shot, then follow the **ADVANCED OVERVIEW** directions. This will give you a solid overview, plus some detail on each topic.

4. **EXPERT TRACK**
   For you high achievers who want an in-depth discussion, simply read straight through.

You should, of course, feel free to mix and match any of these tracks. If a particular topic grabs your interest, by all means keep reading and check out the details. (Amazingly, the topics that grab your interest tend to be things currently happening in your life.) If another topic is a yawn, Fast Track through it.

So let's get going. Everybody starts with Part I.

Your
Team of
Advisors

2

How to Pick a Team

GETTING YOUR TEAM TOGETHER

Let's talk about the professionals you're going to use to maximize your career and net worth. The main players are your:

1. Personal manager
2. Attorney
3. Business manager
4. Agency
5. Groupies

With respect to number 5, you're pretty much on your own. As to the others, let's take a look:

BUSINESS PHILOSOPHY

Before we talk about the specific players, let me share a bit of personal philosophy. (If "share" is too California for you, read "Let me tell you some of my personal philosophy.") Take a hard look at some facts:

1. **You are a business.**
   Even though your skills are creative, you're capable of generating multimillions of dollars per year, and thus you must think of yourself as a business.
2. **Most artists don't like business.**
   This is not to say that you're not good at it. Some artists are unbelievably sophisticated and astute when it comes to their business. However, they are very much in the minority, and even these people recognize that, whatever their love and skill for business, their love and skill for creating and performing are much

greater. Thus, even if you're capable of handling all your own business, it's not the most effective use of your time to do so.

3. **Success hides a multitude of sins.**

   This is true in any business, from making widgets to making records. If you're successful, you can get away with sloppy operations that would bankrupt you if times were bad. For example, putting all your pals on the payroll, buying lots of non-income-producing assets (such as houses, jets, raw land, and other things that cost you money to maintain), as well as an overindulgence in various legal and illegal goodies, can easily result in a crash-and-burn if your income takes even a small dip, much less a large one. You can make more money by cutting costs than you can by earning more income (see page 342 for proof of this), so the time to operate efficiently is *now*, not later.

4. **Your career is going to have a limited run.**

   Please don't take offense at this—"limited" can mean anything from a year to thirty years, but it is nonetheless going to be limited. In most other careers, you can expect to have a professional life of forty-five-years plus, but as an entertainer in the music business, this virtually never happens. And the road is strewn with carcasses of aging rock stars who work for rent money on nostalgia tours. So take the concentrated earnings of a few years and spread them over a forty-five-year period, and you'll find that two things happen: (a) The earnings cease to be quite as impressive; and (b) you realize this money may have to last you the rest of your life.

It is certainly possible to have a long, healthy career, and to the extent you do, your need for caution and preservation diminishes radically. However, even the best entertainers have slumps, and very few truly have lengthy careers. Thus, it's best to plan as if your career is not going to last, and be pleasantly surprised if it does. To spend money as if you're going to make the same amount for the rest of your life is to invite disaster. But to set yourself up so that you never have to work again doesn't stop you from working all you like—it just becomes an option, and not an obligation.

HIRING A TEAM

The way you pick your professional team will either set your career and finances up for life, or assure you a place on the Electric Prunes tour. So be very careful and pay attention *personally* to the process of assembling them. I know you don't like to deal with this stuff, but it's your career and your money, and you have to do it every now and then. If you pick the right people, you can then set your life on automatic pilot and just check in on it periodically. If you pick the wrong people and set it on automatic pilot, you will slam into a mountain before you know what happened.

Pre-team Strategies

Since you wouldn't open a store without something to sell, before you start assembling a team, you want to be sure your music is ready to take you to the big time. And how do you know when it's ready? You ask your tummy. Do you believe, in your gut, that your music has matured to the point that you're ready to seek a professional career? If the answer is yes, then you're ready. (Tummies are reliable indicators once we learn how to listen to them and dismiss the goblins that yell, "You're a phony and nobody wants you." Even the superstars have these goblins—they've just learned how to let their tummies shout them down.)

The first thing to do is get your music down on tape. The people at record companies are much too busy to run around looking at live performances unless they're first intrigued by your music (or unless you have some compromising photos of the executive). The tape doesn't have to be expensive or elaborate, but the better you can make it sound, the better your chances are going to be. Most record executives will tell you that they can hear "diamonds in the rough," but my experience is that the more your demo sounds like a hit, the more likely that you'll get a good reception. This doesn't mean you have to go to great expense—with the advent of relatively inexpensive four-track and eight-track recorders, as well as synthesizers, you can get an amazingly professional sound in your bedroom. In fact, a client of mine recently had six record companies chasing him based on a home demo he made on a four-track. The important thing is to get down your energy, enthusiasm, and drive. You know what I mean.

A word about what kind of music to make. It's simple—you make the music that moves your soul. No one has ever had a serious career imitating others or trying to guess what the record companies want. And I'll tell you a secret: What the record companies want is someone whose music is pure and true to themselves. So whether your music is the commercial flavor of the month, or an obscure blend of reggae and Buddhist chants, you have to put down what's in your heart. All the superstars I've known have a clear vision of who they are and what their music is.

Your tape doesn't need more than three or four songs on it. But these should be the *best* three or four songs that you're capable of doing, starting with the primo masterpiece first. The people who listen to tapes are busy, and if you don't hook them on the first song, they ain't gonna get to the second. If they're interested, they'll ask if you have more songs. But leave 'em wanting more.

So you've got a killer tape and you're ready to boogie. What's next? If you've got photographs, they're a good thing to put in the package because, in this multimedia world, record companies are interested in much more than how you sound. You have to be able to perform live, look good in videos, etc. By the way, "look good" doesn't mean a pretty face, as you and I are both aware of successful artists who are anything but pretty. But it does mean you have to have an interesting look (or at least be presentable).

And now for a bit of a bummer. Unfortunately, the major record companies (not necessarily so the minors) have developed a practice of not taking tapes unless they're submitted by a manager or attorney in the business. (I hate delivering bad news, but look at the bright side: I just saved you three months of waiting for a form letter that says they won't listen because it didn't come from a lawyer or manager.) The reason for this practice is that record companies can get 300 to 400 tapes *per week*, and restricting who can send in tapes is one way they regulate the floodgates. However, it's also a Catch-22: How can you get your tape heard if you're not already connected in the business, and how do you get connected in the business if you can't get heard? But don't despair; I'm going to give you the key to the door. The key consists of finding yourself a lawyer or manager to shop your tape, which leads nicely into our next topic.

Who's on First?

The first person on your team is almost always a manager or a lawyer. In your baby stages, the manager is not likely to be someone already in the business; it's more likely a friend or relative with a lot of enthusiasm. While this can be a major plus (as we'll discuss in more detail when we discuss managers, on page 49), it may or may not get your tape into the record companies. Accordingly, if you have an inexperienced manager, or if you have no manager at all, the lawyer is commonly the first true industry person on the team. The time required of a music lawyer to shop your tape is minimal compared to the time a manager has to devote. While the manager would be expected to help you with songs, image, bookings, baby-sitting, etc., the lawyer need only be involved for a few hours because it's his or her relationships that will get your tape through the door. And a good music lawyer can be a big plus to your efforts for another reason: Record companies prefer to deal with people they know, so your tape will get heard much faster, and by more important people, if the right person submits it.

A word of caution about hiring a lawyer to shop your tape. Most of the lawyers consider it important to maintain their credibility with the record companies, and thus will only shop tapes that they really believe in. However, there are unfortunately a few who will shop any tape that walks in the door as long as they get paid a fee. Being shopped by one of these is no better than sending the tape yourself, because the record companies know these guys don't screen out any of the garbage, and their tapes go to the bottom of the pile. To prevent your tape from being thrown in with those, you should carefully check out the references of any lawyer you're thinking of using. Ask them for the names of people whose tapes they've shopped (both successfully and unsuccessfully, so they don't just give you the few success stories that slipped through the cracks), and then call up the references and find out how it went. You can also check around other industry sources to see who's legit. (We'll talk more about checking references later on.)

A business manager is usually the last on board for almost the opposite reasons why the lawyer is first: It's expensive (in terms of staffing and labor) for a business manager to take you on, and new artists need a lot of work just to keep financially afloat. Also, very few business managers are willing to "take a flyer" with a totally unproven, unsigned artist—the business manager's potential upside is not nearly so great as a personal manager's or agent's, and yet they have to incur substantial expense. (As you'll see in chapter 4, business managers aren't paid as much as agents or personal managers.) However, don't be concerned. Until you have some decent money coming in, you really don't need a full-fledged business manager. A good accountant can take care of your tax returns and answer any questions.

The Search

Where do you find warm bodies to begin assembling your team? Well, start with the age-old ploy of asking every human being you know for a recommendation. Talk to people involved in music, even if it's only your high school choir's piano accompanist. You can lead yourself into any totally unknown arena by diligently following your nose, and the music business is no exception. You'll be amazed how many things fall into your life when you open yourself up to the possibilities. The only frustrating part is that the people you really want to grab don't have time for you in the beginning. (But be assured, as soon as you're successful, they'll fall all over you and say they "knew it all along.")

The major players are almost all in Los Angeles and New York, plus Nashville if you're a country artist. This is not to say there aren't qualified people in other places—there most assuredly are—but the music industry is centered in these three towns, and the people who live there usually have more experience. On the other hand, major managers are increasingly popping up in other places. For example, I've dealt with managers of world-class artists who live in Seattle, Austin, Philadelphia, and Boston. However, the better ones spend a lot of time on airplanes visiting Los Angeles, New York, and/or Nashville.

Here are some specific suggestions on building your list:

1. *Yellow Pages of Rock!*
   Pretty much as it sounds—a book printed on yellow pages listing the names, addresses, and phone numbers of record companies (with the names of executives), managers, agents, attorneys, publicists, retailers, publishers, record distributors, radio stations, etc. It is expensive (currently about $110), but is available in many libraries. Very complete, it also has a number of ads, which list managers' clients and otherwise brag about the various advertisers' wares. *Yellow Pages of Rock!* is published by the Album Network, 120 N. Victory Boulevard, Third Floor, Burbank, California 91502. Telephone: (818) 955-4000.

2. *The Recording Industry Source Book*
   Published annually, lists major and independent labels, publishers, managers, agents, attorneys, and all sorts of other information. The cost is currently about $80. However, it doesn't indicate which artists are represented by the various people and organizations. Their address is 6400 Hollis St., Suite 12, Emeryville, California 94608-9889.

3. *Hits Magazine*
   Hits is the *Mad* magazine of the music business. It's full of current news reported with a college-humor-magazine style, and it's very funny reading. Each year *Hits* publishes an article in mid-August entitled "Who's Got Who." The article lists numerous artists, together with their agents and personal managers. You can contact *Hits Magazine* at 14958 Ventura Boulevard, Sherman Oaks, California 91403. Telephone: (818) 501-7900.

4. ***Billboard International Talent and Touring Directory***
This guide is published annually and lists hundreds of artists, together with their booking agents, personal managers, and record companies. It also has a section telling where to contact the agents and managers. For information, write Billboard Publications, 1515 Broadway, New York, New York 10036-8986. Telephone: (212) 764-7300.

By no means are these four an exhaustive list of sources; they just happened to be the ones nearest by when I grabbed for something to give you. Frankly, I've been doing this long enough to know everybody I need to get to, and so I don't use references on a routine basis. Thus, don't take my suggestions as gospel. You should check your local bookstores and libraries for more references, as well as look for ads and reviews of reference books in music magazines.

Use a bit of caution with published sources. Annual publications are bound to be a bit out of date by the time you pick them up. And the farther you get from publication date, the greater the chance of inaccuracy. Also, I noted from a brief reading that many of them have minor errors of one sort or another (like listing a business manager as an "agent").

Here are some more ideas on adding to your list of potential team members:

1. Read interviews with industry figures in *Rolling Stone* and other music magazines, and note the names. The major industry trade magazine is the weekly *Billboard,* which is available at newsstands. Others are *Radio and Records,* and *Hits Magazine. Billboard*'s and *Hits'* addresses are above. The address for *Radio and Records* is 10100 Santa Monica Blvd., 5th Floor, Los Angeles, California 90067-4004.

   Major consumer magazines (as opposed to trade magazines) are (in alphabetical order):

   (a) *BAM,* 6767 Forest Lawn Drive, Suite 110, Los Angeles, California 90068. Each year *BAM* lists 100 major music businessfolk.

   (b) *Music Connection,* 4731 Laurel Canyon Blvd., N. Hollywood, California 91607.

   (c) *Musician,* 1515 Broadway, 11th Floor, New York, New York 10036.

   (d) *Spin,* 6 West 18th Street, New York, New York 10011.

2. Watch for quotes, stories, or blurbs about music industry people in the newspapers, and on radio and TV.
3. The backs of albums often list managers, lawyers, business managers, or agents in the "Special Thanks" section. Unfortunately, they may only list the people's names and not their roles (so you might end up managed by someone's yoga instructor if you're not careful). Still, when you're compiling a list of names, every little bit helps.
4. Some artists list the names of their professionals, together with their jobs, in their tour programs.

Anyway, using the above and anything else you can think of, write down the names and develop a "hit list." Just let your imagination go—follow any lead that seems promising, and keep moving forward.

Once you assemble a bunch of names, begin the process of prioritizing them, and decide who to contact first. If you've heard any names from two or more sources, the odds are you are on to a person who is "somebody," and he or she should move up in priority. Also look for the professionals surrounding people whose music you admire and whose style is similar to your own. While this is less critical with lawyers and business managers, it's important to be sure agencies, and especially personal managers, handle your style of music. For example, the agent that books the Lawrence Welk Review is not likely to book Slayer, and I guarantee you they have different managers. On the other hand, you may be surprised to find that acts just as diverse are represented by the same agency (with *very* different individual agents involved). And, the legal and business management lives of acts within the realm of popular music are not as different as you might expect. Rock 'n' rollers (like Aerosmith, Rolling Stones, etc.) and balladeers (like Barbra Streisand, Whitney Houston, etc.) have similar needs in music publishing, record royalties, touring, merchandising, sponsorship, etc.

Once you've prioritized your list, start trying to contact the people on it. It's always better to come in through a recommendation, friend of the family, etc., even if it's only the person's dry cleaner. But if you can't find any contact, start cold. You can try calling people on the phone (if it's not too expensive), but expect a lot of unreturned phone calls, or at best to be shuffled off to an underling. That's OK—talk to the underling. Be sure you're brief and to the point if you get someone on the phone—these folks are always in a hurry. (You may even want to rehearse your rap with a friend in advance.) You can also begin mailing out tapes, pictures, and anything else that can get their attention. If you have any local press, that's a good thing to include. Use a yellow highlighter so the guy doesn't have to search the page for where you are. And by the way, I personally hate to get unsolicited letters marked "Personal & Confidential" because I have to open them myself (my office assumes they contain state secrets). Not only do I lose the time while I fumble with a letter opener (I've never been particularly coordinated), but I also find myself annoyed that someone would put me to this extra effort for something that isn't truly confidential. And while we're on the subject of annoyances, I also hate getting letters that are terminally cute (like "Looking for a hit? Here's one!") So be short and straightforward—good people are always busy, and you'll be lucky to get five seconds of their attention. If you can't grab 'em in that time, you're off to the round file. Repeated letters to the same person also help get their attention, and may even have the subliminal effect of making your name sound familiar if anyone ever asks. But expect a lot of unacknowledged letters, and don't get discouraged.

When you get someone's attention, even if he or she hasn't got the time or inclination to get involved, ask who they would recommend for you. This is valuable for two reasons: First, you've got a lead from someone actually in the industry. Second, when you call up the recommended person, you can tell them "So-and-so" told you to call. If "So-and-so" is a big enough name, it should at least get your phone call returned. (Maybe.)

Someone, somewhere, will nibble, and you can parlay it into real interest by being persistent. All the superstars I've known have an incredible amount of drive and perseverance, and will continually hound people to further their career. So hang in there and keep following up, despite whatever discouragements get thrown in front of you. Virtually every record company in America passed on the Beatles and Elton John when they were first looking for deals, so don't expect people to be any smarter about your music. And don't get discouraged—it only takes one enthusiastic person to get the ball rolling.

Screening the Sharks

So you've honed your list, run up large postage and long-distance phone bills, and hopefully found two or three nibbles on your line. At this point, you should fly, drive, bus, or hitchhike to meet these people face to face in their natural habitat. You can't tell everything from a telephone conversation; you want to see their offices, watch their body language, and generally use your instincts to feel how they vibe you. And don't be afraid to trust your instincts. If you think you're meeting with a piece of slime, you probably are. But if they dazzle you, use even more caution—charming crooks are the most dangerous!

Here's how to maneuver through the sharks and evaluate potential team members:

References. Ask for references. The fact that they have a lot of big names is helpful, but not a final determination. There have been a lot of big names associated with disasters over the years. I remember when I was just starting to practice law, my wife and I decided to buy a vacuum cleaner. For some inexplicable reason, we called a door-to-door salesman who came to the house all pumped up with sunshine. After picking up seven-pound metal balls with the vacuum's suction and doing other impressive stunts, he began bragging about how he had sold vacuum cleaners to the wives of several prominent movie stars. While he was on a roll, rattling off big names, I interrupted him and said, "Excuse me, but do these people know anything about vacuum cleaners?"

The point, as I'm sure you see, is that a big name celebrity isn't necessarily a good recommendation. It may just mean the celebrity pays no attention to his or her business, or that the celebrity is a fool. Also, if you're interviewing a lawyer, agent, or business manager, the artist may not really know how good they are—sometimes performers have little contact with these people because the personal manager handles all the business. In that case, talk to the personal manager.

And in getting references, it's important to get recommendations from people *at your level* of success. The fact that someone takes great care of their biggest client doesn't necessarily mean he or she will pay such good attention to you. Odd as it seems, some people don't even pay much attention to their big name clients, usually because the professional is too busy. There's an old joke (based on truth) about a major artist who couldn't get his lawyer on the phone to fire him. And also try to get references from someone who has been using this professional for a while, so you don't just get a report on their honeymoon period.

Although it may seem obvious, be sure this person's expertise is in music. There are brilliant real estate accountants who would be lost in the music business, just as the opposite is true. In fact, even people with extensive film, television, or literary expertise may not understand music. So be sure you're talking to someone who does.

Use Your Other Team Members. You should consult the other members of your team anytime you hire someone, because you want their input and suggestions. Also, these people have to work together. But be aware of this: Benjamin Franklin once said (and I'm too lazy to look up the exact quote, so I'll paraphrase it) that when you gather together a group of people for their collective wisdom, you also gather their collective prejudices and hidden agendas. In other words, there will almost always be a political reason your other team members do or don't want something, and this may or may not coincide with your best interests. For example, a business manager may have just referred a very important client to a personal manager. The personal manager may therefore be pushing you toward this particular business manager in order to pay back the favor, regardless of whether or not the business manager is right for your situation. (I don't mean to make you paranoid; most people are ethical and won't recommend someone unless they genuinely believe he or she would be the best person for the job, even if it's a payback. But a great deal of politicking goes on in the music business, just as in any other business, and you should be aware of it.) Thus, always ask people the *reasons* for their recommendation, rather than just the bottom line of who they think you should use. And make them give you specific, factual reasons. Facts are something you can evaluate yourself, and *you* should make the final decision.

Look Beyond the Sales Pitch. Remember, everybody looks great when they're selling. When you interview someone, all the seller's attention is totally focused on you, and you are absolutely the most important creature on the planet. This is almost never the case when you actually get down to business; the realities of other peoples' needs begin to take their toll. It's extremely difficult to know this in an interview, as "giving good interview" can take people far in their professions. So how do you get beyond this? You check their references very carefully. Ask the references about everything you can think of, such as their reputation for promptness in returning phone calls, how fast he or she gets work done, what's their zodiac sign, etc.

Don't be lulled by promises that sound unbelievably fantastic. If they sound too good to be true, they probably aren't. Many people will promise you things they know they can't possibly deliver, just to get the job. They figure you won't fire them when they can't deliver, because they know most artists don't like to make changes in their lives. (These are the same people who will stop returning your phone calls if your star fades.) They also figure they have to lie just to ace out the next guy, who they assume is doing the same thing. The truth is that there are no real miracle workers; the secret of success in the music business is no different from that in any other business—intelligent planning, solid work, and proper execution. Promises of "shortcuts" usually don't come through.

Who Does the Work? Ask exactly who is going to be involved in your day-to-day work. It may not be the person you're meeting with, and you should know that and meet the people who *will* be involved. All professionals use staff people of some sort, some to a greater degree than others. With some firms the staff people divide and multiply like paramecia, in an ever-changing kaleidoscope of faces. Other firms are more stable. So ask, and also ask your references.

Fees. Never hesitate to ask what someone is going to charge you. I know it's an uncomfortable subject, but bring it up anyway—you can be in for some seriously rude surprises if you don't. And when you do raise the topic, be particularly wary of someone who gives you only a vague answer. (If you really can't stomach a fee discussion, have another team member do it for you.)

Personality. It's a myth to think any one personality style is more effective than any other (assuming you don't hire a wimp). Screamers and table pounders, *if they're smart and knowledgeable,* can get a lot out of a deal; but no more than those who speak quietly, *if they're smart and knowledgeable.* Some people work with a foil, and some with a sabre, but both styles can be effective.

Remember, you're hiring people to guide your professional life, not to travel on the tour bus. It's nice if you strike up a genuine friendship with your professionals, but it's not essential. (However, with your personal manager, I think you need at least a solid rapport, if not a true friendship.) I'm not advocating hiring someone you really dislike, or someone who has the personality of a salamander, but I am saying these folks don't have to be your pals. In fact, some amount of distance is often helpful. Just as doctors can't operate on their own relatives, one of the main things a professional does is bring some objectivity to your life.

There is a wonderful story about Genghis Khan, the great warrior and conqueror. In the midst of a pivotal battle for his empire, involving tens of thousands of troops on both sides, an aide went into Khan's tent and was surprised to find Khan himself sitting there. The aide said, "How can you be in your tent? The troops need your command, and the battle is at a critical point." Khan replied, "I found myself getting angry over a turn in the battle, and I can't think straight when I'm angry. I came in here to cool off before deciding the next move." Think about that. If even ol' Genghis had to be detached from his emotions to function properly, who are you and I to do any better? When I have legal problems, I hire a lawyer. This may sound peculiar to you, but I get emotional about my own problems (just as you do) and I don't trust my judgment when I'm too close to the situation. So I hire someone who isn't.

In sum, a bit of distance from your professionals is not a concern, but you should feel comfortable and open with your team, and have a good, easy communication.

"Trust Me." Be wary of anyone who begins by telling you how honest they are. Honest people don't usually go out of their way to say so. I once represented a client who had managed a major rock group for eight years, and as the relationship was deteriorating, he was facing a potential audit and litigation from the group. He began to tell me the group wasn't going to find anything, because he was so honest that there could never be a question about it. The first time he told me this, I assumed that was the case and moved onward. The second time he told me, I began to get nervous, and when he said it the third time, I suggested he get another lawyer.

Decide Now—Confirm Later. Make a decision reasonably quickly, but confirm it slowly. In other words, once you've decided who to use and have hired them, continue to watch your team very carefully (to the extent you can stand to do it). The fact that someone came in with rave reviews doesn't mean they'll be right for you, so consider them "on probation" until you've seen enough to merit your trust. And don't just take another team member's word that it's working. Force yourself to follow their moves in the beginning—no one pays as much attention to your career as you—and you will earn the right to relax later.

CHANGING A TEAM MEMBER

Here's what to do if something goes wrong on your team.

Even if you never pay much attention to business, I have yet to meet an artist who doesn't have a built-in radar that tells them when something is wrong. It may be that things aren't being handled right, or that you just don't feel comfortable talking to one of the team members. Ignoring the problem doesn't help any more than turning up the car radio to drown out the sound of a rattle in the engine. It's like a quote I once heard attributed to Dick Gregory: "I read so much about how bad smoking is that I got scared and gave up reading." So deal with problems head on.

Talk About Your Problems

I know confrontation is difficult. I have never known an artist (or anyone else, for that matter, other than a few ornery jerks that have been divorced six times) who enjoys confrontation. But for the members of your team to do an effective job for you, you must have an open communication with them. If you can't bring yourself to talk directly to the person who is bugging you, talk to another team member and make sure they carry the message. Fast. Nothing is worse than letting small things snowball to the point that they build into a major drama. If you discuss them when they're small, they can usually stay small, and often they are innocent misunderstandings.

If you talk about your problems frankly, and they still aren't getting solved to your satisfaction, make a change. No one has the right to expect a lifetime contract with you. People and circumstances change over the years; those who were spectacular for you at one point in your life may no longer be interested in you (if your career has taken a nosedive, or if they've lost interest in their job, etc.). Or they may no longer be capable of handling you (if they were unable to grow with you and your career is soaring; if you have changed careers and their expertise is in the wrong area, etc.). I respect and admire loyalty (if for no other reason than because it's so rare), but blind loyalty does no one a favor. To me, loyalty means you don't turn your head and run off with every pretty face that walks by (and as you get more successful, pretty faces come out of the woodwork to try to seduce you, literally and figuratively). But loyalty is a two-way street, meaning you must get the same commitment from your professional. You are only obligated to stick with someone as long as they're doing a good job for you. If you're not getting the service you want, then loyalty means you discuss it with them and tell them what needs to be changed. (Again, if you don't want to do it directly, do it through another team member.) If, after that, things still aren't being done right, and you're sure your complaints were accurately and clearly communicated, make a change. But do it for the right reasons, not the wrong ones.

Lost Confidence

It pains me a bit to give you this next piece of advice, but you should have it. Once you've lost confidence in someone, whether it's for the right reasons or totally wrong reasons, it's almost impossible to continue with them. It's like falling out of love—it isn't easy to fall in again. I say this sadly, because many times we lose confidence in a person for the wrong reasons. It may be that someone with a political ax has buried them unjustly; it may be they are doing a terrific job, but they have the personality of a stop sign and treat you rudely or bore you to death; it may be they have just delivered bad news to you (firing such a person is known as "shooting the messenger," from ancient Greek times, when a messenger bringing bad news was killed); it may be they have done a terrific job on everything important in your life, but screwed up paying your bills one month, so you had no telephone or electricity and your spouse refuses ever to see their face again; or it just may be an uneasy feeling in your stomach that you don't trust them. When you find yourself in this situation, again I urge you to talk to the person openly (directly or through another team member) and tell them how you feel. (I know this is easy for me to say, and I admit it's difficult for me to do as well. But I force myself, and most of the time I find the problem is a simple mistake that is easily fixed. And even if it isn't, I always feel better afterward just from processing it.) If you talk things out and the situation still doesn't get any better, split.

COCKTAIL PARTY TALK

Let me say a word about cocktail party talk. In college, we used to play a kind of poker called "roll your own." In this game you get five cards, and then draw additional cards (like in regular five-card draw). But then you get to arrange your cards in any order you want before flipping them over one at a time and betting on each card. After flipping the first three cards, everybody at the table looks like they have a spectacular hand. There appear to be straights, flushes, straight flushes, three of a kind, high pairs, and every other imaginable configuration to make you want to drop out of the game and give up the pot. However, when it comes to flipping over the last couple of cards, most of the hands are mediocre.

I've always thought that cocktail party talk is the same as flipping only the first three cards. Everyone sounds like a genius; everyone has just pulled off the greatest deal since the Louisiana Purchase. The truth, however, is in the last two cards, which you never see. The $10 million deal turns out to be a $1 million deal, with the other $9 million being there only if the artist achieves success far beyond anything he or she has ever had before (not that $1 million isn't a lot of money, but it ain't $10 million). Nobody talks about their losses and screwups, because self-aggrandizement is part of the dance of the sand crabs that is ritualized at cocktail parties.

The whole point of this is only to say you should not take casual talk at face value, particularly if someone has an editorial point of view—like a manager trying to convince you to leave your current manager for the terrific things he or she can do for you. (Lawyers, of course, would never do such a thing. And if you buy that, I have some land in Florida we should discuss.) So make your own evaluations in the realistic light of day.

3

Personal Managers

ROLE

The personal manager is the single most important person in your professional life. A good personal manager can expand your career to its maximum potential, just as a bad one can rocket you into oblivion. When the job is done properly, a personal manager is the general manager and chief operating officer of your enterprise. (There are, of course, some artists without managers, but they are very much the exception, and they usually have one or more others on the team filling this role.)

The most important aspects of the manager's job are:

1. Helping you with major career decisions, such as deciding which record company to sign with, whether to make a publishing deal, how much to ask for, etc.
2. Helping you with the creative process, such as selecting a producer (you'll find out what a producer is on page 133), deciding which songs to record, hiring band members, selecting photographers, etc.
3. Promoting your career by hyping you to everyone the manager meets, helping you coordinate a publicity campaign, etc.
4. Assembling and heading your professional team by introducing you to lawyers, business managers, and agents, and overseeing these people's work.
5. Coordinating your concert tours by working with your agent to make the best deals with promoters, routing the tour, working with your business manager to develop and implement a budget, assembling your road crew, supervising the road and tour managers to make sure everything runs smoothly, etc.
6. Pounding your record company by coordinating the record company's advertising and marketing campaigns for your records,

making sure your records are treated as priorities, screaming at them when they do wrong, praising them when they do right, etc.

7. Generally being a buffer between you and the outside world, such as fielding inquiries for commercial endorsements, personal appearances, charitable requests (both for money and for your smiling face), taking the rap for tough decisions that you make but don't want anyone to think you did, etc.

Let's first take a look at the structure of your deal with the personal manager, and then we'll talk about picking one.

COMMISSION OVERVIEW

Managers typically get from 15% to 20% of your gross earnings, with the majority earning 15%.

Managers' percentages are usually applied to your *gross* earnings, before deducting any expenses. This means the following:

1. If you're an individual artist, the fee is pretty much what it sounds like for songwriting, publishing, records, etc. We'll discuss some of the finer points later, but basically the manager takes 15% of your earnings. However, when it comes to touring, the 15% means much more than you might think. You'll see when we discuss concert appearances (on page 333) that you're lucky to take home 40% to 50% of your gross income, and thus a manager's 15% of gross can amount to almost *half* of your net. For example, if you earn $100,000 and net $50,000 (50%), your manager's 15% of gross ($15,000) is 30% of your $50,000 net.

2. If you're a group and you have more than five members, the manager's 15% of gross equals almost the same, or more than, any one of you earns (assuming you're dividing equally). For example, if there are seven of you, each receives only one-seventh, or 14.28%, versus the manager's 15%. In fact, since the manager's percentage comes "off the top" before you divide up any monies, you only have one-seventh of the 85% left after the manager's 15%, which is 12.14%. And for touring monies, a manager's 15% of *gross* is several times the share of *net* each of you is taking home.

I don't mean to sound negative, because this is the industry custom. On the other hand, I wouldn't want you to have cardiac arrest when you get your first accounting. But because of the possibility of the manager making more than you, more and more artists are trying to make deals that pay the manager a percentage of the artist's net (which we'll discuss in the next section).

NEGOTIATING THE MANAGER'S DEAL

Despite the powerful personality of many managers (carefully designed to give you the opposite impression), it *is* possible to negotiate with your manager. However, just like any other negotiation, the result depends on bargaining power. If you're a major artist, bringing in $10 million plus per year, you can pretty well get what you want. If you're a brand-new band looking for a record deal, your bargaining power with a successful, powerful manager is not likely to be very good.

Here are the points to discuss.

Compensation. The first and most obvious issue is the manager's percentage. You should try to limit the percentage to 15%, although some managers argue that the risk of taking on a new band is worth 20%. They say it will be years—if ever—before they get paid for a lot of work (which is true). A compromise is to say the manager gets 15%, which escalates to 20% when you earn a certain dollar amount (such as 15% of the first $2 million and 20% of the excess). I've also seen the opposite, where the manager gets 20% up to a certain level, and then 15% after that. The theory is that the manager gets a bigger percentage when you're young and the manager can't make as much, but his or her cut drops to the 15% norm when you're successful. This seems a bit weird at first, because it looks like the manager has no incentive to make you more successful (the more success, the lower the manager's take). But it's really not true—all managers would rather have 15% of a big number than 20% of a small one.

Sometimes managers share in the net of an artist's earnings rather than the gross. This is much better for the artist—for starters, the manager won't get paid if the artist loses money, which is not the case in gross deals. In one deal I'm aware of, the manager got 20% of the net of a four-piece band, which worked out to about 8% of gross.

When a manager has a deal on the net, they will sometimes ask for limits on the expenses. For example, artists who decide to go on the road and charter jets, throw gigantic parties in every city, put inflatable pools in their suites, etc., can easily eat up the net while having a great time. Managers don't usually enjoy these parties quite as much. Thus, the agreement might be that the manager is paid on net touring proceeds, but that the expenses of the tour can't exceed a negotiated percentage of the gross.

A variation on this theme is the idea that a manager gets a percentage of gross, but is capped out at 50% of the net. In other words, the manager will never make more than the artist actually puts in his or her pocket. For example, if you gross $1,000, and have $800 in expenses, your net is $200. If the manager got 15% of the gross, he or she would earn $150. Under this arrangement, the maximum would be 50% of the net (50% of $200, or $100), so the manager gets $100 and the artist gets $100. Note, however, that if you're a group, you all have to share the artist's 50% of the net, which means the manager makes more than any one of you.

In a few situations, where the artist is a superstar and substantially more important than the manager, the deal is sometimes a set salary (no percentage) for the manager (although this salary can run well into six, or sometimes even seven, figures).

Exclusions. It's sometimes possible to reduce (or even exclude) certain types of earnings. For example, if you're a major songwriter hiring a manager to help you become a recording artist, the manager might get 15% of your earnings as an artist, but only 10% (or even 7½%, 5%, or 0%) of your songwriting monies. Or perhaps the manager gets 15% of your songwriting monies from records on which you appear as an artist, and a reduced (or no) percentage on other songwriter earnings. Another example is an established actor in the film industry who hires a manager to help with his or her music career. Or vice versa. In these cases, you normally exclude (or reduce the percentage for) the area where you're already established. The possibilities are as varied as your imagination.

If you exclude any of your earnings from commission, you would of course not expect the manager to work in the excluded area.

Deductions. Certain types of monies are customarily deducted before computing the manager's percentage, and these are never commissionable. Most managers won't commission them (even if their contract says they can), but some try. So it's always a good idea to spell these out, and avoid any misunderstandings:

1. **Recording costs.**
   If the record company pays you monies that you use to pay for recording costs, you should not pay a commission on these. This is because they only pass through your hands (i.e., you don't keep them), and thus they are not really "earnings."

2. Monies paid to a producer.

The reasoning is the same as recording costs. This includes not only advances to the producer, but also royalties. (Producers are discussed on page 133.)

3. Tour support.

This is money paid by a record company to offset your losses from touring (see page 157). Commissioning tour support is a bit controversial. Some managers argue this is money you get from the record company, and, just like any other money, they should commission it. Most of the time, however, they will agree that it isn't commissionable, because it only compensates you for a loss.

4. Costs of collection.

If you have to sue someone to get paid, the cost of suing them to collect the money ("collection costs") should be deducted before applying the manager's percentage. For example, if a promoter refuses to pay your $50,000 fee for a show you performed, and it costs you $10,000 in legal fees and court costs to collect, the manager should only commission $40,000 (the $50,000 recovery less the $10,000 collection costs). Another way to look at this is to say the manager bears his or her proportionate share of the collection costs.

5. Sound and lights.

It's common in contracts for personal appearances that the artist supplies his or her own sound system and stage lighting. The promoter then "rents" the sound and lights from the artist for a specified dollar amount. Customarily, the rent money is considered an expense reimbursement (as opposed to a fee paid to the artist), and so the manager isn't paid on the amount allocated to sound and lights. But you gotta ask for this one.

6. Opening acts.

When you get to the superstar category, your deal for a personal appearance may also include monies you must pay to an opening act (see page 336). Again, since this money just passes through your hands, it should not be commissionable.

Term

The term of a management agreement is generally three to five years. If you're an artist, you want to make it as short as possible; if you're a manager, you want it to be as long as possible.

A trend over the last few years is for managers to have terms that are geared to **album cycles** as opposed to a specific number of years. An

album cycle means a period of time from the commencement of recording an album until the end of the promotional activities surrounding it. Usually that means a tour, as well as promotion of all of the
singles from the album. A management-deal term geared to album
cycles is fairer to the manager. If the term is simply a period of years,
it could end in the middle of an album and the manager could get
locked out of commissions after he or she has done almost all of the
work.

The most common compromise is to say that if the artist doesn't earn
certain minimum amounts, he or she can terminate the agreement
early. For example, if an artist doesn't earn $200,000 over the first two
years of a five-year deal, the artist can terminate the agreement at the
close of the two years. A recent trend has been to use album sales figures, instead of a minimum dollar figure, to determine if the artist can
get out of the deal. The amount of sales varies with the type of artist
involved. For example, if you're a straight-ahead, commercial artist,
you want a fairly high figure. On the other hand, if you're more off-
center and want to build slowly, the figure would be lower. Whatever
the level, it doesn't usually kick in until the second or third album, as
the managers argue that the first album is just the beginning of a building process. Recent deals I've seen used a figure of 80,000 albums for
an alternative, quirky band, and a figure of 250,000 albums for a
straight-ahead, commercial artist. The termination can either be done
by a letter from the artist to the manager containing legal words that
translate as "You're fired," or it can be set up as a shorter deal that
continues if the artist achieves certain earnings (for example, the term
of the agreement is two years, but if the artist earns at least $200,000
over these two years, the manager continues for an additional three
years). The only difference between these two arrangements is whether
the artist has to remember to send the manager a notice.

If the manager has satisfied the criteria, the deal then continues. It's
to your advantage to keep the continuation period as short as possible—say one year, with a minimum earnings requirement for that year
before you go to the next, or one album with a sales criteria to continue. And no matter what, a manager shouldn't have a total of more
than five years or three to four albums.

I hesitate to give you any specific dollar figures for the earnings,
because (1) they'll probably be out of date by the time you read this,
and (2) they also depend on who you are. If you're a heavy metal
touring band, the numbers are much higher than if you write folk
songs and appear only in coffee houses. But here's an example from
one of my recent deals for a beginning rock artist: The deal was for

two years, and the manager could renew for an additional year if the artist earned $300,000 over the first two years. The manager could then renew for another (fourth) year if, during the third year, the artist earned $200,000 (remember, the $300,000 was for two years). Finally, the manager could continue for a fifth year if, during the fourth year, the artist earned $500,000.

The manager, if he or she has any sophistication, will also say the earnings figure has to include offers you turn down. The theory is that you can't refuse to work and then get out of the deal with your manager because you didn't earn enough. I usually agree to this request, but I require that the offers must be similar to those which you have previously accepted, so an offer to appear nude at the Moscow Circus doesn't count (unless that's your act).

Earnings After the Term

One of the most important points you have to negotiate with your manager is what he or she gets paid after the end of your deal. Even though the term of your deal is three to five years, virtually every management contract says the manager gets paid on earnings *after* the term if they're generated under "contracts entered into or substantially negotiated during the term." This language means two things:

1. As to records made *during* the term of the management deal, the manager gets a commission from sales of these records occurring *after* the management deal; and
2. The manager is paid on records made *after* the term of your management deal if the records are recorded under a record contract signed during the term.

All of this could mean—and I've seen it happen—that the manager is still getting paid seven, ten, or more years after he or she finished rendering services. For example, suppose six months before the end of the management deal you sign a five-album record deal. Under this clause, the manager gets paid forever on sales of these five albums, most of which will be recorded years after you've parted company.

I personally think this clause is overreaching, and I've been pretty successful in cutting it way back. Let's analyze the situation:

The major things to be concerned about are records and publishing. Unless you're in a television series or some other nonmusical commitment that could run for several years, records and publishing are the only areas where you're likely to have significant earnings from activities *after* the term *under agreements* made *during* the term. The other contracts you make during the term, such as personal appearance engagements, may be completed after the term, but this happens in a relatively short period (although it can represent millions of dollars). And if a manager is involved in setting up a tour, it's not unreasonable for him or her to be paid on the tour. (So if you're going to dump your manager, do it before the tour gets set up.)

Sunset Clauses. In any event, here are some of my better strategies to cut this back. These are known as **sunset clauses,** because they end the day for commissions:

1. **Records**
   (a) The manager gets paid only on records recorded and released during the term (and not on any others). This is the best for you.
   (b) Another solution is that the manager gets a half commission (e.g., if the manager gets 15%, it's reduced to 7.5%) on records recorded during the term but released afterward. The theory is that the manager only has to do half the work—overseeing the recording, but not overseeing the release and promotion. (As in (a), records recorded after the term aren't commissionable at all.)

2. **Publishing**
   (a) The manager is paid only on songs recorded and released during the term. This is the best for you.
   (b) The manager gets a half commission on songs recorded during the term and released after.
   (c) The manager gets a half commission on songs *written* during the term but recorded afterward. This at least cuts off participation in songs written after the term under contracts made during the term.

3. **Compromises**
   If you can't pull off any of the above, try these:
   (a) The manager gets a full commission on everything made under deals entered into during the term (including records recorded after the term), but only for the first three years after the term. He or she is then reduced to a half commission for another three years, and then everything stops.

(b) The manager gets a full commission for five years after the term, and thereafter nothing.

Notice the above three approaches are not in any way mutually exclusive; you can creatively mix and match. For example, the manager could get a full commission on records recorded and released during the term, but only for a period of three years after the term. Or he or she might get a commission for a period after the term equal to the term itself (if the term were three years, the period afterward would be three years; if it were four years, the period would be four years, etc.), and thereafter nothing else. The limits are only your imagination and the manager's patience.

A particularly thorny problem (and another reason you should pay so much attention to the commissions after the term) is the fact that, after the term, you'll need to hire a new manager. As you can imagine, there aren't too many managers who want to work for free, and there are even fewer artists who want to pay 15% of their gross to two managers (30%!). Thus, it's very important that you limit or eliminate commissions after the term on some basis. In truth, most managers are willing to take reduced or no commissions on earnings that another manager is commissioning. But they're only going to do this for, say, the first album or the first tour, and they'll only do it if you're pretty successful. If they can't start making money relatively quickly, managing you isn't going to be worth their time and effort. So while you can live with paying a prior manager something on after-term projects, you should limit it as much as possible.

Key Man

Another important aspect of your deal is called a **key man** clause (hopefully soon to be called a "key person" clause). For various tax reasons (or sometimes because they have partners), you may have a relationship with a particular personal manager, but your contract is with their corporation or a partnership. It is thus possible that "your person" could leave the corporation or partnership, and since your deal isn't with that manager personally, you can't just get up and go with him or her. Accordingly, you could find yourself managed by a stranger.

To prevent this, you should insert a clause that says the person with whom you have a relationship (the "key man") must personally act as your manager, and if not, you can terminate the deal. If the company buys this concept (some bigger ones won't), you can easily get a clause that says you can terminate if the key man dies or is disabled, or if he or she is no longer employed by the corporation or partnership. But what if they're alive and kicking, still employed by your manager, yet taken off your account? It's much harder to say the key man must be "actively involved" in managing your life, because the manager begins to worry that, even if the key man is still working on your career, you'll try to use this clause to get out of your deal—you would argue that the manager is doing a mediocre job (and thus is not "actively involved") so that the management company is in breach of your contract. (For exactly this reason, from your point of view, the broader you can make the language, the better.)

Double Commissions

If you, for tax planning or otherwise, set up a corporation to conduct your entertainment activities, you want to be certain there are no **double commissions** by reason of your corporation. (See page 187 for a discussion of using a corporation in record deals, and page 313 for corporations used by groups.) Management contracts say that the manager gets a commission based on your earnings at the corporate level. This is perfectly reasonable—otherwise, you could easily pay the gross monies into the corporation, pay yourself only a small salary, and claim the manager gets his or her commission based on the small amount that comes out to you. (For example, if your corporation gets $100,000 for your appearance at a show but only pays you $10,000, it wouldn't be fair to pay the manager only 15% of the $10,000.) However, it's not reasonable for the manager to take a second bite at the money. Once he or she has commissioned it at the corporate level, there should be no further commission when it comes out to you in the form of salary. (In the previous example, this means the manager can't commission both the $100,000 *and* the $10,000.) Most management contracts would technically allow the manager to do this "double dip" (after all, the salary is your gross income), but in practice it isn't done (by reputable managers). Still, it's always a good idea to specifically say so.

Power of Attorney

Another provision to watch for in the agreement is one which says the manager has a **power of attorney** (meaning the power to act for you), such as the right to sign your name to contracts, hire and fire your other representatives, cash your checks, etc. I like to wipe out most of this nonsense. You should hire and fire your own representatives, and the only time I let a manager sign for an artist is (a) if you're unavailable to sign the agreement yourself, (b) after the manager has your verbal approval of the deal, *and* (c) the deal is for personal appearance engagements, of no more than two or three nights, which will be performed within the next four to six weeks. If it doesn't meet these criteria, bless the piece of paper with your autograph.

The Best Deals

Having now discussed managers' contracts at length, you're ready for a well-kept secret. Many of the top managers have absolutely no written contracts with their artists. It's all done on a handshake, and the only discussion is the percentage. Their feeling, and I respect them for it, is that the relationship is more important than any piece of paper, and if the artist isn't happy, they're free to go at any time. Also implicit in the statement is that the artist needs them as much as (or more than) they need the artist.

Please don't misunderstand this point. Many legitimate and well-respected managers require written contracts, and there is nothing wrong with this. But there are also a number who "fly naked" (without a written deal), and ironically they are often the ones who keep their clients the longest.

PICKING THE RIGHT MANAGER

So how do you pick a manager? First, review chapter 2, which applies to your whole team. Then, take a look at these specific tips on a manager.

Let's start with what would be the absolute best. This is the yardstick to use in measuring your candidates: The absolute best manager is a powerful, well-connected manager, with one or more major clients, who is wildly enthusiastic about you and willing to commit the time required for your career. If you're a superstar, you can find such a person without too much trouble. If you're not, this situation hardly ever exists. The reason is that, when a manager is powerful and successful, he or she is usually not interested in anything other than a major money-earning client. The thinking is simple—it takes as much or more work to establish a new artist as it does to service an established artist, and guess which one pays better (and sooner)? (It's true that, every once in a while, a powerful manager gets genuinely revved up over a new band. But this is rare, and you have to be extraordinarily lucky even to get such a person's attention.)

So let's take a look at some more down-to-earth alternatives, which are not in any particular order:

1. A major manager with a young assistant who is genuinely enthusiastic about you.
2. A midsize manager (whose artists' albums sell in the 300,000 to 500,000 range) who is wildly enthusiastic about you.
3. A major, powerful manager who is taking you on as a favor (either personal or professional) to somebody who is *very* important to him or her.
4. A young, inexperienced manager who is willing to kill for you.

There are of course endless combinations of the above, but these are the major categories.

Unless you can get the best possible situation described on the preceding page, you'll have to make some kind of compromise. The compromise is between power and clout on one hand, and time and attention on the other. The reason a manager is powerful is because he or she has at least one powerful client who takes up most of the manager's time. This means you're going to get less of it, and thus less personal attention (although these people can often do more in a five-minute call to the right person than a newcomer can do in a week). On the other hand, a young, bright manager with no other clients will lack the clout and experience but will spend all of his or her waking hours with you and worrying about you, and will go to any lengths to promote your career. And in between lies a rainbow of choices.

I personally like young managers a lot. If they're bright and motivated, I have seen their energy overcome a lack of political clout and knowledge with superb results. And to help you understand why, let me give you the Passman Treatise on Managers' Careers. Managers' careers go something like this:

1. The manager is young and enthusiastic, and attaches himself or herself to a promising young act.
2. Through whatever means it takes, the manager promotes the artist into major stardom, at which point (a) every other manager comes out of the woodwork to try and steal the act, and (b) the manager is offered twenty-seven other acts to manage each week. (The people who previously wouldn't return his or her phone calls are suddenly his or her best friends, and are saying this manager must be a genius to have taken these obscure nobodies to stardom.)

3. The manager is now exhausted from having worked so hard on the first act (back when he or she had nothing else to do and could literally live with the band). So the manager wants to cash in on the fame and fortune while it lasts, and, accordingly, starts hiring assistants and begins taking on more and more superstars.

4. This is the point at which many managers begin to lose it because they're too successful. Some of them have such huge egos that they won't take on assistants of their own caliber (for fear the assistants might steal the artists). So they hire less capable people and give the artists lousy service. Others hire good people, but pay them so poorly that their employees get frustrated and go out on their own (usually stealing the artists in the process). As things unravel, the manager begins to lose artists who are no longer getting the personal attention they once did. (A few managers have been able to pull off a large, successful management company, but they're the exception. They also ruin my theory, so I'm ignoring them.)

5. After these batterings, the manager feels it was a mistake to have tried to get so big, breaks up with his or her partners, keeps one or two key artists, and starts a record label or goes into the movie business.

Remember, everybody was nobody at one time. While I don't suggest that a superstar should take on an inexperienced manager, I do think many new artists are well advised to hire a bright, aggressive young manager. Obviously, you shouldn't do this if you have the opportunity to go with an established manager who is (or has someone in his or her organization who is) genuinely enthused about you. But if this is not an option, the right young manager can be a real asset.

4

Business Managers

ROLE

The business manager is the person on your team who handles all your money. He or she collects it, keeps track of it, pays your bills, invests it, makes sure you file your tax returns, etc.

Listen to me!!! Did you know that, in California, a person needs no credentials whatsoever to be a business manager? Contrary to popular opinion, to be a business manager you don't have to be an accountant (much less a certified public accountant), and you don't even have to be licensed by the state. Technically, business managers who give certain kinds of investment advice need to be "registered investment advisors" (like stockbrokers, who are licensed by the federal government before they can sell securities to the public). However, very few are.

What this means is that you could be turning your money over to someone who has no more financial training than you do. And when you stop to think about it, that's pretty scary.

I know you wouldn't have gone into the music business if you wanted to be a financial whiz—if you were good with numbers, you'd be in some back room with a green eyeshade instead of winning your way into the hearts of millions. I also know that numbers make you nervous and may even intimidate you. On the other hand, there are parts of all of our lives that we don't like, and, while we can get other people to deal with them day to day, we have to be sure we choose good people to do it. For this reason, I urge you to *personally* spend some time investigating all of the people on your team, AND BE ESPECIALLY CAREFUL WHEN IT COMES TO BUSINESS MANAGERS. They can range anywhere from superb to sleazoid, with all variations in between. And their bedside manner and office space may tell you very little of what they're really like—the bad ones can be like a shiny used car that's rotting from rust underneath a new paint job. Financial disasters can come from someone who is an out-and-out crook, or they can come from an honest person, with the best of intentions, who is just a boob. My doctor once told me a story about an orderly he had when he was in the army. One day the orderly decided to go that extra mile and do something on his own initiative. So he decided to sterilize all of the thermometers—which he proudly did, with the best of intentions, by *boiling* them. SO BE EXTREMELY CAREFUL!

Hopefully I've now got your attention, so let's take a look at how to find the right person.

HOW TO PICK A BUSINESS MANAGER

References

The other professionals on your team can be of great help in choosing a business manager. But remember, they may have their own agendas. (See page 42.) For example, a personal manager may have a lot of control over a business manager because he or she handles some of the business manager's most important clients. This is a two-edged sword—it means you may get a lot of attention from the business manager, but it also means that, if you have a fight with your personal manager, the business manager may not necessarily be on your side (if the business manager loses you, it's only one account; but it could mean their whole career if they upset the personal manager). This is particularly so when the business manager also does the personal manager's work. With reputable personal managers and reputable business managers, I have rarely found this to be a practical problem, but it's worth watching.

Wheeler-Dealers

I'm leery of business managers who put together clients' money for deals in which the business manager is a general partner and is being paid by the partnership. For example, a business manager might form a partnership to buy a shopping center for $2 million. The partnership borrows $1.5 million, and the business manager's clients put in the remaining $500,000. As compensation for putting the deal together, the business manager might get 10% to 20% of the profits of the partnership, even though he or she puts up no money.

This practice (of taking a percentage to set up the deal) is a common way for real estate operators to function. However, when a business manager is both the operator and the investors' representative, it is impossible for him or her to be objective in advising the client to put money in the deal. I understand there are advantages to it—having your own representative in there running the investment can be to your benefit—but it strikes me as a bit too cozy. (Frankly, I don't even think this is a particularly smart move from the business manager's point of view. If the deal is a success, the clients resent the business manager's taking a piece. If it's a flop, they not only get blamed for recommending the investment, but eventually get nailed for the conflict of interest. If the business manager had instead invested with a stranger, this wouldn't have been the case.)

A trend over the last few years is for business managers to farm out their investment advice to specialists. There is a reality to the fact that doing investment research can (and probably ought to) be a full-time job. If the business manager doesn't have people on staff to handle it full-time, he or she may well arrange for someone else to take care of the investment advice. Also, some of them like to diversify into a number of different areas and get specialists for each area. I think this is a healthy trend overall, but you should ask how these outsiders get paid.

Family

Inviting family members into your financial life can, barring a very unusual circumstance, be extremely dangerous. Most of them aren't qualified to do the job, and even when they are, it's difficult for them to be totally objective about you. It's something like the reason that doctors won't operate on their immediate family, because they're too involved emotionally. And not only that, if something goes wrong, Momma may stop speaking to you.

BUSINESS MANAGER CHECKLIST

Take a look at chapter 2 again for general questions. And here are some specific ones to ask your potential business manager:

1. What kinds of financial reports are you going to get, and how often? (You should get monthly reports.) Ask to see samples of the reports. Are they clear? Can you understand them?
2. What is the business manager's investment philosophy? Will they

only keep your money in conservative, short-term paper (meaning bank deposits or government notes of thirty days to one year duration), or in highly speculative pork belly futures? Don't settle for the gobbledygook that says "we tailor to every individual's needs"; ask what their philosophy is for *you*, and *why*.

3. Is he or she a CPA (Certified Public Accountant)? Accountants who are certified have passed rigorous accounting exams and at least have that part of the job down. Whether they have the other skills to be good business managers is another question, but at least they're true professionals, who have trained extensively and are responsible for adhering to the CPA's code of ethics.

4. How much do they charge? (This is discussed in detail below.)

5. Find out exactly what the business manager is going to do for you besides paying your bills and keeping track of your income. Are they also going to do your tax returns? (Some charge extra for tax returns or send them to outsiders who charge.) Are they going to handle your investments or hire an outsider? In either case, how are they paid for investments? Do they do projections, budgets, and forecasts of your income? Do they coordinate wills and estate planning? Monitor your insurance needs? Oversee divorces?

6. Does the business manager want a written agreement? Some business managers require written agreements, although many don't. It isn't a bad idea, because it spells out exactly what's going on. However, don't ever agree to a deal with a term—you should be free to leave anytime you want.

7. Will the business manager object to your auditing him periodically? (An **audit** means you send in an independent person to see if the business manager has properly handled your money.) Very few people are willing to audit their business managers because they're embarrassed to do so and they think it looks as if they don't trust the business manager. In fact, the ethical business managers welcome it—they have nothing to hide and know it gives you peace of mind to find everything is as it should be. (You can figure out which ones don't want you to audit.) Auditing a business manager is expensive ($10,000 plus), and thus not worth it unless you earn substantial monies. However, when you get to the big leagues, an audit is important to consider. If you've raised the issue up front, there won't be any question later. It's surprising how few people raise this issue until it's too late.

8. Do they represent music clients? This may seem like a silly question, but some very talented business managers have no expertise in the music industry, and you don't want one of them. The music industry is specialized, and you need someone who understands its intricacies. For example, if they don't really understand publishing, they can't do a good job of making sure you get paid everything you should.

9. Have they handled people with your particular problems and challenges? If you're a new artist, you want to be sure they know how to watch every penny so you can survive. You also want to be sure they have time for you. If you're a superstar, you want to make sure they've handled, for example, mega tours, which require massive financial controls and records (as we'll discuss in chapter 23).

10. If you live outside the United States or plan any extensive activities there, ask if they have any international experience. I probably don't have to tell you that meshing the tax laws between several jurisdictions (much less understanding the tax laws in any one of them) is a major job, and if you have or anticipate these kinds of problems, you need someone who's been down that road before.

11. Do they get "referral fees" from any place they might put your money (such as a purchase of insurance, putting your funds in a particular bank, placing your investments through a particular stockbroker, etc.)? A referral fee is an amount paid to them by the people who receive your money, as compensation for referring you to them. Ideally, they shouldn't get any such fee because it could affect the advice they give you—they might be inclined to put you with someone who gives them a fee, even if it's not in your best interests. However, if the existence of the fee and the amount are fully disclosed up front, and if the business manager is willing to credit it against your fees, and if you get independent advice about the particular transaction, this could be okay. But put your radar up if you see it.

12. The check-signing procedure should be set up carefully, and if possible you should sign all the checks. When you get really busy, it may not be possible to do it, although I know some extremely successful and busy artists who manage to sign all their big checks. Most of the time, larger checks can be either signed in advance or sent to you.

13. Be sure the person you're dealing with wants to educate you, rather than just tell you what to do. Most decisions can be

condensed down to a fairly simple summary, and you should make all the significant decisions yourself. Be wary of someone who just wants to tell you what to do and seems offended if you question it.

FEES

How to pay your business manager varies depending on your circumstance. The custom is for them to work on a percentage (5%), an hourly rate, a flat fee, or some combination. Some people earn great sums of money and have uncomplicated lives, and if this is you, opt for an hourly rate or set fee. Others, who earn much less and always seem to have financial troubles, should go for a percentage. (Ironically, if your finances nosedive, you may need more of your business manager's time than when you're doing well—he or she has to keep the wolves away from the door and turn pennies into nickels. This, of course, comes at a time when you can least afford to pay.)

Some business managers want a minimum fee, because they have legitimate costs just to set up their systems to service you. Unless they're willing to take a flyer with you on the hopes that you'll someday be hugely successful, they normally want their downside covered. Hence they charge a minimum fee, which can range from $500 to $2,500 a month, or more for superstars. Some business managers charge a minimum fee equal to a percentage (for example, 66%) of their hourly rate. Under these arrangements, they get a minimum that varies with how much work they do, and you get a break because they charge you less than if they were merely on an hourly rate. This discounted hourly fee isn't for everyone—if you don't like the thrill of not knowing what you have to pay until the bill arrives, stick to a minimum that's a flat amount. Whatever the minimum, it will be against (meaning a prepayment of) the percentage. If the business manager is young and hungry, he or she may be willing to take a "flat fee" for all services, regardless of the amount of work.

If the charges are based on an hourly rate, spell out what the rate is, and be sure to get the rate for everyone involved, not just the top people. If the fee is a percentage, many business managers will accept a maximum fee, particularly when they're charging you a minimum. This will again vary with the amount of money you earn and the amount of work you require. Maximum fees range generally from $150,000 to $300,000 per year (which means, if the percentage is 5 percent, you are making $3 million to $6 million a year). Minimums for people in this range are roughly $30,000 to $125,000.

If the business manager charges a percentage, ask if it applies to investment income. With some business managers it does, while with others it doesn't. It should also apply only to money *received* (not earned) while they are involved.

Listen again! Let me say this one more time. *Be extremely careful in picking your business manager, more than anyone else on your team.* This is the person who can make sure you have a cozy old age, or can assure that you have to play nightclubs in your fifties just to eat.

YOUR HALF OF THE JOB

Just as important as picking the right business manager is your own attitude. I remember seeing one of Elvis Presley's bodyguards at a press conference for his book on Elvis. A reporter asked why he didn't stop Elvis from taking drugs and destroying himself. His answer was, "How do you save a man from himself?"

I've always felt that answer, which really hit me, was the most telling statement about an entertainer's life. If you don't care about your financial future, it's difficult for anybody else to. If someone is constantly telling you not to do something (like spend money), and you really want to do it, you'll probably get rid of them rather than listen. Remember Dick Gregory's quote (see page 45)? If you're going to spend everything you make, and then start spending money you don't yet have, you're going to end up broke. It's that simple. So don't do it, unless you subscribe to my partner Chuck Scott's philosophy of how to build a small fortune: "The best way to build a small fortune is to take a large one and dwindle it down."

Few things last forever, and an assured stream of earnings at your highest level is not one of them. So even the best business managers can't help you if you're bent on jets, yachts, houses, cars, and overuse of controlled substances when you can't afford them. I know: You're reading this and saying it will never apply to you. But only you can make sure it doesn't.

5

Attorneys

Now for a subject close to my own heart, and one about which it's hard for me to be totally objective. But I'll try.

PICKING A LAWYER

Role

Attorneys in the music business do much more than just look over contracts and advise clients about the law. They are very much involved in structuring deals and shaping artists' business lives.

Lawyers have evolved into one of the most powerful groups in the music industry, odd as that may sound to you. The reason is that the power bases in the music business aren't concentrated in any one group (such as, for example, the major agencies, who are the most powerful players in the film business. In the music biz, the agents are powerful but limited in their sphere of influence, as we'll see in the next chapter). Personal managers are very powerful, but the nature of their job limits the number of clients they can take. The business managers can have a lot of major clients, but they deal only in limited financial areas and are therefore not power bases. Lawyers, on the other hand, are involved in all areas, and because the time required for each client is less than that of a personal manager, they can handle a large number of clients. This means the attorneys end up seeing more deals than anyone else and, thus, have more knowledge of what's "going down" around town. Consequently, they can be influential in determining which company will get a particular deal, which means the companies want to keep them happy. They can also influence which personal manager and which business manager get a client, which means these guys also want to keep the lawyers happy. This means lawyers have power (and are happy).

Style

There are distinctly separate styles of attorneys in the music business. Some are into "hanging out" and acting as if they're one of the band members, while others are more conservative and stick to the business side. There are power broker/agent types, who are good negotiators but not particularly good lawyers, and excellent lawyers who lose sight of the big picture. And of course there's a whole spectrum in between.

Using the techniques in chapter 2, first assure yourself you're talking to a good, competent lawyer. After that, the match-up of style is mostly a matter of your personal taste in people. For example, if you like flash, you may want a flashy lawyer (although I find more often that flashy artists like their lawyers to be staid and solid). If you're honest and straightforward in your business dealings, however, be sure to get an honest and straightforward lawyer (your references will tell you who is and isn't). If you aren't, there are lawyers to match you too.

Clout

It's true a lawyer with clout can get through to people that other lawyers can't (or at least faster). Indeed, one of the major things to look for in a lawyer is his or her relationships in the industry. Let me illustrate with a story about remodeling my house: Over the years I have been through a number of house remodels, always looking for the cheapest possible solution (which meant dealing directly with the workmen). I finally got sick of the whole process and broke down and hired a contractor who came highly recommended. (This contractor was so good that, after the job was finished, I was still speaking to him. That's a serious recommendation.) During this job, for the first time, I realized the value of a general contractor. In the past, whenever I called up a tile man, electrician, plumber, etc., these people couldn't have cared less about me. They came to do the job when it was convenient for them (if ever). If my sink leaked for a few days, they didn't care because they had a lot of other customers. On the other hand, when the contractor called them, they jumped immediately. The reason was pretty simple: If they didn't satisfy the contractor, they didn't just lose one job, they lost their next year's work.

The same applies to lawyers. Record companies can't ignore phone calls from important lawyers, nor can they afford to treat them shabbily in any particular transaction. The reason is the same as with the contractor—they're going to be dealing with these lawyers over and over, and they don't want to make enemies out of them. So a lawyer with good relationships will get your deals done quicker, and, if they know what they're doing, will get you the maximum that can legitimately be had.

You should also know what clout doesn't do. There is only so much you can get from any particular deal, regardless of who is asking. If a record company doesn't like your music, they're not going to sign you because of your lawyer. If they're hot for you, you'll get a deal even if you're represented by Jesse Helms. Put another way, the real "clout" is your musical talent. (Note I'm *not* talking about a lawyer's experience and knowledge—that is truly valuable, and will indeed get you the maximum from the negotiation. But you should have a perspective on the hyped-up importance of "clout.")

Loose Lips

Be especially wary of a lawyer who tells you about other clients' lives. Some lawyers, for example, will tell you exactly what deal they got for a specific client. Apart from the fact that this violates the attorneys' Canon of Ethics, it also means they will be telling other people about your deal. It may appear that these people trade confidential information for secrets they wouldn't otherwise have, but in fact the opposite is almost always the case—because everyone knows they have a big mouth, they're usually only told things that people want spread around town.

FEES

Most lawyers in the music business don't charge just on an hourly basis. For the ones that do, the rates are from $125 per hour for new lawyers, up to $450 or more for biggies. Some of us charge a percentage (usually 5%), while others do something known as "*value billing*," often with an hourly rate or *retainer* against it. (A "retainer" is a set monthly fee [like the business manager's minimum fee discussed on page 67], and it is either credited against the ultimate fee, or it's a flat fee covering all services.) "Value billing" means that, when the deal is finished, the lawyer asks for a fee based on the size of the deal and his or her contribution to it. If the lawyer had very little to do with shaping the deal, but rather just did the contract, I think the fee should be close to an hourly rate (though I'll get heat for telling you this, because it's usually more). On the other hand, if the lawyer came up with a clever concept or strategy that made you substantial sums of money, or the lawyer shaped or created the deal from scratch, he or she will ask for a much larger fee. If your lawyer "value bills," you should get some idea up front what it's going to be, so that there aren't any rude surprises. At a minimum, get a ballpark range.

CONFLICTS OF INTEREST

A lawyer has a **conflict of interest** when his or her clients get into a situation where their interests are adverse. This is easy to see, for example, when two clients of the same lawyer want to sue each other. However, it's also a conflict when two clients of the same lawyer make a deal with each other.

Lawyers are ethically required to disclose their conflicts of interest to you. Your choice is either to hire another lawyer, or you may "waive" (meaning you "choose to ignore") the conflict, and continue to use the same lawyer.

Because the entertainment industry is a relatively small business, those of us who practice in this field are continually bumping into ourselves when our clients make deals with each other. Most of the time these situations are harmless and can be handled simply, in one of several ways:

1. Each of the clients gets another lawyer (rare unless it's a pretty serious conflict).
2. One of the clients gets another lawyer (much more common).
3. The clients work out the agreement amongst themselves (or else the manager, agent, or business manager negotiates for them), and the lawyer merely draws up the paperwork, not representing anyone's interest.

When you are interviewing attorneys, you should ask if they have or foresee any conflicts of interest. Most ethical lawyers will bring it up before you do, but you should ask anyway. For example, your lawyer might also represent your record company, your merchandiser, your personal manager, producer, publisher, etc. It's not uncommon for a personal manager to recommend his own lawyer, his own business manager, etc., and thus it's not uncommon for lawyers to represent both the personal manager and an artist. Most of the time, this isn't a problem. However, if you get into a fight with your personal manager, the lawyer will probably have to resign (at least your side if the manager was there first). Also, you can't expect him or her to represent you vigorously against the personal manager in making your management deal. (On the other hand, as noted above in our discussion of personal managers, many powerful personal managers have no contracts at all, and there isn't much to discuss besides the percentage.)

In short, there are no hard and fast rules about conflicts. If the lawyer is straight and ethical, you can usually live with having him or her represent other people in your life. But if you have any concerns about this, look for a lawyer who's independent.

Conflicts, by the way, are not just limited to lawyers. Business managers can have conflicts when they represent both a personal manager and an artist (for example, if there is a dispute over commissions). Managers can have conflicts when they act in some other capacity (such as becoming the producer of the artist's motion pictures and negotiating a fee for themselves that affects what the artist gets paid). Managers can also have conflicts when they have two artists vying for the same gig. Like I say, it's a small business. But we generally work these things out amicably.

A disturbing thing that's been happening over the last few years is that some lawyers are actually selling conflicts of interest as a *benefit* to their clients. For example, they might suggest that you will get a better deal with a certain record company or publisher because they also represent them. I'll give you my subtle opinion of this pitch: It's utter nonsense. For one thing, if the lawyer is being paid by a record company or publisher, it's human nature that they'll think twice about how hard they want to beat them up and jeopardize a profitable relationship—especially for an artist who may pay them much less. Secondly, it's unethical for them to use any information they gain representing a company when negotiating against that company, and you can bet the company is neither going to like it nor permit it. So be very wary of any pitch along these lines.

It is certainly possible for you to live with a conflict, if you're fully informed and are comfortable that the lawyer will be in your court. But the conflict is a reason for you to be careful, not a plus. Accordingly, the issue must be left to the tummy test. In other words, ask yourself whether your tummy feels like it's OK, or whether you're concerned about it. And, if you're concerned, get another lawyer.

In recent years litigation concerning lawyers' conflicts of interest has increased. Some of the most powerful lawyers in the business have been sued over this. Hopefully, this will make everyone more cautious, including you and me. So always ask about potential conflicts of interest.

ATTORNEY CHECKLIST

Here's a recap of the questions to ask your potential lawyer:

1. Do you have expertise in the music business?
2. What do you charge? In addition to fees, do you charge for costs? (Everyone charges for long-distance phone calls, messengers, etc., but some charge for every page of photocopying, faxing, etc., while others are much looser.)
3. Ask if the lawyer has a written fee agreement. In California, lawyers are required to have their fee agreements in writing in order to enforce them (a major incentive to get them in writing). Ask for a copy of the fee agreement so that you can review it. Also, the lawyer can't insist on your signing it in his or her office—the California Bar considers that too intimidating. So take it home.

   It's unethical in California for lawyers to have an agreement with you that can't be terminated at any time. If it's a percentage arrangement, be careful about what happens to the percentage after the term. See the discussion of this under "Earnings After the Term" on page 55.

   You should ask if they object to your having the fee agreement reviewed by an independent advisor, preferably a lawyer, but at least a personal manager or business manager. No legitimate lawyer will object to this, and in fact they should encourage it. If it's at all possible, you should have your fee agreement with your lawyer reviewed independently—especially if it involves a percentage. And, if it isn't possible to do this, make sure the lawyer explains it to you in detail, and that you understand it.
4. Ask for references of artists at your level, and check them out. Does this lawyer return phone calls? Do they get deals done in a reasonable period of time? "Reasonable" in the music business is not going to be anywhere near the speed you would like. It's not uncommon for a record deal to take four or five months to negotiate, especially if you're a new artist and can't force the record company to turn out a draft quickly. Four to five months is a realistic time frame, but if it goes beyond that, someone isn't doing their job. I've always been amused by a story I heard from a new client when I was a young lawyer. He had been represented by another lawyer, and he said, "I know my record deal is good. It took over a year to negotiate."
5. Do you have or foresee any conflicts of interest?

6

Agents

ROLE

Agents in the music business are very different from agents in the film business. Whereas agents in the film business are the major power brokers in the industry, controlling many aspects of it, agents in the music industry are involved almost exclusively in booking live personal appearances (concerts). Music agents are sometimes involved in commercials, tour sponsorship, television specials, and other areas, but they don't participate in (or get paid for) phonograph records or songwriting, and thus are not players of the same magnitude as film agents. This is not to suggest that agents aren't important—they are extremely so, and very influential. But their sphere of influence is limited.

FEES

Because of their limited sphere, agents are only paid for the area where they render services (primarily concerts, as noted). So *never* give your agent a piece of your income from records, songwriting, or publishing (with the possible exception of film music, as noted on page 77). Usually agents don't even ask for this, but be careful of union forms as noted in the next paragraph.

Agents are regulated by the unions: AFM (American Federation of Musicians) for musicians; AFTRA (American Federation of Television and Radio Artists) for vocalists and taped or live television actors and actresses; SAG (Screen Actors Guild) for film; and Equity for live stage. The maximum the unions allow them to charge is 10%. (For certain personal appearances under AFM jurisdiction, it can be more. However, the agents readily agree to a 10% overall maximum if you ask.) The AFM and AFTRA printed forms have a place for you to initial if the agency commissions your earnings from records. Watch out for it and *never* do this.

The union regulation of agencies is called **franchising,** and unions only allow their members to be represented by "franchised" agents, meaning those who agree to the union's restrictions. Part of being franchised is an agreement with the union that the agency can only represent union members under a contract approved by the union. This system results in each union having its own pet printed form, spelling out that union's particular requirements. So your agency contract looks like a small telephone book. Actually, it's a stack of separate contracts, three for SAG (one for films, one for TV, and one for commercials), one for AFM, one for AFTRA, one for Equity, and two (called "General Services" and "Packaging") to pick up everything that isn't covered by a union.

Don't tell them I told you, but some agents will discount their percentage to as low as 5% for artists generating major revenues. (This is only for concerts. They stay at 10% for films, TV, etc., unless you're a major hitter in those areas—and even then they may not budge.) Sometimes there's a sliding scale, so that as your income goes up, the percentage goes down. The industry goes through cycles as to how easy it is to get this discount, and thus you have to check the situation out when it's relevant to you.

DEAL POINTS

The major things to negotiate in your agent's deal are the following:

Term

The agency will ask for three or more years, and you will want to keep it to one year. Shorter is better for you, because you can split if things don't work out, or squeeze their commission down if things do. The result of the jockeying depends on bargaining power. If you give more than a year, you should have the right to get out after each year if you don't earn minimum levels. (See the discussion of this under personal managers' deals on page 54; agency deals work the same way, except the numbers should be lower because they don't represent all areas of your life.) If you have enough clout, you may never sign any papers at all. However, this varies with the policy of the agency.

Scope

If you're involved in the film business other than doing music for films (for example, if you're a musical artist and also an actress, screenwriter, director, etc.), the trend is for agencies to insist on representing you in all areas. Thus, the agency representing you in the film business will require you to sign with them for your musical concerts, and vice versa. This may or may not be to your advantage, and it becomes more negotiable as your bargaining power increases and the agency's decreases. Some agencies have a firm policy and won't let you in the door without a full package, while others are more flexible.

Exclusions

Whatever the scope of your deal, you can exclude some areas, like the following:

1. As we discussed a minute ago, you can exclude earnings from phonograph records and songwriting or publishing without any difficulty (if you ask). However, some agencies try to commission your soundtrack album royalties if the album is derived from a film in which they got you work as an actor or actress. I have tried to resist this, unless you have no career as an actor or actress at the moment and the agency is instrumental in making one. And even under these circumstances, I like to make sure you're getting a major part in the film before the agency commissions the soundtrack album. It isn't fair for an agent to commission your earnings on the title song just because you're on screen for ten seconds to tell the doctor he has a telephone call. Your argument is that you don't need the agency to get you motion picture music work (unless, of course, you do), and that they shouldn't be commissioning an area in which you already have a career independent of them. Their argument is that, if they move you into a new arena (acting), and the soundtrack album is merely an aid to doing it, they should get paid on everything. Results vary with bargaining power. (There are agencies that specialize in getting motion picture musical work for artists. In that case, of course, the agency commissions your fee for writing music and/or singing, and phonograph record royalties as well. They normally don't commission songwriter performance royalties, which are monies we'll discuss on page 230.)
2. You should further exclude things like commercials (unless you've specifically engaged the agency for commercials), book publishing (if you're so inclined), and record producing.
3. You can also exclude costs of collection before applying the commission (as we discussed in manager's deals on page 53). In other words, if you have to sue someone to get paid, you should

deduct the cost of the lawsuit from your recovery before the agent gets his or her commission.

Even in excluded areas, however, the agents want to be paid if they get you work. I like to say they can only get you employment in these areas with your consent. That way they don't come running in with a flood of offers if you aren't in the market, or if you just don't want them involved.

Termination of the Agency

Remember, your agency deal is a stack of union forms. Each of these union agreements has a clause saying you can terminate if the agent doesn't get you work (or an offer of work) for ninety days. One of the things you need to ask for is that, if any of these agreements terminates, you can get out of all of them. Otherwise, the agency would represent you in some areas but not others, because they all have different termination criteria. This clause is a bit hard to get if you work only in the music area. Since you've never had a film career, the agency can reasonably argue they can't be expected to produce one in ninety days. The usual compromise is to say that, if the AFM or AFTRA agreement (your area) can be terminated for failing to get you work, then you can get out of everything.

Territory

If you're a new, or even midlevel artist, it may be difficult to give an agency less than worldwide rights. However, as you move up the ladder, you can sometimes exclude territories outside the United States. This is often beneficial, because you can use agents in Europe or elsewhere who are skilled in those markets. In fact, many U.S. agencies often employ a local subagent for foreign territories, and you can thus eliminate the middle man. And at a high enough level, you might even eliminate the foreign agent and deal directly with the promoters through your lawyer and personal manager (if they have the expertise). On the other hand, the U.S. agency doesn't just sit idly by while a subagent does the work. The agency oversees the foreign agent and makes sure the shows are properly promoted, that you get paid on time, etc.

Double Commissions

Like personal management deals, there should be no double commissions if you have a corporation. (See page 58.)

PICKING AN AGENT

If you have a personal manager, you'll have only occasional contact with your agent. You'll see him or her at your shows, and you may meet to set up your tours. The rest of the time he or she talks to your personal manager and, to a lesser degree, to your lawyer and business manager. Thus, while you should make the final decision, picking an agent should be primarily handled by your manager (since he or she deals with the agent most of the time).

If you don't have a manager, the agent will report directly to you. In this case, the criteria for picking your agent should be the same as picking a manager. So take another look at page 59.

PART II

Record Deals

7

Broad-Strokes Overview of the Record Business

So now you've got a great team. Congratulations! Let's learn how you can participate intelligently in the work its members do for you. We'll start with records.

INDUSTRY STRUCTURE

Let's first talk about how records make their way from the oven to your table. There are several designer methods to choose from:

Major Record Companies

This is the mainstream way most records are made. An artist signs a recording contract with a major label (Warner Brothers, MCA, etc.) and hands in his or her recorded tapes. The company then turns these into records (as you'll see in a minute, the definition of a "record" isn't so simple). It ships your records to a **distributor,** who is the wholesaler that sells your records to the stores (more about distributors later). The company then gears up its advertising, promotion, marketing, etc., and rockets you to stardom.

Here are the major divisions of fully staffed record companies (in no particular order):

A&R. These are the people with "ears" who find and nurture new talent, and who work creatively with the artists. (See page 133 for a discussion of A&R people.)

Sales. Sales people get your records into the stores—not an inconsequential step in having a million-seller.

Marketing. Advertising, publicity, album-cover artwork, promotional videos, in-store displays, promotional merchandise, etc.

Promotion. These folks live exclusively for getting your records played on the radio. They spend their days "jamming" various radio stations, and saying "baby" and "sweetheart" a lot.

Product Management. Product managers are in charge of whipping up all the other departments (sales, marketing, promotion, etc.) and getting them to work together to push your records. This is to make sure you get pulled forward by a coordinated team of horses, rather than torn apart by horses running in different directions.

Artist Development. This department coordinates the company's efforts while you're touring, such as running promotions in towns where you're appearing, making sure those cities have your records in the stores, etc. These are the ones to bug about tour support (which we'll discuss on page 157).

Production. Manufacturing, cover printing, assembling, and shipping to the distributors.

Finance. They compute and pay your royalties, bless their little hearts, as well as keep track of the company's income and expenses.

Business Affairs/Legal. These executives are responsible for the company's contracts, not only with artists, but with record clubs, foreign licensees, etc. Business affairs people negotiate the deals and, in conjunction with other executives, make the decisions as to what to give and what to hold. The legal department gives legal advice and drafts the contracts. Sometimes business affairs and legal are the same people.

International. As the name implies, the international department coordinates release of your records around the world, and oversees all the functions listed above in foreign territories.

Here's a pictorial chart, suitable for framing:

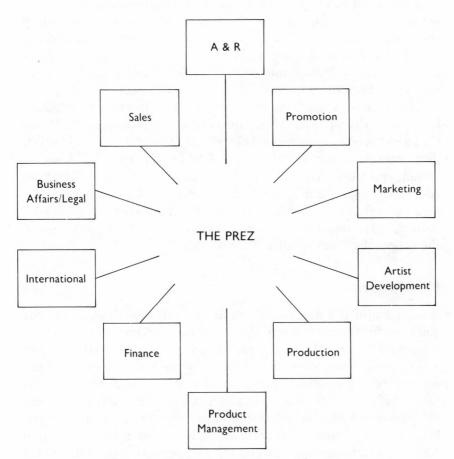

Figure 1. Divisions of a major record company.

By the way, in some companies a number of these functions are combined in a single person or department, while in other companies multiple departments handle just one of them. For example, a smaller company might have its A&R people also act as product managers. And at a larger label, there might be separate departments for advertising, publicity, art, and video (which are all handled by the marketing department at other companies). But the above is a good broadstroke view of the main divisions.

The major record companies are all distributed by **major distributors,** which are gigantic distribution networks that move records from manufacturing plants into the stores. And ramming these little suckers into retailers is more difficult than it sounds. You need a large network to do it, like any other manufacturing business, and it's expensive to set up and maintain the warehousing, shipping, inventory controls, sales force, etc., necessary to move goods into a marketplace. To give you some feel for it, WEA, a major distributor, employs approximately 1,250 people, while Warner Bros. Records (whose records it distributes) has only about 500 employees.

After years of consolidation, there are only six major distributors left, and they're all owned by the major labels (or, more specifically, by the labels' parent companies). They are (alphabetically): BMG (which distributes Arista and RCA Records); CEMA (Capitol, EMI-America, Virgin, and Chrysalis); MCA (MCA, Geffen); Polygram (Polygram, A&M, Motown, Island); Sony Music (formerly CBS, which distributes Columbia, Epic, Work, 550); and WEA (Warner Bros., Elektra, Atlantic). The labels listed after each are only the main labels—all of the majors distribute smaller labels as well.

Mini-Majors

A **mini-major** is a fully staffed company, with everything except the ability to distribute records to the stores. (And, as you now know, this is no small "except.") So the mini-majors are all distributed by majors and in almost every case are co-owned by the major. It isn't just the expense of a distribution operation that drives mini-majors to use major distributors. It's also a question of clout: If a retailer doesn't feel like paying its bills, who will it stiff—a major record company that can keep it from getting the next Janet Jackson album, or Fred Glump Records, which currently has a hit but next week may be in that Great Dust Bin in the Sky? (By the way, *mini-major* is not an industry term. I borrowed it from the film industry because I didn't know what else to call these companies.)

Mini-majors can be important forces in the industry. Examples of them are Maverick Records (distributed by WEA), Interscope Records (distributed by MCA), and La Face Records (distributed by BMG through Arista). There have been a number of others over the years, which have been gobbled up by majors on buying sprees, such as A&M, Geffen, Virgin, Motown, Chrysalis, Island, Sire, and Enigma. The gobbled companies now exist as parts of majors.

Here's a mini-major's distribution set-up:

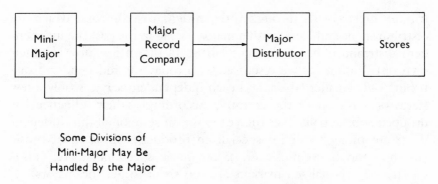

Some Divisions of
Mini-Major May Be
Handled By the Major

Figure 2. Mini-major record company distribution.

Independents

Independents are record companies not owned by a major or mini-major, and they come in two main flavors:

Major-Distributed Independent. This is an independent entity that has little or no staff, but rather signs artists and contracts with a major or mini-major to perform all functions except recording the records. The main thing these companies bring to the party is the ability to find talent and to mercilessly beat the distributing company about the head and shoulders to make sure their product gets promoted. Product released by these companies may be on the independent's own label, or it may be on the distributing company's label (in which case the public may never even know the independent exists). This type of entity is discussed in detail on page 193, in connection with independent production agreements.

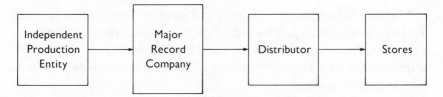

Figure 3. Major-distributed independent record company.

True Independent. A **true independent** has no affiliation with a major or mini-major, but rather is financed by its owners and/or investors. Examples of these labels are Ryko, Sub Pop, Epitaph, Rounder Records, Flying Fish, and SST. The true independents distribute their records through **independent distributors,** which are distributors not affiliated with a major. While in the past the independent distributors handled major labels, all the majors now do their own distribution (as we discussed). So today the independents distribute only smaller labels, and each independent services only a few states or a region of the country. Accordingly, their influence has dropped substantially over the years. But in spite of all this, independents are often better for specialized product such as street music (hip-hop, rap, house music, etc.), folk music, speed metal, etc. This is because (1) specialized markets are too small to get the majors' attention, and (2) the independents are "wired into" the smaller retailers who cater to this trade. Also, independents have recently had a huge resurgence with rap music, some of which can sell millions of albums (like the infamous 2 Live Crew). And because they're smaller and less cumbersome, they can move quicker. I'm told it can take ten weeks for majors to get product into their system and solicit orders, while independents can do it in just a few weeks.

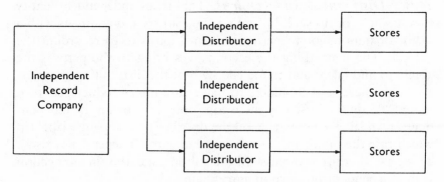

Figure 4. True independent record company distribution.

The line between independents and mini-majors is often blurred. You may find an independent, for example, that distributes through a major but does its own promotion and marketing, just as you may find a mini-major that lays off some of these functions on the major to whom they're married.

There is also a relatively new breed of company in the independent marketplace: independents owned by a major or mini-major record company. For example, Island owns "4th and Broadway," EMI owns "Caroline," and Sony owns "Relativity." Even though these entities are owned by majors, they are distributed by independents and thus have the ability to reach specialized markets, coupled with the clout and expertise of a major.

WHAT'S A RECORD?

Let's now turn to a real basic: What's a record?

As simple and straightforward as it sounds, the answer to this question is not what you'd expect. Of course, the term "record" means the devices you're thinking of—compact discs, prerecorded cassettes, and vinyl discs (R.I.P.). However, in virtually every record agreement made since the 1960s, the contractual definition of **record** says a record is both an audio-only *and* an **audiovisual** device (meaning one with sound and visual images), such as videocassettes and video discs (laser discs), which play video as well as audio material. (This is particularly interesting when you remember that audiovisual devices weren't even invented in the 1960s! Companies anticipated their development, even though none of us knew what form they would take.) The definition of *records* also included (and still does) any other device *now or hereafter known* that is capable of transmitting sound alone, or sound with visual images. As you'll see later, the inclusion of audiovisual devices in record deals can make life a bit tricky if you're a recording artist and also an actor or actress in films. Stay tuned (or peek at page 151 if you can't wait).

By the way, did you know that, originally, records were made by having the musicians and singers perform for each record sold? This was because there was no mass duplication process available, and thus the recordings were made directly onto the wax that was ultimately sold (meaning every record in a store contained a unique, one-time performance). Can you imagine how sick you'd be of performing a particular song if it sold a million copies?

MASTERS

The word **master** has two meanings:

1. The original tape recording made in the studio is called a master, because it is the *master* (meaning controlling entity) from which all copies are made (the machines making the copies are called *slaves*—master/slave; get it?). Master recordings today are **multitrack,** meaning that each instrument and voice part is recorded on a separate track or channel: the drums on one track, guitar on another, voice on another, etc. Most studios today use twenty-four tracks, and some have thirty-two tracks and more, meaning there can be twenty-four or more separate channels of informa-

tion. When the recording is complete, the master is then **edited, mixed,** and **EQ'd.** As in films, *editing* means cutting out the parts you don't like and splicing in the parts you do. *Mixing* means getting the proper level for each track, so that the drums are the right volume during each particular part of the song, the voice is raised a bit on the chorus, etc. (Most mixing today is done with computers, which "remember" the proper level of every track at each point during the song. Also in mixing, the sounds may be enhanced through processes I have never completely understood.) *EQ'ing* stands for "equalizing," and means that the bass, mid-range, and treble are each adjusted to be the right level (so that no one of them overpowers the others). The mixed multitrack is then reduced down to a **two-track** stereophonic master, which is ready for the duplication process. So there are two masters—the original multitrack, and the finished two-track.

2. The word master also means a recording of one particular song. Thus, you might say an album has "ten masters" (meaning ten selections) on it. These individual recordings are also called **cuts,** because of the historical fact that each selection was "cut" into vinyl.

ROYALTY COMPUTATION

Enough about art, let's talk about money. We'll start with your **royalties.**

Basic Concept

My brother-in-law, Jules, is in the used car business. He's famous throughout the West Valley because he'll trade cars for anything. At one point, he traded a car for a silver tea set, a set of golf clubs, and a mule. (Honest.) He then traded the mule, along with a stained-glass window of Daffy Duck, for an English bulldog named Rosie.

About that time, my wife and I were looking for a dog. It was before we had children, and we wanted to test our parenting skills on something that wouldn't use drugs if we failed. In trying to decide what kind of dog we wanted, we used to take Rosie for outings on weekends, and in a perverted way we began to think of her gnarled face and drooling as cute. Anyway, Jules decided he was going to breed her, and we wanted a puppy. So I helped by finding a stud dog, through a sophisticated referral system—the Yellow Pages. I called a place named Royal Family Bulldogs, which conjured up images of pampered dogs reclining on velvet pillows in a castle. Well, it turned out to be a dilapidated house in Pacoima, the most impressive feature of which was its bulldog smells. But Royal Family had a huge brown stud named Winston, who was a champion. So Jules hired Winston, and Rosie got pregnant.

About this time, Jules decided he wasn't interested in the headaches of small puppies. So he enlisted the help of his friend Corky. Corky's deal was that she would take care of Rosie and the puppies, and when each dog was sold, she'd get half of the sales price. Thus, if a dog sold for two hundred dollars, Jules would get a hundred dollars and Corky would get a hundred dollars.

So what does this have to do with records? Well, your record royalty is very much like Jules's share of the bulldog proceeds. In the case of records, the artist (like Jules) turns his recordings (pregnant Rosie) over to the company (Corky), who then sells the finished product (puppies). For each record (puppy) sold, the artist gets a piece of the proceeds, and the company keeps the rest to cover its costs and make a profit.

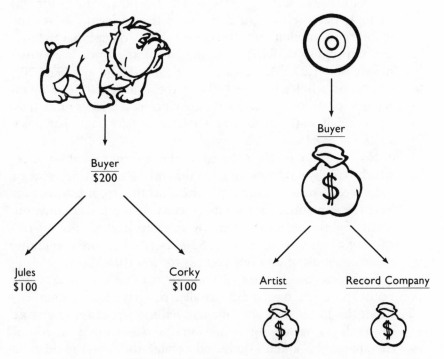

Figure 5. Bulldogs and royalties.

Basic Royalty Computations

For historical reasons, the division of proceeds between the artist and record company is more complicated than the puppy deal. The companies don't simply divide the money they get (that would be too easy and I'd be out of a job). Instead, almost all of the companies compute artist royalties as a percentage of the **suggested retail list price** of records (**SRLP** to its friends). The SRLP is an approximation of the price received by the *retailer,* which has nothing to do with the wholesale price received by the company. (Even those few companies that compute royalties based on the wholesale price don't just divide up the company's actual receipts; instead, there are a bunch of artificial adjustments, as you'll see.)

To follow the next part we'll need to use a little math. Don't worry if numbers aren't your strong suit—I'll keep it simple and go slowly. I've explained these concepts to my cousin David, who has to take off his shoes and socks to count to twenty, and he understood them.

Here's how it works:

1. The artist's royalty is stated as a percentage of the suggested retail list price, such as "10% of retail." I'll use retail for this example because the vast majority of the business uses it. The wholesale computation is the same as retail, except that the royalty is roughly doubled, since the wholesale price is approximately one-half of the retail price. To use simple numbers, 20% of a $4.50 wholesale price (90¢) is the same as 10% of a $9.00 retail price (90¢). (In actuality, the wholesale price is more than half of retail, so the equivalent wholesale royalty is less than twice the retail royalty.)

    Note that the royalty is based on the *suggested* retail list price, which has absolutely nothing to do with what you pay at your local record store (in my experience, no two record stores ever have the same price for the same record anyway). Currently, the SRLP for the majority of newly released analog (nondigital) cassette albums of superstars is $10.98. (As I'm sure you know, you can almost always buy records for less than this.)

    Each percentage point of retail or wholesale is known as a **point.** So if you have a 10% royalty, you have ten "points."

2. From this price, the company first deducts a **packaging charge** (also called a **packaging deduction**). In *theory,* this is the cost of the "package," and it's deducted because the artist should get a royalty only on the record, not the package. In *reality,* it's a

charge of much more than any package actually costs, and is thus only an artificial way to reduce the artist's royalty. The packaging charge is stated as a percentage of the SRLP, and the industry norm is 20% for cassettes and 25% for compact discs and other "new configurations."

3. The result of this (i.e., the SRLP after deducting the packaging charge) is called a **base price** or **royalty base.** This is the figure you apply your royalty percentage against.

Here's an example of an analog cassette royalty base computation:

Retail price of cassette	$10.98
Less: Packaging (20% of $10.98)	−2.19
ROYALTY BASE	$ 8.79

Thus, in this example, if an artist has a 10% royalty, he or she gets 87.9¢ (10% of $8.79) for analog cassettes. (CDs and digital cassettes are more complicated, so I'm saving them for later.)

Free Goods

Royalties are paid for each record <u>sold</u>. Why do I underline the word *sold?* Well, before I can tell you, you need to know more about how records are distributed.

When I was ten years old, I had a soft-drink stand in front of our house. I don't mean a card table with lemonade; I mean a serious soft-drink stand made out of genuine pine (by my stepfather), with Dr. Pepper and Coca-Cola signs that, if I'd kept them, would be worth more than my first car. Anyway, I stumbled on the brilliant idea of delivering soft drinks to the workmen at a construction site about a block away, using my little wagon. Instead of selling the drinks for a nickel, like everyone else, I would sell them for a dime (delivery labor, you know). But for every two drinks they bought, they would get two free. (Although I felt I was putting one over on the workmen, I have a feeling they really knew I was selling the drinks for a nickel each and using mirrors.)

My idea for a soft-drink scam, however, was taken to dizzying heights by the early record company accounting magicians. First, they figured out that selling one hundred records at 85¢ each was the same as selling eighty-five records for $1.00 each and giving the customer fifteen more for "free" for every eighty-five they bought (the retailer

Figure 6. The author invents free goods.

gets one hundred records either way, and the company gets $85 either way). Then, they figured out that, because fifteen of these records were "free," they didn't have to pay the artist for the free records—I mean, how could you have the gall to ask for royalties on a record the company wasn't being paid for? So by raising the price and giving away records for "free," the companies saved royalties on fifteen records out of every one hundred while making the same money. (Remember, the artist's royalty is based on *retail*, so the artist doesn't get any benefit from an inflated wholesale price.) Nifty, eh?

It took the workmen who bought my soft drinks about thirty seconds to figure out the price of my drinks was 5¢ each. But it took recording artists over twenty years to figure out that these "free" records were hardly free, because the economics to the company were exactly the same as if all the records had been sold at a lesser price. Got it?

There are two types of "free goods":

"Phony" Free Goods. Today, about half of the companies give away 15% of the records they ship (although historically, almost all of them did this). Where it's done, these "free" records are known as "phony" free goods because, like my soft drinks, they are nothing more than a cute way of discounting the purchase price. (Technically, they're called **normal distributor free goods**.) And in fact the companies that still use this practice charge a higher wholesale price

than those who don't, and the difference (not surprisingly) is the percentage of "free goods." For example, one major company that uses free goods currently charges approximately $12.12 for a $15.98 CD, while another major company, which has no free goods, charges $10.30. So one hundred CDs from the no-free-goods company cost $1030, while eighty-five CDs from the free-goods folks cost $1030 ($12.12 × 85 CDs = $1030). However, when you buy those eighty-five, you get fifteen "free," which means the cost of one hundred CDs from either company is the same. (By the way, even though it sounds like you should, you don't get more royalties from the companies without free goods, as we'll see in a minute). Back to our example:

Retail price of cassette	$10.98
Less: Packaging (20% of $10.98)	−2.19
ROYALTY BASE	**$8.79**

Using a 10% (87.9¢) royalty for sales of 100,000 cassettes, the artist's earnings would be $87,900 (rounded). However, since the company "gives away" 15% (or 15,000 of the units in this example) for "free," these 15,000 units don't bear any royalties. Thus, the artist is only paid on 85,000 units, and instead of getting $87,900, in fact the artist gets $74,715 (87.9¢ × 85,000 units), or 85% of the $87,900.

Units shipped	100,000
Less: free goods	−15,000
Royalty-bearing units	85,000
Times: Royalty	× 87.9¢
AMOUNT PAYABLE	**$74,715**

As noted before, about half of the companies have done away with the fiction of these "phony" free goods. But do you get more royalties? No; instead of free goods, they pay you only on 85% of the sales. So the result is exactly the same as it used to be with free goods, and it looks like this:

Units shipped	100,000
Royalty-bearing percentage	85%
Royalty-bearing units	85,000
Times: Royalty	× 87.9¢
AMOUNT PAYABLE	**$74,715**

You could get to the same place by simply saying the artist's royalty is $74.7¢, which is 85% of 87.9¢, and paying a royalty on all goods shipped. But no one does this, and I'll tell you why in a minute (on page 100).

"Real" Free Goods. All companies (even those who don't give "phony" free goods) give away **real free goods,** also known as **special campaign free goods.** This happens when a company is trying to push out large numbers of a particular artist's album. To get the stores to stock more of it, they give away 5% or 10% of all records shipped. These free goods are a very real discount of the price and are meant to encourage dealers to buy the record (which they invariably do because the dealers make bigger profits when they sell them). And because they actually cost the record company, they don't bear royalties.

Promotion Copies

Records given away for promotion, such as radio-station copies, are also real free goods and don't bear royalties. They are known as **promotional** or **promo** (pronounced "pro-moe") records. These don't go to retailers and are marked "not for sale."

As with any number of other things in life, unfortunately the theory and reality of promo records don't quite converge. While these records are meant for disc jockeys, they sometimes end up being sold in record stores. And of course they're priced cheaply, for the obvious reason that whoever sold them to the store got them for free.

What is less obvious is that the people who created the record don't get paid for sales of promos. Thus, while someone is enjoying a bargain, it's at the expense of the artist, publisher, songwriter, record company, unions, etc. (I hope I'm making you feel guilty if you buy promo records, since you're taking bread out of the mouths of your creative brothers and sisters.) Some record companies—for example, Sony—have tried to solve the problem by stamping their promotional product with an official-looking statement that says the record is only *licensed* for promotional use, as opposed to being given away. The theory is that the record company keeps ownership of each promo record, and so any resale of it is illegal. In theory the company is absolutely right—it is illegal to sell something you don't own, and Sony could demand return of the record at any time. However, you can imagine how meaningful this concept is to the owners and customers of Mortimer's Used Records and Ski Shop in East Elk, Vermont. So the best cure is an informed boycott. Let's start one.

Return Privilege

To understand this next part, you need to know that records are sold on a **100% return privilege.** This means that, if a retailer orders one hundred records from Epic but can't sell them, it can bundle them up, ship them back to Epic, and get full credit for (or a refund of) the price it paid. Such a practice is unlike most other businesses, because if you buy a load of plastic flamingos and can't sell them, you eat them. The reason is historical—records have always needed to be pushed out quickly in large numbers, and the retailers simply weren't willing to take the risk of getting stuck with too many of them (especially with new artists). Thus the retailers said they would only stock large quantities if the manufacturer agreed to take back the stiffs. (For you sticklers, I'm aware that most companies now charge penalties for returns in excess of 20% of records shipped, which means that, if a retailer buys one hundred records, it is likely to return only twenty of them [unless the record's a *real* dog]. However, since any given artist may have 100% of his or her records returned [the 20% applies overall, to all of the records of the company], I'm simplifying this to a pure 100% privilege, like the old days.)

To see why this is important, let's go back to Rosie's puppies. Jump ahead to the time when the puppies have been born and are crawling all over Corky's living room. A customer comes in to buy one of the dogs, but she isn't sure the puppy will get along with her kids. So she says, "I'll give you a check for the dog and you hold it while I take the puppy home to play with the kids. If, after a week or so, everything is going well, you can cash the check. If not, I'll bring the dog back for a refund." Corky agrees, willing to do anything to move the little nippers out. Later the same day, she tells Jules about the deal. Jules then asks for his half of the check (which of course Corky can't yet cash), and Corky suggests he have intercourse with himself. She says he can have his share when the buyer decides to keep the dog.

Reserves

The **reserves** used by record companies work in precisely the same way (usually without the suggestion for self-intercourse). Because records are sold on a 100% return basis, the companies legitimately don't know, particularly with a new artist, whether all the records they shipped will sell or whether they'll be returned by the retailer at a later date. Because the records may come back, the companies (like Corky) keep a portion of the royalties that would otherwise be payable to the artist (Jules) until they know whether the sales to the retailer are final. This holdback is called a *reserve* against returns.

For example, if a company ships 100,000 records of an artist, they may only pay the artist on 65,000 of these and wait to see if the other 35,000 sell through or are returned. At some point in the future (usually within two years after the shipment), the monies are paid through to the artist. The technical term for this pay-through is called **liquidating** the reserve. Of course, if the records are returned, the reserves are never paid to the artist because the sales are canceled and the royalty is never earned.

The size of your reserves varies with how well the company thinks your *next* album will do. For example, if the record company executives think your next album will sell extremely well, they'll be less concerned about holding big reserves—if they happen to hold inadequate reserves and overpay you, they can just take the money back from your next album. However, if you're a new artist and they're not sure there is even going to be another album, or if this is a "one-off" album such as a soundtrack album, or if this is the last album under your deal, you can anticipate healthy reserves and a record company attitude along the lines of "If you don't like it, tough noogies." (As your bargaining power grows, you can put caps on reserves. See page 161 for more on this.)

Adding reserves to our computation example, and assuming the reserve is 35%, the amount payable to the artist would look like this:

Units (100,000 shipped, payment on 85%)	85,000
Artist Royalty	×87.9¢
Total	$74,715
Less: 35% reserve	−26,150
AMOUNT PAYABLE TO ARTIST	**$48,565**

"90% of Net Sales"

In the early days, records were made of shellac, and were therefore breakable. So the record companies developed a practice of paying the artist on only 90% of the shipment, keeping the remaining 10% to cover their breakage.

Records haven't been made of shellac for the last fifty years, but the practice of paying on 90% of net sales persisted until very recently, and indeed at least two major record companies (I won't use any names, but their initials are A&M and Atlantic) routinely pay on only 90%. Note this 90% deduction is *in addition* to the free goods, and a wholly separate computation. There is no logical reason for this—it is a total rip-off that arbitrarily reduces your royalty by 10%. Thus, where a company pays on 90%, you are being paid on 90% (for "breakage") of 85% (for free goods), *resulting in payment on only 76.5% of shipments!* Resist this with your life, or else raise your royalty rate to compensate (10% on 90% is the same as 9% on 100%).

WHY ALL THIS WEIRDNESS?

The gypsies have a story that goes like this: When a baby is born, he is laid on a sheepskin with a violin to his left and a bag of gold to his right. The elders of the camp stand around the baby, murmuring hushed incantations, and watch closely for the child to act. If the baby reaches for the violin, he will grow up to be a musician. If he reaches for the gold, he will be a thief. In the rare case where the baby takes both, he will head the royalty department at a major record company.

I'm convinced that these bizarre computations came from the earliest days of the record business when artists had little sophistication (and no lawyers). We've all heard horror stories of early pop stars who received little or nothing for their music, and most of these stories are true. I'm certain a number of adult gypsy babies sat up nights trying to think of ways they could take money from the artists by doing anything other than reducing the royalty rate—"How can I tell them they have a 10% royalty and pay them like they have 7%?" You can almost see the "idea light bulb" illuminating the green eyeshade as one of these fellows hit on the brilliant stroke that the artist shouldn't be paid for the package in which the record is wrapped, or for records "given away" as free goods. The reality, as we discussed, is that the packaging deductions bear no relationship whatsoever to the real cost of the packaging, while the "free goods" are just a convoluted way to pay less royalties.

Perhaps more forthright is the story told about the late Morris Levy, a pioneer industry entrepreneur. Morris, a gruff guy whose voice sounded like he gargled with Drano, owned and ran Roulette Records. As legend has it, he was negotiating with an artist who was insisting on an 8% royalty, and Morris wanted to pay him only 5%. After a half hour of arguing, Morris finally said, "Okay, I tell you what. We'll put 8% in the contract. But I'm gonna pay you 5%."

ISN'T THERE A BETTER WAY?

Yes, there is. However, there is little chance it will be adopted in the near future.

Over the years, one or two companies have tried to compute their royalties more realistically, such as using a percentage of wholesale price with no free goods or packaging. But they all abandoned it because their royalty percentages came out so much lower than the other companies that they were unable to compete. In other words, an 8.5% royalty from a company paying on 100% of its sales without free goods doesn't sound as attractive as a 10% royalty from a company that pays on 85% of sales, even though they're exactly the same. Silly as it may seem, artists want to be able to "royalty drop" at cocktail parties, and it's easier to say you have a 16% royalty (and leave out the fact that it's on 85% of sales) than to say you have a "14% royalty with no free goods." In fact, the 14% is a higher royalty: For a $10.98 cassette (with a 20% packaging deduction), the 16% equals only $1.19, while the 14% equals $1.23.

It is also possible to state royalties in pennies, but the companies don't like this for a different reason. When you use pennies, you realize the packaging deduction causes an artist to get less money for the same-priced compact disc than for an analog tape (since the packaging deduction for analog tapes is 20%, while it is 25% for CDs). Also, this would make it too easy to compare what different companies are actually offering. So these deals are rare. Incidentally, if you ever make such a deal, be sure the pennies go up and down in proportion to the retail price, or you'll be locked in and, in effect, have a drop in royalties every time the price goes up. For example, if your royalty is $1.09 for a $10.98 cassette, and if it doesn't change when the cassette price moves to $11.98, your royalty drops from 10% (the ratio of $1.09 to $10.98) to 9.1% (the ratio of $1.09 to $11.98).

So forget being a reformer for now, and just accept the system. Besides, I had to learn how all this crap works, so why shouldn't you?

8

Advances and Recoupment

ADVANCES:
THE BASIC CONCEPT

Back to Jules and his bulldogs. Our friends at Royal Family charged him a $300 stud fee for the services of Winston. Let's suppose Jules didn't have the $300 (or at least didn't want to invest it in this particular endeavor). So Corky comes up with an idea: She agrees to pay Jules the $300, or to pay it directly to Royal Family, and then take her money back from Jules's share of money from the puppies. For example, if the puppies sell for $200 each (so that Corky gets $100 and Jules gets $100 for each dog), Corky would keep Jules's $100 share of the first three puppies ($300) to get back the stud fee.

This is exactly how an **advance** works. The record company pays a sum of money to the artist (the $300 stud fee) and then keeps the artist's royalties (the proceeds from selling the puppies) until it gets its money back. So if a company gives an artist $10,000 to sign a record deal, it keeps the first $10,000 of artist's royalties that would other-wise be payable. The process of keeping the money to recover an advance is called **recoupment,** and we say an advance is **recoupable** from royalties. The amount of unrecouped monies is called your **deficit** or **red position** (from the accounting use of red ink to signify a business loss), since this is the amount that has to be recovered before you get paid. So if you got a $100,000 advance and earned $75,000 in royalties, you have *recouped* $75,000 of the advance, and your *deficit* is $25,000 (you are $25,000 *"in the red,"* or $25,000 *unrecouped*).

Here's another way to look at it:

When I grew up in Texas, it was a big deal to drive just outside the city and see the huge water tanks with the name of the town painted on the side. (It takes very little to make me happy.) In fact,

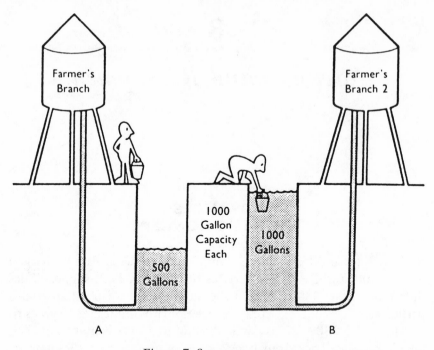

Figure 7. Separate accounts.

Farmer's Branch, a city outside Dallas, had a water tower that was a major local site. (Not as big as its post office, however, because the sign there said "Farmer's Branch Branch." Honest.) Anyway, picture a water tower with a large connecting pipe that runs deep into the ground. The connecting pipe feeds into a narrow dry well that requires a thousand gallons of water to fill it up to ground level. If there were no other access to the water, you'd have to wait until the water tower filled the well up to ground level (that is, until a thousand gallons had been poured in) before you could get any water. If there were only five hundred gallons, you couldn't reach it (see Illustration A), but when another five hundred gallons was added, you could (Illustration B).

Recoupment works exactly the same way. The water represents your sales, and the ditch is your deficit account. If you got a $1,000 advance from the record company, your account is $1,000 unrecouped. Until you earn $1,000 of royalties (i.e., until you have enough water to fill the well), you don't get anything. Just like the first 1,000 gallons of water have to fill the hole before you can get to the water, the record company keeps the first $1,000 in royalties to get its money back before you get any royalties.

Other Goodies

Monies paid directly to the artist are not the only recoupable monies. Recording costs are also recoupable from royalties, and so are (depending on negotiating strength, as we'll see below) video production costs, monies paid on behalf of the artist (for example, to buy equipment or to support a personal appearance tour), and anything else not nailed down.

Recoupable recording costs include everything you can think of, which is often a page-long list in your record deal. It's not just studio time; it includes equipment rental, travel, arranging, instrument transportation, etc. It also includes **union scale** (*scale* means the minimum amount a union requires everyone to pay its members) paid to you and others to perform at recording sessions.

In addition to a specific list of recoupable stuff (like cash to you, recording costs, and video costs), almost every contract has a general provision that says all amounts "paid to you or on your behalf, or otherwise paid in connection with this agreement" are recoupable unless the contract specifically provides otherwise. You can feel the history jumping from the pages on this one—Charlie Artist asked his company to advance the cost of a trip to see his mom, and then argued the money was nonrecoupable because the contract didn't say it was recoupable. This of course is wrong, but the above broad language solution is overbearing and overkill—sort of like using a sledgehammer to squash a fly (which is effective, but messes up the kitchen). In fact, there are a number of costs paid on your behalf or in connection with the agreement that are never recouped under industry custom. These include such things as manufacturing costs, promotion costs, advertising, marketing, shipping, etc. In practice, the companies don't abuse this language, but I like to carve out the items I just ticked off, together with my own broad language saying they can't recoup amounts that are "customarily nonrecoupable in the industry."

Risk of Loss

What happens if you don't sell enough records to get back the full amount of the advance? With very rare exceptions, advances are **nonreturnable,** which means it's totally the record company's risk. So if you don't sell any records, it will never get back its advances. (This nonreturnable aspect is also significant because it means advances are taxable income when you get them, as opposed to when they're recouped.)

CROSS-COLLATERALIZATION

An important concept tied to recoupment is that of **cross-collateralization.** Remember the illustration on page 102, where there are two towers side by side, and two 1,000-gallon dry wells? The water tank for one of the wells contains exactly one thousand gallons, and that well is filled and the water usable. The other water tank has only five hundred gallons, and you can't reach the water. Suppose we dug a hole in the ground connecting these two wells. In that case, the same 1,500 gallons (five hundred from Well A and one thousand from Well B) would be distributed evenly between the wells (750 gallons in each), and you couldn't reach the water in either of them. (See figure 8 below.)

Cross-collateralization works exactly the same way, and it's built into every deal. Let's assume you get a $100,000 advance for album number 1, plus another $100,000 for album number 2. Let's further assume album number 1 earns royalties of $10,000, and album number 2 earns royalties of $120,000.

If the two albums were *not* cross-collateralized (the two wells were *not* connected), you would get nothing for album number 1 (it only earned back $10,000 of the $100,000 advance, so it's $90,000

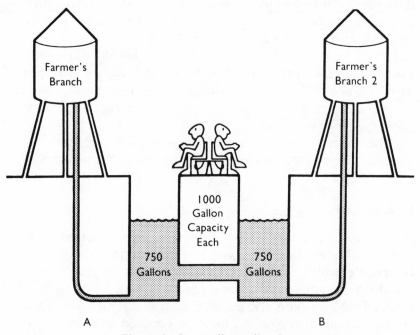

Figure 8. Cross-collateralization.

unrecouped), but you would be paid $20,000 for album number 2 (the $20,000 earned in excess of the $100,000 needed to recoup the $100,000 advance). However, this only happens in Fairyland. In the real world, the two albums are *always* cross-collateralized (i.e., the wells are connected), which means the entire $200,000 deficit ($100,000 for each album) is recouped from the entire $130,000 earnings ($10,000 from album number 1 plus $120,000 from album number 2). Accordingly, your account is $70,000 unrecouped ($200,000 less $130,000), and this deficit carries forward against the next album(s).

Cross-Collateralization of Deals

Besides referring to royalties and recoupment on different albums, cross-collateralization can also refer to different agreements. These can be simultaneous agreements (for example, an artist signing a recording and publishing agreement with the same company), or they can be sequential (such as an artist who, at the end or renegotiation of one record agreement, signs a new deal with the same company). In either case, the concept is that advances under either agreement can be recouped from royalties under both. This is *never* good for the artist. NEVER.

Most companies include language in their form contract that automatically cross-collateralizes the deal with all other deals. Major record companies don't really try to cross-collateralize a record deal with a publishing deal, but small labels may (see page 262). However, everyone tries to cross-collateralize *sequentially,* meaning that advances under your current recording deal are cross-collateralized with royalties under past and future record deals, and vice versa. The language that does this is buried innocently in the recoupment language and can easily be missed by the untrained eye. It says that advances can be recouped from royalties payable, and royalties can be used to recoup advances paid, "under this *or any other agreement.*" (Your eye is now trained—so don't miss it!) I've been reasonably successful in knocking this language out in artists' first deals by arguing that the issue should be discussed later, if and when there is a second contract. My argument is that there is no other deal to cross-collateralize with, and until there is, the language is meaningless. That reduces the point down to who is more likely to forget about it—the artist or the company—at the time of the new deal. (Don't worry: The company won't forget.)

9

Real-Life Numbers

OVERVIEW

Let's start to plug some real industry figures into these concepts. Before we get into specific numbers, however, you should know they are continually changing, and that they're affected by when the deal is made. Here's the Passman Theory of Record Industry Cycles:

1. The record business is a cyclical business, and by that I don't just mean they sell more records at Christmas (which they do). What I mean is that, contrary to other entertainment industries (which tend to do well in bad economic times), the music business follows the general economic cycle. When the economy is depressed, sales drop; when it booms, so do we.

2. In addition, the industry follows a cycle that it creates itself, as bargaining power shifts back and forth between companies and artists. In periods of prosperity, the companies work each other into a feeding frenzy and bid the price of artists through the roof. During this time, there are plenty of artists willing to oblige, and they negotiate agreements under which record companies have a gigantic downside risk but only a minimal upside potential. (Record companies can't be wrong about too many of these deals, because one loser can eat up several winners.) Also, during these times, new artists don't tend to do very well; when a record company has huge investments in superstar talent, you can guess where their priorities are. So new artists get ignored, despite the fact that they are the lifeblood of the business.

3. This cycle moves along swimmingly until there is a general economic downturn. At this point the limousines and parties come to an abrupt halt; the executives begin flying coach; and the record company gets sold to a foreign power. Next comes a

period of contraction, where artists get dropped by the carload (meaning their options aren't exercised—see page 117 for what options are); the companies stop bidding so hard against each other; and the deals move in the other direction. Ironically, this is a good time for new artists, because their deals are cheap, and cheap is in. As with any generalization, there are always exceptions. Even when the stock market is at its worst, some company is always hitting its new high, and even in the worst of times, some artists are getting record deals (pun intended). But even these exceptions are not as rich as they would have been in good times, for the simple reason that no one is selling as many records. This is usually because consumers aren't parting with their money (since they don't have as much), but it may also be for other reasons, such as consumer dollars going into other forms of entertainment (for example, the brief surge of video arcades, or huge blockbuster movies).

4. Following the gloom, the industry begins its recovery, and we start all over again (or, as musicians say, "D.C. al Coda").

Despite the doomsayers when times are bad (and the doomsayers when times are good), now that I've lived through several up/down cycles, I'm certain the music business is a long-term major industry. Records are one of the cheapest forms of permanent entertainment you can buy, and music is one of the few things that enhance other activities (as opposed to a motion picture or a book, for example, which require your total concentration). Also, the power of music to vividly conjure feelings, visions, and emotions is staggering. (I still can't listen to Johnny Mathis's *Greatest Hits* without thinking of slow [and close] dancing as a teenager. Am I dating myself?)

What's Your Clout?

And now, back to earth.

To discuss the range of real numbers, we have to know how strong your bargaining power is. Broadly, I'll divide it into three categories:

New Artist. This is someone who has never before had a record deal, or someone who has been signed but never sold over 150,000 or so albums per release. It can also mean an artist who was once successful but lost his or her following and is having difficulty finding a record deal (or, as one of my clients lovingly put it, someone who has "crashed and burned").

Midlevel Artist or New Artist with a Bidding War. Either (1) an artist whose last album sold in the 200,000 to 500,000 range, or (2) a new artist being chased by a lot of labels. Since I first wrote this book, the proliferation of record companies and the intense feeding frenzy for new artists has radically changed the rules of the game. Now, the distinction is not so much between new artists and midlevel, as it is between a situation where there is a bidding war versus a situation where there is a begging war (i.e., where the artist is begging for the privilege of being recorded). When a number of companies are chasing an unsigned artist, it's not uncommon for the deal to look like a midlevel deal, and on occasion even higher. I'm aware of one situation where an unsigned artist was offered over $1,000,000 for two albums. (Just so you don't get too jealous, that artist's records have only had mediocre success.)

Superstar. Sales from 750,000 into the stratosphere. (If you're between 500,000 and 750,000 your deal will be in between midlevel and superstar.)

These categories are only rough approximations, as there are so many variables. For example, you might be a midlevel artist but have six record companies chasing you and bidding each other up, which means you will get a superstar deal. On the other hand, you may be a relatively successful artist who is perceived as "out of step" with "what's happening," so you therefore get only a lukewarm reception. But we gotta start somewhere, and this range is close enough for rock 'n' roll.

For your point of reference, a **gold album** is one that sells 500,000 U.S. units, and a **platinum album** is one that sells 1 million U.S. units (see page 109 for gold and platinum singles). The sales figures are certified by the RIAA (Recording Industry Association of America, an industry group comprised of record companies), which awards "gold" or "platinum" status. We also have an industry joke that bombs are "certified lead." And since we're on the topic of grading a record's performance, you may have heard the term **bullets.** Each of the major trades (see page 39 for who they are) have charts that rank records numerically based on sales and/or airplay. A bullet is a dot or a star next to a record's number on the chart, and it means the record is moving up strongly. The lack of one means it's weakening or on its way down. So "Number One with a Bullet" is the best you can do.

And of course there's an industry joke for turkeys: "Number 99 with an Anchor."

ROYALTIES

Range of Royalties

Using the above categories, and bearing in mind that different record companies will have slightly different computations (meaning these percentages will be worth different pennies at different places), the following is the current industry norm for royalties on United States album sales:

1. **New Artist Signing to Independent Company:**
   9% to 13% of SRLP. (See page 87 for what an independent company is, and page 92 for what SRLP is.) As we'll discuss on page 192, you may do a deal in which you get a percentage of the label's royalty instead of a set rate.
2. **New Artist Signing to Major or Mini-Major:**
   12% to 14% of SRLP.
3. **Midlevel:**
   16% to 18% of SRLP.
4. **Superstar:**
   19% to 20% or more of SRLP (royalties over 20% are rare).

If the company computes royalties on wholesale, you should roughly double the above figures (see page 92).

The above rates are all for sales of analog cassette albums. (Compact discs are discussed on page 170.) Singles are typically at a lower royalty rate, on the theory that record companies make very little profit on singles (which is true). (Indeed, these days the sales of singles are shrinking substantially; within the last several years the "gold" award for a single was dropped from 1 million to 500,000 units, and the "platinum" award was dropped from 2 million to 1 million.) The singles rate is normally three-quarters of the album rate, but it tops out in the 12% to 14% range. New artists can, with some bargaining power, get to the 10% range no matter what their overall rate, and it may be possible to get escalations in your singles royalties based on sales of singles (in the United States only).

It's always a good idea to compute the pennies your royalties are worth at each company when you compare proposals, so you can compare apples to apples. As we discussed, the pennies can vary for the same percentage (see page 100 for an example), and you wouldn't want to find your apple was a persimmon.

Escalations

It's also common to escalate royalties based on sales of records. Typical escalations are .5% to 1% at some level between 500,000 and 1 million album sales, and another .5% to 1% at 500,000 to 1 million albums beyond that point. For example, if your royalty is 12%, it might escalate to 13% for sales over 500,000 and to 14% for sales over 1 million. The lower your royalty rate, the sooner you can expect the escalations to kick in, and in fact you may even be able to get a third bump. These escalated rates usually top out around the 14% to 15% range for new artists (10% to 13% if you're signed to an independent label), 17% for midlevel, and 19% to 20% for superstars.

Escalations are on an album-by-album basis (meaning that if the first album sells 10 million, it doesn't escalate the royalty on the second). Also, the escalations are based on *royalty bearing* units, which means (since virtually all companies pay on 85% of net sales) that only 85% of the records sold at retail count toward your escalation.

These escalations only apply to sales occurring after the level is reached, and are called **prospective** escalations. For example, if you have 16% on the first 1 million units, escalating to 17% thereafter, you don't get 17% on the first 1 million. If you have sufficient bargaining power, you can sometimes get the escalations on *all* sales (called a **retroactive** escalation). This is rare, and when you can get it, it is usually for stratospheric sales. For example, at sales of 4 million units, you might get an increase on the first 1 million.

Typically, escalations are limited to sales in the United States, but as your bargaining power goes up, so does your ability to get escalations in other major territories (such as Canada and certain European markets). Escalations also apply only to full-priced retail sales, through normal retail (record store) channels.

"All-In"

The above royalties are known by the technical term **all-in,** which means the artist is responsible, out of his or her royalty, for paying the record producer. (If you're not sure what producers do, their role and how they're paid are discussed in chapter 11. However, I suggest you wait till we get there before tackling how they're paid unless you're already pretty familiar with royalties.) The practice of paying artists an all-in rate began in the early 1970s, and is now the industry norm (excluding country music). Producers are paid a U.S. royalty in the range of 3% to 4% of SRLP. Some producers, who become "superstars" in their own right by producing hugely successful records, can get 5% or (very rarely) 6%. Accordingly, the "all-in" rate is not what the artist puts in his or her pocket; that amount is the all-in rate *minus* the amount paid to the producer.

ADVANCES

In the 1950s, artists would go to the studio, sing their little hearts out, and have almost no other involvement in the creative process. In those days, companies paid the artist a set amount of money as an advance (for example, $10,000 for an album). The record company in addition paid the recording costs (which, remember, are recoupable from royalties, just like an advance), and everybody went their separate ways. It took maybe two weeks to do an album.

Funds

Today, again with the exception of country music, virtually all recording agreements are structured as **funds.** A fund is a set amount of money, which includes both recording costs and any amounts that may be payable to the artist as an advance (the term *recording costs* also includes the producer's advance, which we'll discuss later). Whatever the artist doesn't spend on recording costs goes into his or her pocket. For example, if the recording fund for an album is $200,000, and the recording costs are $150,000, the artist would pocket $50,000 as an "advance." On the other hand, if the recording costs are $200,000, the artist pockets nothing.

Here's a rough range of recording funds:

1. **New Artist Signing to Independent Company:**
   $5,000 to $125,000. (See the discussion below for more detail.)
2. **New Artist Signing to Major or Mini-major:**
   $175,000 to $350,000.
3. **Midlevel:**
   $250,000 to $500,000.
4. **Superstar:**
   $750,000 and up. It's not unusual for a major artist's fund to run into millions of dollars. At this level, funds are computed on

the basis of past track record and future expectations, as well as the bidding in the marketplace.

New Artist/Independent Company Funds

Let's take a closer look at funds paid by independent labels. (See page 87 for what an "independent" is.) When you're a brand new artist and can't get signed to a major label (or in fact even get their attention), your best alternative to busing tables may well be signing with an independent. However, unless you're dealing with an independent owned by an industry "biggie," such as a major producer or manager, doing deals at this level is really shopping in the Kmart of the music biz. You're not going to get a lot of money, and your album will be recorded, shall we say, "economically." So, as noted above, expect an album fund of anywhere from $5,000 (for this price range I strongly suggest a kazoo chorus) up to the equivalent of what you could get from a major label. However, albums at this level typically don't exceed funds of $50,000 to $75,000.

These deals often mean you'll be working with less sophisticated studios, producers, engineers, etc. However, "cheap" and "unsophisticated" don't always equate to "lousy." In fact, many low-budget records have an energy that is totally lost in slick, highly produced recordings. Most people recording low-budget product are the most excited and enthused about their music, willing to make records for the devil if necessary to get ahead. (As you probably know, we have no shortage of devils in the music biz.)

Budget Problems

If your fund is $200,000, what keeps you from recording a super-cheapo album for $25,000 and pocketing $175,000? In virtually all of these deals, unless you have a lot of bargaining power, the record company has to approve your recording cost budget for precisely this reason. In truth, however, they're usually more worried about the other end—that you'll have an unrealistically low budget and not be able to finish your album at a cost less than the fund. This is particularly common with new artists, because their funds are low; an album can easily cost $150,000 or more, and this is often the entire fund.

So what happens when you've spent your full recording fund and have three-quarters of an album? Most of the time the record companies pay to finish the record, under the age-old business strategy of "What the hell are we going to do with three-quarters of an album?"

However, they will grumble and stomp the floor in the process, and, if they do pay, they'll take the excess from your next album's recording fund, from your publishing royalties (I'll explain what those are later), and from anything else they can think of. Almost all recording contracts require *you* to write a check for the excess, but in practice this can't happen with a new artist (who doesn't have the money), and rarely happens with a superstar (whose feathers they don't want to ruffle by asking).

Formulas

If you know enough to ask for it, a substantial number of record companies will agree to something called a **formula** for advances. This is a mechanism designed to automatically increase (or decrease) your deal if you are successful (or a flop). It works like this:

The advance for the second album recorded under an agreement is equal to a percentage (usually 60% to 70%) of all royalties *earned* (as opposed to paid) by the first album under the agreement. The advance for album number three is a percentage of album number two's earnings, and so forth. Thus, for example, if the first album earns $1,000,000 in royalties and you have a 60% formula, the advance for album number two is $600,000. The formula percentage is usually based only on earnings in the United States, or sometimes the United States and Canada. The earnings are also limited in time (usually six to nine months after release), so that sales trickling in over a two- or three-year period won't increase the advance for an artist who is slow in delivery. The last thing a company wants to do is reward late delivery.

Variations include delaying a formula until the third or a later LP; averaging the earnings of the previous two LPs (as opposed to using the earnings only of the previous LP); and a limitation (or elimination) of reserves for purposes of determining the formula (reserves are discussed on page 97, and reserve limitations are on page 161).

But what, you say, if the first album is a dismal failure, and earns only $20,000? How can anyone make an album for $12,000 to $14,000 (60% to 70% of the $20,000)? Well, you can't, so this is handled by establishing a **floor** for the formula. This means that no matter how lousy the earnings of the previous album are, the fund will be no less than an agreed amount (the floor). Not surprisingly, as soon as record companies hear the word *floor*, they think of a concept called a **ceiling,** which means that no matter how wildly successful the prior album is, the fund won't *exceed* an agreed dollar figure. (The prospect of owing you $4,000,000 for an album makes them nervous.)

Both the floors and ceilings normally escalate for later albums, varying with the bargaining power of the parties. Here's a set of floors and ceilings I got in a recent new artist deal:

LP No.	Floor	Ceiling
1	$175,000	(no formula)
2	$200,000	$400,000
3	$225,000	$450,000
4	$275,000	$550,000
5	$350,000	$700,000
6	$400,000	$800,000

Don't get excited about the big numbers for the last albums. The company isn't really committed to them, as you'll see on page 117.

LOOK HOW MUCH YOU ALREADY KNOW

A couple of years ago, I got a call from a television producer. She was doing a special about the music business, and had stopped people on the street to ask how much they thought an artist made from a gold album (sales of 500,000 units). The guesses ranged from $500,000 to over $2 million, and the producer wanted to know the real answer.

Now you know enough to answer the question the same way I did. Here's what I told her:

If a new artist has a royalty of 14% all-in, pays a producer 3%, and has recording costs of $200,000 for the album, his or her royalty for sales of 500,000 units of that album looks like this:

Cassette (suggested retail price)	$10.98
Less: Packaging (20%)	−2.19
Royalty Base	$8.79
Royalty Rate (14% all-in, less 3% for the producer)	×11%
Gross Royalty (11% of $7.99)	$.96
× 500,000 units	×500,000
	$480,000
Less 15% "free goods factor"	−72,000
	$408,000
Less: Recording Costs	−200,000
Less: 50% of independent promotion (see page 155)	−75,000
Less: 50% of video costs (see page 180)	−75,000
TOTAL	$58,000

To the extent that these sales are CDs, the royalties on those units will be higher (see page 170). However, remember that the artist doesn't get a check for this all at once; the company holds back a reserve of at least 35% to 50% in case the records boomerang (see the reserve discussion on page 97). This percentage is applied to the *gross* royalties (i.e., the $408,000 total in our example, which is the gross before deducting costs). This means the artist gets zippo on the first statement.

If you're on the *Fast Track*,
go to chapter 11 on page 133.
Everyone else, forward ho . . .

IF YOU DON'T UNDERSTAND THE WORDS IN THE BOX, IT MEANS YOU SKIPPED PAGE 29. IT ALSO MEANS YOU NEVER READ THE DIRECTIONS WHEN YOU BUY A NEW STEREO.

10

Other Major Deal Points

The other major things you want to know about your record deal are "How much?" and "How long?" The "how much" part of this doesn't mean royalties and advances, which we discussed, but rather the number of albums you have to record. The "how long" is pretty straightforward, but has taken a peculiar twist over the last few years, as you'll see.

AMOUNT OF PRODUCT

Pay or Play

Did you know that most record deals for both new and midlevel artists (and even some superstars) don't require the company to even make a record? Almost all of their forms contain a provision whereby the company, instead of recording the album, can merely pay the artist a sum of money equal to (in the first draft of their agreement) minimum union scale for an album or (after negotiating) the difference between the recording fund and the cost of the last album. This is called a **pay-or-play** provision, meaning, as the name implies, that the record company has the option either to allow you to "play your music," or to "pay you off." Should you come across this and are unable to get it out of the deal, at least be certain that, once they pay you off, the deal is over. This shouldn't be hard to get, but it isn't in any form agreement, and without it the company could in theory hold you without making records. (On the other hand, since they don't want your records, they probably don't want you around either. But it's cheap insurance to add language making sure.)

Options

Record deals are traditionally structured with the company having the smallest obligation that it can negotiate, while keeping the option to get as much product as possible. For example, a company may commit to record one album of an artist and have the option to require the artist to record an additional five to seven albums, each one at the company's election.

Options in New Artist Deals

With new artists, the companies like to commit to only one album but insist on the right to get six to eight albums total. This is an improvement over recent years—the companies used to insist on options for up to eight to ten albums. Optional albums might be one at a time for the first, second, and maybe third albums, but thereafter I make the company take at least two albums at a time (or else they have to let the artist go). In other words, the company can opt out of the agreement after the first, second, or perhaps even third album, but if the deal continues beyond that point, the company must accept the fourth *and* fifth albums before it can again opt out; similarly with the sixth *and* seventh, etc. (If there's an extra left over at the end, they of course only have to commit to that one album.)

Farm Teams

In baseball, when you're not quite ready to play in the majors, they send you to a minor-league team called a *farm team*. The major teams all have affiliated "farm teams" (so named, I think, because they use them to grow their players from seeds into turnips, or whatever). In the minors, the scouts watch you in real game situations, and as soon as you're good enough, they move you up to the majors.

Record companies over the years have developed a similar system. Originally, if they were reluctant to commit to an album, they would sign you up to record only a single (two songs). If the single did well, they'd go ahead and record an album. But this was when single sales were profit centers, and the times have changed. As we discussed on page 109, single sales now hover somewhere between minimal and obscure. Also, singles now serve primarily to push album sales, and if you have no album, the single is useless. (There's a Texas expression about mammary glands on bulls that I won't stoop to, but it's accurate.) Accordingly, this system has dropped out of vogue.

Today's farm teams are **demo deals** (sometimes called **develop-**

ment deals). Under this arrangement the record company gives you some money ($500 to $5,000, sometimes a bit more) to go into a studio and record demos. The term "demo" is short for "demonstration recording," which is less than a full-fledged master but gives the company some idea of what you'll sound like on a professional record. They listen to the demo and then decide whether they want to sign you. If they do, the deal will be along the lines we just discussed for new artists. (We're going to discuss how to protect yourself in demo deals later, on page 144.)

Options in Midrange and Superstar Deals

With a midrange artist, the company typically commits itself to two albums firm, and its additional options are two albums each. It's rare that a company doesn't have the right to at least six albums from a midrange artist, and eight is the norm. At the superstar level, deals of four albums or less are possible but rare; the norm is five to six albums. With superstars, firm commitments of three to four albums are not uncommon, and the options (if any) are typically limited to one (or two at most), each one requiring two or more albums.

Options Aren't Good for You

I remember a friend of mine from the high school choir who came in one day, jubilant, because she had signed a "ten-album deal" with Capitol Records. In reality, it turned out to be a deal for one single only, and she had merely given Capitol the option to require up to ten albums. While my friend has faded into obscurity after recording that one single, her attitude is not unusual. Many artists still think of record company options as being good for them (the numbers are so high at the end!), but in fact this is never the case. If you're a flop, you'll never see the money; if you're a success, it will probably be less than you're worth. So train yourself to think of options only as the chance for the record company to get out of your deal. They are never good for you.

Making the Best of Options

Despite my high-minded speech, the reality is that you have to live with options at all but superstar levels—this industry custom is too well entrenched to buck. However, since you're giving the company a chance to drop you after each album or two (in other words, to protect their tushies if there's no success), I think you're entitled to more goodies if they keep you. This can be done in two different ways:

Royalties. For optional albums, you should get increased royalties. Typically, the increase is around .5% to 1%, both in your basic rate and in any escalated rates. For example, I recently did a midlevel deal that looked like this:

LP No.	Royalty on sales of 0–500,000 Albums	Royalty on Sales of 500,001– 1,000,000 Albums	Royalty on Sales of 1,000,001+ Albums
1	17%	17.5%	18%
2	17%	17.5%	18%
3	18%	18.5%	19%
4	18%	18.5%	19%
5	19%	19%	19%
6	19%	19%	19.5%

Funds. You should also get increased recording funds for optional albums. Page 114 cites an example of a new artist deal, and here's the numbers from a recent midlevel deal:

LP No.	Floor	Ceiling
1	$300,000	(no formula)
2	$300,000	$600,000
3	$350,000	$700,000
4	$350,000	$700,000
5	$400,000	$800,000
6	$400,000	$800, 000

Don't the numbers look delicious in the later option periods? What a great deal! What a genius negotiator! DON'T BE FOOLED! OPTIONS ARE NEVER GOOD FOR YOU!! They only mean you'll get dropped if you're not worth the price, or you'll get too little if you're a smash. So repeat after me: "OPTIONS ARE NEVER GOOD FOR ME!!!" Now write it on the blackboard twenty-five times.

HOW LONG?

Term

How long the record company keeps you under an exclusive agreement is called the **term** of your deal. Record deals used to be for a term of one year, with options to renew for additional periods of one year each. The artist was usually obligated to deliver two albums each year. This worked terrifically in the days when records were banged out like pancakes, since most of the time the artists just showed up, sang, then went back to the beach. As we discussed, in those days it was not unusual to make an album in two weeks (three if the artist was a prima donna). But all this has gone the way of the dinosaurs.

Every contract is a history lesson, and the clauses dealing with the length of deals have had a particularly colorful past. Behind each clause is a story that ends with "I'm going to write language so that, if this ever happens again, I won't get shafted." And unraveling these bits of history can be fun, so let's take a look.

Late Delivery of Albums

As artists took more creative control, albums began to take longer to make. Indeed, the more successful the artist, the longer (with rare exception) the next album seemed to take. Today, periods of years between albums are not at all unusual for superstars (or for flakes at any level). Many reasons for this are legitimate—if an album is successful, you need to be out touring and promoting it, which means you can't be in the studio. In fact, the more successful it is, the longer you'll be out touring and promoting, and the record company won't even want you to start the second album. However, many of these delays don't have such a noble purpose. I'm convinced (but can't prove) that one of the reasons for delay is that artists, particularly following a major success, are a bit frightened to put out their next record. When it's actually released, they have to find out whether it's as successful as the prior one; until then, it's only speculation and their track record stays intact. So, they continue to fine tune, tweak, poke, re-record, ponder, rethink, etc., which delays the day of reckoning. And second albums are particularly troublesome. It's interesting to realize that someone's first album can actually be ten years or more in the making. This is because they were accumulating songs for a long time before they ever got a record deal, and thus had a huge catalog to choose from in making the first album. However, when the artist gets to the second album, all the cherries have been picked, so it's a matter of writing new material or going into the second tier of old stuff. And this process now has to take place within a year or two, as opposed to the unlimited time that preceded the first album. So there is much more pressure.

Record companies historically solved this slow-delivery problem by having the right to extend the term of the agreement if an album wasn't delivered on time—in other words, if your album was six months late, the current one-year term of your deal was extended by six months. This worked terrifically until Olivia Newton-John filed a suit against MCA Records seeking termination of her agreement. (The case cite is 90 Cal.App 3d. 18 (1979), for you technical freaks who like to read court cases.) In this case, she argued that her deal should be limited to the actual number of years stated in the contract, without regard to any extensions. In other words, since her contract was for a two-year term with three one-year options (a total of five years), she argued that MCA could not enforce the deal beyond five years from the start date, even though she had not given them all the product due. To everyone's surprise, the court (sort of) agreed. It reduced the duration of MCA's injunction (meaning the order saying she couldn't record for anyone else) to the five years, rather than allowing any extensions. However, I say "sort of" because the five years wasn't over at the time of the case, and so the court technically didn't deal with the issue in full. Nonetheless, the case's language was strong enough to make all the companies nervous, and it forever changed the way record contracts are drawn.

Nowadays, the terms of record deals are not stated in specific time periods like one or two years. Instead, the contracts say each period ends six to nine months after delivery of the last album required for that period, and can be no less than a specified time period (e.g., eighteen months). For example, if you have to make two albums, the period might start upon the signing of your deal and end six months after delivery of the second album, but no sooner than eighteen months after signing.

This language solves the Olivia Newton-John problem, but the companies had to add additional provisions to deal with these little snippets of history: In 1970, Dean Martin signed an agreement with Warner Bros. Records. The agreement was unusual for those days (although it is the norm today) because the term continued until delivery of all the albums. Approximately six years later, after everyone had forgotten about him, Dino came in and announced he was about to start recording a new album (for which he expected the substantial amount of money specified in the contract). This sent Warner into a tizzy, since Mr. Martin's star was not of the same brightness as when he signed the agreement, and they began scrambling to find a way out. So Dino sued them. Ultimately the case was settled, but it taught the companies a lesson—that contracts shouldn't be geared only to delivery of albums, or else they can go on forever. Accordingly, you will now find provisions stating that, if the artist has not delivered an album within a certain period of time after delivery of the previous album (usually six to eighteen months, depending on bargaining power), the company can get out of the deal.

At the other end of the spectrum comes a history lesson from Frank Zappa. Also picking on our friends at Warner Bros. Records (so that they could have the distinction of being clobbered with both ends of the same stick), Mr. Zappa showed up one day with four albums under his arm. He said he was delivering all the remaining product required under his deal, and thus was free to sign elsewhere. As you can imagine, this didn't go over much better than Mr. Martin's arrival.

The Zappa lesson is now handled by stating that you can't start *recording* an LP until you have delivered the prior album, and that the new LP can't be *delivered* sooner than six months after delivery of the prior album. Record companies have a legitimate point in saying they don't have to take more than one album at a time, on the basis that (a) they can't reasonably market more than one album at a time, and (b) if they put an album on the shelf for later release, it may not be in touch with the trends in the music business (which, in case you haven't noticed, change hourly) at the time of release.

MEGA DEALS

Background. Over the last few years, there have been a rash of "Mega Deals" in the music business that I'm sure you've read about. Janet Jackson, R.E.M., Michael Jackson, Prince, Madonna, U2, etc., have all had multimillion-dollar extravaganzas.

What's the truth behind all of these? Well, first you need to know about what happens to an artist when you reach superstardom.

Remember, as we discussed before, the record company takes options on new artists for up to eight albums (see page 117). Putting this together with how long it can take to do a new album (as we discussed on page 120), you realize that, the more successful you are, the longer it takes to fulfill the commitment. The other reality is that most new-artist deals have low royalties and advances or, at best, are in the midrange (and then only if there were wolves snapping at the door when the deal was made). So as soon as an artist has any success, they show up at the record company's door and ask for more substantial advances and royalties. And what do you suppose the record company wants? You got it—more albums.

All of this adds up to the fact that record companies continue extending their deals, and artists rarely end up in a position to change companies. This is why artists tend to spend their entire career at one company. They would rather get better terms on their next album (which is for sure) than live out a mediocre deal on the hopes that they'll be as hot when it's over.

On the other hand, artists do occasionally get free, and if they're important at the time, they can set new benchmarks in the industry. They don't even have to get completely free to do this—there are people out there who will make a deal with them that doesn't begin until they deliver one or two more albums to their current record company (this was the case with Aerosmith). And the fear of this can sometimes cause the current record company to come to the party in a big way.

The other reality is that, when one artist is able to raise the standard in the industry, all of the other superstars go back to their record companies and ask for similar treatment. And in fact the recent rash of mega deals was triggered by just such a frenzy.

The Deals. So what makes a deal "mega"? Several things:

1. *Advances*
   The advances are in the multimillion-dollar range. At this level, the deal becomes a banking transaction—the record company makes its best guess as to what the artist will sell and then computes its potential profit versus risk.
2. *Royalty*
   Superstar deals tend to be 20% or more of retail.
3. *Product*
   The amount of product in a mega deal has two aspects:
   a. There will be many more firm albums—at least three or four—and there may be only one option, which is normally for more than one album (e.g., two or three firm).
   b. The total amount of product tends to be less. This is less applicable in the case of the superstar who owes a lot of product to the existing company, but if the deal is with a new company, or if there are only a few albums left, the company will get fewer albums than a normal deal (maybe four to six).

The Hype. Some of these mega deals were nowhere near what was reported in the press. Not that they weren't substantial deals, but they weren't all in the magnitude that the public was led to believe. Also, a number of the deals (such as Madonna's and Michael Jackson's) were multi-media deals, involving not only a record deal but also a record label (i.e., funding a company to sign other artists), publishing company, film projects, and perhaps merchandising (see page 349 for what that is), books, etc.

Note also a key distinction (which the public, and indeed the press, have never fully understood) between an artist who is re-signing with his or her own record company versus an artist signing with a new company. When re-signing, the company has its entire catalog of old product from which it can hedge its bet against the future. If the deals are cross-collateralized (see page 104 for what that is), and they often are so the artist can push up the advances, the company's risk is substantially different from the risk of a new company that has no catalog against which to get back its money. Now you know something that very few people, even many in the industry, understand.

I'm often asked whether the industry has lost its mind in making these mega deals, and whether I think they'll continue. As to the first part, I answer that there are sophisticated business players on both sides of every mega transaction. Also, if an artist is free, there is always more than one company willing to step to the line on these deals. Thus, I see it more as a question of dividing up the pie of profits, and I don't think anyone has lost their mind. I use the analogy of what happened to the L.A. Kings hockey team when they signed Wayne Gretsky—their season-ticket sales immediately went up substantially, and this paid for much (if not all) of the deal. And there is also an intangible "trophy value" to having these artists, not to mention how it attracts new artists who want to be on the same label as their heroes. These aspects are impossible to measure with precision, but can be worth quite a bit.

Whether these deals will continue is a question of when and how many superstars become available or get in a position to renegotiate. They have slowed down radically over the last few years, but my prediction is that there'll be another wave of them within the next five years. And if there's not, I'll delete the previous sentence from my next edition.

DELIVERY REQUIREMENTS

Apart from the number of recordings, contracts also talk about the kind of recordings you can deliver. **Delivery** is a magic word, because it means more than dumping the stuff on their doorstep. It means the company has to *accept* the recordings as complying with your deal, and the contract will specify what standards the company can use in deciding whether to accept. The standard that applies to your deal depends on your bargaining power. The extremes are:

Commercially Satisfactory

If your contract says you must deliver **commercially satisfactory** recordings, it means the record company only has to take recordings it believes will sell; in other words, recordings it finds satisfactory for commercial exploitation (translation: recordings it likes). If your contract has this language and they don't like your record, then (a) at best, they send you back to the studio (at your expense), or (b) at worst, they take the position that you haven't delivered an album as required by the deal, and thus you're late and they can terminate the contract.

Technically Satisfactory

If you only have to deliver **technically satisfactory** recordings, then as long as a recording is technically well made (without hissing and warp, not made in a Karaoke bar, etc.), the company has to take it.

There was a period in the early seventies when "technically satisfactory" was pretty easy to come by. However, it is very rare today because of abuses that I'm sure you can imagine (for example, one of my record company clients got an album which was supposed to be a secret group of superstars, but turned out to be a previously released flop from an unknown group). Newer artists can expect to live with "commercially satisfactory." Midrange artists may get a "technically satisfactory" standard subject to the company's approving the songs and the producer, plus the same limits described in the next two sentences. Superstars can expect an even more favorable version of technically satisfactory: the company may not have any approvals, but it will have language saying the recordings must be of a "style" (and perhaps even a "quality") similar to your previous recordings. They will also exclude any "specialty" or "novelty" recordings, so you can't give them a children's record, Christmas record, the Ella Fitzgerald songbook (unless, of course, you *are* Ella Fitzgerald), polka records, Gregorian chants, etc.

Other Delivery Criteria

The other requirements for your recordings (regardless of your level) are that they must be:

1. Recorded during the term (to keep you from pulling out those old garage tapes).
2. Studio recordings (as opposed to "live" concert recordings—see page 128 for a discussion of "live" albums).

3. Songs not previously recorded by you (I'm sure you can figure out the history lesson behind this one).
4. Recordings that feature only your performance (to keep you from bringing in the kids and your aunt Sally as guest soloists).
5. Not wholly instrumental selections (unless you're only an instrumentalist).
6. Material that doesn't cause the company any legal hassles, such as infringing somebody's copyright, defaming someone, or using obscene language (to the extent that's still possible, which unfortunately it may be since I first wrote these words).
7. Songs of a minimum playing time (usually two minutes).

CONTROLLED COMPOSITIONS

One of the most important provisions of your record deal is the controlled composition clause, which limits how much you get paid as a songwriter. However, to understand it you need a fairly extensive knowledge of publishing, which we're going to discuss later. So let's put it off until you have the background. (If you really can't wait, flip ahead to page 221. Don't forget to come back.)

If you're on the *Advanced Overview* track, go to chapter 11 on page 133.
Experts, straight on.

GREATEST HITS

A **Greatest Hits** (also called a **Best Of**) album is a compilation of songs from your prior albums, perhaps with one or two new songs. (I've always been amused by the term *Greatest Hits,* since the album is usually neither.) Traditionally, releasing a Greatest Hits album was a record company's way of blowing taps over an artist's career that had passed away. However, in the 1970s Elton John released a Greatest Hits album at the height of his career and sold eight gazillion copies. Suddenly everyone rethought their position, and today a Greatest Hits album is common at any point in an artist's life cycle.

If you don't say anything, the company will put out as many as it likes, whenever it likes, and pay you no advance. While some things about Greatest Hits albums aren't negotiable—no company will count a Greatest Hits album against your delivery requirement—you can fix other issues if you know what to ask for. These are:

Limits

From the midrange level and up, and sometimes at the new artist level (depending on the company), you can often limit the number of Greatest Hits albums the company can compile from your material. (Incidentally, don't ever assume there's a practical limit if you don't have one contractually—I've heard of one company that managed to put out eleven different albums of an artist that only recorded two LPs' worth of masters in their entire career!) The usual limit is that the company can release no more than one (or two) Greatest Hits LPs during the term, plus one (or two) after the term.

Greatest Hits Advances

You should be able to get an advance for your Greatest Hits albums. The amount will depend on your bargaining power, and typically it will be reduced by the amount of your deficit if you're unrecouped (see page 101 if you don't remember what a "deficit" is). You want the date of determining the deficit to be as late as possible, so you can get in the maximum sales to reduce it. The date of release of the Greatest Hits album is the best.

A typical Greatest Hits advance for a new artist signed to a major label might be $75,000 less the unrecouped deficit. So if the artist is unrecouped by $25,000, he or she would receive $50,000 ($75,000 less the $25,000 deficit). Independent labels will pay nothing, or perhaps $10,000 less the deficit. For a midlevel artist, the number is closer to $150,000 (again less the deficit); and for a superstar, $250,000 to $500,000 and up (less the deficit).

A superstar might also have a "floor" to his or her Greatest Hits advance, regardless of the deficit. For example, I did one artist's agreement that had a Greatest Hits advance of $400,000 minus the unrecouped deficit, but in no event less than $150,000. Here's how this advance would work under different circumstances:

1. If the artist was recouped, the advance would be $400,000.
2. If the artist was unrecouped in the amount of $100,000, then $400,000 minus the $100,000 deficit equals a $300,000 advance for the Greatest Hits album.

3. If the artist's deficit was $350,000, then $400,000 minus the $350,000 deficit equals $50,000, but the floor is $150,000, so the artist would get a $150,000 advance.

4. Can you figure the advance if the artist was $200,000 unrecouped? How about $600,000 unrecouped? (Answers on page 132.)

New Songs for Greatest Hits

It's becoming more and more customary to require an artist to record one or two new songs for a Greatest Hits package. This is in the best interests of all concerned, because a hit single pumps up the sales of the Greatest Hits album (it's the only place to get the song). At a minimum, the record company will agree to pay the recording costs of the new masters even if you're unrecouped (but don't assume the form agreement will say so), and you may also be able to negotiate a higher advance for the Greatest Hits album if you deliver these recordings.

LIVE ALBUMS

A **live album** is recorded during a live concert (with lots of screaming and applause), rather than in a studio. Don't assume a live recording is inferior because it isn't made in a studio; there are mobile recording studios in trucks that rival the highest-tech equipment in town. These trucks are simply backed up to the auditorium, and the concert is recorded with a quality that isn't noticeably different from a studio.

"Live" albums go through periodic ups and downs (sort of like space movies). They were historically something the company did to keep the artist happy, because they didn't really make any money. Then, in 1976, Peter Frampton broke all the rules with an album called *Frampton Comes Alive*, which was not only a live album, but also a *double* live album (double albums are a traditional handicap at retail). This album sold in multimillion numbers that blew out all the traditional wisdom. After the predictable glut of live albums following Mr. Frampton, the popularity again faded. Currently, live albums sell reasonably well, but are no great shakes. However, an exception to this (and a major exception) is the special genre created by MTV's "Unplugged" series. Eric Clapton's "Unplugged" album, I understand, sold over 9 million copies, and Mariah Carey, Rod Stewart, Neil

Young, and others are charting along swimmingly. However, this hasn't translated into an upsurge in the sales of traditional "live" albums.

Unless you have a lot of muscle, record companies won't let you deliver a live album (or even one live cut on a studio album) without their consent. On rare occasions, superstars can get the right to deliver one live album during the term of their deal. But it will usually be for a reduced advance, both because of live LPs' dicey sales history and the fact that most of the material will have been previously recorded.

GUARANTEED RELEASE

Very few form record contracts guarantee to release your records. Indeed, as we discussed on page 116, very few build in an obligation even to record, much less release.

With only moderate bargaining power, however, you can get a **guaranteed release,** and you should always ask. But this clause will *never* obligate the company to release your product; rather it will only say you can get out of the deal and go elsewhere if they don't. With more bargaining power, you can sometimes get the right to buy back an unreleased album. After all, if the company doesn't think enough of it to put it out, why not let you take it elsewhere and get its money back?

Guaranteed release clauses basically turn you into a notice factory. If, within a certain period after delivery (usually 90 to 120 days) the company hasn't put out your album, you have earned the right to give it a written notice saying "You haven't put out my album." After receiving this shocking news, the company has another period (usually sixty days) within which to actually put out the album (if they feel like it). If they don't, you now have the privilege of sending a second notice, usually within 30 days after the 60 days (and if you're late, you lose your rights). This notice says the company still has failed to put out your album; that you really meant it when you said you wanted it to; and that you are now terminating the deal. At this point you can say good-bye. (But note the company still doesn't have to put out the record.)

By the way, the period after delivery in which the company must release is usually extended if any of it falls between October 15 and January 15. This is because no one other than the most super of superstars can release product after October 15. Beginning in early December, the radio stations start thinking about Hawaii or Aspen, and they "freeze" their playlists (meaning they add no new records until after January 15). In response, the record industry closes up around the middle of December. And since a record by an artist who is not well known doesn't have time to make its climb before the December shutdown, everyone has to wait until the next year. Thus, the record companies want to extend their release commitment period to make way for this phenomenon.

As your bargaining power increases, as well as your international fame, you may be able to negotiate a similar release provision for foreign territories. Certainly you should try to get this in the "major" territories (see page 167 for what they are) and anywhere else you are big. Normally you can't get the right to terminate the entire deal for failure to release outside the United States—you can only terminate for the particular territory where they blew it, and only for the specific album not released (so you can get another distributor to release that album in the territory). If you keep pushing, the company may agree that, if it fails to release two consecutive albums in a particular territory, you can have back that territory for the rest of the deal. While this is not likely to be meaningful (if you're that much of a stiff in the territory, odds are no one else will want you either), it's better than a sharp stick in the eye.

Whatever your guaranteed release, get it on the company's **top-line label.** This means the main label of the company, as opposed to a smaller, obscure, or low-priced label. (See page 181 for a discussion of budget and mid-priced records, which are sometimes released on a different label than full-price records.) Companies will usually agree to this for *initial* releases only, meaning they can put you on a budget or mid-price label in subsequent releases if they want. It will also be for the United States only, because in foreign territories (a) many records are first released as mid-price, and (b) foreign distributors are often uncontrollable no matter what the U.S. company says.

DEAL PECULIARITIES FOR INDEPENDENTS

When you're recording for an independent who is not a "true independent" (see page 87 for what all that means), you have concerns in addition to those we just discussed.

Distribution

When you sign to an independent, you have to ask whether this company can get anyone to distribute your album. Remember, these companies aren't distributors, and thus they have no way to get your records into the stores unless they contract with someone else to do it. So here's how to cover yourself:

1. First of all, put a clause in your contract that says the independent must enter into an agreement to distribute your product within a certain period of time. Ideally you should get six months after either execution of the contract or completion of your album, but I've gone as long as nine to twelve months. If the time period is measured from completion of your album, be sure you have some outside date—otherwise, if the company never records you, the date will never arrive. For example, you might require a company to make an agreement within six months after completion of your album, but in no event later than twelve months after execution of your deal.

2. If you have a bit more muscle, you should say the company must enter into an agreement with a *major* distribution entity. If you don't, you may find your records shipped out in Uncle Herbert's U-Haul. The best way to handle this is to get approval of the distributor. If the independent agrees, it will say you must be "reasonable" in your approval so you can't use this clause to get out of the deal when some prettier face dangles more money in front of you. (You wouldn't do that, would you?) And by the way, when I represent the independent, I insist that the artist preapprove all the major distributors (which I then list).

3. If the independent does make a deal with a distributor, but the distributor doesn't pick up its option with the independent, can the independent continue to hold you? For example, if your deal is for two albums with options for more, but the distributor drops the company (and you) after one album, can the company hold you for the second album even though they have no way to put it out? Part of your protection is a guaranteed release—if they don't put your album out, you can terminate the deal (see page 129). However, as you'll remember from page 116, companies don't even have to make a record to hang on to your contract. And if they don't record any product, the guaranteed release never comes into play. Knowing this, various sleazeballs in our business have sunk their teeth into an artist and not let go if they smelled that somebody might pay them for the privilege. So the way to cover yourself is to say the independent has six to twelve months after a distribution deal lapses within which to get a new deal, or else you're out.

The Great Publishing Grab

Independent companies are the ones most likely to try and take your publishing (your earnings as a songwriter, as opposed to your earnings as a performer on records). Since we haven't discussed publishing, I want to defer the ins and outs of this until we do. The way to protect yourself from an independent is on page 260 if you want to look ahead, but I suggest you do it only if you understand publishing pretty well.

Answers to quiz on page 128

If $200,000 unrecouped: $200,000 advance ($400,000 minus the $200,000 deficit).

If $600,000 unrecouped: $150,000 advance ($400,000 minus the $600,000 deficit is zero, but the floor is $150,000 no matter what).

11

Producer Deals

WHAT'S A PRODUCER?

A record producer's role combines the roles of director and producer in the motion picture field. He or she is responsible for overseeing and bringing the creative product into tangible form (a recording), which means (a) being responsible for maximizing the creative process (finding and selecting songs, deciding on arrangements, getting the right vocal sound, etc.) and (b) taking care of all the administration (booking studios, hiring musicians, staying within a budget, filing union reports, etc.). The mechanical aspects of administration (actually calling the musicians, doing the paperwork, etc.) are often handled by a **production coordinator,** whose life purpose is these chores.

History

As we discussed earlier, artists in the 1950s were for the most part people who would only show up to sing, and then go home. My friend Snuff Garrett, one of the most important producers of the fifties and sixties, considered it burdensome if it took him more than five days to record an album (and the artist wasn't even there all that time). Using this technique, Snuff produced records of Cher, Sonny and Cher, Gary Lewis and the Playboys, Bobbie Vee, Bobby Vinton, and a host of other successes, including such strange choices as Telly Savalas and Walter Brennan.

Snuff started out (as did all the early producers) as an **A&R** man (the letters stand for "Artists and Repertoire"). A&R men (in those days there were no A&R "persons") were executives of record companies whose job was to find, sign, and guide talent, including matching songs to singers and running recording sessions (in other words, doing almost exactly what producers do today). A&R executives still exist, and indeed are amongst the most important industry people.

But today most don't actually produce the recordings (although many of the better ones come quite close to producing). They are responsible for finding and signing talent, as well as finding songs, matching producers and artists, and generally overseeing projects.

Anyway, Snuff began working for Liberty Records, which was then run by its founder and chief executive, Simon Waronker (the father of DreamWorks Records' current president, Lenny Waronker), its president, the late Alvin Bennett, and its chief recording engineer, Theodore Keep. (Do the first names of these gentlemen sound familiar? Do they remind you of a recording artist on Liberty? See page 143 for the answer if you can't guess.) Snuff (who is one of the smartest businesspeople I have ever met, but hides behind a country cornpone) figured out early on that he was making millions of dollars for Liberty while drawing a generous but small salary in comparison to what he was generating. So he summoned up all his courage and asked Alvin for a royalty of 1¢ per record. This was unheard of—the radical idea that a guy instrumental in creating product get a royalty—and Snuff was almost fired in the process. But due to his value to Liberty, he held out and won the point. And in so doing, he started a trend that is the reason producers get royalties on records today.

ROYALTIES

We talked before about the range of royalties for producers, on page 111. However, there are some major distinctions between artists' and producers' royalties you should understand, and some fine points that will bite you in the tush if you don't know about them. For whatever historical reasons, *producers' royalties are computed more favorably than artists' royalties.*

"Record One" Royalties

Most important, it is customary for producers, at some point, to be paid for *all* records sold, meaning recording costs are *not* charged against their royalties (while those costs, as you know, are always charged against artists' royalties). These are called **record one** royalties, because they are paid from the first record ("record one") that the company sells. (All producers, of course, have to recoup any advances they have received, but if you think of these advances as a prepayment of royalties, this is the same as getting royalty on all records.) The key question is *when* the record one royalties are paid, and there are three methods:

Superstar producers are paid for *every record sold*, without recoupment of anything (except their advances). Let's look at an example:

Suppose an artist's "all-in" royalty (artist and producer combined) is 60¢ a record, and the producer's royalty is 10¢ a record. Assume the producer gets a $10,000 advance, and that the recording costs (including the producer's advance) are $120,000. (These numbers bear no relationship to reality but make for easy math.) If the producer is paid from "record one," and the album sells 150,000 units, the producer will get $15,000 in royalties (10¢ × 150,000 units). Since he got a $10,000 advance, this is deducted, and he gets the balance of $5,000.

Units sold	150,000
Producer Royalty	× $.10
	$15,000
Less: Advance	− 10,000
NET PAYABLE	**$5,000**

So as not to mislead you, you should know it's extremely difficult for even superstar producers to be paid from record one. The most common methods are those described in the next two sections. (A major exception to this has been producers based in the United Kingdom, where being paid from the first record was the norm. It was also customary for these producers to get the same royalty rate throughout the world, without reduction for any territories, which is not true for artists and U.S. producers, as we'll see on page 166. In recent years, however, the trend is for UK producers to be paid like U.S. producers.)

Hot producers can get a royalty that is **retroactive to record one** after recoupment of recording costs at the **combined rate.** What this means in English is that (a) before recordings costs are recouped, the producer gets *no royalties* at all; (b) once the recording costs are recouped, the producer gets paid from record one "retroactively" (meaning the company "goes back" and pays on sales previously made that didn't bear royalties at the time of sale); and (c) the recording costs are recouped at the artist's "all-in" rate (the "combined" artist and producer rate). This is easier to see with numbers:

Assume the same facts as in the first example. By changing the deal so that the producer is paid retroactively, however, the producer makes less. This is because, at 150,000 units, the artist will have only re-couped a total of $90,000 (60¢ × 150,000), which is short of the $120,000 recording costs. Thus, the recording costs have not been recouped, and the producer is not entitled to any royalties. So, instead of the additional $5,000 paid in the first example, the producer gets nothing (except, of course, the $10,000 advance).

Producer's Recording Cost Recoupment Computation		Producer's Royalty Account	
Units Sold	150,000	Units Sold	150,000
"Combined" Royalty	× $.60	Producer Royalty	× 0
	$90,000		0
Less: Recording Costs	– 120,000	Less: Advance	– $10,000
DEFICIT	**– $30,000**	DEFICIT	**– $10,000**

If the album later sells another 50,000 copies (a total of 200,000 units), the recording costs are now recouped (200,000 × 60¢ = $120,000 in costs), which means the producer gets paid for *all* 200,000 units ($20,000, which is 10¢ × 200,000 units), less, of course, the $10,000 advance. At this stage, note the producer is in exactly the same position as if he or she had been paid from the first record sold:

Producer's Recording Cost Recoupment Computation		Producer's Royalty Account	
Units Sold	200,000	Units Sold	200,000
"Combined" Royalty	× $.60	Producer Royalty	× $.10
	$120,000		$20,000
Less: Recording Costs	– $120,000	Less: Advance	– $10,000
DEFICIT	**$0**	NET PAYABLE	**$10,000**

Most producers are paid retroactively after recoupment of recording costs at the **net rate.** This means that, instead of recouping at the combined producer and artist (all-in) rate, the recoupment is only at the artist's rate *after deducting the producer* (i.e., the all-in rate "net" of the producer's royalty). In our example, this would mean 60¢ less the 10¢ producer's royalty, or 50¢. Thus, under this example at 200,000 units, the producer still doesn't get any royalties, because 50¢ × 200,000 equals only $100,000, which is short of the $120,000 needed to recoup the recording costs.

Producer's Recording Cost Recoupment Computation		Producer's Royalty Account	
Units Sold	200,000	Units Sold	200,000
"Net" Royalty	× $.50	Producer Royalty	× 0
	$100,000		0
Less: Recording Costs	– $120,000	Less: Advance	– $10,000
DEFICIT	– **$20,000**	DEFICIT	– **$10,000**

In this case, the producer wouldn't get his record one royalties until the artist sells a total of 240,000 units (50¢ × 240,000 = $120,000). Once this sales level is reached, the producer is paid retroactively ($24,000, which is 10¢ × 240,000), less the $10,000 advance. At this point, there is no difference between this deal and the deals under the first two examples.

Producer's Recording Cost Recoupment Computation		Producer's Royalty Account	
Units Sold	240,000	Units Sold	240,000
"Net" Royalty	× $.50	Producer Royalty	× $.10
	$120,000		$24,000
Less: Recording Costs	– $120,000	Less: Advance	– $10,000
DEFICIT	**$0**	NET PAYABLE	**$14,000**

For you sharp-eyed purists, I'm aware that the $10,000 producer's advance would *not* be included in recording costs to determine the *artist's* royalty once it's recouped from the producer's royalty—if it were, the company would be getting it twice. But for simplicity, I've ignored this in the examples, because it is an issue in the artist's deal and doesn't bear on the producer computation issues.

Other Royalty Computations

Except for the record one aspect, producers' royalties are customarily calculated in exactly the same way as the artists' (except for home video, as noted in the next section). This means they get the same packaging deduction, the same "free goods" reduction, and (as we'll discuss in chapter 13) the same proportionate reduction for foreign, budget, mid-price, CDs, etc. For example, if an artist gets 75% of his or her U.S. rate in England, the producer will get 75% of his or her U.S. producer rate in England. In situations where the artist gets a percentage of the company's net receipts (such as a license to use a recording in a motion picture, where the artist gets 50% of the fee paid by the motion picture company), the producer gets a pro-rata share of the artist's earnings, based on the ratio that the producer's royalty bears to the all-in rate. For example, if the artist's all-in rate is 12% and the producer gets 3%, the producer would get three-twelfths (one-fourth) of the artist's receipts. So if the record company gets $20,000 to use a master in a film, and pays $10,000 to the artist, the producer would get $2,500 (three-twelfths of the $10,000), and the artist would get $7,500 (the remaining nine-twelfths).

Home Video Royalties

For home video devices, producers generally get half of their otherwise applicable rate. The theory is that the master is only half of the product (the video portion is the other half). Accordingly, in the above example of 3% and 12%, instead of getting 25% (three-twelfths) of the artist's video monies, the producer would only get 12½%.

ADVANCES

Producers, like artists, also get advances. These advances are recoupable from the producer's royalties, regardless of how the producer's royalties are calculated. The range is something like this:

1. **New Producers:**
   Anywhere from nothing to $2,500 or $3,500 per master ($25,000 to $35,000 per album).
2. **Midlevel:**
   $3,500 to $7,500 per master ($35,000 to $75,000 per album).
3. **Superstar:**
   $10,000 to $15,000 plus per master ($100,000 to $150,000 plus per album). If a major producer is doing a major artist, advances in the $150,000 plus range aren't uncommon.

   A distinct category of superstar producers are those people (today mostly in the R&B area) who are considered by the industry to be as important (and in some cases more important) than the artist. These folks often write the songs as well. For their services, the range of advances can be $75,000 to $100,000 per *master*, and sometimes even more.

There's also a trend for producers at all levels to do "funds," meaning the producer gets a chunk of cash that includes recording costs and the producer's advance (just like the artist funds we discussed on page 111). This is especially so with producers who own their own studios.

WHO HIRES THE PRODUCER?

Until about ten years ago, record companies routinely hired the producers. However, one day they woke up and found their in-house lawyers spending so much time negotiating producer deals that it was costing them a fortune. So they hit on the brilliant idea that the artist should hire the producer, which has not only shifted the paperwork burden to the artist, but has also shifted the financial burden to you. Let's analyze the issues separately.

Who Actually Hires (Contracts with) the Producer?

The question of who does the paperwork to hire the producer is really a question of whether you or the record company bear the legal fees for negotiating the producer's deal. Can you guess which arrangement is better for you? Can you also guess which one is *very* hard to come by?

Who Pays the Producer?

Remember, in an all-in deal, you are responsible for the producer's royalties, regardless of who actually contracts with him or her. This is a much more serious issue than it may appear at first glance. For reasons we'll discuss in a minute, the producer may be entitled to royalties *before* you are recouped under your deal with the record company. This means you could owe money to the producer at a time when the record company doesn't owe you anything. This means you could have to write a check to the producer from your own pocket. This is not a good thing.

A MAJOR POINT—PAY ATTENTION

In case you've been dozing, now's the time to wake up—I'm going to talk about something that can mean a lot of money out of your pocket if you don't do it right. This is true whether you're an artist or a producer, even though it concerns the same point.

Let's take another look at our example from page 136:

Units Sold	150,000
Producer Royalty	× $.10
	$15,000
Less: Advance	− $10,000
NET PAYABLE	**$5,000**

Notice the producer is owed $5,000, but 150,000 units times the artist's 60¢ rate is only $90,000, meaning the $120,000 recording costs have not been recouped. Now remember that we talked about how the *artist* is responsible for paying the producer's royalties in an all-in deal (see page 110). If you put these two points together, you'll see the artist is obligated to pay $5,000 to the producer, but the artist is getting no money because he or she is unrecouped. A major bummer.

And the situation can get *much* worse. Watch this Parade of Horribles: The artist may have received substantial advances in which the producer did not share. For example, if the artist spent $120,000 on recording costs (as in our example) and got another $100,000 as an advance, the artist won't get any monies until both the recording costs *and* the $100,000 advance are recouped. Meanwhile, the producer (who didn't share in the $100,000 advance) is owed royalties.

Observe what happens if you double the sales to 300,000 units:

Artist's Account		Producer's Account	
Units Sold	300,000	Units Sold	300,000
Royalty	× $.60	Royalty	× $.10
	$180,000		$30,000
Less: Recording Costs	− $120,000	Less: Advance	− $10,000
Less: Advance	− $100,000	NET PAYABLE	**$20,000**
DEFICIT	− $40,000		

If the $20,000 number doesn't impress you, try adding a zero to make it $200,000. Do I have your attention?

This is one of the times when success can kill you, because the more records you sell, the deeper in the hole you go! (In a sense, I'm misleading you. First of all, at some level of success the artist *will* recoup and earn enough royalties to pay the producer off. Secondly, part of the reason the artist isn't getting royalties is because of an advance, which is in his or her pocket. Thus, if you think of advances as prepaid royalties, the artist has really received these royalties and is only required to pay a part of them to the producer. However, unless you're very different from the artists I know, you won't be setting any money aside for your producer. And much of this problem is caused by the fact that *recording costs* have not been recouped, which is not money sitting in your pocket. So you can't put that aside to cover the producer even if you want to.)

Now let's see how the above example can get truly miserable. Suppose the deal we just discussed was the artist's first album, which ultimately sold only 50,000 units. This means the album didn't recoup its recording costs, and the producer didn't recoup his or her advance. So far, the artist doesn't owe the producer anything, and so everything is fine (from the point of view of our example, that is—the artist's career is of course in the toilet). At this point, the artist ditches this producer in favor of a better one, who produces the second album, which also costs $120,000. For good measure, let's assume the artist's recording fund is $200,000 per album, so that the artist pockets $80,000 (the difference between the fund and the $120,000 recording costs) on each album. Finally, assume the second album sells 500,000 units, so that it recoups its recording costs and the producer of album number two is entitled to retroactive royalties. This means he or she is owed $50,000 (10¢ × 500,000 units), less the $10,000 advance, or $40,000.

Now let's look at how the accounts stack up. First, the *artist's* account with the record company:

ARTIST'S ACCOUNT WITH RECORD COMPANY

	Royalty Earnings	Charges Against Royalties	Net Due Artist (or Unrecouped Amount)
Album 1	+ $30,000 (60¢ × 50,000 units)	– $200,000 ($120,000 recording costs and $80,000 advance)	– $170,000
Album 2	+ $300,000 (60¢ × 500,000 units)	– $200,000 ($120,000 recording costs and $80,000 advance)	+ $100,000
TOTAL	+ **$330,000** ROYALTIES	– **$400,000** CHARGES	– **$70,000** NET DEFICIT

Now here's the computation of Album Number 2's producer royalties (Album Number 1's producer is not owed any royalties):

ALBUM NUMBER 2 PRODUCER'S ACCOUNT WITH ARTIST

	Royalty Earnings	Charges Against Royalties	Net Due Producer
Album 2	+ $50,000 (10¢ × 500,000 units)	– $10,000 (advance)	NET PAYABLE + $40,000

As you can see from the above, the producer of Album Number 2 is owed $40,000, and yet the artist is unrecouped by $70,000. If you add a few more unsuccessful albums prior to the big hit, and/or add a few zeros after these dollar amounts, you have the makings of a 10 on the Richter scale for the artist. And the producer ain't gonna be much happier when he or she doesn't get paid—instead of having a nice solid record company to send out the producer's royalty checks, he or she now has to chase Fred Flake the artist, who may be vacationing in Venezuela for the next five or six years. If either of these people is you, take two Valium and call me in the morning.

So what happens in real life? **Any producer who has the slightest idea what they're doing will insist on the record company paying his or her royalties.** Any artist who has the slightest idea what they're doing will insist on the record company paying the producer's royalties. Any record company that knows what it's doing (and they all do) will avoid this obligation like the plague.

It's simple enough to get the record company to pay the producer after the artist is recouped. This is because there are royalties from which it can deduct the producer's royalties. This is also relatively meaningless because the artist then has the money anyway. (It is, however, still better than not having the record company on the hook at all.) But it's when the artist *doesn't* have the money that this issue is critical.

If you have a reasonable amount of bargaining power (or if the producer does and requires this in the producer's agreement), you can get the record company to pay the producer and treat the payments as additional advances under your deal. In our example, this means the company would pay the producer $40,000 and you would then be $110,000 in the red (the original $70,000 plus the $40,000 paid to the producer). This makes you further unrecouped, but it's vastly superior to taking the money from your own pocket (few things aren't). If the company does agree, it will insist on approving the producer's deal, so that the amount it has to pay while you're unrecouped can't get out of hand. Also, as your bargaining power declines, the sources from which the record company will get these monies back increase geometrically—not only will the company take it back from your royalties, but it will also want to take it from:

1. **This album's budget,**
   meaning they'll hold back part of the money until either (a) the producer earns it, or (b) you flop so bad it becomes obvious the producer will never get it. For example, out of a $250,000 recording fund, they might hold back $50,000 in anticipation of paying producer's royalties before the artist is recouped. If in fact the producer gets $50,000 in royalties, the artist never sees this money. If, after a period of time from release of the album it becomes clear that it's a turkey, and the producer will never be entitled to the royalties, the artist gets it (more specifically, the artist gets the portion of it not earned by the producer).
2. **Your mechanical royalties**
   (we'll discuss what these babies are on page 209).
3. **The next album's budget**
   (assuming there is a next album).
4. Some record companies attempted to take **first-born children,** but this practice died out in the late sixties.

If you don't have much bargaining power, you're going to end up giving the company whatever it wants in exchange for an agreement to pay these royalties. Whatever it is, though, it beats the hell out of writing a check or selling your prized squeegee collection, so I suggest you take it. But don't let them know I said so until after you fight valiantly. And burn this page after you read it.

If you're on the *Fast Track,* go to
Part III (chapter 15) on page 205.
Everyone else, read on.

Answer to question on page 134:

The Chipmunks.

12

Advanced Record Deal Points

ADVANCED DEMO DEAL NEGOTIATION

If you're making a demo deal (see page 117 for what that is), read this section. If you're going right into a full deal, you can skip to the section on exclusivity on page 148, or read this section for general education.

First Refusal

Suppose you make a demo deal and record a spectacular demo. Can you thank the company very much for their help, and then go shop the demo to other companies, thereby running the price of your deal through the roof? Not very likely. The company that paid for the demo attaches the following strings:

1. In exchange for the company's giving you demo money, you have to give it a period of time after it gets the demos (about thirty to sixty days) before it has to decide whether or not it wants you. You're sitting in limbo while the company decides—you can't go to another company during this period—so the shorter it is, the better for you.
2. If the company decides it wants you, one of two things happens:
   (a) Many companies, in their demo deals, spell out the terms on which they have rights to your services if they go forward. (These terms will be within the parameters of new artists deals, which we've already discussed.) So if they want you, the deal is all set.
   (b) Some companies don't spell out the terms in the demo deal, but instead just require you to negotiate with them and try to make a deal (called a **first negotiation right**). If you make a deal, everything's great. If you don't make a deal,

however, the company gets a **first refusal** (also called a **last refusal**). This means that, if you get an offer from another company, you can't just accept it. Instead, you have to come back to the original company and give it a chance to match your offer.

Here's an example of a first refusal:

After making a demo, you first negotiate with the record company making the demo (let's call them the Demo Company). You insist on $200,000 for your first album, but the Demo Company only offers $125,000. You say you're insulted and, in a beautifully choreographed fit of righteous indignation, you walk away to shop your deal around town. Finally, another company offers you $150,000. In steps the Demo Company, saying, "Not so fast, Charlie." Under the first refusal, you have to go back and offer the deal to the Demo Company at $150,000. If the Demo Company wants it at that price, you have to sign with that outfit; if not, you're free to go elsewhere (although you can't sign for less than the offer you told the Demo Company about without giving it a chance to match that deal, for reasons I'm sure you can figure out).

Here's some goodies to negotiate on your first refusal:

1. You only have to come back to the Demo Company if the offer you get from somebody else is less than the last offer that the Demo Company made to you. So in our example, since it only offered you $125,000, you wouldn't have to come back to it if somebody else offered you $150,000 (it's more than the Demo Company's last $125,000 offer). This is pretty hard (read "next to impossible") to get. Remember, when you're making a demo deal, you haven't got a lot of bargaining power (if you did, you'd be making an album deal).

2. You only have to come back if the offer you get is less than the last offer *you* made to the Demo Company. Note this wouldn't change anything under our above example. Since the new company offered you $150,000, and you last offered the Demo Company $200,000, you'd still have to come back (the $150,000 is less than the $200,000 you offered the Demo Company). This provision is a bit more possible to get, but the Demo Company may still insist on your coming back with any offer, higher or lower.

3. However you end up under (1) or (2), you should limit the time within which the Demo Company can accept or reject your

offer. The best for you is the shortest possible. Ideally, I'd like to see five business days, but more realistic is ten or fifteen business days. ("Business days" are Monday through Friday, excluding holidays. So ten business days is two weeks if there are no holidays.) Companies may want as long as forty-five to sixty days (regular "calendar" days, not business days), which is an outrageous amount of time to hold you in never-never land. You could sit around all this time only to discover that (a) they decided not to take you, and (b) your other deal has gone away. Try never to go beyond 30 days—after all, the company heard your demos a long time ago.

Cost Reimbursement

If the Demo Company doesn't want you after you do the demos, or if it passes on your deal when you come back under a first refusal, you are free to go elsewhere. When you do sign with another company, however, the Demo Company will want its demo money back. Since you're not likely to be in a position to write a check, the Demo Company will want it from your new record deal.

Most record companies "second in line" (meaning the ones that follow the Demo Company) are willing to put up money to reimburse the cost of demos. (After all, sometimes they're the Demo Company and they want their money back too.) This cost, of course, will be recoupable from your royalties, and thus it's ultimately your money. However, it still beats smashing your piggy bank.

Here are a couple of things to negotiate in anticipation of this possibility:

1. The Demo Company should *only* get its money back *if* you make a new record deal. *Period*.
2. There should be a time limit. Otherwise, five years later you might get a deal based on totally different music and find you owe money to the Demo Company. Try a year or so.

Non–Record Company Demos

Record companies aren't the only places that may be willing to fund your demos. I've seen deals where demos are funded by recording studios, producers, engineers, rich people who want to be in rock 'n' roll, poor people who want to be in rock 'n' roll, etc. Indeed, one of the more bizarre stories I came across was a guy who funded an entire album, but would never tell any of us where his money came from. He lived in a walled estate and always paid in cash (I have my guess about his occupation; how about you?). Ultimately, after the album was finished, this guy literally disappeared, and we haven't heard from him in the last several years. It would really round out the story to tell you this was a hugely successful album, but to date they still don't have a record deal. (Sorry.)

Since non–record company sources can't actually make you a record deal, their contracts don't look anything like the demo deals offered by majors or independents. Also, because they are not mainstream deals, there are basically no rules, and I've seen them run all over the map. Here are some of the more common arrangements:

1. If and when you get a record deal, you reimburse them the cost of the demos, and the demo funder (let's call them the Funder) gets a 1% or 2% of retail royalty on your records. This royalty is known as an **override,** because it rides on top of your deal. However, the record company will take it out of your royalties, under the age-old theory that "It's your problem, not mine."

2. You want to limit the override to as few records as humanly possible. The minimum is where the Funder gets an override only on the specific demo recordings that are finished into masters on your record. Your argument is that the other demos didn't interest the record company. I've also seen deals where there is a smaller override if a song in a demo is re-recorded, as opposed to the demo being turned into a master. For example, the Funder might get a 2% royalty if you fix up and use their actual recordings, versus a 1% royalty if the same song is re-recorded.

3. At the other extreme, the Funder may ask for an override on every record under your deal, which I think is overreaching. If you agree to this, you'll be married to this yutzo forever, in exchange for their relatively small investment in your career. Ideally the override should only apply to the first album, but perhaps you can throw in a couple more if it's necessary to make the deal. Another compromise is not to limit the number of albums on which the Funder gets an override, but to say they only get the override until they get back twice (or three times) their investment. So if the Funder puts up $10,000, they only get an override until they receive $20,000 (or $30,000).

4. If the Funder only gets a royalty based on the use of specific

recordings or songs, then be sure to specify their royalty is **pro-rata** (see page 173 for a discussion of pro-rata).

5. The Funder's royalty should only be payable after recoupment of the amounts charged to you in connection with the records on which they have a royalty, such as tour support, videos, etc. (Note this is recoupment at *your* rate, not from the Funder's royalties.) It's not fair, however, to charge the Funder for recording costs of records on which they don't get an override, nor should they be charged for advances they don't share in.

6. If you make one of these deals, you should thoroughly understand the discussion on page 139 concerning payment of producer's royalties when you have no royalties from which to pay them. The exact same thing can happen here on the override—you could owe the Funder money before you are recouped. Ideally, when you make your record deal, try to get the company to pay the override obligation even though it's taken out of your royalties (in the same manner as discussed on page 142 for producers).

EXCLUSIVITY

It's no startling revelation that every record contract includes a provision stating the deal is **exclusive.** In other words, during the term of the agreement, you can't make records for anybody else. However, there are some related clauses and subtle side effects you should know about:

Re-recording Restrictions

It may surprise you to learn that all contracts say you can't re-record any song you recorded during the term of a deal for a certain period of time *after* the term. This is known as a **re-recording restriction.** When you think about it, it's perfectly logical—without it, you could go out the day after your deal is over and duplicate your albums for somebody else, and/or put out a greatest hits album. The usual period is five years from the date of recording, but with a minimum of three to five years from the end of the term. The minimum keeps you from re-recording an album delivered in year one of a six-year deal immediately after the term, even though it is more than five years since recording it.

Re-recording restrictions used to apply only to "records," which meant there was no restriction on re-recording for motion pictures, commercials, etc., which fall outside the definition of records (see page 89 for the definition). However, the companies realized that their artists were re-recording songs for commercials instead of using the master for which the record company could charge a fee, and now most forms provide that the re-recording restriction applies to these as well.

By the way, the world's record for re-recording restrictions belongs to Decca Records, which structured a deal whereby Bing Crosby had a *perpetual* re-recording restriction on the song "White Christmas."

Motion Picture and Television Soundtracks

Exclusivity clauses are limited to "records," which, as we discussed before, are devices sold for home use (see page 89). This means that the exclusivity provisions do not prevent you from recording for the *soundtrack* of a motion picture, or for a radio *transcription,* as long as these recordings are *not* sold as records. That's nice. But what about a soundtrack album, you ask? You've seen lots of artists with recordings on soundtrack albums, often on different labels. That's a real sticking point.

Record companies do not want you freely dropping recordings on others, for the legitimate reasons that (a) they want to be exclusively identified with you, and (b) they don't want someone else releasing a record of yours at a time that would conflict with one of your own albums (incidentally, neither should you, as you normally make a lot less on a soundtrack album).

So how do people get to put out soundtrack albums? Well, it's handled one of two ways in your record deal:

Forget It. At some record companies, this is an absolute "religious issue" ("sacred cow," "irrefutable principle," etc.—you get the idea), meaning you have no right to let anyone else put out a soundtrack album with your recording on it. In these cases, the artist throws him- or herself on the mercy of the record company each time a film company asks them to perform a song in a movie. The record company either agrees to let the artist perform (with restrictions—see below), or it refuses and the issue is closed (unless your manager can yell loud enough to reopen it). The other choice is to force the film company to give the soundtrack album to your record company, because then there is no conflict. If you're important enough, you can do this, even if you're only on one track.

If your company allows you to go elsewhere, and provided there is no conflict with your own product, then the album can be released on another label. Companies historically have been much more reluctant to allow a single to come out on another label, but this is changing as singles become less and less profitable items. If you can help it, it's best to get the single released by the same company that's releasing the soundtrack album. This is because their incentive is greater—they make money on the album even if they lose on the single, and the single helps sell the very profitable album.

Contractual Exclusions. *If you have clout,* you can negotiate an automatic contractual soundtrack exclusion in your record deal with some companies (or even with the sticklers if you're King Kong). These typically have some or all of the following laundry list (which will also apply if you have no exclusion but the company consents):

1. You can't perform on more than one (or two at most) selections for inclusion in the album.
2. You can't do more than one of these during any one-year (or two-year) period of the term.
3. You must not be late in delivery of your product at the time.
4. All of the royalties and advances must be paid to your record company. (Note here we're talking about advances against your royalties, as opposed to a fee that you may get for performance in the film [which, as you'll see on page 390, is normally not fully recoupable from royalties]. Some companies also attempt to grab part of your fee for performing, but I think this is wrong and I slap their hands.) After the company gets your royalties or advances, it will want to keep 50% of them for releasing you from the exclusivity and allowing you to go elsewhere. The other 50% is credited to your royalty account, which means (if you're un-recouped) you won't see any of it but it will reduce your deficit. If the soundtrack album is being released on your own company's label, you should be able to get 100% of the monies credited to your account (to reduce your deficit) or paid if you are recouped. If you really have a lot of bargaining power, you can get 50% to 100% of the royalties paid to you even if you're unrecouped, on the theory that this recording is in addition to the product they're entitled to under your deal, and thus should be handled separately.
5. The company having the exclusive contract must receive a courtesy credit in the film and on records, such as, "[Artist] appears courtesy of Atlantic Records."

6. You must try to get the right to use the recording on one of your albums, and perhaps also on a Greatest Hits album. The film company, if it gives these rights at all, will ask for a hold-back period before you can do so. (This is discussed on page 391.)

Home Video Exclusivity

Let's suppose you're signed to a record company that never gives soundtrack album exclusion rights in their contracts, and in fact refuses to do so for a specific film. The producer of the film tells you that's no problem, because they won't be putting out a soundtrack album. So you don't need the record company's consent and everybody's happy, right? Well, not really. Can you guess why?

The problem comes up when a home video device of the movie comes out. Remember, a home video device is a *record* (see page 89), and you can't make *records* for anyone else. So you are in violation of your recording agreement. What do you think of that?

In truth, and technically, you are indeed in violation of your recording agreement. If you raise the issue when making your record deal (and you always should), it can be resolved easily for a legitimate film (as opposed, for example, to a film of your concert that goes out on home video, which the record companies view as competitive with sales of audio records). If you have a career as an actor, this is particularly important, or you'll find yourself rather embarrassed when your record company shows up claiming it owns the home video distribution rights for the film. (In fact, the record companies don't seriously push this position, but at least one company has tried it in the past on a major film, and there's no reason to take a chance when it's easily fixable up front. If you ask, that is.)

Sideman Performances

Isn't it nice how all the superstars seem to be playing instruments and singing background on everybody else's records? These nonfeatured appearances are known as **sideman** performances, and there is hopefully a trend toward calling them **sideperson** performances. Now that you're educated, don't you wonder how this is possible? Doesn't it violate the exclusivity provisions of the superstar's agreement when she sings background for her pals on another label?

The answer is that there's a strong custom in the industry (and indeed you can have the provision inserted in your contract just by asking) that sideman performances are freely permitted, on the following conditions:

1. The performance must be truly a background performance, without any solos, duets, or "stepping out."
2. Your exclusive company must get a "courtesy credit" in the form of "[Artist] appears courtesy of ___ Records." (Before I started in music, I always thought they did that just to be nice.)
3. You can't violate your re-recording restriction (see page 148) for any selection, even as a background performer.
4. If you're a group, no more than two of you can perform together on any particular session. This is because your record company doesn't want your distinctive sound showing up on another label.

There is an exchange of correspondence between the record companies giving sideman clearance in each specific instance, but this is usually just a "rubber stamp" process (unless one company is having a fight with the other about something unrelated to the sideman). After all, if one of the companies makes an issue of it, they won't have such an easy go the next time that other company's artist shows up as a sideman on their label. The process is something like porcupines dancing carefully with each other.

VIDEOS

Promotional videos are the videos you see on MTV and (if you're over a certain age, physically or mentally) on VH-1. They're paid for by the record company to promote the sales of your records, and all the provisions concerning them are in your record deal. On a good day, a company can spend ten to twenty pages of its form agreement talking about these suckers, which have yet to break even (with extraordinarily rare exceptions), much less make a profit.

History

Did you know that music videos (which only became popular in the United States when MTV started in 1981) have been around since the 1960s in Europe? They started originally because it was cheaper for artists to make videos than to tour Europe. But videos have an even longer history than that. There are some great treasures that came from something called a "Scopitone" (pronounced "scope-ih-tone"). This was a jukebox that played videos on 16mm film, and it enjoyed a brief life in the late 1950s and early 1960s. Today the Scopitone videos are collectors' items, and they include a number of wonderful color videos from such artists as Sonny and Cher, Neil Sedaka, Dion, Nat King Cole, Bobby Darin, etc. And if you *really* want to delve into the past, there are black-and-white videos that were shown in cinemas in the 1940s and 1950s, with such artists as Fats Waller, Louis Jordan, Lena Horne, Bing Crosby, Spike Jones, and many others. But back to today.

Commercial Market

At the time of this writing, and probably for the foreseeable future, there is little (if any) profit in single-song (MTV-type) videos. This is because most of the uses are promotional (read "free") or for a nominal charge (which covers only duplicating and shipping), to gain exposure for the record. So far, you only get monies for home video sales (videocassettes and video discs) using these videos, either as (1) a **compilation** (meaning a program "compiled" from a number of individual video clips, of the same or different artists), or (2) occasionally a video plus a "making of." (For the royalties from both of these, see page 178.) However, with rare exception, these usages generate only minimal income, so neither you nor the company can expect to make anything on videos. No matter how hard everyone has tried (again with rare exception), videos have ended up being money losers that the companies hope will sell enough additional records to justify the videos' existence. Nonetheless, it is almost impossible to successfully promote a record these days without a video, so I think they'll be around for a while. Maybe.

Now to the issues you need to cover in your deal.

Is the Company Going to Make a Video of Your Song?

This is the first question, because if the answer is no, there's not much else to talk about. Until you have quite a bit of bargaining power, the record company, totally by itself, decides whether or not to make a video. As your bargaining power increases, you can require the company to do one or two videos per album. But even in this case, almost every company will say they only have to make videos for as long as it is doing so for artists of a stature similar to yours. Their concern (with justification) is that videos may someday not be a useful means of promoting records, and I usually agree to this request—if videos don't help sell records and aren't profitable, who cares?

Control

Control concerns two areas: (1) the content of the videos, and (2) the manner in which they're exploited. Unless you have an enormous amount of bargaining power, you generally can't control the commercial exploitation of your videos. This is because the company wants every opportunity to get its money back, and it doesn't want you stopping them over some silly concept like artistry. You may get the company to agree it won't commercially exploit a video if you repay the cost of it, but this is not of any practical value unless you're an extremely rich prima donna. You may be able to limit the exploitation a bit, however. For example, you can (with some bargaining power) prevent the company's putting your videos in a home video package that also contains videos of other artists.

The creative controls, when it comes to the content of videos, tend to be very limited. Except at the highest levels, you get only a bare bones approval of the story, song, director, and perhaps producer. Companies don't want to be in the position of having spent $100,000 for your video merely to have you say the "vibes" don't hit you right and you don't approve. That would mean they're stuck with a turkey they can't unload. If you have serious bargaining power, however, you may be able to pull off approval of all elements and the final video, or indeed take complete creative control of making the video.

Budget

Budgets for shooting a video will normally be either designated or approved by the company, but as your stature grows, you may be able to put in a minimum amount. Today, it's difficult to make a video of more than garage quality for less than $25,000 or so, and the majority of new and midlevel artists spend $70,000 to $100,000. Superstars routinely spend closer to $125,000 to $250,000, and there are occasional forays that take people into the $400,000 to $500,000-plus range (I think the record is $3,000,000). When you go upscale like this, you get a video that can compete with *Independence Day* (or *Waterworld*).

INDEPENDENT PROMOTION

There is an important phenomenon known as **independent promotion.** Promotion people (as noted on page 84) get records played on the radio, and they have relationships with station programmers to help ensure this. Some of these people are independent of record companies; they work for themselves and are hired by the companies on a project-by-project basis. They are cleverly called *independents,* to distinguish them from record company employees who also do promotion.

The independents are paid handsomely for their services by a record company (in most cases) or by the artist (in others). And by handsomely, I mean $50,000 or so per single. If the record company pays it, 50 percent to 100 percent is recoupable from the artist's royalties.

It's almost impossible to get companies to commit in your contract to pay for independent promotion, but it's always worth asking for. Whether they commit or they don't, however, it's a great idea to ask for a "cap" on how much they can charge you for independent promotion. The usual compromise is $50,000 per single, meaning that the company can't charge your royalties with more than $50,000 (or $25,000 if you're only charged with 50% of the amount) paid for independent promotion of any particular single. Without the cap, it's a blank check out of your royalties.

MERCHANDISING RIGHTS

In recent years, some record companies have begun trying to take artists' merchandising rights. These are the rights to put your name on a t-shirt, poster, etc., and we'll discuss them in great detail in chapters 24 and 25. (Note that I'm *not* talking about the rights to put out promotional posters, t-shirts, etc., which are distributed free to promote records, and for which all record companies have the rights. This section is about record companies wanting the right to sell merchandise at concerts, in stores, etc.)

If the companies get merchandising rights, they pay you the royalties we discuss in chapters 24 and 25 if they exploit the rights themselves, or else they pay you 50% of their receipts if they license the rights to merchandiser. They will also try to cross-collateralize the merchandise earnings with your record deal (see page 104 for what that means).

This is something you should resist if at all possible, since these are valuable rights and you don't want your record company's sticky fingers grabbing them. But expect some resistance. For example, most of the major record companies are affiliated with significant merchandising companies (Time-Warner owns Warner Bros. Records and Giant Merchandising; Sony owns Columbia Records and Sony Signatures Merchandising; BMG owns RCA Records and Nice Man Merchandising, etc.). And these affiliated companies will be particularly insistent on getting the rights for their pals. Other companies aren't affiliated with merchandisers but are greedy.

Whatever the company's reasoning is, put up a good fight, and try to get one of these:

1. Ideally, the company should not have any merchandising rights. You'll need some clout for this.
2. Next best is that the company gets no merchandising but keeps a matching right. This means that you can go out and shop around all you like, but you must come back and give them a chance to make the deal on the same terms as your best offer. (We discussed the details of a matching right in connection with demo deals, on page 144.) This system isn't ideal: The requirement to come back makes your shopping more difficult because bidders aren't interested in negotiating a whole deal if someone else can waltz in and take it away. But it's better than giving away the rights.

   Some record companies not only want a matching right, but also want a discount. For example, they may want to pay only 80% of what someone else offers. So if you had an offer for $10,000, they would be able to take the deal for $8,000. And in case you didn't figure it out, this is not good for you. If you must give a matching right, try very hard to keep it at 100%.

   In the real world, when the record company has a matching right, you usually go to them first and, if they're interested, just make a deal. If they're not interested, sometimes they'll let you go and forget about the matching right. But under the contractual language, they don't have to.
3. If all else fails, and you have to give up merchandising rights, make the best possible royalty deal (see chapters 24 and 25), and don't let them cross-collateralize merchandise earnings with your record deal. You can usually knock out the cross-collaterialization just by asking.

TOUR SUPPORT

And now for a bit of my personal finances. Remember my soft-drink stand (on page 94)? Well, here's that summer's take: 250 drinks, at 5¢ each, equals $12.50. Not bad for sweating in the sun for seven days a week over ten weeks, eh? But here's the real coup: I convinced my mother to pay for the drinks, so it was *all profit*. (I hope you're impressed.) If she hadn't, the drinks would have cost me $6.25, and the lumber for the stand was $18.00. So the expenses were $24.25, and I took in $12.50, resulting in a loss of $11.75. If it hadn't been for Ma, I'd have had to file bankruptcy.

This is not unlike the situation of a new band going on tour. As we'll see in more detail later (on page 335), it's virtually impossible for a new artist to go on the road and do anything besides lose money. Even assuming the band members only have a "share of profits," and therefore don't have to pay salaries to the players, the costs of rehearsal and putting together a show, travel, hotels, agents, managers, etc., are more than any band can earn in their baby stages. Indeed, even by the time you're midlevel, you'll be doing well to break even on the road.

This raises the question of why you should tour under these circumstances. (As the joke goes, if you buy widgets for $1.00 and sell them for 50¢, how do you make a profit? Answer: Volume.) The reason, of course, is to become better known, build an audience, sell more records, play bigger concerts, and generally further your career. The question, then, is "Who's going to pay for the loss?" The answer is one of two possibilities: (1) A rich relative; or (2) A record company. Guess which one happens more often?

Monies that record companies give you to make up tour losses are called **tour support.** Tour support used to be much easier to come by than it is nowadays. Record companies are more and more skeptical about whether an artist really sells more records by going on the road, and it also depends on the type of artist you are. If you're a heavy metal band, being on the road sells records better than anything else—in fact, you may never even get on Top 40 radio (Top 40 is today called **CHR,** standing for "contemporary hit radio"), but there will be a direct relationship between your appearing in a town and the sales of your records in that town. If you're more the ballad type, it's much harder to convince the company you should go out. If you fall in between, the amount of your tour support will depend on how well your manager does the Tijuana Two-Step.

Tour support is defined as the actual amount of your loss (you'll be required to give accountings to the company), but of course it has a maximum limit, usually in the range of $30,000 to $50,000 per tour. Many record companies are reluctant to commit to tour support in the contract, but are pretty good about doing it when the situation seems appropriate. If you can get it up front, it's a great thing to have; if you can't, go in and pound the table when you need it.

Tour support used to be nonrecoupable. For a while, the record companies bought the argument that it was "promotion" of their records, and wrote it off just like any other advertising and promotion expenses. But those days are gone with the wind. Today, tour support is always 100% recoupable (if you need it, your bargaining power usually ain't so great), and if you use any of the money to buy equipment, the company now wants to own the stuff.

If you're on the *Advanced Overview* track,
go to chapter 13 on page 164.
Experts, read on.

TERRITORY

For United States artists in the new-to-midrange category, the **territory** of your recording agreement (i.e., where the company can exclusively sell your records) is almost always the world. In fact, the territory is usually defined as "the universe," because our early thinking was that someone might argue satellites weren't covered by a contract that only said "the world."

This "universe" wording was the cause of one of my most bizarre negotiations, as well as my initiation by fire to the music business. I had only been practicing entertainment law a few months when a label I represented signed a strange jazz artist. This guy said he was a reincarnated Egyptian, and had recorded records in the pyramids (for real). Anyway, his lawyer called me up to say that it was unacceptable to grant the universe, and that our territory must be limited to the Earth Zone. At first I thought he was kidding, so I said I would give him everything beyond our solar system, and maybe Neptune and Pluto, but that the Moon and neighboring planets were mine. I also asked if we had to pay him in Earth money. The lawyer, very seriously, said this was not negotiable and would blow the deal. So I added "satellites" to the territory of "the world" and caved in on the rest. (That lawyer owes me one.)

More normal negotiation of the territory comes at the superstar level, or when the artist is not based in the United States. In this case, the artist may divide North America (United States and Canada) from the rest of the world, thus making two separate recording agreements. The advantages of this are (1) the fact that these two territories are not cross-collateralized (meaning unrecouped amounts in North America aren't offset against foreign royalties, and vice versa), and (2) you can always get a higher royalty outside of North America because you're eliminating the U.S. company's share of it. The disadvantages are (1) the advances may be lower (because there is no cross-collateralization), and (2) it's a pain for the artist to deal with two record companies. Dealing with two companies means shipping two sets of master tapes and artwork, "schmoozing" (hanging out) with two sets of executives, and most importantly, coordinating releases. If one territory releases prior to the other, you may (and you will, if you're an important artist) find records manufactured in one territory exported to the other, much to the dismay of the company with the exclusive rights in that territory.

In recent years, more and more companies have been refusing to sign you for anything except the entire world. So this type of deal is getting harder to come by.

UNION PER-RECORD CHARGES

It's important that you not be charged with any union payments based on the *sales* of records, as these are customarily borne solely by the record company. (This is different from union scale—see page 103 for what that is—paid to you for recording sessions, which has nothing to do with sales and is due even if the recordings are never released. Session scale payments are always recoupable as recording costs, as we discussed on page 103.) The most significant per-record union charges are payments made to the AFM (American Federation of Musicians) Music Performance Trust Fund (MPTF) and the AFM Special Payments Fund. Through various computations, these currently total about 4.6¢ per cassette and 5.6¢ per CD, for worldwide sales during (a) the first five years after release for the MPTF portion of these monies (28%), and (b) ten years after release for the balance. These royalties aren't paid on the first 25,000 albums or on any singles. There are some reductions of these amounts built into the record company/union deal over the next few years, but these monies can still add up to a chunk of change.

There is also an AFTRA contingent scale compensation based on record sales, which is much less money. This is only payable if you have nonroyalty background singers, and it has a ceiling (meaning it stops after the union gets a certain amount). The ceiling is currently four and one-half times scale for a one-hour session. So, because one-hour scale is currently about $60 to $130, the maximum AFTRA contingent scale is $270 to $585 per singer.

ALBUM COVER ARTWORK

At almost any level you can usually get some involvement in your album cover artwork, but you have to ask for it.

"Involvement" at lower levels means they tell you what they're doing, then go ahead and do it whether you like it or not. This process is called **consultation,** which means they talk to you but don't have to get your approval. Consultation is actually more valuable than I'm making it sound, because you can at least make your feelings known before the horse leaves the starting gate, and many companies will actually listen to you.

The next step up is **approval,** which means you can approve the artwork the company prepares. When you have approval rights, the company has to please you or you can stop them from using it.

Top of the line is the right to create your own artwork, subject to the company's approval. You can get this as your bargaining power grows. If you're a superstar, the company's only approval rights may be as to legalities, obscenity, and other major grossness—otherwise it's your show. When you get the right to create artwork, the trick is to make sure you have an adequate budget, or your creative juices will be severely hampered. So build in a set figure and escalate it over time (for inflation). I hesitate to give you specific figures because they may be out of date by the time you read this, but as of now a normal (no particular frills) artwork budget is in the range of $10,000 to $15,000.

CREATIVE, MARKETING, AND OTHER CONTROLS

There are a number of controls you should ask for, some of which you may actually get. These are:

1. Consent to coupling (see page 173 for what this is and the details on controlling it).
2. Consent to usage of your masters in commercials.

3. Consent to licensing your masters for films or television.
4. Approval of your photographs and biographical materials used in advertising and promotion.

If you can't get approval of any of these, at least try to get consultation rights (see page 160 for what those are).

RESERVE LIMITATIONS

When you're a midlevel to major artist, you can often get a limit on album reserves, usually 35% to 50% of the records shipped. (Reserves are discussed on page 97.) You won't get a limit for singles, because the market is so weird, as noted on page 109.

At midlevel and up, you can also force the company to liquidate the reserves over a set period of time, usually two years. Try to make the liquidation **ratable,** meaning they have to pay an equal amount each time. For example, if the company has to liquidate your reserves over two years, this is four six-month accounting periods. If they must liquidate ratably, they have to pay you one-fourth of the reserves in each of the four periods. If you don't say this, they could pay you a small percentage in the first three periods and hold the bulk of your money until the end.

As a newer artist, the best you normally get is contractual language saying reserves must be "reasonable." This is helpful in banging on your record company to release monies held in reserve, but as you can imagine, it leaves a lot of room for argument. Also, the amount of reserves a record company holds will be larger if you're a new artist. When you're new, they hold more because there's no history to judge whether your sales will stick or bounce back like little rubber balls.

SOUNDSCAN

A company called SoundScan, which began in 1991, measures how many records are sold *at retail.* They do it by reading the register tapes of the reporting stores, thus measuring records that walk out the door with consumers. (In the past, the companies only knew how many records were shipped *to* the stores.) SoundScan's data are used for *Billboard*'s charts and are also sold to record companies and other users.

SoundScan isn't 100% accurate—at the time of this writing, they have about 70% of the retail market, and they statistically extrapolate the other 30%. For mainstream records, I understand it's a very good snapshot of the marketplace. However, I'm told that records which sell primarily in independent stores and other outlets that aren't measured by SoundScan may be reported low. Still, it's substantially more accurate than anything we've ever had in the past, and they continue to add new reporting stores. So, by the time you read this, it should be even more accurate.

As its accuracy improves, it's going to be interesting to see what SoundScan does to reserves. It will be hard, for example, for a record company to argue that they have a right to hold reserves on records that SoundScan shows moving out the door. Watch this area for lots of action.

SPECIAL PACKAGING COSTS

Most record companies believe that, other than massaging an artist's ego, printed inner sleeves, special inserts (Alice Cooper once included a pair of girls' panties with each copy of an album), inflatable ducks, etc., add little, if any, to the sales of records. With vinyl discs disappearing, this has become virtually a non-issue, because CDs and cassettes don't lend themselves to this kind of abuse. However, there is still an issue over extra panels in cassette paper linings and CD booklets. The cassette linings are called **J-cards** because they're folded to fit the box and look like the letter *J*. If you print your song lyrics, add "special thanks," write a letter to your mom, etc., you need more than the standard three panels. CD booklets are normally 16 pages (i.e., 4 sheets folded and stapled in the middle), but you can easily get carried away and fill up a small volume of prose. At the superstar levels you can negotiate for more than the normal allowance, but if you don't have it in your contract, most companies charge artists with the excess that the fancy stuff costs over a standard package. And this can be significant money out of your hide. Since the variations are so infinite, and costs change quickly over time, it's hard to put any real parameters on them. But this provision could reduce your royalty by 5¢ to 10¢ or more per unit, which is serious money if you sell millions of units. So be aware that this attack of ego could happen to your pocketbook.

ACCOUNTINGS

When do you get your royalties? Twice a year, within sixty to ninety days after the close of each calendar six-month period (except for some companies that use weird, noncalendar six-month periods).

Objections

Your contract will say that each accounting becomes "final" (meaning you can no longer argue it's wrong) within a period of one or two years after the statement is sent to you. If the companies didn't say this, you would have until four years after the statement (in California) or six years thereafter (in New York) within which to sue them. That is, of course, precisely why they say it. You can increase the contractual period to a minimum of two years, and often three years, with minimal clout. Always do it, because it's uneconomical to audit unless you can do two or three years at once. What's auditing? Funny you should ask . . .

Audit Rights

Closely following the accounting clause is an audit clause, which says you can audit (meaning send in an accountant to verify) the record company's books. This is a way of assuring that you're getting a fair reporting, and if you have any success you should do it. Audits are expensive ($25,000 to $50,000 or more), so you'd better be recouped before you start. (There's not much joy in proving to the record company that, instead of being $1,000,000 unrecouped, you're only $900,000 unrecouped.) Most reputable auditors will give you an indication of whether an audit is worthwhile before you engage them—they do this by looking at your accounting statements and contracts, and knowing what the various record companies do.

Nowadays almost every record contract has a built-in right to audit, although in the past you had to ask for it. The audit clause will also say you can't audit more than once in any twelve-month period; that you can't examine any particular accounting statement more than once; and that you have to audit before the period to object has expired (see the above section).

13

Advanced Royalty Computations

DISTRIBUTION METHODS

Before we can get deeper into royalties, you need to know a little more about distribution. Records are distributed by four major methods: wholesale distribution entities, one-stops, rack jobbers, and licensees. Here's a brief look at each.

Wholesale Distribution Entities

Record wholesalers are by far the major means of distributing records. They're just like wholesale distributors in any other business—they buy from the manufacturing company (like Warner Bros., Epic, MCA, etc.) and sell to retail stores. (These are the major and independent distributors we discussed on page 83.)

One-Stops

One-stops buy from the major distributors and then sell to "Mom and Pop" record stores, who buy quantities too small for the majors to bother with. The one-stop buys in bulk (like a big retailer, so the majors will sell to them), and then sells onesies and twosies to the stores at a markup (which makes the price higher to Mom and Pop than to the chain stores).

Rack Jobbers

Rack jobbers are people who lease floor space from department stores and put in "racks" of records. Although it looks like Sears and Target are selling your records, in fact they only turn the space over to someone who decides what product to carry, delivers it to the racks, pays rent to the store, and keeps the profits. (After all, could you really expect the shoe buyer at Kmart to decide how many Metallica records to buy?)

Licensees

Records are also distributed by **licensees.** A licensee is someone who signs a "license agreement" with a record company, which allows them to *actually manufacture* and distribute records, as opposed to merely buying and distributing goods manufactured by the record company. Typical examples of licensees are:

1. Foreign distributors of U.S. recordings;
2. Record clubs (you know, the ones you signed up for in college so you could get 10 records for a penny and then move out of that dormitory before you got the bill for the next six at full price); and
3. Television-advertised packages (such as *Psychedelic Hits of the Sixties, The Best of Slim Whitman,* etc.), which are packages advertised on television and usually sold through direct mail ("Not Available in Any Store!"). These are still referred to as "K-Tel" packages, after a company named K-Tel that was the biggest in this field; the name still sticks even though K-Tel is now a much smaller player. (A friend of mine accurately observed that you know you're getting old when you watch commercials for the *Great Love Songs of the Eighties* and you want one.)

In addition to these four major methods, there are a variety of other weird ways to get records to the public. None of these are particularly meaningful at this time, but we'll touch on them because companies include royalty computations for most of them in their deals. They are things like direct mail by the record company (which almost never happens), distribution through armed forces post exchanges, and sales to educational institutions and libraries. There are also a host of new technologies, such as the currently nonexistent system of delivering records via satellite or cable to your home, with a special decoder that allows you to copy it on a blank tape and thus "buy" the record, for which you get a monthly bill. Royalties for these are discussed on page 186.

So how does all this affect your royalties? To paraphrase George Orwell in *Animal Farm,* some record sales are more equal than others. Royalties for the exact same record can be quite different, depending on how and where it's distributed. For example, a record that sells in a U.S. record store at full price will bear a higher (substantially higher) royalty than the same record when it's sold through record clubs, or outside the United States, or through other assorted methods. It's especially fun to watch new technologies (such as compact discs and digital audio tapes) go through predictable patterns of royalty shifts as they work their way from obscurity to the major way we deliver music. (See page 169 for an in-depth discussion of these patterns.)

Now you're ready to get into advanced royalty discussions. Let's take a look.

ROYALTIES FOR UNITED STATES SALES

We'll start first with United States sales, because, if you're signing to a U.S. company, all other sales are based on (i.e., a reduced percentage of) the rate for the United States.

The royalties we discussed in chapters 7 and 9 are for records sold:

1. In the United States; *and*
2. On a "top-line" label (see page 130 for what this means); *and*
3. At full price (meaning, today, $10.98 for cassettes and $15.98 or $16.98 for CDs. Some superstar CDs are priced at $17.98); *and*
4. Through normal retail channels (record stores); *and*
5. By the company's normal distribution channels (meaning the customary wholesale distributor—remember that some television advertised packages, for example, occasionally turn up in record stores, but these are sold by the television marketer's distributors [not the company's], and the royalty computation is totally different).

Sales that comply with 1 through 5 are known as **United States normal retail sales,** or sales through **USNRC,** meaning U.S. Normal Retail Channels. The royalty rate for these sales is usually defined in record deals as something like the **U.S. basic rate.** For simplicity, let's assume that your U.S. basic rate is 10% of retail; this makes the percentage reductions easy to follow.

FOREIGN ROYALTIES

The royalty reduction for sales outside the United States varies widely from company to company, and artist to artist. As a broad rule, companies usually give a higher rate in territories where they have an ownership interest in the foreign distributor. Conversely, they give a lesser royalty where they are only licensing their product to a wholly independent third party.

Let's look at the most common patterns.

Canada

Canada seems to have evolved into 85% of the United States rate with most companies, although some still treat it as just another "major" foreign territory (see the next paragraph). Using our example of a 10% U.S. basic rate, an 85% rate means you get 8.5% of retail for normal retail sales in Canada.

Majors

There are a number of markets in which American product sells particularly well, and these are known as the "major" territories. They of course vary from artist to artist, but in general they are (in no particular order): United Kingdom, Australia, Italy, Japan, Holland, Germany, and France. (By the way, France is one of the strangest record markets on this planet. Records that are total dogs in all other territories can be gigantic smashes in France, and vice versa. France is also the only country in Europe to have a television system totally incompatible with the rest of Europe, as well as with the United States.) The remaining EEC countries (Western Europe) and Scandinavia can be treated as "majors" if you have enough clout. The royalty for major territories again varies for the reasons set forth above (ownership versus licensing), but it's generally 60% to 75% of the U.S. basic rate, or 6% to 7.5% of retail in our example.

As you probably know, in 1993, Western Europe opened its borders and became one big, happy economic community. Since then (with clout), it's become a little easier to treat all of these territories as "majors."

R.O.W.

R.O.W. stands for **rest of world** and includes the grab bag of countries left over, which I'll leave to you and your atlas to name. The royalty for these generally runs around 50% to 60% of the U.S. basic rate, or 5% to 6% of retail under our assumption.

Having stated the general rules, let me also say that if you're an artist with a huge following in any particular foreign territory, you can usually negotiate a better royalty for that country. Superstars can also get better royalties than others, but the top for an artist signed to a U.S. company is around 16% for the major territories and 14% elsewhere, unless you have extraordinary bargaining power.

An interesting aspect of foreign royalties is that, in U.S. deals, they are almost always based on SRLP. That sounds logical, until you learn that virtually no other territory in the world has an SRLP. What really happens is that the companies "uplift" the wholesale price to create an SRLP, in a way that is identical to some U.S. companies' 130% uplift for CD royalty computations (see page 170). For example, if the wholesale price is $10.00 and the uplift is 130%, the SRLP is deemed to be $13.00. The actual uplift percentage varies from territory to territory (depending on local pricing), from a low of 125% to a high of 140%.

Incidentally, foreign territories don't use the term "wholesale." Instead, they say **Published Price to Dealers** or **Published Dealer Price** (both of which are abbreviated as PPD), or **Base Price to Dealers** (abbreviated as BPD). There is a trend for some companies simply to state foreign royalties as a percentage of PPD (after a packaging deduction), and in this case your royalty should be "uplifted" to compensate for the fact that the base is lower. My guess is that, in time, all of the companies will move to a royalty that is a percentage of PPD or BPD, because it's simple, logical, and avoids any dispute about the proper percentage for uplift.

COMPACT DISCS, DAT, MD, DCC, AUDIOPHILE RECORDS, AND THINGS NOT YET INVENTED

As of this writing, CDs and prerecorded analog cassettes are the dominant means of delivering music, with about 70% of sales being CDs. (Individual artists may vary from this—for example, Baby Boomer Crooners sell more CDs, while street artists sell more cassettes.) Vinyl discs have gone to that Great Schlock House in the Sky, which was formerly occupied by 78s and monaural records (to find out about "schlock," see page 183).

Digital Audio Tape (DAT), Mini Disc (MD), and Digital Compact Cassette (DCC)

As you probably know, audio cassettes utilize a technology known as *analog* recording, whereas compact discs are recorded *digitally*. The next generation of cassettes is going to be digital, but so far all that's happened is that people have spent millions of dollars unsuccessfully trying to come up with a new format. The carcasses strewn along the road are: **Digital Audio Tapes (DAT), Digital Compact Cassettes (DCC),** and **Mini Discs (MD).** A Mini Disc is a tiny compact disc, but is also recordable. Digital Audio Tapes (DAT) are small cassettes that are important in recording studios and professional work, but they have failed in the mass marketplace. DCCs are the same size as regular cassettes, and the machines can play both analog and digital cassettes. However, they have also crashed and burned.

All of these formats sounded good on paper: They have CD sound quality, as well as "random access" (in other words, you can tell them to go directly from cut 1 to cut 7). However, consumers haven't wanted them and I doubt if any of these devices are going to make it long term. Someday there will be a recordable, digital medium, but it's still on the other side of the horizon.

The Passman Theory of Technology Cycles

There are predictable, and fascinating, patterns that take place every time a new technology hits the record industry. It goes something like this:

1. The record companies scramble to see what their contracts say about these devices. Since they didn't exist when the deal was made, the contract either doesn't deal with them at all, or if it does, it usually pays a royalty that proves to be too high now that the fantasy is a reality. (To see how companies now do it, look at page 170.)
2. This means the companies are forced to go to every single artist and negotiate a new deal for the technology.
3. Because the technology is so new, no one (including the record companies) really understands its economics. Also, when it's first introduced, the device is expensive, because it's not being mass-produced.
4. The result is a grace period during which royalties on these devices are not particularly favorable to the artist. This is to give the technology a chance to get off the ground, and to help the record company justify the financial risk.
5. Invariably, this grace period carries on far beyond its economic life, during which time the companies make huge profits and the artist gets a smaller portion of them than he or she gets on the dominant technology. As artist deals expire and are renegotiated, the rate goes up.
6. Finally, an industry pattern develops and royalty rates stabilize.

Compact Disc and Other New Technology Royalties

Compact discs have long passed the "it's brand new and I don't know what to do with it" stage, as they are now the major means of delivering music. The royalties have settled into an industry norm, although they still vary substantially from company to company, and are less than the royalty for cassettes (on a percentage basis, that is—the royalties are higher in pennies [today] because the price on which the percentage is based is higher than the price for cassettes). The companies justify this by saying that manufacturing compact discs is more expensive than cassettes (which is true), although the manufacturing costs of CDs are falling. In the beginning, CDs required very high technology and expensive factories. They were manufactured in "clean rooms," where workers had to wear "space suits" because even one particle of dust could disrupt the process. They also had to be made in factories insulated for vibration, the manufacturing process being so precise that a highway over a mile away could upset it. However, the capacity to manufacture compact discs has so expanded that, while getting sufficient inventory used to be a problem, now so many factories are onstream that they produce more CDs than can be sold. And the CD manufacturing machine (called a "monoliner") is now a closed unit, creating its own "clean room" inside, so there's no more need for workers to look like Darth Vader. Accordingly, the price has tumbled radically, but CD manufacture is still more expensive than duplicating cassettes at high speed (which is done on a machine that your grandmother could run by pushing a button).

Let's now look at how the royalties work. Most companies have a royalty provision that covers not only compact discs, but also DATs and DCCs (as and when they exist), **audiophile** recordings, and any other new technologies that may exist. Audiophile recordings have been around a while, but have never accounted for substantial sales. They are extra-high quality recordings, sold mainly through stereo hardware outlets, as opposed to record stores. They're mastered at half speed for higher quality, embedded on a gold CD, and packaged by little elves wearing velvet gloves.

Virtually all the companies use a 25% packaging deduction for CDs and these other records (as compared to 10% packaging for vinyl discs and 20% for tapes), and most of the companies further discount the royalty rate itself (e.g., you might get 75% to 80% of the analog cassette rate). Others give you a full rate but play games with the retail price, and one company adds an additional 5% distributor free goods (i.e., a total of 20% for CDs when there's only 15% for analog cassettes) (see page 93 for what free goods are). In other words, it's a holy mess.

In preparing for my class recently, I called all of the major distributors and asked how they computed compact disc royalties. To my surprise, almost every one of them was different! They have asked me not to give out the precise methods that each of them uses, but the truth is that it really doesn't matter; the methods used by companies change over time and may be subject to negotiation. The real lesson is that, if you're considering signing with a company, you *must* sit down and make them walk you through their compact disc royalty calculations. This is the only way you can really figure out what your royalty is worth, so you can compare it to another company's.

Here are a couple of examples to guide you in your computations:

Example. Assuming an artist has a 10% royalty rate, and the company pays 85% of this for compact discs (8.5%), here's a computation of the CD royalty with a $15.98 SRLP:

Retail Price	$15.98
Less: 25% Packaging	– 3.99
Royalty Base	$11.98
Royalty Rate	× 8.5%
ROYALTY (ROUNDED TO PENNY)	**$1.01**

Many companies also use an artificial retail price, which they define as a 130% **uplift** of their wholesale price, meaning the wholesale price is increased (uplifted) to 130% of itself. How this got started is beyond me, but several companies have picked it up since they figured out it's a further reduction of artists' royalties. But even this practice isn't uniform. Companies that have no free goods use a wholesale price that is lower than the companies that do have free goods, but remember they both pay on only 85% of the records sold. However, the companies without free goods tend to pay a CD royalty equal to the full analog cassette rate (e.g., 10%), while the ones that have free goods pay more like 80% to 85% of that rate (e.g., 8% to 8.5%), so you end up in about the same place.

Confused? It's a little easier to see with the numbers. Assuming an artist has a 10% analog cassette royalty rate, and the company has no free goods (but pays on 85%), here's the computation of an uplift:

Wholesale Price	$10.30
Uplift Factor	× 130%
Imputed Retail Price	$13.39
Less: 25% Packaging	− 3.35
Royalty Base	$10.04
Royalty Rate	× 10%
ROYALTY (ROUNDED TO PENNY)	**$1.00**

On the other hand, if the company has free goods, the wholesale price is going to be higher. But they usually pay an 85% royalty, so in fact you end up in about the same place:

Wholesale Price	$12.12 (note the higher price)
Uplift Factor	× 130%
Imputed Retail Price	$15.76
Less: 25% Packaging	− 3.94
Royalty Base	$11.82
Royalty Rate	8.5% (note the 85% rate)
ROYALTY (ROUNDED TO PENNY)	**$1.00**

It used to be, if you had enough bargaining power, you could muscle a provision that says the royalty for sales of your record in any new technology will be negotiated at the time of release. But this is extremely hard to come by nowadays because new technologies have been arriving by the busload. (If you do get this clause, however, the record company will clearly state that it can go ahead and sell these formats even if you don't reach agreement, subject only to working out the royalty with you later.) Most likely your company will insist on a prenegotiated rate that is a percentage (usually 75% to 80%) of your analog cassette royalty.

Enhanced CD/CD Plus

An **Enhanced CD,** or a **CD Plus,** is a normal album when played on your stereo. But when put into your computer, it's magically transformed into (1) an audio album that can sound relatively lousy through your one-inch computer speakers, and (2) a device that displays one or two mediocre-looking videos, copies of reviews, interviews, lyrics, and so forth. Did I sugarcoat it too much?

The original CD Plus had a slight glitch: the audio CD players had a nasty habit of thinking the video information was supposed to be sound, so they played it through your speakers. That blasted out a lot of eardrums before they fixed the problem and hid the information where audio players couldn't find it.

Royalties at the time of this writing are treated the same as normal, audio CDs (i.e., your audio CD royalty rate after a 25% packaging deduction, although some companies take a 30% packaging on Enhanced CDs. For a discussion of CD royalties, see page 170). Full-blown CD-ROMs are discussed on page 372.

COUPLING AND COMPILATIONS

The practice of putting your performances together with those of other artists is known as **coupling,** and albums with a bunch of different artists are called **compilations.** Samplers (see page 184) are a form of coupling, but the practice also exists at a much higher end of the scale. It includes television-advertised compilation albums (*Texas Punk Bands of the Sixties,* etc.); soundtrack albums from motion pictures with diverse music (*Forrest Gump, Dirty Dancing,* etc.); and any other marketing device the record companies can dream up. For example, several companies have tried (so far unsuccessfully) a system that lists a number of individual cuts and allows the customer to create a custom tape of only those cuts selected. This is also a form of coupling.

Royalties

The royalty on coupled product sold by your record company is pretty much what you would think—if there are ten cuts on the album and you've done one of them, you get one-tenth of your normal royalty; if you've done two cuts out of ten, you get 20%, etc. This process is called **pro-ration,** and you are said to have a **pro-rata** royalty (meaning your royalty is in proportion to the number of cuts on the album). (Every once in a while pro-ration is based on the playing time of your cut versus the total playing time of the record, but this is pretty rare. It's almost always based solely on the number of cuts.)

The royalty on coupled product that is licensed to someone else by your record company is usually 50% of the company's licensing receipts. For example, if a record company licenses your song to a TV-packaged album and gets 6¢ or 7¢ per selection for CDs, and about 4¢ or 5¢ for cassettes (these deals are often done in pennies rather than as a percentage of retail), they pay you half (e.g., 3¢ or 3.5¢ for CDs). Remember, in an all-in deal, your half includes the producer's royalty (the producer's share of this is discussed on page 137).

Control

You should always try to control coupling, both for (1) the artistic reason that you don't want to be on a record with someone you hate, and (2) the financial reason that you don't want to be the major cut selling an album of dorks when you only get a small part of the royalty. With moderate bargaining power, you can control this completely during the term of your deal. With more bargaining power, you can control it after the term if you're recouped, and with massive clout you can control it forever. Restrictions normally are only for the United States, unless you have really strong bargaining power. These compilation albums are major sources of revenue in foreign territories, and the foreign licensees tend to do whatever they feel like, regardless of what your contract says. Also, even if you have ultimate control, companies will insist on the right to couple for **in-transit uses** (such as in-flight programs for airplanes) and samplers (see page 184) without your consent—they view these as promotion.

Even as a new artist, you should at least be able to get a limit on the number of couplings. A common provision is to say the company can't couple more than two of your selections per year, and on no more than two albums. Note the difference between these two concepts: If the company's only limit is two selections per year, they could put one of your hits on 37 different compilation albums.

JOINT RECORDINGS

Related to coupling is the concept of **joint recordings.** A joint recording is where more than one royalty artist gets together on the same song, such as a duet.

Royalty

The most common arrangement is for the royalty to be split amongst the artists in proportion to their numbers, so that if it's a duet, each gets half; if it's a trio, each gets a third; etc. While this is usually pretty straightforward, here are a couple of twists:

1. If you do a duet with a five-piece group, be sure in your deal that the group only counts as one entity. Otherwise, the company might say there are *six* royalty artists instead of two (you and the group), and you'll only get one-sixth of the royalty instead of one-half.

2. Whose royalty gets divided, yours or theirs? If you're the star, be sure your price is a share of *your* royalty. If you're new and singing with a star, try for a piece of theirs.

Control

It's easy to get control over joint recordings. Just ask. The record company will readily agree you don't have to make a joint recording without your consent. The reason why is pretty simple—no one goes into the studio with someone he or she doesn't like.

"GREATEST HITS" OR "BEST OF"

The royalties on Greatest Hits albums (see page 126 for what a "Greatest Hits" album is) are pro-rata royalties (see page 173), based on the album they come from. For example, if your first two albums were at 12%, and the others at 13%, and if half the Greatest Hits album was from the first two albums (12%) and half from the others (13%), your royalty on the Greatest Hits album would be 12.5% (50% times 12%, plus 50% times 13%). But these calculations are trickier than they look at first glance.

For example, suppose that some of the albums from which you take the selections had escalations because of sales success (see page 110). Which royalty do you use? The initial release royalty? The escalated royalty? And do you also get an escalation based on sales of the Greatest Hits album itself?

The answer is usually one of three:

1. You get the lowest royalty for the album from which each selection is taken (i.e., the royalty before any escalations based on sales of that album), and then a negotiated escalation based on sales of the Greatest Hits album. Under this formula, the starting royalty is pro-rated based on nonescalated rates.

2. You get the highest royalty rate achieved by the album from which the selection is taken (i.e., the escalated rate based on sales of that album) with *no* further escalations for sales of the Great-

est Hits album. These rates are then pro-rated the same way we did it in the first example.

3. You get the lowest possible rate and no escalations for anything. This is what you get if you don't ask.

Let's look at examples of the first two:

1. Suppose a Greatest Hits album contains ten selections, consisting of three selections from the initial term, when your rate (before escalations) was 10%; two selections from the first option period when your (nonescalated) rate was 11%; and five selections from the second option period, when your (nonescalated) rate was 12%. Under the first approach (no escalations count), the result would be the following:

Masters	Album Royalty
3 Masters recorded during initial term: These masters are ³⁄₁₀ of the album (30%), because 3 of the 10 selections on the album are at this rate. Thus, the royalty for these cuts is 30% of 10% (the initial period royalty):	3.0%
2 Masters recorded during first option term: 2 of 10 (20%), at 11%:	2.2%
5 Masters recorded during second option term: 5 of 10 (50%), at 12%	6.0%
TOTAL ROYALTY ON ALBUM	**11.2%**

This 11.2% royalty might then escalate based on sales of the Greatest Hits album. For example, you might get an additional 1% (to 12.2%) at 1 million units, and another 1% (to 13.2%) at 2 million.

2. Now let's look at the second method (where escalated royalties are pro-rated). We'll use the same figures as the first example, but assume the royalties on early albums escalated because of sales, to 12% for the album made in the first option period, and to 14% for the album made in the second option period. (Assume there are no escalations for the initial term album.)

Here's how the royalties look:

Masters	Royalty
Initial Term: 3 of 10 (30%) at 10%:	3.0%
First Option Term: 2 of 10 (20%) at 12%:	2.4%
Second Option Term: 5 of 10 (50%) at 14%:	7.0%
TOTAL ROYALTY ON ALBUM	**12.4%**

As noted above, under this method there are no escalations for sales of the greatest hits album.

MULTIPLE ALBUMS

The **multiple album** has gone through an enormous change lately. Originally, it meant an album that couldn't fit on one vinyl disc, since vinyl discs were limited to a maximum of about 60 minutes of playing time. However, cassettes and CDs can hold substantially more than this, so it takes a lot of material to require two CDs or two cassettes. Also, these two-in-one sets don't sell as well as single albums, if for no other reason than because they're more expensive (at the time of this writing, a double cassette is approximately $20.98 to $24.98, and a multiple CD package is approximately $24.98 to $29.98). Thus "multiple albums" (in the classic sense of a two-CD or two-cassette package) are rare.

Virtually every form contract says you can't put out a true multiple album without the company's consent. And if they do consent, your royalty may be reduced. The reduction used to be pretty radical, because the price of a double album was only about 60% more than a single album, but the manufacturing costs were approximately double. Now the prices of these babies are just about double the single album price (as noted in the prior paragraph), so there's only a small royalty reduction, if any. The reduction works like this: Your royalty is adjusted downward in the ratio that the selling price of the multiple album is less than two times the single-album price. That's not as confusing as it sounds if we use numbers: If a single-album cassette price is $10.98 (let's use $11.00 for simplicity), you'd only get a full royalty for a multiple album if its retail price were doubled to $22.00 (i.e., if the company were getting the full price of two single albums). If the price of the double album is $20.98 (let's use $21), that is only 21/22 (or 95%) of $22.00. Accordingly, you'd get 95% (21/22) of your normal royalty, applied against the $20.98 price. So if your normal royalty is 10% of retail, you'd get 9.5% (21/22 of the 10%) for a $20.98 multiple-album set.

If a single album has more than 14 selections, some form contracts consider it a multiple album. But, if it only consists of one cassette or CD, it's priced the same as, or perhaps a dollar more than, a single album. Your royalty shouldn't be reduced for a single CD or a single cassette album just because it has a lot of tracks, but a lot of forms do. And because the price is not increased (and thus is nowhere near double that of a single album), the formula in the prior paragraph could cut your royalty in half! So watch out for this. (There's a related discussion of multiple albums in connection with mechanical royalties on page 229.)

Regardless of how you define it, and no matter how your royalty gets computed, all record companies treat a multiple album as only one album for purposes of your delivery commitment. Accordingly, if you thought you'd knock out your obligation to deliver two albums with a multiple album, they got there ahead of you. Sorry.

Note here I'm discussing multiple albums that are sold through retail stores. The multiple albums sold through TV campaigns are an entirely different story, as we discussed on page 173.

VIDEOCASSETTES, VIDEO DISCS, AND OTHER HOME VIDEO DEVICES

After years of groping, there now seems to be a general industry norm (although the specifics still vary) for home video devices.

Manufactured Units

If home video units are manufactured and distributed by your record company, you get a royalty which falls in the 10% to 20% of wholesale range for U.S. normal retail top-price sales. You should not be charged a packaging deduction on videos (although some companies try), and several companies vary their royalty depending on the retail price. For example, the royalty might be 10% for a retail price of less than $17.00, 15% for a retail price of $17.00 to $20.00, and 20% for a price of more than $20.00. Foreign royalties tend to be around 8% to 15% of wholesale, and all royalties are reduced for budget line (usually to a one-half royalty) and for free goods (only real ones). (Budget line records are discussed on page 182, and the same idea applies to home video devices.)

Licensed Sales

Where video rights are licensed by the record company to someone else (meaning another company manufactures, distributes, and pays a royalty to the record company), the company pays you 50% of its net receipts. "Net receipts" are what's left after the company takes its gross receipts and deducts the following:

1. **A distribution fee**
   for the record company, which is a percentage of gross and therefore taken first. This is a key lesson in computing fees: If you get a percentage of something, always take it first so that it's against the biggest possible dollar amount. The distribution fee is to cover the company's overhead in handling the licensing, and it ranges anywhere from 10% to 25%, depending on your bargaining power. It can sometimes be eliminated (if you're the ruler of a moderate-size nation).
2. **Distribution expenses,**
   meaning the costs of duplicating, shipping, etc., necessary to distribute the product.
3. **Third party payments**
   to unions and guilds.

The result of this is net receipts, and you get 50% as your share.

All-in Video Royalties

When you have an all-in record deal (see page 110), out of *your share* of proceeds (whether designated as a royalty or a percentage of receipts), you are responsible for:

1. All copyright royalties payable for compositions used in the videos. (See page 229 for what these are.)
2. All third-party payments, which include the *audio* producer of the master recordings used in the video, the unions, and anyone else entitled to a royalty.

Digital Video Discs (DVD)

A new format, which should be in the marketplace by the time you read this, is called **DVD**, which stands for **Digital Video Disc**. These little critters are the same size as compact discs, yet they can hold a full motion picture. Translation: they hold tons more information than compact discs.

The most obvious market for DVDs is the video cassette business, as movies will be released in this format and will probably blow out VHS. But DVDs will have implications for the music business as well. Apart from the fact that concerts, video compilations, etc., which are now on videocassette, can be put out on DVDs, DVDs will also have the ability to hold a great number of albums (like the entire catalog of an artist). I know several companies have serious questions as to whether doing this will cheapen the product—in other words, would buying five albums on one little piece of plastic detract from the value of each album? It will be interesting and fun to see what DVDs do to the music world.

Recoupment of Video Costs

All the costs of making the video go into a pot, to be charged against your video royalties. With some companies, only half the costs go into this pot, because the other half are charged against your audio record royalties. Other companies say that all costs go against video royalties, less the half charged to audio royalties which are actually recouped. (With this second method, if there are no audio royalties [because you're unrecouped], 100% of the video costs are charged against your video royalties. With the first method, only 50% would go against your video royalties under the same scenario. However, using either method, if your record isn't successful enough to earn any audio royalties, the video isn't likely to be meaningful, and neither will the charge on the video side.) When you make your deal, be sure you don't end up getting charged twice for the same cost—in other words, once the costs have been taken from your audio record royalties, the same amount shouldn't also be taken from your video royalties, or vice versa. Many record company forms would technically allow this, although I'm not certain it's intended, and I've never seen them do it.

So now we have a pot with chargeable costs in it. The company next takes your video royalties and throws them into this pot. When these monies equal the costs charged, then from that point forward your royalties are paid out or credited to your audio royalty account if you're unrecouped (in the same way that audio record royalties are paid or credited after recouping recording costs). However, as noted on page 153, the reality of video royalties is elusive. Accordingly, please write me if you ever get to this point and actually earn video royalties, so we can both savor the moment.

MID-PRICE RECORDS

After a record has had its initial run in current release, it is known as a **catalog item,** meaning it's listed in the company's catalog of available titles, but isn't being currently promoted. Most record companies' catalog items are now issued at **mid-price,** meaning a reduced price that's designed to encourage consumers to buy older titles. Today, a typical mid-price for a cassette album originally released at $10.98 would be $7.98, and for a CD originally released at $15.98 would be $11.98. The contractual definition of a mid-price record (with slight variations from company to company) is one "with a suggested retail price between 65% and 80% of the price for newly released top-line records." Some companies also say it's a record with a price at least $2.00 below the new release prices, so that if it fits either category, it's considered mid-price.

Royalty

The royalty rate for mid-price is usually 75% of the U.S. basic rate (7.5% if you have a 10% royalty). Note this is a double whammy—not only is the royalty rate lower, but the retail price on which it's based is also lower. The record companies justify this because their wholesale price is lower, and accordingly, so is their profit margin. Their thinking is that the lower price will generate extra sales to more than make up the lost revenue.

Here's an example of a mid-priced cassette royalty computation:

Retail Price	$7.98
Less: 20% Packaging	− 1.60
Royalty Base	$6.38
Royalty Rate	× 7.5%
ROYALTY (ROUNDED TO PENNY)	**$.48**

Compare this to your royalty of 87.9¢ when this same record is sold at full price (see page 93) and pray the companies are right about the extra sales.

As you gain clout, you can negotiate a period of time after initial release before a record can be released at mid-price in the United States (usually twelve to eighteen months), or perhaps even a flat prohibition without your consent. This provision used to be easier to get than it is today, because it's a relatively recent practice to issue catalog items at mid-price.

In some territories of the world mid-price is customary for the first release, and there is little, if anything, you can do about it. Presumably, your interests and the record company's are the same, since they want to maximize their profits in that territory. Thus they won't put something out a mid-price unless they feel the reduced price will promote the sale of enough additional copies to justify the lower profit margin.

BUDGET RECORDS

The next step down from mid-price is **budget,** which means a record the company doesn't think it can sell unless it knocks the price way down. These are the ones stuck in bins (with a handwritten sign saying "Big Savings!") selling for $4.98 or less for cassettes, and $9.98 or less for CDs. The contractual definition of budget records is one with a price of less than 65% of the top-line price, but sometimes there is no mid-price defined and the contract says everything under 80% of the top-line price is a budget record.

Royalty

The royalty on budget records is usually 50% of the top-line royalty rate, or 5% in our 10% example. With some clout, you can hold back budget records for a period after initial release. Because being on a budget line is a statement about what the company thinks of your career, you can usually get a longer holdback than you can for mid-price. For example, in the United States, the company might agree to wait eighteen months to two years after initial release. Again, foreign markets have their own peculiarities, and there will be little you can do unless you're a major artist in a particular territory. As your muscle increases, you may be able to get a flat prohibition against budget, at least during the term of your agreement. And, if you can't get the right to consent to budgets after the term, a compromise is to say they can't do it as long as your account is recouped. The idea is that, if they've lost money on your project, they can do whatever they want to get even, but otherwise they must keep you off the budget line.

RECORD CLUBS

Record clubs are mail-order "clubs" which you join by agreeing to buy a certain number of records. (We touched on them on page 165.) Royalties for record-club sales are usually half of the top-line royalty rate, but not more than 50% of the company's net licensing receipts from the record club (remember, these sales are licensed to record clubs, who manufacture and distribute the records). With a little clout, you can get a straight 50% of the company's net licensing receipts.

The lower rate is justified on the grounds that the marketing cost is higher (advertising, shipping, etc.) and there are lot of "bad debts," meaning people who don't pay for records they've ordered. Also, the companies make less on these sales than if they sold the records themselves. So they say they do it only because they believe these are sales to people who wouldn't buy at retail (and thus the sales are gravy).

Record-club free goods are also a lot of fun. Guess how many records they can give away for every hundred they sell? Remember (from page 94) that the norm for retail sales is 15%, or fifteen free albums for every eighty-five sold. With clubs, it's a bit more. What's your guess for each hundred sold? If you said one hundred, you're right—the company's contract with the club only limits them to giving away *100%*, meaning one free for every one sold! In other words, out of every two hundred shipped, one hundred can be free!

So you should ask for a limit in your contract of one free record for every sale, right? Wrong. The one-to-one limit is for the company's *entire catalog,* which means they might give away more of your records and less of someone else's, as long as the *total* doesn't exceed one to one. At superstar levels you can get your own one-to-one limit (the companies have the right to do it for a few artists, but they don't like to tell you this). Even with your own limit, however, they only "settle up" the difference between one to one and whatever they did to you every couple of years. So until you reach superstardom, just smile; you can't do much else.

CUTOUTS, DELETES, SCRAPS, AND OTHER FOOD FOR BOTTOM FISHERS

Every company publishes a catalog of records it currently offers for sale. **Cutouts** and **deletes** are records that have been taken out of the company's catalog, and this isn't done until a title is really dead. When a company finds an album isn't selling at mid-price or budget, either because nobody cares about it or because the company has overmanufactured and/or had gigantic returns, it deletes the title and looks for a way to bail out for whatever it can get. These leftovers are sometimes sold as **scrap,** to be broken up for their component parts. If not, they're sold as **schlock,** which means they're put in the bins where the prices are 99¢, $1.50, etc. (I've always felt it adds insult to injury when these bins are on the sidewalk in front of a record store, because it shows they don't even care if people steal them.) Artists get no royalties whatsoever for these, as the company says (correctly) that they are sold at cost or below, just to get rid of them. With negotiating power, you can provide the company can't *schlock* your records until they're deleted from the catalog, and in any event not within twelve or eighteen months after initial release. (Note you can do this for *schlock,* not scrap. You can't restrict their ability to sell as scrap because the public never knows about this; schlock, however, tells the world that your records are worthless.) You can also get the right to buy these records at the best price offered to the record company, but I've never felt this is of any practical value. You're not likely to be able to sell them at a better price than the company, and what are you going to do with 100,000 dogs?

PREMIUMS

Send in a Wheaties box top and get the latest Megadeth single. Records sold this way are called **premiums,** which means they're sold in conjunction with a product or service, typically at a very low price. The royalty is correspondingly low—usually at half rate—and is based on the price at which the record company sells the record to the advertiser (also very low). (There may in fact be no other price, because the records are often given away or sold at less than cost to the public.)

If you know enough to ask, even with very little bargaining power, you can prohibit premiums without your consent. This is because they really constitute a commercial use of your name, likeness, and voice (by tying you into the product of the people offering them).

SAMPLERS

Virgin Records put out a record called *The Tape That Ate My Brain,* consisting of one track each from a number of new bands it had signed. This is a **sampler,** meaning it gives you a "sample" of a number of different releases. Samplers are typically sold at a low price (like $7.98 for a CD), and they bear no royalties because they're promotional (not profit) items. Rather than limit them, for a new band, I've always thought it would be fun to *require* the company to include you, but so far no one at the record companies appreciates my sense of humor. While there is potential for abuse (sometimes they include a major artist to get people to buy the sampler and listen to the minor artists), they're pretty harmless. In fact, they are becoming scarce these days.

DART MONIES

Recording artists are entitled to monies payable under the Audio Home Recording Act of 1992, also known as the DART Bill (standing, I think, for "Digital Audio Recorders and Tapes"). All of that, of course, sounds like gibberish because I haven't given you any background to understand what it means. The reason is that I want to do it after we've discussed publishing, because this also involves songwriting/publishing monies. So use a little of the patience that driven musical artists are so famous for, and wait till we get to it on page 245.

PUBLIC PERFORMANCE OF MASTERS

In many countries, the *record company* is paid a royalty every time a recording is played on the radio. (This is different from public performance royalties that are paid to a *songwriter and publisher* of the *musical composition* when a recording is played on the radio, and which have always been paid in the U.S., as we'll discuss on page 230.) Public performance monies for recordings didn't exist in the U.S. until 1995, and the law enacting them is so narrow that it means virtually nothing today (as we'll discuss in more detail on page 300). Still, since the monies are going to be there, you should ask for a share of them.

You aren't entitled to share in the company's monies if you're directly paid a share of the earnings. In other words, if the society that collects record performance monies pays both the record company and the artist separately, you don't share in each other's monies. (This is the same concept as songwriters getting paid directly by the songwriting performance societies, which we'll discuss on page 232.) However, not all of the U.S. performance royalties will be paid separately, and so you need to ask for 50% of the money that isn't.

In foreign territories, these monies not only exist, but are substantial. Record companies don't like to share their foreign public performance royalties, on the theory that the artists can get their share by directly applying to the foreign performing rights society (see the previous paragraph). The problem is that most U.S. artists aren't allowed to collect foreign performances under the local rules, and while this should move the companies to tears, somehow it doesn't. They simply dig into the position that they don't have to give the artist any part of the record company's share, and this is an extremely difficult point for the artist to win.

HOME DELIVERED RECORDS

Some companies have a provision in their form dealing with records delivered to your house by satellite or cable (we touched on these previously, on page 165). This comes from an idea some guy had a few years ago to deliver a signal via satellite (or phone line) direct to people's houses. With a decoder, you would be able to dial up specific LPs, which you could then record on a home cassette, and your account would be billed for the charge. The system was never implemented, but another paragraph got added to some companies' contracts. The ones that deal with it say it bears the same royalty as a CD sale—i.e., you get the same pennies as if a CD were sold at retail.

14

Loan-out, Independent Production, Label, and Distribution Deals

LOAN-OUT DEALS

Loan-out Corporations

As you begin to get more successful, you will undoubtedly want a **loan-out corporation,** since everybody on the block has one. It's called a *loan-out* because the corporation (not you) enters into the deals, and "loans" your services to others for recording, concerts, etc. This is the entity you see people naming with cute little phrases (my favorites are "Disappearing, Inc.," and "I Want It All"). As the tax laws have changed over the years, particularly in the pension area, it is questionable whether it makes sense to have a loan-out company. I personally think it's marginal whether the expense of maintaining such a corporation is worth the benefit, but it has to be looked at in each individual case. Consult your accountant, lawyer, or bartender.

Anyway, for record deals it works like this: You sign an exclusive recording contract with your own corporation, on a form that looks like the record company deal. In turn, the record company signs a recording agreement with your corporation, which agrees to supply your services (*Figure 9*).

Inducement (Side) Letters

As you can see, this means you have no direct deal with the record company. So what's to keep you from walking out on your own corporation (after all, you could fire yourself, or quit), and then thumbing your nose at the record company? You personally have no deal with the company—only your bankrupt corporation has a contract, and its secretary/treasurer is now in Lithuania with the masters.

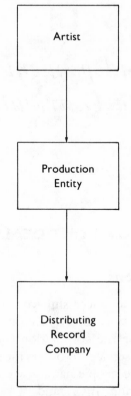

Figure 9. Loan-out deal structure.

Well, you know the companies won't let that happen, so they have you sign something known as an **inducement letter** or **side letter.** This is simply a piece of paper saying that if your corporation doesn't perform by delivering recordings, you will deliver them directly to the record company. So the real picture looks like *Figure 10.*

The side letter is an integral part of an independent production deal. It's like an emergency detour. If the highway is flooded, the company sends a jeep down a back road to get you.

Structure of Loan-out Deals

Loan-out contracts are very similar to contracts directly between the record company and artist (known as **direct agreements**), except that:

1. The parties, of course, are the record company and the corporation, instead of the company and you;
2. The corporation agrees to supply your services and recordings;

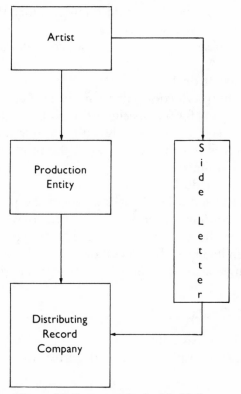

Figure 10. Loan-out deal with side letter.

3. There are additional legal clauses, such as assurances that the corporation has the right to your exclusive services, that it has the right to deliver your recordings, etc.; and
4. You have to sign an inducement letter saying the loan-out is really a phony, and if you or it try anything cute, you'll perform directly for the record company as if the loan-out didn't exist.

INDEPENDENT PRODUCTION AGREEMENTS

An independent production agreement is what a major-distributed independent label (we discussed these companies on page 87) signs with the major. These deals are just like loan-outs, except that the artist doesn't own the corporation in the middle (let's call the corporation the "production entity," because it "produces" the recordings). Typically, the production entity is owned by a producer or other record mogul, whose "magic ears" have found you. It then signs to a major or mini-major (let's call it the "distributor") to deliver the artist's recordings. As we'll see in a minute, under these deals, the inducement letter is even more critical.

There are two basic types of these production deals:

1. **A single-artist deal**
   is where the production entity makes an agreement with the record company for one specific artist. Note, by the way, that the production entity may have signed more than one artist; we're talking only about the deal between the production entity and the record company.
2. **A multi-artist deal,**
   sometimes called a **label deal,** is where the production entity supplies recordings of various artists, many of whom (or perhaps all of whom) have not yet been signed by the production entity. As you can imagine, this type of deal is much more complicated than a single-artist deal. So let's start with the simpler one.

Single-Artist Deals

A single-artist deal is basically the same as a loan-out deal, but because the production entity isn't owned by the artist, there are a couple of differences:

1. The deal between the artist and the production entity is now a real, arm's-length transaction, as opposed to one the artist makes with himself or herself. This means there is a true negotiation— i.e., one where the parties are at "arm's length" from each other—and the artist asks for most of the things he or she would get from a record company, like guaranteed release, approvals, etc. (When you sign to a production entity, there are some points you should get in this type of deal that you don't need from a record company. We'll discuss these in a minute, on page 192.)
2. There is a possibility that the artist can get into a fight with the production entity. This means it's more likely that the record company will exercise its rights under the inducement letter, and thus the terms of the inducement letter are critical.

Why Do It? So why should you as an artist make a deal like this? Wouldn't it be better to have direct contact with your record company? Well, the answer is "maybe." A production deal has its pluses and minuses compared to a direct deal, and whether it's better for you depends on your specific situation.

Here are the negatives:

1. The production entity in the middle takes some of the royalty. Traditionally its deal with the record company provides a somewhat higher royalty than direct artist deals (by 1% to 2%) for precisely this purpose. But you still normally get less of a royalty than under a direct deal, and this is especially so when you're successful. The reason is that, with success, the production entity's deal with the record company "tops out" and leaves no room for them to keep anything without getting it from you.
2. It may be harder for you to coordinate marketing, promotion, etc., if you and your manager have no direct contact with the record company.
3. There may be problems auditing the distributor directly (see page 163 for what auditing is). In its contract, the production entity has the right to audit the distributor. But the distributor doesn't want two different people (you and the production entity) doing the same audit, and since it has no direct contract with you, it doesn't have to let you in at all.
4. Production entities are more likely to ask for your publishing and/or your management at the same time they make a record deal, and this is rarely to the artist's advantage.
5. The production entity might go south with your money.

On the positive side:

1. The production entity may be owned by someone who really brings something to the party. For example, there are production companies owned by major producers who will only work with a new artist if the artist signs to his or her entity. Other production companies are owned by important managers, promotion people, or industry people with good track records (translation: They have a lot of clout). Examples are ZTT (Seal), Michael Bivens (Boyz II Men), and Maurice Starr (New Kids on the Block, New Edition).
2. You may be able to get the same calculation of royalties the production entity gets (meaning the same reduction for foreign sales, free-good limits, reserve limits, etc.). If you're a new artist and they're an established company, this can be more favorable than you could get on your own.
3. And I saved the best for last: Nobody else may want to sign you.

On balance, this is not your ideal choice (barring very unusual circumstances, like a great producer), but it can be a very desirable alternative to flipping Big Macs.

Artist Deal Points. If you're making a deal with a production entity, you want to be sure that, in addition to all the other items we talked about for record deals (guaranteed release, advances, approvals, etc.—see page 116), you get the following:

1. You want to get the same computation of royalties that the production entity has (for packaging, free goods, foreign, budget, CD, etc). Indeed, you may want to ask for a percentage of the production company's receipts. It's not uncommon to structure an agreement whereby the artist gets 75% of the production entity's royalties (with the artist paying the producer from his or her share), or perhaps 50% or 60% (with the production entity paying the producer from its share). This percentage should also apply to advances in excess of recording costs.

2. Try to get direct accountings from the record company. This may or may not be possible, depending on the production entity's own deal. Your worry is the situation we talked about on page 139, where a producer is owed money by an artist and no royalties are payable, but in this case the roles are reversed: You're the one due money, and the production entity may not have any royalties coming in. This can easily happen to your production entity—especially if it has signed several artists (as you'll see in excruciating detail on page 195).

Production Deal Points. Now, let's jump over the table and get the production entity's point of view. (Come on—it will make you a better-rounded person.) Here are two major areas of concern:

1. Remember how the artist wants the same computation of royalties as you? (See paragraph 1 of the previous section.) In representing production entities, I've rarely found it worthwhile to recompute the royalties. First of all, it's difficult, complex, time-consuming, and usually given to a low-level bookkeeper who doesn't quite understand what to do. So half the time they end up paying *more* than you would if you just used the same computation. Second, even when done correctly, the advantage you pick up is often minimal. Third, if and when the artist finds it out (which of course will only happen if there's a great deal of success), you look like a pig, which is not usually good for artist relations.

2. Make sure you don't give the artist any rights you don't have in the first place. I've seen clients who (before I was involved, of course) gave artists such things as approval of coupling, approval of album cover artwork, guaranteed release, etc., when they themselves didn't have these things from the record company. At best this is embarrassing, and at worst the artist can walk away from your deal when you don't deliver. (Note the artist isn't going very far—if he or she succeeds in walking away from you, they'll still have to record for the record company under their inducement letter. However, this doesn't do you any good—the record company won't pay you any royalties if you lose the artist because of your screw-up. This position is known in show biz as "sucking rocks.")

Multi-Artist (Label) Deals

A **multi-artist deal,** as the name implies, is one where the production entity has a deal with a record company to sign and deliver a number of artists. It is sometimes called a **label deal,** as nowadays the production entity usually has its own label on the product. Examples of this are Qwest Records (Quincy Jones) and Maverick (Madonna), where these artists own the entities signing the artists, and Warner Brothers Records is the distributor. Sometimes, however, the producing entity has no identification on the records, and the public doesn't even know they exist.

Differences from Single-Artist Deals. A multi artist deal between the distributor and the production entity looks a lot like a single-artist loan-out deal, but:

1. In addition to paying a recording fund for each album, there is often some form of overhead payment to the production entity. This is usually an advance (although it can at times be nonrecoupable, at least in part) and is used to pay the entity's rent, payroll, phone, light bills, etc. For bigger deals and mini-majors (see page 86), it will also cover marketing, promotion, etc.
2. The term of the deal is usually two or three years firm, with the distributor having options for one or more additional one-, two-, or three-year periods.
3. The number of artists the production entity can sign, and whether the distributor can approve these artists, is a matter of great negotiation. A new production entity will perhaps be allowed to sign one, two, or three artists over the term, but a more

established company may get to sign two or three artists per year. More and more, the distributors want to approve the artists before signing, but if you have a lot of bargaining power, you may be able to negotiate (a) no approval (very difficult today), or (b) for each one or two approved artists, you have the right to sign an artist that isn't approved.

4. The minimum and maximum number of albums the production entity can deliver is also prenegotiated, both in terms of the overall number per year, and the number per artist. Normally, the distributor doesn't want you delivering more than one album per artist per year without its consent.

5. And speaking of albums, how about this great idea (see if you can find the history lesson): You are a production entity in the last year of your deal with a distributor, and you suddenly have the opportunity to sign a hot new band. So six months before the end of your term, you deliver an album with this band. You say, "Please make these guys into superstars so that, six months later when my deal ends, I can (a) beat you to death in a renegotiation, or (b) better yet, take them to another company, leaving you with a gigantic deficit from any prior flops, while I take the royalties from this band and buy that little farm I've always wanted." Sound too good to be true? Of course; the deal will provide that you must deliver the distributor a minimum number of albums for each artist—usually three or four—even if the term is over. (Note this will put you in the position of having your deal expire for some artists, but continue for others.)

6. The recording funds for the artists are spelled out up front. If you're a new entity, you'll probably have to live with something like $150,000 to $200,000 per album. You may be able to negotiate a preapproved formula for artists with previous track records (for example, a fund of $250,000 to $300,000 for an artist who has sold 200,000 albums or more). To exceed these figures, you need the company's consent on each specific deal. This means, if you have the chance to sign a major artist, you must sit down with the distributor and work out a special arrangement. (It happens, on occasion, that the production entity and the distributor are both bidding for the same artist. You can imagine, since the distributor approves how much the production entity can spend, which one is likely to come out the winner. In this case, unless there's a personal relationship or some other good reason the major artist would rather sign to you, you can pretty well kiss it off.)

7. It's sometimes possible, although difficult, to get ownership of

the master recordings under a label deal. Even in this situation, however, you normally wouldn't own the recordings during the term. (In fact, other than for tax planning, you probably wouldn't want to own these suckers at all. One of the fringe detriments of ownership is the joy of showing up in places like Fargo, North Dakota, to testify against record counterfeiters. This is because the judge requires the copyright owner of the master to be at the trial. See page 297 for more information on the copyrights in sound recordings.) So even if you win this point, the distributor owns the masters and assigns them to you some period after the end of the term (usually seven to ten years or so). The distributor may insist on your being recouped before they'll assign; if this is the case, you should get the right to pay back the unrecouped deficit for an immediate reassignment.

Cross-Collateralization. Remember our story about the two different producers being entitled to royalties from the same artist, and how the artist went further in the hole with every success? (See page 139.) Well, when you get to a multi-artist deal, this scenario gets to be a high-speed drilling rig. It is entirely possible (even easy) to have two or three real losers, together with one smash, but not get any royalties because the record company is recouping the losers' deficit from the winner's royalties. Here's a simple example:

Suppose a production entity has signed three artists. Assume the following (*the numbers bear no relationship to reality;* they're just for easy math):

Multiple-Artist Deal

All-in Royalty to Production Entity:	60¢
Royalty to Artist A:	50¢
Royalty to Artist B:	50¢
Royalty to Artist C:	50¢
Recording Costs:	$60,000/album
Advance for Production Entity's Operations	$100,000

Sales:		
	Artist A:	Album 1: 60,000 units
		Album 2: 40,000 units
	Artist B:	Album 1: 20,000 units
		Album 2: 40,000 units
	Artist C	Album 1: 60,000 units
		Album 2: 500,000 units

Under these assumptions, let's look at everyone's accounts:

Artist A's Account with Production Entity

	Charges	Earnings	Balance
Album 1	– $60,000	+ $30,000 (50¢ × 60,000 units)	– $30,000
Album 2	– $60,000	+ $20,000 (50¢ × 40,000 units)	– $40,000
TOTAL	–$120,000	+ $50,000	– $70,000

Summary: Artist A is *in the red* (*unrecouped*) *in the amount of $70,000* (the $120,000 deficit less the $50,000 earnings), and is thus owed nothing.

Artist B's Account with Production Entity

	Charges	Earnings	Balance
Album 1	– $60,000	+ $10,000 (50¢ × 20,000 units)	– $50,000
Album 2	– $60,000	+ $20,000 (50¢ × 40,000 units)	– $40,000
TOTAL	–$120,000	+ $30,000	– $90,000

Summary: Artist B is *in the red* (*unrecouped*) *in the amount of $90,000* (the $120,000 deficit less the $30,000 earnings), and is thus owed nothing.

Artist C's Account with Production Entity

	Charges	Earnings	Balance
Album 1	– $60,000	+ $30,000 (50¢ × 60,000 units)	– $30,000
Album 2	– $60,000	+ $250,000 (50¢ × 500,000 units)	+ $190,000
TOTAL	– $120,000	+ $280,000	+ $160,000

Summary: Artist C is *in the black* (*and owed*) *$160,000* (the $280,000 earnings less the $120,000 deficit).

Production Entity's Account with Record Company

	Charges	Earnings	Balance
Overhead Advance	–$100,000		–$100,000
Artist A	–$120,000	+ $60,000 (60¢ × 100,000 units)	– $60,000
Artist B	–$120,000	+ $36,000 (60¢ × 60,000 units)	– $84,000
Artist C	–$120,000	+ $300,000 (60¢ × 560,000 units)	+ $180,000
TOTAL	–$460,000	+ $396,000	– $64,000

Summary: The production company entity is *in the red* (*unrecouped*) *$28,000* (the $460,000 deficit less the $432,000 earnings), *and is thus owed nothing.*

Grand Summary

Artist A:	Unrecouped and not entitled to royalties.
Artist B:	Unrecouped and not entitled to royalties.
Artist C:	Owed $160,000
Production entity:	Owes Artist C $160,000, but is in the red $28,000 and thus not entitled to royalties.

Owing $160,000 and having no royalties due you is certainly the fuzzy side of the lollipop.

So how do you get out of the box? Well, if you have enough clout, you make the distributor pay the artists' royalties without regard to cross-collateralization. Thus, if you and Artists A and B are deeply unrecouped, but Artist C is recouped, they have to pay Artist C's royalties. In other words, they can't cross-collateralize any artist's royalties with either your or any other artist's deficits.

If you don't have enough bargaining power for this, then at minimum you should require the distributor to pay the recouped artist's royalties and to treat these payments as additional advances against your share of royalties. Thus, in the above example, the record company would advance the $160,000 owed to Artist C, and the producing entity would then be $188,000 in the red (the $28,000 original deficit plus the $160,000 paid to Artist C). You wouldn't make any money under these circumstances (until you have an awfully big success and eventually recoup), but at least you won't be breaking your kids' piggy banks to pay the artists.

JOINT VENTURES

A **joint venture** is the same as a multi-artist or label deal, except the production entity doesn't get a royalty. Instead, the production entity and the distributing record company are in effect "partners." This means they take all of the income which comes in (the gross wholesale price) and put it into a pot. Then they take all the expenses of operations out of the pot, and whatever is left over is split between the two entities, usually 50/50.

In fact, these agreements are never true "joint ventures" or "partnerships" in the legal sense. A true partnership or joint venture means one partner can commit both of them to legal obligations. For example, if one partner signs a bank loan for $200,000, *both* partners can be sued if it isn't paid back. And neither you nor the record company wants this, so the agreements specifically state they aren't legally part-nerships or joint ventures. Thus, the name "joint venture" is not technically correct; it just describes a multi artist deal where the profits are shared as if a joint venture existed.

Computation of Profits

The economics of a joint venture look like this:

Income Side. Gross receipts are the wholesale price received by the record company, which is easy to compute if the distributor is inde-pendent. However, as we discussed on page 85, all the major dis-tributors are owned by the major record companies. This means you need a different definition of gross receipts when the joint-venture distributor is a major—since the price the distributor pays is set be-tween two related parties, it can be anything they want it to be. Thus, gross receipts are usually defined as the *price paid by the dealers* (to the distributor, *not* to the company), less a charge for the distributor's op-erating expenses and profit. Typically, the companies reduce the price the distributors charge to the dealers by 10%, and the 90% balance is treated as the joint venture's gross receipts. For example, if the distrib-utor's wholesale price to a dealer is $5.00, the joint venture's gross is $4.50 ($5.00 less a 10% [50¢] charge for the distributor).

Income from licenses is all treated as gross.

Expenses. From this gross, the joint venture deducts its expenses and charges. These consist of the following:

1. The first thing deducted is a **distribution fee** for the record company. (We already discussed this concept in the context of home videos, on page 179. And remember the rule we discussed there: If you're getting a percentage, take it out first.) The dis-tribution fee is a charge to cover the cost of the record com-pany's overseeing the distribution of records, meaning the accounting, invoicing, manufacturing, etc., of the venture. (Note the difference between this and the fee charged in com-puting gross *income*, which was for the *distributor's* expenses. The fee here is for the *manufacturer's* expenses in overseeing the distribution.) Typically, these fees range from 15% to 25%, de-pending on bargaining power. It's also possible to reduce this fee as volume increases, usually on a yearly basis. For example, the fee could be 25% of the first $5 million each year, 20% of the

next $5 million, and 15% thereafter. At the beginning of the following year, the fee would start again at 25%.

2. The record company may also charge an **overhead fee.** In theory, this is to compensate it for indirect, general overhead expenses (salaries of people who work on this and other projects, rent, light bills, stationery, etc.). In truth, it is just a matter of how many dollars the record company gets to keep before splitting profits, and it's subject to negotiation—with enough clout, you don't have to pay it. Where an overhead fee is charged, it is usually in the range of 10%.

3. Next come all the costs of operation. In addition to the costs you would normally expect (recording costs, advances, etc.), there are a number of costs that aren't charged under royalty deals. These include:

   (a) Manufacturing
   (b) Shipping
   (c) Advertising
   (d) Mechanical royalties (we'll discuss these later, on page 209)
   (e) Per-record union payments (for a definition, see page 159)

4. Lastly, the record company takes back payments it has made to the production entity, such as reimbursements for promotional and operating expenses of the company. It's a matter of negotiation whether these are charged "off-the-top" of the venture (so that each party bears 50%), or whether they're charged solely against the producing entity's share of the profits.

Profits. The amount left after the above calculation is the profit, and 50% goes to each party.

Royalty Versus Joint Venture

So how about the key question: Are you better off with a joint venture or with a royalty arrangement? To answer this requires a crystal ball. If you're extremely successful, you're better off with a joint venture. With modest success, you're better off under a royalty arrangement. (If you're a turkey, it really doesn't matter.) Here's why: As we discussed, you're charged for more costs in a joint venture than you are under a royalty deal, and thus with only modest success, you're behind. However, many of these costs are not "per unit," meaning they're only paid once at the beginning, as opposed to "per-unit" costs that are incurred for each record ("unit") made. (Examples of per-unit costs are costs of manufacture, mechanical royalties, union per-record charges, freight, etc., which must be paid to manufacture and ship each unit. Costs that are *not* per unit are such things as artwork, promotion, and advertising, which are unrelated to specific units.) Thus, with a great deal of success, the non–per-unit costs are eaten up by the first dollars that come in, and thereafter the profit per unit is far greater than any royalty arrangement is ever likely to be.

PRESSING AND DISTRIBUTION (P&D) DEALS

If you are truly a record company in your own right, then this is the deal for you. It gives you the most autonomy and control of your life, as well as the highest profit margin.

A **pressing and distribution agreement** (or **P&D** deal) is exactly that—the record company agrees to manufacture your records for you (although in some situations this isn't even so; the product is manufactured elsewhere), and then to distribute them solely as a wholesaler. This means you sell the records to the distributing entity for a wholesale price less a negotiated distribution fee to help cover the distributing company's overhead, operations, and profit. The distribution fee ranges in the 18% to 25% range (less if you're a big label), and the balance of the monies is paid to the production entity. For example, if a cassette wholesales for $5.00, under a deal with a 25% distribution fee, the production entity gets $3.75 per cassette ($5.00 less 25%). Out of this, the production entity pays manufacturing, mechanicals, artist royalties, promotion, overhead, salaries, and everything else.

This arrangement is not for the weak-hearted:

1. In these deals, the entire risk of manufacturing falls on the production entity. Remember how records are sold on a returnable basis (see page 97)? This means that, if you guess wrong, the returns come back home to roost. So not only are you losing your potential profit on the sale, but you're also coming out of pocket and losing the cost of manufacturing and shipping a record you can't sell (although they make passable doorstops). Many deals also require you to pay a distribution fee even if the record is returned, adding injury to insult.
2. The distributing company typically offers no services whatsoever in terms of marketing, promotion, accounting, etc. You really are on your own.
3. You may well be treated as a second-class citizen. This is because

the distributing company will favor its own product over yours—they make a bigger profit on their own stuff, and they have a bigger investment in it.

These types of deals can be made at the highest level (for example, A&M Records was distributed by BMG under such an arrangement for many years), and the true independent record companies (see page 87 for what those are) make these deals with independent distributors. P&D deals can also be made at a more modest level by anyone insane enough to want to try, or anyone desperate enough to get their records out even when no one else wants to pay them for the privilege. However, unless you're a *real* record company, with a full staff, I strongly recommend against this type of deal.

PART III

Songwriting and Music Publishing

15

Copyright Basics

Before you can understand what songwriting and music publishing are all about, you really have to understand how copyrights work. But when you deal with something intangible like a copyright (which you can't see, feel, or smell), it's a challenge to nail it down. Copyrights are a tremendous amount of fun—they're squiggly little critters that, every time you think you have a handle on them, take an unexpected turn and nip you in the tush. Moreover, many of the concepts have been around for close to a hundred years, but remain unchanged; always a challenge in today's world. But don't worry. I'll guide you through the maze.

BASIC COPYRIGHT CONCEPTS

When you own a copyright, it's like playing Monopoly and owning all the properties on the board. But unlike Monopoly, you're not limited to the rents printed on the little cards. (As we'll see later, there are some preset rents, but for the most part you can charge whatever the traffic will bear.)

Definition of Copyright

The legal definition of a copyright is "a limited duration monopoly." Its purpose (as stated in the U.S. Constitution, no less) is to promote the progress of science and useful arts by giving creators exclusive rights to their works for a while. As you can imagine, if you created something and everybody immediately had the right to use it without paying you, not very many people would go the trouble of creating anything (including you and me).

What's Copyrightable?

To be copyrightable, the work has to be original (not copied from something else) and of sufficient materiality to constitute a work. There's no specific test to cover this; it's decided on a case-by-case basis. For example, the five notes played by the spaceship in *Close Encounters of the Third Kind* are copyrightable because of their originality, even though they're just five notes.

How to Get a Copyright

Under United States Copyright Law, as soon as you make a **tangible copy** of something, you have a copyright. *Tangible* simply means something you can touch. If the work is a musical composition, for example, it can be written down (if you write music, which many creative people don't these days), or just sung or played into a tape recorder. Once this tangible copy exists, you have all the copyright you need.

Many people think you have to register in Washington to get a copyright. Not true. There are some important rights you get from registering, but securing a copyright isn't one of them. (More on this later.)

So it's that simple. If you sing a song in your head, no matter how completely it's composed, you have no copyright; if you write it down or record it, you have one. If you'd like to take a few minutes right now and copyright something, I'll wait.

WHAT ARE ALL THESE RIGHTS YOU GET?

When you have a copyright, you get the following rights at no extra charge. These rights are **exclusive,** which means that **no one** can do these things without your permission. (For you technical freaks, the rights are listed in Section 106 of the Copyright Act.)

You get the exclusive right to:

1. **Reproduce the work.**
   Keeping with a musical composition as our example, this means no one can record your composition, publish it as sheet music, put it in a movie, or otherwise copy it.
2. **Distribute copies of the work.**
   Apart from the right to reproduce your song, there is a *separate* right of *distribution* which you also control. Note the difference between making a copy of the work (for example, recording it

and manufacturing records of it), which is a use of the copyright (it's a reproduction, as we discussed in number 1), and the *distribution* of this copy (for example, selling records to the public), which is another, separate right. One illustration of this would be a record company that hires a plant to duplicate their cassettes. The plant gets the right to reproduce the songs, but not the right to distribute copies of them.

3. **Perform the work "publicly."**
   With a song, this means playing it in nightclubs, on the radio, on television, in amusement parks, supermarkets, elevators (you know your career is either soaring or history when you hear your song in an elevator), or anywhere else music is heard publicly. It doesn't matter whether the performance is by live musicians or a DJ playing records, you get to control this right. (If you're wondering how you could ever police this or get paid, stay tuned.)

4. **Make a derivative work.**
   A **derivative work** is a creation based on another work. In the music industry, an example is a parody lyric set to a well-known song (like what Weird Al Yankovic does). The melody may be a copyrighted original work (say "Gangster's Paradise"), but with parody lyrics (like "Amish Paradise"), it constitutes a new work. This new work is called a derivative work because it's *derived* from the original. The concept is even easier to see in the motion picture area. Any film made from a novel is a derivative work (the novel is the original work). And *West Side Story* is a derivative work based on *Romeo and Juliet*. Anyway, you get the idea. (By the way, the original doesn't have to be copyrighted. If it isn't, the only parts of the derivative work that are protected are the newly created ones.)

5. **To display the work publicly.**
   This really doesn't apply to music; it's for things like paintings, statues, etc.

EXCEPTIONS TO THE COPYRIGHT MONOPOLY

As we discussed before, the copyright law gives you an absolute monopoly, which means you don't have to let anyone use your copyright if you don't want to. If you want to write poems and throw them into the sea, so that no human being can ever make use of them, that's your prerogative. You may be cold and poor in your old age, but you will have entertained a lot of fish.

Compulsory Licenses

On the other hand, there are six major exceptions to this rule, and they're known as **compulsory licenses.** The term *compulsory license* means that you *must* issue a license to someone who wants to use your work, whether you like it or not. The six compulsory licenses are:

1. **Cable television rebroadcast.**
   Basically, this is designed for an area that has poor television reception and sets up a big antenna to receive weak signals. The cable company boosts the signals electronically, and then distributes them to the homes in the area. The cable television compulsory license provisions require the broadcasting stations to allow this, in exchange for payment of set fees. (Without this license, the rebroadcast would be an unauthorized distribution of copyrighted programming.)

2. **Public Broadcasting System.**
   The PBS lobbyists were terrific in requiring copyright owners to license works to them at cheap rates.

3. **Jukeboxes.**
   It may surprise you to know that, until the 1976 Copyright Law, jukeboxes paid nothing for the right to use music. They were considered "toys" in the 1909 Copyright Act (really). Now they pay set license fees, the details of which have never been relevant to me, and so I don't know them.

4. **Digital performance of records.**
   This baby was also added in 1995, and it requires the owner of the *recording* to allow its performance on digital subscription radio. We'll discuss it in more detail on page 300.

5. **Digital distribution of records.**
   This looks forward to the day when records will be sold over telephone lines, satellites, etc. by means of sending a digital signal that is copied at home. The compulsory license requires the owner of the song to allow its use in this way. As you can imagine from the subject matter, this compulsory license was only recently created (in 1995). This topic is discussed in some detail on page 303.

6. **Phonorecords of nondramatic musical compositions.**
   This is the biggie in the music business, so we'll discuss it in detail. It's called a **compulsory mechanical license.**

COMPULSORY MECHANICAL LICENSES

To understand how compulsory licenses work for records, you first need to know about mechanical royalties.

Mechanical Royalties

The term **mechanical royalties** (or "mechanicals," to its friends) developed in the 1909 Copyright Law, and referred to payments for devices "serving to mechanically reproduce sound." Even though devices haven't reproduced sound "mechanically" since the 1940s, the name has stuck and the monies paid to copyright owners for the manufacture and distribution of records are still called "mechanical royalties." And the rights to reproduce songs in records are known as **mechanical rights.**

The concept of a *compulsory* license for these mechanical rights grew out of a concern in Congress that the music industry was going to develop into a gigantic monopoly (we may still make it). This desire to keep copyright owners from controlling the world resulted in the compulsory license for records, which accomplishes its mission nicely. It says that, once a work has been recorded, the publisher is *required* to license it to anyone else who wants to use it in records. (The old law had quite a number of ambiguities and problems with it, but there's no point in discussing them because they were cured in the 1976 law. You get off easy—I had to study the damn stuff.) Let's take a closer look at what the law says:

Compulsory Mechanical Licenses

The compulsory copyright royalty provision for records is in Section 115 of the Copyright Act. It provides that, once a song has been recorded, a copyright owner must license it: (a) to anyone else that wants to use it in a *phonorecord* (which is a defined term in the Copyright Act), and (b) for a specific payment established by the law (more on this later). You can get a compulsory license *only if*

1. The song is a nondramatic musical work; *and*
2. It has been previously recorded; *and*
3. The previous recording has been distributed publicly in phonorecords; *and*
4. Your use of the recording will be in phonorecords only.

All of these conditions must exist before you get a compulsory license. Let's look at them separately.

Nondramatic Musical Work. For you to get a compulsory license, the song must be a *nondramatic musical composition*. It's not clear what a "dramatic" musical composition is, but it's probably a song used in an opera or musical—i.e., a song that helps tell the story. No one knows whether or not the term includes a "story song," such as "Ode to Billy Joe" or any of Harry Chapin's works. My guess is that it doesn't, but it's just a guess.

Previously Recorded. You can't get a compulsory license for the very first recording of a work. The law allows the owner to control who gets it the first time, which is known as a **first use.** Once it's recorded, however, anyone can get a compulsory license if the first recording was *authorized by the copyright owner.* The fact that someone sneaks off and records the composition without consent doesn't trigger the compulsory license.

Public Distribution. The first recording must have been *distributed to the public.* This closes a loophole from the prior law, and is of course eminently logical. It's not enough that the publisher allowed a recording to be made if it wasn't released.

Phonorecord Use. A compulsory license is available only for **phonorecords,** which is defined in the Copyright Law to mean *audio only* recordings. This definition was the publishers' finest lobbying accomplishment in the 1976 Copyright Act, because it excluded home video devices from the definition of phonorecords. This means there is no compulsory license for home videos, and the result has been that motion picture companies must now negotiate with every copyright owner (publisher) for home video usage of each song, and that the owners are free to charge whatever rate they choose. More on how this is done when we get to publishing (on page 229).

If all of the above conditions exist, then anyone who wants to use a song in phonorecords can do so merely by filing certain notices and paying a set fee per record. This fee is called the **statutory rate** (because it's a rate set by the Copyright Statute), and has had a rather bizarre history itself. The rate was 2¢ from 1909 to 1976 (inflation didn't exist in those years, but record company lobbyists did). The 1976 Copyright Act raised it to 2.75¢, with provisions for further adjustments by a Copyright Royalty Tribunal, which is a committee that meets periodically and reviews the rate. It is currently the larger of: (a) 6.95¢, or (b) 1.3¢ per minute of playing time *or fraction thereof.* Thus, if a song runs 5 minutes or less, the rate is 6.6¢. However, if it's over 5 minutes (even by a second or two), but not over 6 minutes, the rate is 7.8¢ (1.3¢ × 6 = 7.8¢). If a song is over 6 minutes but not more than 7 minutes, the rate is 9.1¢ (1.3¢ × 7 = 9.1¢), and so forth.

To its credit, Congress did a thorough job of research in working out the compulsory licensing legislation. There are specific accounting provisions (monthly), limits for the amount of reserves (see page 97 for a definition of reserves) that can be withheld, and requirements when the reserves must be liquidated (paid out). Also, in perhaps its most sophisticated move, the royalty is payable on all records "made and distributed" (as opposed to "made and *sold*"), which means the compulsory royalties are payable on "free goods" (see page 93 for a discussion of free goods).

Back to Real Life

Having told you how this works, I will now tell you the compulsory license is almost never used. Record companies hate to use it because the monthly accounting provisions are too burdensome. The copyright owners (publishers) would rather give a direct license because they can keep track of it easier. (Would you want a Washington bureaucrat to handle your licensing?) However, it's still very significant because the "statutory rate" is the benchmark for setting mechanical rates in the industry. The reason is that, once a musical composition is recorded, the "statutory rate" is the maximum mechanical royalty anyone is willing to pay for it (if a publisher refuses to license it at that rate, the manufacturer just gets a compulsory license). Whether the rate for a particular song is less than statutory is a subject of negotiation (see page 219).

First Use

Implicit in the above (which I'll now make explicit) is the fact that the compulsory license section does not apply to a **first use** (the first recording of a song). In other words, until a song has been recorded under authorization of the copyright owner (until a "first use" has been made), the publisher can charge anything it wants. Customarily, the publisher does not charge more than the statutory rate, but there is no reason other than industry custom (and the refusal of the user to pay more) why it can't.

Foreign Mechanicals

For contrast, it's interesting to note that, other than the United States and Canada, most countries of the world use an entirely different copyright royalty system. Mechanicals there are a set percentage of wholesale price, which covers *all* songs on the record. This means the rate has nothing to do with the length of the composition or even the number of songs. The same amount of mechanicals is paid for an album containing eight compositions as is paid for one with twelve. Also, as we'll discuss later (on page 239), the mechanicals are usually paid to a government agency.

Currently, mechanicals in the U.K. are 8.5% of PPD (see page 168 for what PPD is), without any packaging deduction (see page 92 for what that is), and the only free goods allowed are "real" free goods (see page 96), which are clearly marked as being "free." The rate in the rest of Europe is set by an organization called **BIEM** (**Bureau International des Sociétés Gérant les Droits d'Enregistrement et de Reproduction Mécanique;** is that a mouthful, or what?). BIEM is a group of agencies in each territory that collect mechanical royalties for their affiliates. Currently, the BIEM rate is 9.504% of PPD.

16

Publishing Companies and Major Income Sources

PUBLISHING OVERVIEW

Now that you're a maven on copyrights, understanding publishing is pretty simple. It works like this:

What Does a Publisher Do?

As a songwriter, you may be interested in business, but your talents are best spent in creating. However, someone needs to take care of business, and this is where the publishing industry came from.

A publisher goes to a songwriter and makes the following speech: Your strength is writing songs, and mine is taking care of business. Let's make the following deal: You assign the copyright in your song to me, and in exchange I'll be responsible for all the business. I'll find people to use your song, give them licenses, make sure they pay you, and split the money with you.

Administration

The rights I just described—finding users, issuing licenses, collecting money, and paying the writer—are known as **administration rights.** When a publisher makes a standard deal with a writer, it takes on the obligations to do these things (as well as all rights of the copyright owner), and thus "administers" the compositions (*Figure 11*).

Traditionally, the publisher splits all income 50-50 with the writer (with the exception of sheet music and performance monies, which we'll discuss later). The publisher's 50% is for his overhead (office, staff, etc.) and profit. The share of money kept by the publisher from each

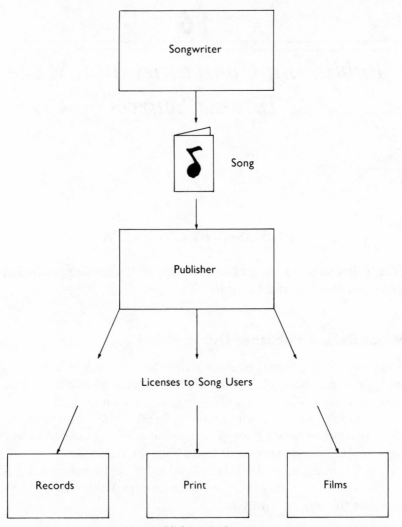

Figure 11. Publishing industry structure.

dollar earned is called the **publisher's share** (clever, huh?), and the balance is just as imaginatively called the **writer's share** (*Figure 12*).

History

Publishers have enjoyed mixed reputations over the years. There is a story about a songwriter who went on a camping trip one weekend with his publisher. They were hiking with their backpacks when they came around a bend and suddenly saw a mountain lion. Both of them

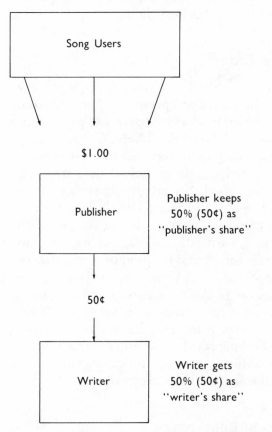

Figure 12. "Publisher's share" and "writer's share."

froze in place, and the cat began snarling and moving slowly toward them. As they stood there, the writer noticed the publisher was quietly taking off his backpack. The writer said, "What are you doing? You can't outrun a mountain lion." The publisher replied, "I don't need to outrun the mountain lion; I only need to outrun you."

Following the turn of the century, and well into the 1940s, publishers were the most powerful people in the music industry. (Ever heard of Tin Pan Alley? That's where the publishers were located.) Most artists didn't write their own songs in those days, and thus, because the publishers controlled the major songwriters, the artists were at the publishers' mercy. Remember, no one can use a song for the first time without the publisher's permission (see page 211), and so the publishers would decide which artist was blessed with the right to record a major new work. Also, because of this power, it was difficult, if not impossible, for songwriters to exploit their works without a major publisher behind them.

Publishers Today

History has now evolved to where the major publishers are often not much more than banking operations. They will compute how much they expect to earn from a given deal, and pay a portion of it to obtain the rights involved. Some publishers are "creative" publishers, in the sense that they put their writers together with other writers, help them fine-tune their writing, match writers with artists, etc. However, regardless of how good they are, the publishers do not have as many heavy writers under contract today. This is because a lot of major songwriters keep their own publishing (i.e., they are their own publisher, retaining ownership of their copyrights and perhaps hiring someone to do the clerical function of administration). The reason is that, once a writer is well known, he or she can get to artists as easily as a publisher can (indeed, the artists often call them). Also, more and more artists are writing their own songs, so there's no need for a publisher to get songs to them. So for all these factors, the role of the publisher has diminished. The major publishers remain a powerful force in the industry, by dint of their gigantic size, but they are not nearly as influential as they were in the past.

Mechanics of Publishing

A publishing company has a lot fewer moving parts than does a record company. (Record company anatomy is discussed on page 84.) You only need the following (and some of these functions can be performed by the same person):

1. An administrator to take care of copyrighting songs, issuing licenses, collecting money, paying writers and copublishers, etc.

2. A "song plugger" who runs around and gets songs recorded.

3. A creative staff person, who finds writers, works with them to improve their songs, pairs them up creatively with co-writers, etc. If the publishing company has no writers under contract to deliver newly written songs (in other words, it just administers existing songs), you don't even need this function.

Thus, unlike the record business, it takes only a small capital investment to call yourself a publisher. You don't need a large staff (until you get to be huge), and there's no need for the expensive distribution network, warehouses, inventory, etc., necessary for records, since you're dealing with intangibles. Indeed, there's an industry term, **vest-pocket publisher,** which refers to one person, with administrative help, acting as a publisher.

Types of Publishers

For this reason, there are a lot of smaller players and the publishing business is not nearly so dominated by the majors as is the record business. There are, to be sure, megaton publishing companies (such as Warner/Chappell and EMI, who have worldwide operations and generate tens of millions of dollars per year), but there are hundreds and hundreds of others running the gamut from a one-person show to the giants. Here's a broad-stroke view of the different types:

The 900-Pound Gorillas. These are the major companies, most of which are affiliated with a record and/or film company. Examples are: Warner/Chappell, EMI, MCA, BMG, Rondor (owned by the former owners of A&M Records), Jobete Music (formerly affiliated with Motown Records), Famous Music (owned by Paramount Communications, Inc.), etc. Actually, the weight of these gorillas varies considerably. EMI and Warner/Chappell are clearly 900-pounders, while Jobete, Famous, and Rondor are closer to 500-pounders.

Major Affiliates. There are a number of independent publishing companies, with full staffs of professionals, whose "administration" is handled by a major. Interscope Music, for example, Ted Field's publishing company, is administered by MCA. And there are hundreds of smaller examples as well. The publisher's affiliation with a major may be for the world, or it may be for only certain territories. For instance, a publisher might be affiliated with a major for the United States and have separate subpublishing deals (with other publishers) for the rest of the world.

Stand-Alones. *Stand-alone* is my term (borrowed from the cable TV business) and not an industry one. I'm using it to mean a company that's not affiliated with a major, but rather which does its own administration. In other words, it collects its own money, does its own accountings, etc. It may, however, be affiliated with a major for territories outside the United States.

Writer-Publishers. Many writers keep their own publishing. Examples are well-established writers who don't need a publisher because people are constantly begging them for songs, and writer/artists who record their own works. In fact, if you're a writer/artist whose material doesn't lend itself to being recorded by others (such as rap, jazz, or heavy metal), then you should only part with your publishing if you need (or want) money up front. Otherwise, you can hire people relatively cheaply to do the administration (see page 277). (If your publishing really generates a lot of money, you can hire someone on an hourly or flat-fee basis and pay even less.)

Just because the publishing game has a low entry price doesn't mean it's an easy gig. So you have to check out your publisher thoroughly. The difference between a good publisher and an unqualified one can mean a lot to your pocketbook. For example, a good publisher knows how much to charge for various licenses (see page 238) and where to look for hidden monies (see, for example, page 244, discussing how foreign monies get lost when nobody claims them properly). The bad ones can lose you money just by sitting there and not doing what they're supposed to.

An inexperienced publisher affiliated with a major is a quantum improvement over an unqualified publisher trying to go it alone. However, the major will not have the same incentive to take care of the independent's songs as it will to take care of its own. Also, a major owns tens of thousands of copyrights, so you can get shoved on the back shelf. On the other hand, a good independent publisher affiliated with a major can often do better for you than if you signed to the major directly. If the publisher has enough clout to become a "squeaky wheel" on your behalf (and remember the squeaking is on its behalf as well), it can prevent you from getting lost in the shuffle.

SOURCES OF INCOME

Now let's take a look at what monies a publisher collects. I'm starting with publishing income, not songwriters' royalties, because the writer gets a percentage of the publisher's monies.

The majority of revenues come from mechanicals and performance monies. So let's examine these first.

MECHANICAL ROYALTIES

As we discussed on page 209, "mechanical royalties" are monies paid by a record company for the right to use a song in records. The publisher issues a license to the record company that says for each record manufactured and distributed, the record company will pay a royalty equal to a specified number of pennies. Often this rate is tied to the "statutory rate" (see page 210), and thus it increases as the statutory royalty increases. However, it may be tied only to *today's* statutory rate, meaning it's fixed in pennies and won't go up even if the statutory rate does. This is most likely when the songwriter is also an artist, for reasons we'll discuss later (on page 222).

The fixed rate can either be at the full statutory rate, or it can be a reduced percentage of that statutory rate. If reduced, it's called a **rate,** which means a mechanical royalty of less than statutory. The customary reduction is 75%, usually for lower-priced records such as midprice or budget (see pages 181 and 182 for what these are), or for compilation packages (see page 173). For compilation packages, if a record company wants a "rate," it may offer an advance against the royalties, which means that, even though the publisher gets less, at least it gets it sooner. For example, a record company might offer to prepay on fifty thousand units of a particular record in exchange for the publisher agreeing to accept 75% of the statutory rate. You'll also see, when we discuss the mechanical royalty provisions in record agreements (on page 222), that record companies routinely ask artists at all levels to issue licenses at less than the statutory rate. They often get turned down by artists at higher levels, but they usually get a "rate" for midlevel and new artists.

Canada

Until a few years ago, Canada also had a compulsory copyright rate (2¢ Canadian; it didn't go up when the United States did). However, this was repealed. Currently, there is a contractual agreement between the Canadian Record Company Association and a number of major publishers setting the "industry royalty rate" at 6.6¢ for the first five minutes, plus 1.32¢ for each additional minute or fraction thereof (all in Canadian pennies). This rate gets adjusted periodically for inflation. Record companies try to get three-quarters of this rate as well.

Harry Fox and CMRRA

There are two major organizations that are delighted to issue mechanical licenses for publishers. One is the Harry Fox Agency (originally known as the Harry Fox Office), which in the United States is the largest organization of its kind, and its Canadian counterpart, CMRRA, standing for Canadian Mechanical Rights Reproduction Agency. (There have been a few competitors over the years, but none has succeeded to any real degree.) Basically, these organizations act as a publisher's agent, issuing mechanical licenses for the publisher, policing them (that is, making sure the users pay), and accounting to the publisher. They also periodically audit record companies on behalf of all their clients, and they allocate the recovered monies amongst their clients in proportion to their earnings. This is particularly significant for a smaller publisher, as the cost of an audit for small earners is prohibitive. (At the time of this writing, a typical publishing audit can cost $10,000 to $20,000 or more, and unless the recovery is likely to be several times this amount, it's not economical.)

For their services, Harry Fox currently charges 4½%, and CMRRA currently charges 5%, of the gross monies collected. It may surprise you to know that many midsize and large publishers use this service, because the cost of hiring a staff to issue numerous licenses and police them is more expensive than the 4½% to 5% these organizations charge.

The Harry Fox Agency and CMRRA will also issue synchronization licenses (see page 238 for what these are) on behalf of its members. CMRRA's fees for this are currently 10%, and Fox's are 10% for motion picture synchs, but 5% for all other synchs (television, commercials, in-flight, etc.). Fox (but not CMRRA) puts a cap on how much it takes for issuing synch licenses. Currently the caps are $250 per song for motion pictures, and $2,200 per song for all other usages. Issuing synch licenses is a separate service, and you don't have to take it just because you use them for mechanical licenses. The advantage is that they continually monitor the marketplace and thus have expertise in what to charge. The disadvantage is that it costs a percentage.

Accounting

Unlike record deals, publishers are paid by users quarterly, meaning four times each year. They're usually paid sixty to ninety days after the close of each calendar quarter, meaning sixty to ninety days after each March 31, June 30, September 30, and December 31.

Reserves

In reporting mechanical royalties to publishers, record companies take substantially larger reserves than they do in accounting to artists for record royalties. These reserves can run anywhere from 50% to 75% of the amount due, as opposed to 30% to 50% for record royalties. Why such a huge amount? Remember, as we discussed (on page 97), that reserves protect the record company against overshipping (i.e., shipping more records than it can sell). If a company overships and therefore overpays a publisher, the only way it can get the money back is to offset the overage against future royalties for *that composition*. (Once, in 1911, a publisher actually repaid an overpayment to a record company, but he was promptly executed by his fellow publishers.) This is different from record royalty overpayments, which can be charged against royalties on *any* records.

For example, suppose a publisher issues two licenses to the same record company, one for Song A and the other for Song B (written by two different songwriters). If the record company overpays on Song A, it has no right to offset this amount against royalties for Song B. The reason is that, even though the overpayment was made to the same publisher, it's a different song and there are different songwriters involved. This is not the case with an artist, where, if the record company overships on the first album, it can take the excess out of royalties payable on the second, third, fourth, and later albums (because it's dealing with the same artist and one royalty account). Accordingly, a record company can take smaller reserves in record deals than it can on publishing licenses, because it has more ways to get back an overpayment.

It's going to be interesting to see if SoundScan affects reserves for publishers. We discussed this in connection with record-company reserves on page 161.

CONTROLLED COMPOSITION CLAUSES

Congratulations!! You now know enough to talk about controlled composition clauses in record deals. These clauses are one of the most significant provisions in your recording arrangement, and you needed to understand both record deals and publishing to grasp the concepts, which you now do. So let's do it.

A **controlled composition** is a song written, owned, or controlled by the artist (in whole or in part). However, it's usually defined more broadly than that, and includes:

1. Any song in which the artist has an income or other interest. This means that, even if the artist doesn't own or *control* it, it's a controlled composition if he or she wrote it or otherwise gets a piece of its earnings.

2. The definition sometimes also includes (depending on the record company) compositions owned or controlled by the *producer* of the recordings. You really have little, if any, control over a producer's publishing, and thus you should try hard to get this provision knocked out. (You'll see why the producer won't like it in a minute.) It's hard to get rid of it, except at superstar levels, but do your best. I say this not only because it's hard or impossible to get a producer to comply with it, but also because, with a producer of any importance, you could end up blowing your producing deal with him or her because of it.

The Controlled Composition Clause

The controlled composition clause puts a limit on how much the company has to pay for each controlled composition. Because these are not artist royalties, the companies don't recoup advances, recording costs, or anything else from mechanicals. Thus, since it's money going out before they break even, they're very touchy about the amount. And you should be just as touchy because this may be the only money you're going to see for quite a while. As we discussed, you get your artist royalties only after you've recouped recording costs, video costs, etc. (which means they may never come, or if they do, it may not be for a couple of years), and, as we'll discuss in chapter 23, you won't be making any money from touring in your early stages. So take extremely good care of your mechanical royalties—they may have to last you through a few cold winters.

The rate limit on controlled compositions is twofold:

1. **Rate per Song.**
   The ink was hardly dry on the 1976 Copyright Law, raising the statutory rate from 2¢ to 2¾¢, when the record companies hit upon the idea that they should require their artists to license controlled compositions at 75% of the statutory rate, with further reductions (to 50%) for record club or budget records. (Controlled composition clauses existed before the 1976 Copyright Law, but they didn't reduce the rate below statutory.) To a large degree, the companies have been successful in getting these 75% and 50% rates with almost all new, and many midlevel,

artists. Even the biggest superstars have some form of controlled composition clause, although the "limit" may be 100% of statutory.

2. **Rate per Album.**
   There is usually a limit of ten times the single song rate for each album, which means several things, as we'll see in a minute. Superstars can sometimes increase this limit to ten times the statutory rate.

These issues are more complex than they appear at first glance. So let's take a more in-depth look, and I promise to go slowly.

MAXIMUM RATE PER SONG

Because the maximum rate per album is a multiple of the single song rate, we need to first look at what they do to you in connection with each song. Here's the skinny:

Percentage of Statutory. The first argument is to see if you can get more than the standard, off-the-shelf "75% of statutory." If you're a new artist, you probably won't. If you're mid-level or up, or if you have some bargaining power, try to get the percentage over 75%—anywhere over 75% would be nice. If you can't, one compromise is to ask for an escalation on later albums. For example, you might have a 75% rate on albums 1 and 2, an 85% rate on albums 3 and 4, and 100% after that. Or another possibility is an escalation based on sales: For example, you might get 75% on the first 500,000 (1,000,000) albums, 85% on the next 500,000 (1,000,000), and 100% thereafter.

Minimum Statutory Rate. The limit per composition is based on the *minimum* statutory rate. This means all compositions are treated as if they are five minutes or less in duration, regardless of their actual playing time—in other words, there is no additional payment for lengthy compositions. For example, the current statutory rate for a seven-minute song is 9.1¢ (see page 210 for why), but under these provisions, you're only paid 6.95¢ if you get 100% of statutory, or 5.21¢ (75% of 6.95¢) if you have a 75% rate.

Changes in Statutory Rate. As we discussed, the statutory rate changes over time (see page 210). But controlled composition clauses set a rate that doesn't go up. Thus, even if you get full statutory rate in your deal, it's normally locked to the statutory rate on a particular date, and there's no change if the statutory rate later escalates. This is tough to change, even for superstars.

The companies lock into the statutory rate in effect on one of these three dates: (a) the date of recording; (b) the date the master is delivered to the company; or (c) the date of first release of the master.

The general thinking (and historically this has been correct) is that *the latest possible date* is best for you—the statutory rate has never gone down, and thus the longer you wait, the most likely that it may go up.

Free Goods. The controlled composition clause will say you get no mechanicals on free goods (see page 93 for what free goods are). Actually, it's usually stated in language that's a little sneaky: It says that you only get mechanicals on records "for which a royalty is payable under this agreement." This means you don't get paid on free goods (because they don't bear royalties), but it isn't so obvious. As a new artist, you may have to live with this. When you begin to have some clout, you can sometimes get paid on 50% of album free goods, and superstars sometimes get paid on 100%. However, even superstars usually aren't paid on single free goods, and no one gets paid on special campaign free goods or promotional records (see page 96 for what all these things are).

Multiple Uses. Controlled composition clauses say that, even if a particular song is used more than once on the same record, you get paid as if it were only used once.

Reduced Rates. The company will typically ask for a 50% rate for record clubs, budget, K-Tel, and so forth. I like to resist these, saying we can work them out at the time. I don't always succeed.

Public Domain Arrangements. If a song is an arrangement of a public domain composition, the record company doesn't want to pay you for it. Your argument is that songs like "Scarborough Fair," "Sloop John B," and "Turn, Turn, Turn" were extremely successful public domain songs, and if you're brilliant enough to have this concept, you should be paid. (Sorry to use old stuff, but I can't think of anything more current.) The typical compromise is that you get a proportionate royalty for public domain material, in the same ratio as ASCAP or BMI (more about them later) pay performance royalties for the composition involved. In other words, if ASCAP pays you 50% of normal performance monies for the song, you get 50% of the mechanical rate. Everyone routinely accepts this.

Non-controlled Songs. The rate limits may be imposed not only on *controlled* compositions, but on *every* composition in the album. Not every company does this, but many do. If you're using **outside songs** (meaning songs that are *not* controlled compositions), this may be impossible to deliver—the owner will tell you to get lost. Remember, you can't force an owner to license you at all for a first use (see page 211), and even if the song was used before, the owner doesn't have to take less than the full statutory rate (see page 210). The only way to pay less for outside songs is to beg or else to threaten ("We'll drop your song if you don't reduce the rate"). But if you're dealing with major songwriters, you can forget it unless you sell a *lot* of records. And if you have to pay more than your contractual limit, the company takes the excess from you.

Here's an example for an eight-song album:

4 Outside Songs at Statutory (4 × 6.95¢)	27.8¢
4 Controlled Compositions (4 × 75% of 6.95¢)	20.9¢
TOTAL MECHANICALS PAYABLE	**46.7¢**
Maximum Allowed (8 × 75% of 6.95¢)	41.7¢
Less: Amounts Due Outside Songs	−27.8¢
MAXIMUM PAYABLE FOR YOUR 4 CONTROLLED COMPOSITIONS	**13.9¢**

As noted above, since you promised the record company the outside songs wouldn't cost more than 75% of 6.95¢, the excess comes out of your mechanicals on the other songs. In this example, the excess is 6.95¢, which is the difference between the 27.8¢ (4 × 6.95¢) due to the four outside song publishers and the allowable 20.9¢ (4 × 75% of 6.95¢). This 6.95¢ excess is deducted from your 20.9¢ for the controlled songs, so you get only 13.9¢ for your four songs (20.9¢ less the 6.95¢ excess). This equates to only 3.47¢ per song for you (13.9¢ divided among four songs), which is less than 75% of statutory (75% of 6.95¢ is 5.21¢). And if you don't have enough controlled songs from which to take the excess, it comes out of your record royalties or your advances.

So now you're a master of the single song limit. You're ready to conquer:

Maximum Rate Per Album

Standard Clause. All controlled composition clauses impose a limit on the total mechanicals for each album, usually ten times 75% of the statutory rate (or ten times the full rate if your rate per song isn't reduced). Note that this is in addition to, and independent of, the per-song limit—in other words, you must deliver each song at the specified single song rate, no matter what the total album limit, but you can't exceed the total album limit no matter how you license each individual song. This is to keep you from delivering, for example, fourteen songs at a 75% rate, which totals more than the company wants to pay even though you haven't exceeded your per-song limit. And remember: All of these limits are based on a multiple of the *minimum* statutory rate (the rate for songs five minutes and under), as discussed on page 223.

Nowadays, it's common for CDs to have eleven or twelve songs on them, even if the cassette has only ten. The practice of putting "bonus" (meaning extra) tracks on CDs is pretty common, but it usually takes you over the maximum album mechanical rate. With some amount of bargaining power, you can get a higher limit on CDs for exactly this reason. For example, you might have a ten times limit on cassettes, and an eleven times limit on CDs. This is always worth asking for.

Just for consistency in these examples, I'm going to assume that you have a maximum album rate of ten times 75% of statutory, or 52.1¢. The same principles apply even if it's a different limit (e.g., eleven times 75%, or ten times full statutory, etc.), but let's use ten times 75%.

No Limit on Non-controlled Songs. As your bargaining power goes up, you may be able to get a clause with no limit on outside compositions (other than statutory rate), even if you have a 75% statutory limit on controlled compositions, as long as you don't exceed the overall limit for the album (which in our example is ten times 75% of the statutory rate). Thus, while the maximum mechanicals for the album is 52.1¢, you would be allowed to pay statutory rate to each outside composition. This sounds a bit odd at first, but it's much better for you than a flat 75% of statutory limit on each composition (as in the example on page 225). The advantage is that you can now pay the outside publishers full statutory without reducing your royalties, because you're not limited on outside songs if you stay under the album limit.

Let's look at this using numbers. Here's what happens to the example on page 225 under this clause:

4 Outside Songs at Statutory (4 × 6.95¢)   27.8¢
4 Controlled Compositions (4 × 75% of
6.95¢)   + 20.9¢
_____
TOTAL MECHANICALS PAYABLE   **48.7¢**
Maximum Allowed (10 × 75% of 6.95¢)   52.1¢

Note the amount payable (48.7¢) is less than the maximum allowed for the album (52.1¢), which is ten times 75% of 6.95¢. So you get the full 20.9¢ for your songs, which is 75% of statutory. This contrasts with the result under the clause discussed on page 225, where you got less than this (only 13.9¢) for the exact same album. And by the way, 6.95¢ can add up to a hefty sum if you sell millions of albums.

On the other hand, if the mechanical royalties total more than ten times 75% of statutory under this clause, the excess comes out of your royalties. So if you pay outsiders at the statutory rate, you either have to put fewer than ten songs on your album or else take a reduced rate on your songs. For example, if there were five outside songs and five controlled compositions, you would get less than 75% of statutory for the controlled songs under this same clause. This is because the maximum per album applies to *all* of the compositions on the album, not just the controlled compositions. Thus, in a sense, the company is imposing a rate on outside compositions under this restriction, even when there is none under the maximum-rate-per-song provisions. Take a look at the numbers:

5 Outside Songs at Statutory (5 × 6.95¢)   34.75¢
5 Controlled Compositions (5 × 75% of 6.95¢)   + 26.06¢
_____
TOTAL   **60.81¢**
Maximum Allowed (10 × 75% of 6.95¢)   52.12¢
Less: Amounts Due Outside Songs (5 × 6.95¢)   − 34.75¢
_____
MAXIMUM PAYABLE FOR YOUR 5
CONTROLLED COMPOSITIONS   **17.37¢**

So, for each of your songs, you don't get 75% statutory (5.21¢), but rather only 3.47¢ (17.37¢ divided among five songs).

No Penalty for a Limited Number of Outside Songs.
The next step up is to say that you can pay statutory rate for the outside songs, and that you are allowed to *exceed* the overall album limit in order to pay this to the outsiders. If you can get this, it's usually limited to one or two songs per album.

This concept is easier to understand with an example:

Assume your overall album limit is ten times 75% of statutory (52.1¢). If you have ten songs on the album and two of them are outside songs licensed at statutory, you will exceed the maximum by the difference between the 75% limit and the full statutory amount (100%) that has to be paid for each of the two outside songs. (The difference is the 100% paid less the 75% maximum, or 25% of statutory, for each of the two songs.)

8 Controlled Compositions (8 × 75% of 6.95¢)	41.7¢
2 Outside Songs at Statutory (2 × 6.95)	13.9¢
TOTAL	**55.6¢**
Maximum Allowed (10 × 75% of 6.95¢)	52.1¢
EXCESS	**3.5¢**

If your clause allows up to two outside songs at full statutory, the company will pay the excess to the outsiders and won't take it back from you. Another way to look at it would be to say that the overall album limit is eight times 75% of statutory plus two times statutory, or 55.6¢. But this is not strictly true, because you get the extra amount only if you use two outside songs. If there was only one outside song, the maximum would be 53.9¢ (nine times 75% of statutory plus one times statutory), and if all ten songs on the album were yours, the rate would drop back to ten times 75% of statutory (52.1¢).

No Penalty for Any Outside Songs. With still more clout, you can get a clause that allows you an overall album limit of ten times the *full* statutory rate, even though controlled songs are limited to 75%. This means you're not penalized at all for the outside songs (unless you exceed ten songs on the album, and/or unless you have outside songs over five minutes). Here's an example using five outside songs under this kind of clause:

5 Outside Songs at Statutory (5 × 6.95¢)	34.75¢
5 Controlled Compositions (5 × 75% of 6.95¢)	+ 26.06¢
TOTAL MECHANICALS PAYABLE	**60.81¢**
Maximum Allowed (10 × 6.95¢)	69.5¢

Since the maximum allowed (6.95¢) is now more than the amount payable for both outside and controlled songs, you get the full 26.06¢ (five times 75% of statutory) for your songs.

The Ultimate. The ultimate is to say that the only limit is ten (or sometimes even eleven) times statutory, and the only per-song limit (on either outsiders or you) is statutory. However, you still have to live with the *minimum* statutory rate, as described on page 223, as well as the other provisions in the prior section on per-song rate limits (rate lock-in, multiple uses, free goods, public domain songs, reduced rates for club, etc.).

Multiple Albums. Most form controlled composition clauses don't distinguish between normal albums and multiple albums (for example, a double vinyl disc set, which today is usually a single cassette or single CD; we covered multiple albums on page 177). If you don't raise the issue, you'll have a ten-song mechanical limit on multiple albums that can have twenty or more songs. If you ask, you may get more than a "ten times" limit, but it may not be "twenty times": The companies will only increase the mechanical royalties in the same proportion that the suggested retail price increases over that of a single-disc album. If the multiple album has two CDs or two cassettes in the package, you will come close to twenty times. But, if it takes two CDs, it's probably more than twenty songs. If the multiple album is contained on only one CD or cassette, there is only a small (if any) increase in price, and you won't get much more for mechanicals. For example, if a single disc album is $10.00, and a double album is $11.00, you would get 11/10, or 110% (the ratio that $11 for the double album bears to $10 for the single album) of the mechanical royalties payable for a single album. (This formula is very similar to the one used for your artist royalties on multiple albums, which we discussed on page 177). If there is no price increase, you won't get any more mechanicals.

This can be serious business if you have a lot of outside songs, because the outsiders will insist on getting paid (greedy pigs that they are), and it will come out of you. For example, if there are sixteen songs and six are outsiders, all six are in excess of the allowed ten and would be deducted from mechanicals (leaving only four songs' worth for your ten songs). And if you pay the outsiders full statutory, while your limit is ten times 75% of statutory, you're even further reduced. Not good. So, if you have an attack of multi-album-itis, negotiate the mechanicals with your record company, and ideally with the outsiders as well, before you start.

Videos. The first draft of almost every controlled composition clause requires you to license your songs for free use in videos, forever. This may be overreaching, but it's hard to change. Let's look at two parts of it:

1. **Promotional usage.**
   I don't think it's unreasonable to give the company a free *promotional* video license. When it's using the video to promote your records, it's not making any money.

2. **Commercial usage.**
   When it comes to commercial usages (primarily home video at this time, although there may be other outlets in the future; see page 153), you should at least argue for some compensation. Independent publishers (those not subject to a controlled composition clause, who can charge what the market will bear) usually get in the range of 5% to 7% of wholesale for all compositions (see page 413), but with the agreement that the publisher will get no less than 8¢ to 12¢ per song. Also, there is almost always a 10,000 unit guarantee, meaning, for example, if you got 8¢ per unit, you would get an $800 advance (8¢ × 10,000 units). It's very difficult to get compensation if you're the artist, for the simple reason that companies don't like to do it—videos are not a big profit center, and they hate paying you when they're losing money. But it's worth asking. Sometimes you can get a small fee ($250 or so) if the video recoups its costs (which is no small "if," as we discussed on page 153).

Postscript

Now that you've read it (I didn't want to prejudice you before you did), I can tell you that controlled composition clauses are one of the most complicated critters in the music business (you probably figured that out though, didn't you?). This section is packed full of numbers and weird concepts, so it may take a few times through to get the flavor. Don't feel bad if you don't get all of it the first time or two—it took me years to get a decent handle on it. But mechanicals may well be your only monies for quite a while (see page 222 for why), so it's worth an investment of time to understand these clauses.

PUBLIC-PERFORMANCE ROYALTIES

Remember, when we discussed copyrights, that one of the exclusive rights you get is the right to perform your composition in public (see page 207). These rights are known as **performing rights,** or **public-performance rights,** and each user needs your permission to play the song on the radio, on television, in nightclubs, in amusement parks, at live concerts, etc.

As you can quickly see, it's impossible for every radio station, night-club, etc., in the country (of which there are thousands) to get a separate license for every song they play (of which there are also thousands). The paperwork alone would send them off to buy that trout farm in Idaho. So out of this situation developed the **blanket license** and **performing rights societies.** Here's how the system works:

Performing Rights Societies

The major performing rights societies in the United States are ASCAP (standing for American Society of Composers, Authors, and Publishers), BMI (Broadcast Music Incorporated), and SESAC (standing for SESAC). Of the three, ASCAP and BMI are by far the largest, as SESAC has only about 1% of all performing rights. Virtually every foreign country has the equivalent for its own territory, most of which are government owned, such as SACEM for France, STEMRA for Holland, PRS for the U.K., etc. The societies go to each publisher and say, "Please designate us as your agent for the performing rights in *all* your songs. We'll then go to the people who want to use them (radio stations, nightclubs, etc.) and give them a license to use *all* the songs of *all* the publishers we represent. For each license, we will collect fees, divide them up, and send you your share." And this is exactly what happens. Publishers sign up with (known as "affiliating with") ASCAP or BMI, who then issues licenses to the users, collects the monies, and pays the publishers.

There may be some interesting storm clouds brewing on the performing-rights-society front. SESAC was recently purchased by a private investment group and intends to embark on an aggressive campaign for market share. Because it's privately owned (as opposed to BMI and ASCAP, which are nonprofit organizations), and because it's not bound by a consent decree (that's a fancy legal term for a procedure whereby BMI and ASCAP agreed to certain restrictions in a court settlement of antitrust problems), SESAC can make deals that ASCAP and BMI can't. It's going to be fun to see what happens.

Blanket Licenses

The license that ASCAP and BMI give each music user is called a **blanket license** because it "blankets" (i.e., "covers") all of the compositions they represent. In other words, in exchange for a fee, the user gets the right to perform *all* the compositions controlled by *all* the publishers affiliated with ASCAP and BMI. The fee can range from a few hundred dollars per year for a small nightclub, to millions of dollars per year for television networks.

Separate Writer Affiliation

It isn't just publishers who affiliate with these societies. The writers do also, and even more important, *the writers are paid directly* by the society. This means performance earnings, unlike any other type of publishing monies, are *not* paid to the publisher; instead, the society bypasses the publisher and sends the checks to the writer. This is designed to protect the writer (which it does very well) from flaky publishers who might steal the money.

Writers can only affiliate with one society.

Allocation of License Proceeds

So here are the societies sitting with all those millions of dollars of license fees. How do they know how much to pay each publisher and writer?

First, the monies are used to pay the operating expenses of the society. Then, everything left over is divided among the participants (ASCAP and BMI are nonprofit, so everything not used for expenses gets paid out). The division is based only on (a) radio airplay, and (b) television airplay. (If you're an artist who constantly performs his or her own compositions in live concerts, but you're not on the radio or TV, you can sometimes make special arrangements with BMI [but not ASCAP] to get paid.) So, you ask, how do they know how much a song is played on the radio or on television?

1. **Radio.**
   BMI requires its licensee radio stations to keep logs of all the musical compositions they play. This is done on a rotating basis, from station to station, and each station has to log for about seven days (twenty-four hours per day) each year. BMI then projects from these logs to the whole country.

   ASCAP does it differently. It hires an independent statistical firm to listen to selected radio stations on a rotating, unannounced basis, writing down the compositions played. Based on this, it then makes the same extrapolations to the whole country.

   It looks as if the allocation of radio performance monies may be headed for major changes. There's a new system called **BDS** (the letters stand for Broadcast Data Systems), which is owned by *Billboard* (the trade publication). BDS is used to determine *Billboard*'s charts, and its innovation is a computer that's learned how to listen to the radio. As I understand it, the computer is fed a number of compositions, which it digitizes. The computer then monitors radio broadcasts, matches songs played with its memory bank, and keeps track of which songs are played, the dates, and times. Should the performing rights societies have enough confidence to treat a system like this as gospel, we may have a much more accurate record of performances.

2. **Television.**

   Television stations are required to keep **cue sheets,** which are lists of every musical composition used, how long it was played, and how it was used (theme song, background, performed visually, etc.). The cue sheets are then filed with ASCAP or BMI, and there are specific dollar amounts allocated for each type of use (theme, background, etc.) and for the size of the broadcast area (local or network).

BMI pays "bonuses" for musical compositions that are performed heavily, and this can result in substantial increases in the amount of performance monies paid. ASCAP has no such concept, but its fees tend to be comparable anyway. Both societies pay quarterly (four times per year), and both societies pay about a year after the quarter in which monies are earned.

Motion Picture Performance Monies

Due to some fancy footwork by the film industry a number of years ago, ASCAP and BMI are not permitted to collect public-performance monies for motion pictures shown in theaters in the United States. There is no logical reason for this (the movies are certainly a public performance); it's just historical and political. However, in foreign territories this is not the case, and motion picture performance monies are significant. This is because the performing rights society fees are based on a percentage of the box office receipts. In fact, the composer of a major smash film score can earn hundreds of thousands of dollars in foreign performance monies alone.

Which Society Is the Best?

Today, we can answer this question better than in prior years. The societies historically were so persnickety that, unless all writers of a particular song were affiliated with the same society, neither one could end up getting paid. For example, if a BMI writer and an ASCAP writer created a work together, no one got paid. Nice, eh? Beginning about 1972, however, the societies finally allowed **cross-registration** of songs, meaning that a BMI publisher and an ASCAP publisher could each register its portion of the composition with its society. Thus, if a song is owned 50% by a BMI publisher and 50% by an ASCAP publisher, it is registered 50% with BMI and 50% with ASCAP. However, the shares of each publisher must match that of the writer; in other words, if ⅓ of a song is written by a BMI writer and ⅔ by an ASCAP writer, a BMI publisher must have ⅓ of the publish-ing, and an ASCAP publisher must have ⅔ of the publishing.

So with cross-registered songs, we finally got to see who pays more. This is because ASCAP collects its half of the song and remits to the ASCAP writer/publisher, while BMI does the same for its writer/publisher on the same song, each independent of the other. And the result? In the comparisons I have seen, ASCAP seems to do a bit better in general, but for some compositions, BMI beats them. Also, BMI pays more for certain usages under specific circumstances, and BMI changes its payment schedules periodically. Thus (unfortunately) there are no hard and fast rules.

Source Licensing

This is going to be a hot topic in the not too distant future. The broadcasters (specifically the networks) realized they were paying mil-lions of dollars for public-performance fees every year. They struck upon the idea that, if they went to the individual publishers, they could "divide and conquer" (meaning beat each one up individually for cheaper fees than they can get from ASCAP or BMI, who represent so many publishers that they are powerful bargainers). Broadcasters, of course, have an entirely different story—they say that publishers will do better if they bypass ASCAP and BMI, because they can save the percentage of performance monies that these societies keep.

This idea is called **source licensing**—so named because the license comes from the source (publisher), as opposed to the intermediary performing rights society. The broadcasters first sought the right to do this through a court case (Buffalo Broadcasting), but the court found against them. (The cite for this case is *Buffalo Broadcasting* v. *American Society of Composers, et al.*, 744 F.2d 917 [1984].) Their next move has been to try and do it legislatively in Congress, and they're pushing slowly and steadily forward.

Does it seem strange that the broadcasters would take such a tack?

It's difficult to see how source licensing could work as a practical matter. It would mean thousands of licenses have to be issued by the networks and stations to individual publishers, which is largely impractical. But the real goal line of all this is for the networks to require producers of their programming to obtain performing licenses as part of the package. This means that, whenever you create a song for a television program (or perhaps even a motion picture), your contract grants the film company a performing license for your work. They will then grant this license to the broadcasters as part of the program license deal, presumably for an additional fee. In the short run, I think it's likely the amount of money allocated for the performance monies will be comparable to what is now paid. But you can imagine it will ultimately end up a lot less than would be payable if a society representing thousands of copyrights were negotiating it. In fact, my guess is that the extra fee will ultimately disappear.

Source licensing is a terrific idea if you're a broadcaster, and probably neutral if you're a film producer. It's a lousy idea if you're a writer or publisher, who have so far mounted a formidable resistance to this effort. If it really goes through, it could cripple or even end the performing rights societies, because it cuts off their largest sources of revenue. So stay tuned for further results. Film at eleven (ten Central).

17

Secondary Publishing Income

Let's take a look at other sources of publishing income: print, synchronization, and foreign monies.

PRINTED MUSIC

The majority of printed music revenues comes from **sheet music** (printed music of a single song—the kind you stuff inside your piano bench) and **folios** (which are collections of songs, such as *Greatest Hits of the Eighties, The Complete Led Zeppelin*, etc.). Collections of songs by a number of different artists and writers are called **mixed folios.** Another popular type is a **matching folio,** which has all the songs of a particular album (i.e., it "matches" the album). Matching folios are usually printed with the album artwork on the cover and various posed candid shots of the artist inside.

Royalties

The royalties paid to a publisher for a single-song sheet music are 20% of the marked retail price (currently about 70¢ for a $3.50 retail price). Royalties on folios are 10% to 12½% of the marked retail price, and the current marked selling prices of folios range from about $14.95 to $16.95. A **personality folio** is one that has the picture of the performing artist plastered all over it, such as *Whitney Houston's Greatest Hits.* (A matching folio [see the prior section for what that is] is also a personality folio.) For a personality folio, there is an additional royalty of 5% of the marked retail selling price for use of the name and likeness of the artist, and it goes to the artist (who may or may not be the same person as the songwriter).

Unless the folio represents the selected works of a particular songwriter and only one publisher, it will contain songs written and/or published by a number of different people. Thus, the royalties are pro-rated, in exactly the same way as royalties are pro-rated for records that have recordings by different artists (see page 173). For example, if there are twenty compositions in the folio, and ten are owned by you, you would get $^{10}\!/_{20}$ths (one-half) of the 10% to 12½% royalty. When you negotiate a pro-ration provision, be sure to insist that the royalty can be pro-rated only on the basis of *copyrighted, royalty-bearing works* in the folio. Otherwise, your royalty gets reduced by "Mary Had a Little Lamb" and "The Star-Spangled Banner," even though the printer isn't paying anyone for these songs.

The balance of print music consists of things like instructional music (such as putting your songs in *How to Play the Zither*), marching band arrangements, choir arrangements, dance arrangements, etc. The royalty for these is generally 10% of retail. Print rights also include reprints of lyrics in books, magazines, etc., usually for flat fees of $50 to $250. Reprints of lyrics on albums are customarily free.

Term

Print music licenses (other than lyric reprints) are for limited periods of time, usually three to five years. Because of this, you have to spell out what the printer can do with the stuff at the end of the term. Certainly they can't manufacture any more inventory, but can they continue to sell what they have?

Normally these licenses give the printer a *nonexclusive* right (meaning someone else can sell the same materials at the same time) to sell their existing inventory for a period of six to twelve months after the term expires. At the end of the six to twelve months, they have to trash any inventory left over. For folios (because they're so much more expensive), the printers try not to have any time limit on their sell-off rights.

When you make these deals, make sure there's no **stockpiling** and no **dumping** or **distress sales.** *Stockpiling* is where the printer runs out and manufactures eight quadrillion units right before the end of the term, so that they have tons of your inventory to sell after the term. (Your new printer won't like it if the market is already flooded with the same books it's trying to sell.) You stop this by saying the printer can only manufacture enough to meet their reasonably anticipated needs during the term.

Dumping and distress sale mean the printer sells your inventory at less than customary wholesale prices. *Way* less. You don't want this because, if they end up with a ton of goods left over, they'll blow it out at whatever rock-bottom price they can get. (Since they have to destroy everything they don't sell, they use the age-old theory that it's better to get something than nothing.) This practice, shall we say, "perturbs" your new printer, who is trying to sell the same stuff at full price. You solve this by saying your materials can be sold only through normal retail channels, at normal wholesale prices.

SYNCHRONIZATION AND TRANSCRIPTION LICENSES

A **synchronization license** (also called a **synch** [pronounced "sink"] license) is a license to use music in "timed synchronization" with visual images. A classic example is a song in a motion picture, where the song is synchronized with the action on the screen. It also includes, however, television commercials, home video devices, etc., although interestingly it doesn't include radio commercials (since they're not synchronized with visuals). Radio commercial licenses are called **transcription licenses.**

Fees

The fees for synchronization licenses are really all over the board, and they vary with the usage and the importance of the song. An example of the lowest end would be a ten-second background use of an unknown song in a television show (perhaps being played on a jukebox while the actors are talking and ignoring it). A high-end example would be an on-camera, full-length performance of a well-known song in a major studio's high-budget film, like the use of "Unchained Melody" in *Ghost*. And when we get into the realm of commercials, the fees go even higher.

In order to give you a range, the low-end television usage I've just described can be anywhere from free (the publisher may do it just for exposure and performance monies) to more typically around $1,000 to $2,000. If it were a film instead of a television show, the fee would be about $10,000 or so. Television licenses are typically for a period of five years, while motion picture licenses are in perpetuity. As the composition gets better known, and the usage more important, the price rises to the range of about $1,200 to $3,000 for a television show, and $15,000 to $25,000 for films. For the major film usage I've described (particularly if it was a theme song), the cost can be $50,000 to $75,000 or more. (Again, the rules are fluid and also based on how badly the film producer is hooked on a song. For example, I recently got $35,000 for a ten-second usage of one of my client's songs because it was well known and really "made" the scene.) For commercials, a song can command anywhere from $25,000 to $500,000 plus per year. The typical range for a well-known song is $75,000 to $200,000 for a one-year national usage in the United States, on television and radio. These figures get scaled down for regional or local usages for periods of less than a year.

This subject is discussed in more detail when we get to film music (on page 412).

If you're on the *Fast Track,*
go to the Bonus Section on page 249.
Everyone else, onward.

FOREIGN SUBPUBLISHING

Barring the worldwide conglomerates, publishers don't have branch offices in all territories. So how do they collect their monies when your records sell in Abu Dhabi? Well, they do it by making agreements with local publishers in each territory to collect on their behalf. The local publisher is called a **subpublisher.**

Foreign Mechanicals

Before talking about deals with the local publishers, you should know about an unusual creature that lives in most territories outside the United States. This is the *mandatory* mechanical rights collection society, and it works like this:

Most countries have a mechanical rights collection organization (usually government owned) that licenses *all* musical compositions (regardless of who owns them) used by *any* record company in that territory. It's like the Harry Fox Agency (see page 220), except that it's mandatory. The society collects mechanical royalties from the record companies, holds them for as long as they can get away with it (remember, they can earn interest on these monies and not have to pay it to anybody), and finally sends them out to the appropriate publisher. (As noted on page 212, mechanical licenses are not issued on a per-song basis outside the United States and Canada. Rather, the entire record is licensed for a percentage of the wholesale or retail price, regardless of the number of compositions. This greatly simplifies the centralization process of putting all the monies through one organization.)

How do they know which publisher to pay? Under this system, each local publisher files a "claim" with the organization, saying it owns a particular composition. It can either be a claim for the entire song, or a percentage share if the rights are split among several publishers in that territory. If a claim is contested (and in some territories even if it isn't), the publisher is required to file proof of its claim, such as a copy of the contract with the U.S. publisher.

Foreign Performances

All foreign territories have some sort of performance rights society, usually government owned, and these societies pay the *publisher's share* of performance monies to local subpublishers. The foreign performing rights societies pay the *writer's share* to ASCAP/BMI/SESAC (which in turn pays the writer), again keeping these monies out of the publishers' hands (as we discussed on page 232). If there is no foreign subpublisher, the publisher's share will ultimately wind its way back to the U.S. publisher through the U.S. society. However, it takes a substantially longer period of time, and it's worth paying the subpublisher a piece so you can get it earlier.

Subpublisher Charges

The range of deals for subpublishing allows the subpublisher to retain anywhere from 10% to 50% of the monies earned, the vast majority of deals being from 15% to 25%. The contracts are actually written the opposite way, stating that the subpublisher collects all monies and remits 75% to 85% of it to the U.S. publisher. The shorthand industry expression of these deals is "75/25" or "85/15" (referring to the percentages kept by each party). I have heard of one deal where the local subpublisher kept no percentage whatsoever of the earnings (i.e., they remitted 100%). Can you figure out why anyone would do this? See page 248 for the answer.

Covers

It is customary for the local publisher to get an increased percentage for **cover records.** A cover record, also called a **cover,** is a recording of a U.S. composition by a local artist in the local territory. The subpublisher usually gets 40% to 50% of the earnings from cover recordings (meaning it remits 60% to 50%). When you make a subpublishing deal, be sure to limit the subpublisher's increased percentage to the *cover recordings' earnings only*, or else you will decrease your money on the U.S. version if the local publisher's nephew records the song.

Performance Monies

A number of subpublishers try to charge a bigger percentage of performance royalties than they do for other monies. For example, they may keep 25% of all monies except performances, and 50% of performances. Here is their reasoning:

Assuming the subpublisher gets 25% of all earnings other than performances, for every dollar of earnings it gets 25¢. The 75¢ paid back to the U.S. publisher includes both the publisher's share and the writer's share (as did of course the dollar paid to them in the first place), and thus their percentage applied to the total writer/publisher combination. On performances, however, remember that the writer's share is paid to the U.S. performing rights society, and not to the local subpublisher (see page 240). This means that, instead of getting the full $1.00 of performance monies, the subpublisher only gets 50¢ (the publisher's share).

Here's a chart:

	Mechanicals	Performances
Total Writer/Publisher Earnings	$1.00	$1.00
Amount Paid to Subpublisher	$1.00	$ .50
		(other $.50 paid to writer directly by society)
Subpublisher's 25% Share	$ .25	$ .125
Percentage of Dollar Earned	25%	12.5%

Accordingly, subpublishers argue, they're really only getting 12.5% of the performance dollar. Thus, they want 50% of performance monies, so they can get 25% of the full performance dollar and be in the same position as they are with other monies. This 50% equals 25¢ (50% of the 50¢ publisher's share of performance monies), or 25% of the total writer/publisher performance dollar.

This reasoning, while clever and not without merit, usually gives way to sheer bargaining power. If the subpublisher has enough bargaining power, they will pull it off. Otherwise, the U.S. publisher simply says no.

Printed Music

For printed music, if the subpublisher actually manufactures and sells the stuff, it pays the U.S. publisher from 10% to 15% of the marked retail selling price, the norm being 10% to 12½%. If the print music is licensed out by the subpublisher, the subpublisher keeps the same percentage as all other monies (15% to 25% of licensing income) and remits the balance.

Advances

It's customary for subpublishers to pay the U.S. publisher an advance against their ultimate earnings. This is largely a banking transaction—if the U.S. publisher's catalog has a track record, the subpublisher pays an advance based on historical earnings. It will vary, of course, with the size of the territory and size of catalog. The range is anywhere from zero to millions of dollars for major catalogs in major territories. If it's a new artist or a so-so older catalog, there may be no advance at all. A deal with no advance is known as a **collection deal,** meaning the subpublisher merely collects on behalf of the U.S. publisher. Also, if there is no advance, the percentage kept by the subpublisher is often lower, usually in the 10% to 15% range. Again, as with all other rules, there are exceptions. For example, if the publisher controls a new artist whose record is doing extremely well in the U.S., the advance can get driven up despite the lack of historical base.

Advances are also affected greatly by the currency exchange rates. When the dollar is weak, high U.S. dollar advances are relatively easy to come by; the opposite is true, of course, when the dollar gets stronger. In other words, the same number of English pounds equals more or fewer dollars at any given time, depending on the current exchange rate. When it equals more, you can get a larger advance.

"At Source"

One of the most important points to have in your subpublishing agreement is a requirement that all monies be computed **"at source."** This means the percentage remitted to you must be based on the earnings in the country *where earned,* which is the source. So if you have an 85/15 deal at source in Germany, and $1.00 is earned there, you get 85¢.

Requiring computation at source is an important protection because, while the practice has largely disappeared, it was popular a number of years ago to play the following game:

A subpublisher in the United Kingdom makes a 75/25 deal with a U.S. publisher for all the territories of Europe. The subpublisher in Germany (owned by the U.K. publisher) collects a dollar, keeps 50¢ as its collection fee, and pays 50¢ to the U.K. publisher. The 50¢ received in the U.K. is then split between the U.S. publisher and the U.K. publisher. Here's a play-by-play:

Earnings in Germany	$.100
Less: German Company's 50% Share	– .50
Amount Remitted to U.K.	$.50
Less: U.K. Company's 25% Share	– .125
AMOUNT REMITTED TO U.S. PUBLISHER	**$.375**

It doesn't take a genius to see that the $1.00 earned at source (in this case, Germany, where the actual earnings were generated) gets dwindled radically before it finds its way into your pocket. And the 75% deal you thought you had becomes 37.5% (you only got 37.5¢ out of the $1.00 earned in Germany).

As I said earlier, this scam has pretty well gone away, but it's cheap insurance to add a clause requiring your percentage must be computed "at source."

Translation/Adaptation Shares

One particularly interesting aspect of subpublishing deals is that of a **translator** or **adaptor**. If your song is a popular one, many territories want to release a version with lyrics in the language of that territory. This all sounds innocent enough, but it creates some problems:

1. First of all, the local lyricist automatically gets a share of royalties, which is paid by the local societies. Most societies require that the lyricist receive about one-sixth of gross (meaning combined writer and publisher shares) for mechanicals, and one-sixth of the writer's share only for performance royalties.
2. Subpublishers, naturally, want to charge you for this share. If you have sufficient bargaining power, you may be able to muscle them into absorbing it out of their percentage. As their percentage decreases, however, so does the likelihood of your making them eat it. So, more commonly, the translator's percentage comes off the top, which means you pay your share of it. In

other words, if you get 60% of the earnings from covers, you are absorbing 60% of the translator's share, and the subpublisher absorbs the other 40%.

3. You must be certain the translation is registered separately with the society (since it will have a foreign title, this is not so difficult), and that the publisher makes sure the translator doesn't get paid on the English language version. This can be done in most territories, but some (notably Germany) insist on paying the translator on the original composition no matter what you do (in the case of Germany, however, the translator gets only a piece of mechanicals and not other income).

The upshot of all this is that you should have the absolute right to approve whether the subpublisher can authorize a local translation, because it may take money out of your pocket. Also, artistically, you should make them send you an English version of the translated lyrics for approval. Otherwise, your ballad may find itself associated with a number of perverse sexual practices, drugs, etc.

The Black Box

Remember, the societies collect mechanicals of *all* songs, not just those registered, but they only pay out for the songs that are registered (see page 239). By now your sharp eye has probably figured out there may be some songs not claimed by any local publisher. And you're right—there are always unclaimed songs. For example, through sheer inadvertence, a U.S. publisher may not have a subpublishing deal in a particular territory, or perhaps the rights are disputed in the U.S. and no foreign publisher has been given the rights.

These unclaimed monies are called **black box** monies. In some countries (notably Germany, Italy, Spain, France, and Holland), if the funds aren't claimed after a set period of time (usually three years), the monies are paid to the local publishers. Each publisher gets a portion of them based on the ratio that its earnings bear to the total earnings of the society, and also based on seniority. So if a publisher earned 100,000 drapkes and the society collected 1,000,000 drapkes, it might receive 100,000/1,000,000, or 10%, of the black box monies, and perhaps another 3% because it has been around for twenty years. This can be a substantial source of additional revenue, and the local publisher keeps it all because the monies aren't earned by any particular compositions.

If you get into the "major leagues" of publishers, you may be able to negotiate for a portion of the black box money. The usual formula is to take a proportionate amount, based on the ratio that your earnings for the subpublisher involved bears to the total earnings of that subpublisher. For example, if your songs earned a total of $200,000 for the subpublisher, and its total earnings were $1 million, you would get 20% of the black box monies, because your $200,000 is 20% of its $1 million total.

DART MONIES (AUDIO HOME RECORDING ACT OF 1992)

Congress passed the Audio Home Recording Act of 1992, not surprisingly, in 1992. This act is the DART (Digital Audio Recorders and Tape) Bill we touched on before (on page 185), and it did two things:

1. It said that consumers who copy tapes at home for their private, noncommercial use are not committing copyright infringement. I'll bet you're sleeping much better now. Actually, this was not such a big deal. The legislative history accompanying the 1976 Copyright Act made it clear that home taping was not copyright infringement.
2. It imposed a tax on digital audio recorders and digital audiotapes. This will become a *very* big deal.

In other countries of the world (most notably Germany), there has been a tax on blank tape and recorders for a number of years. It's paid to the record companies, musicians, and songwriters who are deprived of income because of home taping, and it amounts to substantial sums of money. The U.S. act is a step in that direction, but it applies only to *digital* audio recorders and tapes, which at the moment are not significant. However, since digital recordings will undoubtedly replace analog (see page 169), these monies are going to be very meaningful in the future.

Here's how it works: The act imposes a tax on blank audiotape equal to 3% of the wholesale price, and a tax on digital audio recorders equal to 2% of the wholesale price. The tax on machines has a minimum of $1 and a maximum of $8, unless the machine has two or more digital records, in which case the maximum is $12. After five years, the $8 and $12 can be adjusted, but the $1 never moves. The tax does not apply to professional models (such as recording-studio consoles), nor does it apply to recorders "not generally used to record music" (such as answering machines, dictating machines, talking toaster ovens, etc.).

The act also requires each digital recorder to have a **Serial Copyright Management System (SCMS),** which, in English, means that you can't make a copy from the copies. In other words, your machine can record a digital tape from a CD, but you can't make another copy from that copy. There is no limit on how many copies you can make from the original.

So here sits Uncle Sam with a big bag full of taxes. Who gets it? Basically, one-third of the money goes to songwriters and music publishers, and the other two-thirds goes to record companies, featured artists, and unions (who are collecting on behalf of nonfeatured artists). Here's the exact breakdown:

Recording Portion

Record Companies	38.41%
Featured Artists	25.60%
AFM (see page 75 for what AFM is)	1.75%
AFTRA (see page 75)	.92%
	66.68%

Songwriter/Publishing Portion

Songwriters	16.66%
Music Publishers	16.66%
	33.32%

The act says that the Recording Portion is to be allocated to the various companies and artists based on the distribution of records. So you can easily calculate how much you're owed by comparing exactly how many of your records were distributed as compared to *all* of the records distributed in the United States in the same time period. (Somehow I don't think that's how you want to be spending your time.) And the allocation of the Songwriter/Publishing Portion is even more complicated, because it can be distributed on the basis of either distribution of records (like the recording portion) *or* "dissemination to the public in transmission" (which presumably means airplay). So even if you wanted to, there's virtually no way to figure that one out.

What's happening in real life? Various industry groups are going to collect for each set of interested parties, do the allocations, and disburse the money to the individual record companies, artists, publishers, etc. (Somehow I get the image of a mother bird standing over a nest full of babies with their mouths open.) It was clear from the beginning that ASCAP and BMI would collect the songwriters' portion of these monies. However, there was a brief paper war between ASCAP, BMI, the Harry Fox Agency, and a newly formed industry group called the Alliance of Artists and Recording Companies (also known as the **Alliance** or **AARC**), who were all vying to collect for the featured artists. The Alliance, which is administered by the RIAA (see page 108 for who they are) and a board of artists and artist representatives, was the clear winner on the featured-artist front. The Fox Agency is collecting the publishers' portion of the tax, and the Alliance will collect for the record companies. This all makes pretty good sense because these parties can then access whatever information they need to divide up their monies.

Because this tax only applies to digital equipment and tapes, the monies are not likely to be significant for some time to come. Indeed, the cost of administration (i.e., collecting and figuring out who gets what) may well exceed the monies collected in the beginning. However, as analog cassettes ride off into the sunset, I believe these taxes will amount to a sizable chunk of dough.

Regardless of the fact that it doesn't mean much money now, the record companies have already begun adding clauses in their contracts to grab the featured artist's share of these monies. The record companies want to collect the funds and apply them to the artist's account. Thus, if the artist is recouped, they will pay them through with record royalties, and if not, the monies will reduce the artist's deficit. The companies' argument, and it's not without merit, is that the tax is meant to compensate for lost record sales, and so the income should be treated as if it came from these sales. In other words, if the consumer had not been able to home tape, he or she would have bought another copy and generated income for the record company. If the artist had earned a royalty from this sale, it would of course be recoupable, and thus DART monies should also be.

Whether the publishers will be able to grab the writer's share of these monies is still up in the air. As you already know (from page 232), the publisher can't touch the writer's share of public performance monies. Because the writer's DART monies are being handled by BMI or ASCAP, they will probably be treated the same way, and in fact ASCAP and BMI have both told me they intend to pay DART monies directly to the writers. So my best guess is that these monies will stay "untouched by publisher's hands."

Answer to question on page 240:

While it was a stupid business deal, the subpublisher's thinking was that (a) it would enjoy a certain amount of prestige from having landed a major catalog (which prestige of course immediately vanished when everyone found out what an idiotic deal they made), and (b) even though the subpublisher kept no piece, it collected the monies locally and held them for a period of six months, which meant the company could earn interest on them. If you find someone ready to make a deal like this, give me a call because I still have that land in Florida to sell.

Bonus Section!

HOW TO SET UP A PUBLISHING COMPANY

I am now about to save you an enormous amount of time and frustration in setting up a publishing company. The tips I'm giving you here, revealed in print for the first time, were gained by yours truly through a series of hard knocks that will become obvious as you see the proper way to do it.

The Absolute First Thing to Do

Before you do anything, and I mean before you do *anything*, you positively must take the first step. *Affiliate your company with ASCAP or BMI.* The reason you have to do this first is that these societies will not let you use a name that is the same (or similar to) the name of an existing company. They don't want to accidentally pay the wrong party, and so they're tough about the name you can use. And you don't want to have label copy, printed music, copyright registrations, and everything else in the name of a company that can't collect performance royalties.

   You can affiliate and secure your name by completing an application and giving the society three name choices, ranked in order. That way, at least one of the names should clear. If you're also a songwriter and haven't yet affiliated, you should affiliate as a writer with one of the two societies at the same time (they won't let you affiliate with both). You'll have to affiliate as a publisher with the same society in which you affiliate as a songwriter. This is because, as we discussed on page 234, the societies insist on having a song's publisher affiliated with the same society as the song's writer. And for this same reason, if you're going to be a "real" publisher (meaning you're going to publish other people's songs, as opposed to only your own), you'll need to have two companies, one for ASCAP and one for BMI.

The publishing company affiliation forms are pretty straightforward; they ask you who owns the company, the address, and similar exciting, provocative questions. You also need to give them information about all songs in your catalog (writers, publishers, foreign deals, recordings, etc.), so they can put the info into their system and make sure you're credited (read "paid") for them. You can get affiliation applications by contacting ASCAP or BMI at the following addresses and telephone numbers:

BMI

320 West 57th Street
New York, New York 10019
(212) 586-2000
FAX (212) 489-2368

10 Music Square East
Nashville, Tennessee 37203
(615) 401-2000
FAX (615) 401-2120

8730 Sunset Boulevard
3rd Floor West
Hollywood, California 90069
(310) 659-9109
FAX (310) 657-6947

ASCAP

One Lincoln Plaza
New York, New York 10023
(212) 621-6000
FAX (212) 724-9064

2 Music Square West
Nashville, Tennessee 37203
(615) 742-5000
FAX (615) 742-5020

7920 Sunset Boulevard
Suite 300
Los Angeles, California 90046
(213) 883-1000
FAX (213) 883-1049

And get started early—it can take about five weeks to get an approval.

Here's a tip in picking a name. The more common your name is, the less likely you're going to get it. So steer clear of names like "Hit Music" and similar choices that, because they're obnoxiously obvious, won't clear. Names using just initials, such as "J. B. Music" and the like, also seem to have a hard time clearing (so save that concept for your license plates). For some reason, many of my clients enjoy naming their publishing companies after their children or their streets, and these seem to clear routinely. (For the record, I once owned a publishing company, "Holly Kelly Music," that I named after my dogs.)

Setting Up Business

If you're not a corporation using the corporate name, the next step is to file what, in California, is known as a "fictitious name statement." This is a document filed with a county recorder and published in a newspaper, and it has its counterpart in most states. It tells the world you're doing business under a name that isn't your own and makes it legal to do so. At least in California, you need this statement to open a bank account and, even more important, to cash checks made out to that name. You can imagine the screaming phone call I got as a young lawyer when I learned this lesson.

Copyright Registration

Next, register the songs with the Copyright Office in the name of your publishing entity (see page 303). If they have been previously copyrighted in your name, you need to file an assignment transferring them to the publisher's name.

Society Registration

To the extent you didn't do so when you originally affiliated, you must register all your songs with the performing rights society. The societies will send you the forms, which are self-explanatory. You only have to register the songs as either the writer or the publisher, not both.

After that, you're in business. You can begin to issue licenses to record companies and other users, as well as make foreign subpublishing agreements, print deals, and so forth. However, there's no particular need to rush into these deals, nor will anybody be interested in making them, until you have a record released. In fact, unless you've got a record coming out (or some other exploitation, like a film or TV show using your songs), the societies won't even let you affiliate, and frankly there's not much point in doing any of this. You'll just be all dressed up with no place to go.

18

Songwriter Deals

Now let's look at the terms of the agreement between the songwriter and the publisher. Remember, as we discussed, the songwriter signs a contract transferring ownership of the copyright in the musical composition to the publisher. In exchange for this, the publisher agrees to handle the business and pay royalties to the writer.

SONGWRITER ROYALTIES

The reason we discussed publishers' receipts first was because a songwriter gets a piece of the publisher's collections (with the exception of performance monies and possibly DART monies, as we discussed on page 245). This is almost invariably 50% (except for print music), and as we discussed before, the monies kept by the publisher are called the **publisher's share,** while the monies that the writer gets are called the **writer's share.**

STANDARD CONTRACTS

For some reason, all songwriter contracts seem to be labeled "Standard Songwriter Agreement." However, I've never seen any two Standard Songwriter Contracts that looked like they were even distant cousins, much less twins. So don't take any comfort in the words at the top of the page. Here's really what to look for:

"Catch All." Some contracts say the songwriter gets 50% of the publisher's receipts from "mechanical, synchronization, and transcription income," or words to similar effect. The problem is that it is sometimes a *limited list* of monies from which the songwriter is paid. This means the publisher could be collecting monies that it doesn't

share with the writer, and this is definitely something to avoid (if you're a songwriter). And the problem isn't cured by adding everything you can think of to the list. For example, even the most complete list of income sources anyone could put together in the 1950s would have omitted income from videocassettes, since they didn't exist. The same would be true of arcade games that play music, computer software that reproduces copyrighted songs, and so forth, which not only didn't exist but weren't even contemplated. What you really need, at the end of the list of items, is a **catch all.** This is a phrase that says the writer gets 50% of "all other monies not referred to in this agreement." Often, you'll find the contract states just the opposite—that the writer is *only* entitled to a share of monies set forth in the contract. So cross this out, and add your "catch all." (Tell them I said you have to have it.)

Share of Advances. Most contracts also say you don't share in any advances the publisher may get. In most instances, this is legitimate—if the publisher gets an advance for its entire catalog of songs (of which you're only a part), you really have no right to share in that advance until your song has earnings that are used toward recoupment (see page 101 for what recoupment is). There's no way to know whose songs will earn back the advance, and thus there is no reasonable way to allocate the advance to a particular song until royalties are earned.

The exception to this is an advance paid specifically for your composition. One example is when a publisher issues a license at less than the statutory rate and gets an advance (or guaranteed payment for a certain number of units), *for one particular song.* (We touched on this on page 219.) Since this advance or guarantee is recoupable only from your song's earnings (and doesn't have to be repaid if there are no earnings), you should get your share of it when the advance/guarantee is paid to the publisher. So add language saying you *do* share in advances and guarantees which are specifically for your composition.

No Playing Footsie. If the publishing company is affiliated with a record company, you want to make certain they don't issue "sweetheart" licenses (i.e., licenses at less than customary rates) to their own record company. In other words, you don't want them playing footsie with their sister companies at your expense. For example, they might license your songs to their company at half of the statutory rate. Sure, their publishing company makes less (it only gets its share of a smaller amount), but the record company more than makes up the loss, and you don't.

"At Source." It's also important (and again cheap insurance) to make sure your *publisher's deals* with its subpublishers are all "at source" (see page 242). You have no right to have your *writer's share* computed "at source," because that would eliminate or radically reduce the publisher's participation. But you should make sure the publisher's deals are "at source," so that the *publisher's* income (in which you share) is the largest possible amount. This is especially so when the publisher owns a number of publishing companies around the world.

PERFORMANCE MONIES

As we discussed on page 232, unlike all other forms of income, the performing rights societies pay songwriters directly (that is, they don't pay the publisher, who in turn accounts to the writer). Indeed, the societies are so protective of a writer being paid directly that they won't honor an assignment of performance royalties by the writer. In other words, if the writer tries to sell his performance monies, the society will simply refuse to pay the buyer and continue paying the writer. (There is an exception for assignments of performance monies to a publisher who has paid the writer an advance, and for assignments to a bank securing a loan, but these assignments are limited to the amount of the advance or loan.)

Because the writer is paid directly, all songwriter contracts say the writer doesn't share in any performance monies received by the publisher. And since the performing rights societies are collecting DART monies, these are covered under the same provision (see page 245). Without this language, the writer would get all of the writer's share (from the society), and a part of the publisher's share as well. It's a good idea, however, to provide that, if a society no longer pays writers directly, the publisher must share its receipts. This could happen someday (see page 234).

PRINTED MUSIC ROYALTIES

As we discussed on page 236, printed music consists primarily of single-song sheet music and multisong folio books.

Structure of Business

There are only four major manufacturers of secular printed music in the United States these days, namely Warner/Chappell, Columbia Pictures Publications, Hal Leonard, and Cherry Lane. This means that, unless your publisher is one of these companies, it will be licensing print rights to one of them. Thus, in songwriter deals with publishers who license out these rights to a printer, it would be eminently logical for the writer to get 50% of the publisher's licensing receipts. Logic, however, has never been a major impediment to the music business, and for some twisted historical reason (guess who it favors), print music royalties are expressed as either a percentage of the retail or wholesale price (on folios), or in pennies (for sheet music).

Sheet Music

When we get to single-song sheet music, we really enter the Twilight Zone. For at least the past thirty years, sheet music royalties have hovered in the range of 5¢ or 6¢ per copy. Occasionally some superstars get as high as 10¢ to 12¢, and the publishers act as if this is removing their eyeteeth. If you recall from our earlier discussion, however (on page 236), the publisher gets 20% of the marked retail price, which today is about 70¢.

Why the songwriter gets such a small amount of the sheet music pie bewilders me. I've been told by major publishers it's because they have **favored nations** (meaning a contract that says its rate goes up if anyone ever gets more) with a number of old writers, and that raising the pennies for the new guys would cost them a fortune on the older deals. (Favored nation clauses can be in any kind of agreement, not just publishing.) But whatever the reason, this practice is soundly entrenched in the business. There is some comfort in the fact that sheet music doesn't represent a significant amount of money anymore, so it's tough to get too excited about it in absolute dollar terms. Still, it's a rip-off.

Folios

With regard to folios, remember the printer pays the publisher from 10% to 12½% of the marked retail price (see page 236). Most songwriter agreements pay the writer 10% of *wholesale* (you can kick it up to 12½% with a bit of clout), which approximates 50% of the publisher's receipts. However, to my knowledge, none of the major print houses accounts to publishers on the basis of wholesale, so most publishers merely split their income and call it good. Remember to allow pro-ration only on the basis of copyrighted, royalty-bearing songs (see page 237).

Name and Likeness

In addition to the writer's portion, if you ask, most publishers will give you 5% of wholesale for use of your name and likeness in a personality folio (see page 236), which is about half of the publisher's receipts. You can often hold out for the full 5% of *retail* the publisher gets, arguing this payment is for your name and likeness, and the publisher shouldn't share in it.

Charges Against Royalties

Often a publisher pays the costs to create a **demo** of your song. A demo is an informal recording made solely for the purposes of pitching a song to artists (similar to those for record deals, discussed on page 117). It is usually made by an unknown singer (or the songwriter), accompanied by one or two instruments (which, since the advent of synthesizers, can sound like the London Symphony Orchestra). The publishers try to charge 50% to 100% of the demo charges against the writer, and as your bargaining power increases, this amount decreases, ending up at zero.

No songwriting agreement should charge you for anything other than the following: (1) demos; (2) collection costs (monies spent by the publisher to collect your song's earnings, such as Harry Fox fees (see page 220) and the cost of chasing deadbeats who don't pay); and (3) subpublishing fees (see page 240).

All other costs of administration, copyrighting, advertising, etc., should be borne by the publisher. This is their cost of doing business and the reason they get 50% of the income. (When you share in publishing, you're charged with much more. We'll get to that on page 275.)

Accountings

Publishers typically account and pay within sixty to ninety days after the close of each calendar semiannual period (June 30 and December 31). Some superstar songwriters get quarterly accountings, but this is rare. A quarterly accounting comes after each calendar quarter, meaning March 31, June 30, September 30, and December 31. The advantage, of course, is that you get your money earlier.

Contracts typically limit the period in which you can object to your accounting statements, and most first drafts say you have to object within one year or you lose your right to do so. You can usually get this extended to at least two years, and often three. Beyond that is rare.

The other considerations about statements, auditing, etc., are the same as for record deals, which we discussed on page 163.

DART MONIES

As we discussed on page 245, DART monies are paid to writers and publishers based on the sale of digital audiotapes and recording equipment. Since ASCAP and BMI are collecting for the writers, these monies are treated like performance monies and not subject to publishers' sticky fingers (see page 232 for why performance monies don't get to the publisher).

ADVANCES

The advance for a single-song agreement is usually not very significant. It ranges anywhere from nothing (the most common) to $250 or $500, if we're talking about unknown songwriters and no unusual circumstances (such as a major artist who is committed to record the song, which of course changes the whole ballgame). Major songwriters rarely sign single-song agreements other than for films (which are another story entirely, as we'll discuss on page 394); if they own their own publishing, they keep the song, and if they don't, they're probably under a term songwriter's agreement. Significant advances are paid under these term songwriter agreements, which by coincidence is our next topic.

TERM SONGWRITER AGREEMENTS

A **term songwriter agreement** is just like a record deal except that, instead of making records, you agree to give the publisher all the songs you write during the term. In a sense, it's also like a bunch of single-song agreements hooked together, because it's similar to signing a single-song agreement for each composition when it's created. The difference is that there is one overall contract which sets out the terms on which each song will be delivered.

Term

The term of the agreement (the period during which you must assign over everything you write) is usually one year, with the publisher having two to four additional one-year options. If it's tied to a recording agreement (i.e., if it's with a publisher affiliated with your record company), it may simply adopt the same term as the record deal. If it's tied to delivery of songs (which we'll discuss in a minute), it may have a flexible term ending after delivery of the required songs (like record deal terms, as we discussed on page 119). Note the term only denotes the period during which you exclusively agree to *deliver* your songs—the songs you deliver are owned by the publisher for the life of the copyright, which of course extends far beyond the term. (As we'll see on page 268, however, this is sometimes negotiable.)

Advances

Term songwriter agreements almost always require the publisher to pay advances to the songwriter. Historically, "true songwriters" (meaning songwriters who don't come with access to someone who uses their songs, as opposed to, for example, a writer who is also an artist or producer, or someone who writes regularly with well-known performers) received weekly advances. This is still the practice in Nashville, but it's not so easy for true songwriters to get these deals in rock and roll. If you do get such a deal, new writers signing to a major publisher might get an advance of $350 per week or so, and less if they sign to a smaller publisher. (Don't get discouraged if you're a true songwriter—there's always a need for good talent. And there are true songwriters who make multimillions of dollars per year writing hits for other people.) If you're an established writer, the advances are based on some historical analysis, plus whatever additional "gouge" factor you can leverage. These advances can range from $500 to several thousand dollars per week, and up. Some superstar writers get hundreds of thousands of dollars per year.

More common these days is a deal based on songs being recorded and released. In other words, the publishers have become less interested in what I called "true songwriters" in the prior paragraph, and more interested in people who have the ability to use songs or access someone who can use the songs. For example, if you're an unsigned artist and songwriter, a typical deal might be $15,000 on signing, another $15,000 when you secure a record deal, and another $20,000 to $30,000 upon release of the album. There are often further advances at certain U.S. sales levels, such as an additional $25,000 at sales of 150,000 albums, and another $25,000 at sales of 300,000. Also, the publisher may help you get a record deal, since that enhances their position as well. If you don't get a record deal within a period of time (usually twelve to eighteen months), the publisher has the option to require you to deliver a minimum number of songs (around ten to twelve) over the coming year, and it pays advances for these (in the range of $15,000 to $25,000 for the year, paid quarterly).

If you do get a record deal, as noted above, the advance on release of the first album is a set amount. If you ask, you can often get a "formula" for advances on release of future albums. The formula is similar to those used in record deals, but based on your earnings during the prior twelve months. (See page 113 for a discussion of formulas in record deals.) Here's a recent deal where the advance for the second album was 75% of the earnings during the first year after the release of the first album, less the unrecouped balance, and with a floor and ceiling. This is the structure:

Formula: ⅔ of one year's earnings, less deficit, but not less than the floor or more than the ceiling.

	Floor	Ceiling
Album 1	$ 75,000	(Not applicable)
Album 2	$100,000	$200,000
Album 3	$125,000	$250,000

Under this deal, if the writer earns $60,000 during the first year, meaning only $60,000 of the $75,000 is recouped (and he is thus $15,000 unrecouped), his advance for the second album would be $25,000: ⅔ of $60,000 (which is $40,000) less the unrecouped balance ($15,000) equals $25,000. Since he has a floor of $100,000, however, he gets a $100,000 advance (because the formula result is lower than the floor). If he earns $120,000 (and thus recoups) during the year, there is then no deficit to be deducted from the ⅔-of-earnings formula, and he gets ⅔ of the $120,000 earned, or $80,000. If he earns $600,000 in the year, he would only get the ceiling of $200,000 for album two, because ⅔ of $600,000 ($400,000) exceeds the maximum ($200,000).

As discussed in the record section (see page 108), new artists for which there is a bidding frenzy can command deals that used to be reserved only for artists with track records. The same is true for publishing. For example, where an artist is the fox with a bunch of hounds yapping behind, bids of $200,000 to $300,000 per album are not uncommon. Indeed, these deals often commit the publisher to more than one album, and can thus get into the million dollar plus range. Since publishing pays much less than record royalties, these are quite astounding sums.

Delivery Requirements

Advances are sometimes geared to delivery of songs. The problem with this structure is that songwriters (shocking as it may seem) have been known to throw together a batch of crummy songs for the sole purpose of satisfying a delivery requirement and getting an advance. So publishers want to approve each song before they allow it to satisfy the delivery requirements. Publishers may also gear the advances to a certain number of songs being recorded and released. As noted above, if you're a recording artist, your advances may be specifically tied to how many of your compositions end up on your album, and the advances (at least the bulk of them) may not be payable until your album is released. There will also be a requirement that you have a minimum number of songs on the album, or else the advance gets reduced. For example, if your deal requires you to have ten songs on the album, but you only have five, you would get 50% (the ratio of the five songs you actually had to the ten you were supposed to have) of your advance.

If you have a song-delivery requirement, be sure to add a formula saying that fractional compositions count toward the delivery requirement in proportion to your ownership. For example, if you deliver half the publishing of a composition (because you only wrote half the song; see page 263 for an in-depth discussion of this), it should count as one-half of a song for your delivery requirements. Most forms don't provide this, and the net effect is that you get no credit whatsoever for fractional songs. Since these little guys earn money just like the others, there's no reason you shouldn't.

Prior Songs

Most "standard" term agreements have an innocuous-looking provision that quietly picks up all of the songs you have written *before* the term of the deal. Unless this is something the publisher specifically negotiated for, resist such a clause, or at least get paid for these songs with an additional advance.

Record Deal Tie-Ins

As noted on page 132, independent production entities like to grab your publishing when they sign you to a record deal. If there's any possible way to resist this, I strongly urge you to do so. Most of the time these entities aren't real publishers, but are rather just looking for another way to make money from you. If you're going to give up your publishing, it should ideally be to a fully staffed publisher (see page 216). These folks can add real value to your songs, by teaming you up with creative co-writers, helping you write for existing artists, and otherwise forwarding your career as a songwriter. The independent label publisher often just makes a deal with a major publisher, under which the major administers your songs (something you could do directly, and for which the independent takes a nice chunk of change by being in the middle), or worse yet, they sometimes do nothing but sloppily collect your money. This scenario isn't always the case—sometimes the independent advances you its own money, helps you creatively, professionally administers your songs, and thus brings a real benefit to the party. But unfortunately this is the exception.

If you must give your publishing to an independent, then, in addition to the normal publishing deal points we're discussing in this chapter, ask for these:

1. Try to keep control of your publishing, and merely pay them a piece of the income. (You'll lose this; they won't trust you to pay them. Also, publishing isn't as valuable for them to sell if they haven't got the administration rights.)
2. Try to limit their participation to mechanical royalties from your recordings. This means they wouldn't share in performance monies, print, etc., and they wouldn't share in any money (even mechanicals) from recordings of your songs by other artists. Your argument is that they're getting publishing only because they're the record company, and are thus involved only in generating mechanicals. This is very hard to get.
3. If you lose number 2, agree to let them share in all earnings (not just mechanicals), but only of those songs recorded by you as an artist. Ideally, you should also limit them to the *earnings of your recordings* of the songs. In other words, if you record a song that becomes a hit, and it's then recorded by three other artists, they would share in the earnings from your version but not the other artists. (There are some allocation problems connected with this, as we'll discuss on page 278.) If you can't get this, at least try to exclude the earnings of songs not recorded by you.
4. No matter how you do with the above, try for all the points in paragraphs numbered 1 through 4 of the next section (for majors).

Sometimes you may make a deal with a major and at the same time make a deal with its affiliated publisher. The majors almost never require you to do this, so you make the deal only because you think it's good for your writing career. The following points deal with these kinds of arrangements, but they're applicable to independent record/publishing situations as well:

1. Try to get advances for your publishing in addition to your record advances.
2. Since they share in publishing, ask them not to reduce the mechanical rate they pay you (as a record company) for your songs (see page 221). You should get this from a major, but the independents will argue the distributing record company forces this reduced rate on them, and they want the maximum mechanicals just like you. Both of these arguments are true, but try it anyway.
3. Be sure they can't exercise an option under your publishing deal without also picking you up as an artist. The argument is that you're only giving them publishing because they're making you a record deal, and if that's no longer true, they should get their hands off your songs. (Unless you're getting fat advances under the publishing deal, you probably don't care if they pick up your record option and drop the publishing deal.)
4. *Never* let them cross-collateralize your record and publishing deals (see page 104 for what cross-collateralization is). This is not customary, but it's done. Remember the language about cross-collateralizing "this or any other agreement" between you and the record company (see page 105)? It could pick up a publishing deal as well, because often it's the same parties to both contracts.

Bluntly, if you're dealing with independents who can muscle your publishing, it means your bargaining power is close to zip. So there's not a lot of room. But at least give 'em a good fight, and *never* give up points 3 and 4. **NEVER.**

POP QUIZ

Now that you have carefully digested all of the above, here's a pop quiz:

What is a major source of money that a publisher can't (normally) use to recoup its advances? (Answer on page 269.)

If you're on the *Fast Track,*
go to chapter 19 on page 270.
Everyone else, keep movin'.

COLLABORATION (TWO OR MORE SONGWRITERS)

One provision to be especially careful of is the one that concerns your writing with other people (people you write with are called **collaborators**).

Most of the older term songwriter agreements, and a good number of the ones currently used, take the strong position that the publisher gets 100% of the copyright and publishing (meaning both your share *and* the collaborator's share) of compositions you write with other writers. This is virtually impossible for you to do. It requires you to bind somebody you have no control over and who may not want to be bound. Even worse, it may be someone who *can't* be bound because they already gave these rights to another publisher. In fact, if your collaborator has this same requirement in their term deal, *they* are obligated to deliver 100% of the composition (including your share) to *their publisher*.

Obviously two people can't each own 100% of the same horse. So as a practical matter, this gets worked out between the two publishers, by either splitting the copyright and administration between them (see page 270) or, if there are going to be a number of songs written by the same two people, alternating administration rights. In other words, one publisher gets administration of the first song, the other publisher gets to administer the second, and so forth.

Many of the newer forms adopt a compromise position, which says you must deliver no less than 50% of the song to your publisher. This works fine if you've written 50% or more of the composition, but it's not so hot if you've written less than 50%. In that situation, your publisher takes part of your *writer's* royalties to make up the difference in income between the publishing they actually get and 50%. For example, if you wrote 25% of a song and delivered 25% of the publishing to your publisher, your publisher would take *all* of your songwriter royalties. This is because 25% of the publishing, plus your entire 25% of the songwriting royalties, equals the same dollars the publisher would get if it had 50% of publishing at the outset. This is easier to see using money:

For every dollar received, 50¢ belongs to songwriters (songwriter's share) and the remaining 50¢ is divided among the publishers (publisher's share). Since your publisher has 25% of the publishing, your publisher's 25% of the 50¢ share is 12½¢, and your 25% of the writer's 50¢ is also 12½¢. However, the contract says your publisher must get at least 50% of the publishing (which equals 50% of the entire 50¢ publisher's share, or 25¢). Since it only has 12½¢ (25% of the publisher's 50¢ share), the publisher takes all of your writer's share (which is also 12½¢), to equal the 25¢ (50% of the publisher's 50¢ share) that you promised. This has the net effect of meaning you will make little (or nothing, in this example) for your collaborative efforts. Such a situation does not make for a healthy career, and it certainly turns you off collaborating.

Because of this, the most you should do is agree to deliver that percentage of publishing which equals your percentage of the writer's share. In other words, if you have written 25% of a song, you should only agree to deliver 25% of the publishing; if you wrote one-third, 33⅓% of the publishing, etc.

How Are Songs Divided?

Traditionally, 50% of a song goes to the writer of the music, and 50% to the lyricist. No muss, no fuss. So if one person writes all of the melody, and one person writes all the lyrics, they each get 50% of the song. If two people equally write the lyrics, and one person writes the melody, then the lyricists each get 25% of the song, and the melody writer gets 50%. You get the idea.

There has been a trend in the last few years, however, to credit the people creating the **track** in this formula. The track is the background rhythm and instrumentation, on which the melody and lyrics are laid. Unfortunately, there are no hard and fast rules about how a track gets treated. It's usually negotiated by the parties at the time, depending on their sense of who contributed what to the song. I've seen deals where the track gets one-third, with the melody and lyrics each getting one-third, and I've also seen deals where the track merely becomes part of the music/melody side of the equation. So sit down, slug it out, and have the survivor call me.

Writing Teams

If you write with one particular partner on a continual basis, and your publisher is signing both of you, there are some special points of concern. (If you don't regularly write with a partner, you can skip to the section on **creative controls** on page 266). The writing team issues are:

Advances. Despite what your first thought might be, the advances don't double for a writing team. The reason is rather simple—even though there are two of you, you're each only writing one-half of a song, and so the total output is about the same as for one person.

Delivery Requirements. By the same token, if you have a song delivery requirement, that shouldn't be increased either.

Cross-Collateralization. If the publisher hands you one contract for both of you to sign, listen up. You want to make *absolutely certain* that you each have a separate account for your earnings and advances, and that your two accounts are *not* cross-collateralized (see page 104 for a discussion of cross-collateralization). If you always split the songs 50/50, and get equal advances, this point doesn't make any difference—your earnings are going to be identical, as are your advances. But since that almost never happens, look at the result of cross-collateralization in the following instances:

1. One or both of you may occasionally write songs without the other (in which case you'll want to be sure those earnings aren't used to recoup the other guy's advances).
2. You might stop writing in the same ratio that you get advances (e.g., you take the advances 50/50, but on some songs you split the earnings 60/40 or 75/25). This means the advances get recouped unevenly (see the example below).
3. You may break up as a team completely, and begin writing on your own, in which case you absolutely don't want the other person's advances charged to your account.

Here's an example: Suppose you and your co-writer, Louise, are each getting $10,000 a year under a songwriting agreement. At the end of year one you have written a number of songs on a 50/50 basis that have earned a total of $5,000, and each of you has been credited with $2,500 in royalties. This means you are each $7,500 unrecouped. Now, you write a song by yourself, which earns $20,000 in royalties. If your accounts are not cross-collateralized, the $20,000 earnings recoup your $7,500 deficit, and the publisher pays you $12,500. *If your accounts are cross-collateralized, the publisher will deduct not only your $7,500 deficit but also Louise's $7,500 deficit.* Thus, out of the $20,000 your song earned, you'd only get $5,000 ($20,000 less your

$7,500 deficit and less your partner's $7,500 deficit). Since you didn't get the other $7,500 (your collaborator did), this will not sit too well with you, and has been known to break up otherwise excellent teams. So separate your accounts.

Separate Obligations. Another problem with signing one agreement is that you have to be sure your obligations are separate, and that you're not responsible for a breach by the other guy. For example, if your partner wrongfully terminates his or her agreement and walks out, you don't want to find *your* royalties being used to pay for the publisher's damages and/or legal fees in a fight with your co-writer.

Separate Contracts. On the other side of the fence, suppose the publisher hands you two separate contracts. The odds are they won't be cross-collateralized (although you should always make certain that they aren't). But does that solve everything? Not really. The problem with two contracts is that, at option time, the publisher may decide to drop one of you and keep the other, effectively breaking up your team. Thus, be careful to provide that the publisher can't do this. If the publisher continues with one agreement, it must continue with both.

These problems are easy to fix if you ask up front, but can be an enormous pain if you forget. So don't.

CREATIVE CONTROLS

Moral Rights

In a number of countries outside the United States, there is a legal concept known as **moral rights,** or by the snooty term **droit moral** (which in French means "moral rights," and in Czech means "no parking"). The concept is that an author can stop any mutilation of his or her work, even though they may have parted with it long ago. For example, the creator of a painting (even though it has been sold four or five times) could stop someone from cutting it into smaller paintings, drawing mustaches on it, etc. Similarly, the author of a musical work can stop substantial changes in the music or lyrics.

Contractual Approvals

The United States has never recognized a moral rights concept for music (although there is a limited one for art). Accordingly, to the extent you want any protection, you must put it in your songwriter/

publisher contract. You do this by saying the publisher needs your approval before it can do certain things like:

1. **Make changes in the music.**
   The publisher will normally say that's fine as long as they don't have to ask about simple changes merely to conform to the mood or style of a particular artist.
2. **Make changes in the English lyrics.**
   Again, this approval right usually excludes minor changes for mood or style.
3. **Add foreign lyrics.**
   If you have enough clout, you may be able to approve translations. This is much harder to come by, but it's worth fighting for because it's also a financial issue—remember, translations reduce your royalties (see page 243).
4. **Make changes in the title (in English).**
   Usually no sweat—just ask for this and you'll get it.
5. **Grant synch licenses.**
   If you have some bargaining power, you may be able to get consent to all motion picture synchronization licenses. (These are defined on page 238.) If you have a lot of bargaining power, you might also control television synch licensing, but this is much harder to get. If you can't get either, a compromise is to say the song can't be licensed for X-rated films, or for any scene in a film involving illicit drugs, sex, violence, or anything else that rings your particular bell.
6. **Use the song in commercials.**
   At best, you should have the right to approve any usage of your song in commercials. (If you have approval of synch licenses, you automatically control TV commercials. But this doesn't cover radio commercials because radio recordings aren't made under synch licenses, as we discussed on page 238.) If you haven't enough clout to control commercials entirely, you can compromise by requiring your consent to certain categories, such as alcohol, tobacco, firearms, political candidates, and my personal favorite, sexual hygiene products.

REVERSION OF COPYRIGHT

Smile whenever you hear the words **reversion of copyright,** because this will always be good for you (unless you're a publisher, in which case you can frown). This is different from the termination of copyrights under the Copyright Law, which we'll discuss later, on page 288, because reversion is a *contractual* provision, negotiated specifically. It means the publisher must give your song (copyright and all) back to you at some point in the future.

Conditions of Reversion

What should trigger reassignment? The best (short of the automatic reversions discussed below) is that the song reverts to you if it's not recorded and commercially released. If you really have bargaining power, you can say you get the song back unless the recording is by a major artist (or at least on a major label) and/or achieves a certain chart position (say Top 50). (The publisher of course can't guarantee you success; it can only agree to give back your song if it doesn't hit the target.)

In these clauses, be sure to require that the recording/release must happen within some time frame. Otherwise, the publisher can keep each song for the life of copyright, telling you every week that a recording is just around the corner. If it's a single-song agreement (rather than a term deal), the publisher customarily has from six months to two years after signing within which to get the song recorded and released. Try to break this into two parts—it must be recorded within six months (or twelve months) after signing the deal, and released within six months (or twelve months) after that. This is better for you, because it comes back sooner if nothing happens. For term deals, this period usually begins at the close of the deal, although songs delivered in the later years sometimes have longer time periods (because the publisher hasn't had time to work them). A typical provision is one or two years after the end of the deal, but no less than two or three years from delivery of a song.

The smaller your bargaining power, the less likely you'll be able to pull off a reversion. However, even at the most modest levels, you should be able to get a publisher to give your song back at some point (say four or five years after the term) if it hasn't been exploited. The theory is that the song is of no value to him or her on the shelf, but potentially could be to you in a new situation. This gets more difficult if the publisher has paid you an advance, particularly one that hasn't been recouped (which is probable if the song is unexploited). However, you may be able to negotiate an option to get the song back by repaying the advance (be sure to say you don't have to pay back an advance that has been recouped). The publisher will want to put a time limit on this right to repay (say a year or two after the first date the song can revert), but even with this limit, the option is a plus.

Be certain it's your *option* to pay the money back. You don't want to be obligated to buy back your losers, because all that does is guarantee the publisher against a loss.

Reversion of copyright for nonexploitation is something you should *always* ask for. You may not always get it, but you should *always* ask for it. Is it clear I mean *always*? Did I say *always*?

Automatic Reversion

When you move into the super leagues, you can ask for a reassignment of all compositions, whether or not they're recorded. Time frames on these usually run something like seven to ten years after the close of the exclusive term, and it is usually also tied to recoupment—in other words, after the ten years, the publisher has to reassign only if you're recouped. In this case, (1) take the right to pay the unrecouped balance (remember to keep it at your option), in which case you get the songs back sooner, and (2) be sure you get the songs back if and when you do eventually recoup, even if it's five or ten years later. Don't assume the contract will say either of these if you don't ask, because it usually won't.

Answer to quiz on page 262:

Performance monies. (See page 232 for why.) And maybe DART monies (see page 245).

19

Copublishing and Administration Deals

COPUBLISHING DEALS

A copublishing agreement is simply one under which two or more people share in the publishing of a song. Nothing more, nothing less. The variables are:

1. Whether all parties own a piece of the copyright (some may just have a right to income, with no ownership); and
2. Whether there is a sharing of the administration rights (the rights to issue licenses, collect monies, etc., which we discussed on page 213).

Unfortunately the industry terms of art in this area are not very precise. So for our purposes, I'm going to use the term **copublishing agreement** to mean a deal that lasts for the life of the copyright (whether or not there is a sharing of copyright ownership). If the deal is for a shorter term, I'm calling it an **administration agreement** (which is discussed on page 277) even if ownership is shared.

Because the labels are fuzzy, these are not universal definitions—some people refer to deals for shorter terms as "copublishing agreements" if they involve copyright ownership, and others call life of copyright deals "administration agreements" if there is no ownership. However, we gotta start somewhere, so I'm using these terms *only* to make the distinction of how long the deal lasts. This will keep us from getting lost in overlapping labels.

This first section will discuss only copublishing deals, meaning arrangements for the life of the copyright, whether or not there is shared ownership.

Parties

Copublishing agreements (again, meaning arrangements that last the life of the copyright) are usually made between two publishers. An example is the situation where two writers who are each signed exclusively to different publishers write a song together. In this case, the publishers of the two writers make a copublishing deal that defines the ownership, administration rights, and percentage of income belonging to each party. A copublishing agreement may also be tied to a songwriter's agreement, meaning that the songwriter assigns a song to the publisher (under a songwriter's deal), and the publisher simultaneously signs a copublishing deal to share the publishing income (and perhaps also the copyright ownership, but usually not the administration rights) with the songwriter. An example of this is a songwriter with substantial bargaining power who signs a term agreement with a publisher (see page 257) and insists not only on songwriter's royalties, but also on a share of the publishing income. Another example is a motion picture company that hires a songwriter to compose a song for a film and assigns back half the publishing to the writer. (See page 394 for film stuff.)

Non-monetary Deal Points

There are two major non-monetary points in these deals: ownership and administration.

Ownership of the Copyright. One of the major provisions of a copublishing agreement defines who owns the copyright and in what percentages. The actual ownership of copyright is not terribly significant, other than the fact that:

1. If your name is not on the copyright, you run the possibility that the owner could defraud you by selling the copyright to a third party in violation of your interests. The buyer might not even know you exist. If your name is on the copyright, however, this fact is registered with the Copyright Office. Thus the buyer is aware of you, and for the buyer to be certain he purchases *all* rights, he has to check with you before completing a sale.
2. If you didn't write the composition, there may be tax reasons why you would want to own the copyright, primarily dealing with the fact that it is a depreciable asset if you own it, and it qualifies for capital gains taxes. An in-depth discussion of taxes

is beyond the scope of this book (and possibly your pain tolerance as well. And besides, I gave up tax work for music years ago).

On balance, I would rather own a piece of the copyright.

Who Has Administration Rights? Remember that administration rights are the exclusive bundle of rights bestowed on the copyright owner (see page 213). When there is only one copyright owner, it's pretty clear who has these rights. However, when there is more than one, the rights of the parties have to be defined. We'll talk later (on page 282) about what happens when there's no agreement, but usually the parties negotiate this issue. When they do, it's customary to handle administration in one of several ways:

1. **One administrator**
    One party has the exclusive right to administer on behalf of all, and the other party (or parties) only has the passive right to be paid a share of income from the administrator, with no control.
2. **One administrator with restrictions**
    One party has the exclusive administration rights, but can't license certain usages without the other party's consent. This can mean that a consent is necessary for *every* usage, or it can mean only that a consent is required for certain specific areas (for example, there could be no usages in commercials without consent). We discussed examples of specific restrictions on page 267, in the context of songwriter deals.
3. **One administrator with direct payment to other parties**
    One party has exclusive administration rights, but certain monies are paid directly to the other parties. For example, performance royalties are paid directly by the performing rights society to each copublisher, or mechanical royalties are paid directly by the record company to each party. Other monies, such as foreign, print, etc., are usually paid through the administrating publisher. While this arrangement gives no control to the recipients, it does save them time (they don't have to wait for the administrator to collect and disburse), and it assures they will in fact get paid (i.e., they needn't worry that the administrating publisher will go bankrupt, use the money to buy a duck farm, etc.).
4. **True coadministration**
    Both parties have the right to administer their own shares of the

composition. This concept is known as a **coadministration agreement** (and it can apply to both copublishing and administration deals). This and the system discussed in number 5 are the most common solution for songs cowritten by writers of approximately equal status.

5. **Coadministration with exceptions**
   Both parties coadminister (as in number 4 above), but one party acting alone can issue certain licenses. We'll discuss the details of this in a minute.

True Coadministration. The mechanics of coadministration (the arrangement described in number 4 above) work like this: Assume you and I are 50/50 owners of a song. Under a typical coadministration deal, I can issue a license for my 50%, but not for yours, and vice versa. This means no one can use the song without getting a license from *both* you and me.

Coadministration with Exceptions. A coadministration deal may have exceptions to the requirement that both of us are necessary to issue a license. If it does, the common ones include the following:

1. **Statutory rate licenses**
   Either of us can give a mechanical license for the whole song (both your and my shares) at the statutory rate (see page 210 for what that means). As long as it's not a first-use license (see page 211), this is something we would both have to do anyway (remember, the user can get a compulsory license if we don't, as discussed on page 209). Thus, some agreements say either party alone can issue these licenses, but that the record company must pay each party its respective shares. So if a deal allows this, I could give a license to Warner Bros. Records, but in it, I must require Warner to pay half the money to me and half to you.
   I usually object to this clause, on the basis that the other party may never know about the license, and thus it's hard to keep track of the earnings. I think it's better for each to issue their own license, and the record companies are used to getting licenses from a bunch of people for one song.

2. **Print**
   One of the parties might have an exclusive agreement for print music, while the other may not. In this case, it's not uncommon to license print rights only under that person's exclusive print deal. However, the deal should require the print company to pay

each party directly, and of course you shouldn't allow them to charge you with costs or advances unrelated to your song.

3. **Controlled compositions**

   If one of the parties is a performing artist, he or she will have a controlled composition clause in the record deal requiring such things as a mechanical license at less than statutory rate, a free license for promotional videos, and several other goodies that will affect the copublisher (see page 221 for a discussion of these clauses). The requirements of these clauses are usually spelled out in the copublishing agreement, along with a requirement that the copublisher comply.

How the Money Gets Divided

As you can imagine, dividing the money is where most of the shouting takes place. There are two aspects to this:

What's Divided? The first issue is defining exactly what gets divided. The money being whacked up is called the **net publisher's share** of income, and the definition of this is a major source of back and forth.

How Much Does Each Publisher Get? Once you've defined what you're dividing, you then need to deal with the question of how much each party gets. Normally this is directly in proportion to the contribution that each publisher's songwriter makes to the song. For example, if each writer creates 50% of the song, each publisher gets 50% of the rights (see page 264 for how songs are divided up). But this is not always the case. A publisher with superior bargaining power may have a disproportionately higher percentage of the publishing. For example, if you and I are publishers and our respective writers have written a song 50/50, but my writer is a major artist/songwriter, while yours is a new writer, I may tell you that I want 75% of the publishing, and that you get only 25%. Your writer still gets 50% of the songwriter's royalties, but I get the majority of the publishing. There is no logic to this; it's just brute force.

Net Publisher's Share

Now, let's take a look at how the *net publisher's share* is defined, since this is the crux of every copublishing deal. It's defined as *gross income* (which is everything the publisher receives, meaning writer's and publisher's shares combined), less the following deductions: administration fee, writer royalties, and expenses.

Administration Fee. The first deduction is an **administration fee,** which is a percentage of the gross income (writer's and publisher's shares combined), usually from 10% to 20%. It's always deducted first, because it's a percentage. (Let's repeat our golden rule together: "One who gets a percentage applies it to the largest possible number.")

Sometimes the administration fee is based on the gross monies after deducting the songwriter's royalties (meaning it's applied against our old friend the publisher's share). For example, 10% of the $1.00 gross is 10¢, but 10% of the publisher's share (gross less the writer's 50%) is 10% of 50¢, or 5¢. This practice, however, is really just playing word games. It's the same as cutting the percentage in half (10% of the publisher's share is the same as 5% of gross), but cosmetically it makes the publisher look like they're getting more. So it persists.

Administration fees apply only to a situation where one party is doing all the administration. In a coadministration agreement, neither party charges a fee because each collects only his or her own share of money. Thus neither publisher ever touches the other publisher's share, and there is nothing from which to deduct a fee (taking it from yourself isn't much fun).

An administration fee is, in theory, designed to reimburse the publisher for its indirect expenses of operation—rent, secretarial help, telephone, utilities, executive salaries, etc. In reality, it's just a function of leverage, because it gets eliminated as soon as the other party has any appreciable bargaining power.

Writer Royalties. The next amounts deducted are the songwriter's royalties. These were discussed on page 252.

Expenses. Finally, the administrating publisher deducts its **direct expenses,** which are usually spelled out in a list that ends with something like "and anything else we can think of." **Direct** means the expense is a specific item relating only to this song, as opposed to a general, unallocated overhead cost (like rent, secretarial, etc.). To my mind, there are only a few legitimate direct expense deductions, and none of them amounts to substantial monies. They are:

1. The preparation of **lead sheets.** A lead sheet (pronounced "leed" sheet) is a piece of paper with the words and musical melody line of a song. It's used for copyright registration and promotion. The use of lead sheets has diminished radically over the last few years. Until the 1976 Copyright Act, the U.S. government required lead sheets to be deposited with the Library of Congress (see page 305). Since then, the Library accepts cassette copies of songs, and publishers stopped going to the expense of lead sheets.
2. The cost of making **demos**—informal recordings, not for commercial release, made to promote the song (as discussed on page 256).
3. Copyright Office registration fees.
4. Collection costs, such as charges by the Harry Fox Agency, subpublishers' fees, and legal expenses to chase deadbeats.

Beyond these, I don't think anything should be deducted, and I've been pretty successful in limiting costs to the above. The other items publishers try to charge you are advertising, promotion, legal fees for contracts to exploit the songs, and "all other expenses concerning the composition." Hold firm against these, and don't wimp out.

If one party administers the entire song, it simply deducts these costs from monies due the others. In coadministration deals, however, everybody is collecting their own money, which means there's nothing to deduct from. In this case, the one who pays the costs sends a bill to the other publisher(s) for their respective share(s). For example, if a 50% publisher pays $400 for a demo, it sends a bill for $200 (50% of the $400) to the other 50% publisher.

It's also a good idea to require that costs can't exceed a certain dollar amount (say $500) without the consent of the other party, and be *absolutely sure* the publisher isn't taking these costs twice. I say this because, as we discussed on page 256, demo costs (and every once in a while, other costs) are sometimes charged against songwriter royalties. If so, they shouldn't be also charged against copublishing royalties. Observe: if a publisher pays $500 for a demo and charges it against the songwriter, it should not also charge it to a copublisher in computing the net publisher's share. However, many agreements would allow the publisher to do exactly this, which means it not only charges $500 against the writer, but also charges $250 against a 50% copublisher. Thus they would collect $750 for a $500 expenditure. A bit hard to justify on the grounds of fairness, but a good business to be in.

ADMINISTRATION AGREEMENTS

As I noted earlier, the prior section on copublishing only concerned agreements that divided rights for the life of the copyright. Now let's look at **administration deals,** which are arrangements that grant the right to administer a particular composition (or catalog of compositions) for only a limited period, which is less than the life of the copyright. (Remember, this is my definition, and *not* a strict industry term.) Administration deals are usually for periods of three to five years, although they may provide for extensions up to the life of the copyright under certain conditions.

The party getting the administration rights under the deal is called the **administrator,** and I'm going to refer to the party granting these rights as the **original publisher** (not an industry term).

Administrator's Share

Under an administration deal, the administrator takes an administration fee, reimburses itself for any direct expenses, and pays 100% of the balance to the original publisher. The administrator also customarily (but again not always) takes care of accounting and paying the songwriters and any other participating publishers. These monies are of course also deducted before remitting to the original publisher.

Administration fees range from 10% to 25% of the *gross* dollars (writer's and publisher's shares combined). Note (as we discussed on page 275) that a percentage based on the gross dollars is equal to double that percentage of the publisher's share alone. This means that an administrator taking a 20% administration fee is in reality getting 40% of the publisher's share of income. In other words, if a dollar comes in (including writer and publisher money), the administrator gets 20¢, which equals 40% of the 50¢ publisher's share. The original publisher gets the balance, less the songwriter royalties. It looks like this:

Gross	$1.00
Less: Administration Fee (20%)	–.20
Less: Writer's Share (50% of the $1.00)	–.50
ORIGINAL PUBLISHER'S SHARE	**$.30**

Here's another way to look at what everybody gets out of the $1.00 in this same example:

Each Party's Share

	Administrator	Publisher	Writer
Original Dollar Amount	$ .20	$ .30	$ .50
% of Gross	20%	30%	50%
% of Publisher's Share	40%	60%	0%

As noted above (on page 275), any direct costs are deducted "off the top" and are therefore borne by the administrator and original publisher in proportion to their share of publishing (60%/40%). Of course neither of them bears costs that are recouped from the writer's royalties.

Cover Records

Often administration deals give an incentive for **covers.** A cover is a recording obtained by the administrator, and the incentives can be one of several:

1. **The administrator gets an increased percentage on covers.**
   For example, if the administrator has a 15% administration fee, this might increase to a 25% fee on income from cover recordings.

   This is the fairest approach, because it rewards the administrator's efforts directly. But it's not as simple as it looks if the cover isn't the first recording of a work. The problem is that you can't always tell which version of the song is generating the money. It's easy enough for mechanical royalties—the royalty statements list the company and record number. But when it comes to performances, the songs are only listed by title, and there's no way to know which version was played on the radio (the original or the cover?).

   One way to deal with the performance issue is by using a formula based on the ratio that the mechanical royalties from the cover version bear to the mechanical royalties from other versions. For example, if the cover version earned $100 in mechanical royalties and all other versions earned $200 in a particular period (total of $300), then one-third (100/300) of the performance monies are treated as being earned by the cover. This works reasonably well, but it's subject to aberrations under circumstances where (1) the cover version was not a single, and thus generated very little airplay even though it was on a successful album (singles get substantial airplay, while album cuts usually don't, and little airplay means there's little performance money generated by that recording), or (2) the song generated enormous amounts of airplay (meaning lots of performance monies) but didn't sell records particularly well, which would skew the formula the other way. So I have sometimes written into deals that we would use the mechanical royalty formula unless it generates an unreasonable result, in which case the parties would negotiate in good faith as to an appropriate allocation.

2. **The administrator gets an increased percentage of all income.**

   Another possibility (although I don't like to agree to this) is that, if the administrator gets a cover, it gets an increased percentage of *all* earnings of the composition, not just those from the cover version. This eliminates the allocation problem, but it dents your pocketbook.

3. **The administrator retains administration rights to the covered song for an additional period of time.**

   For example, if the administration term is three years, the publisher might continue to administer covered compositions for a period of five years from a particular date (the start of the deal, the date of the cover recording, the end of the deal, your mom's birthday, etc.). I don't particularly like this, because it breaks up your catalog and makes it difficult to move the songs away. This is of course precisely why publishers like such a clause (as well as the fact that it gives them a longer period to participate in the money).

4. **The administrator gets copyright ownership for covers.**

   Getting a cover may even mean the administrator gets copyright ownership (usually 50%). If you do this, try to make sure it's an *extraordinarily* successful cover record. For example, require that it reach a certain level on a major chart. (See the next section for more on this.)

5. **Any combination of 1, 2, 3 and/or 4.**

6. **None of the above.**

What's Really a Cover? You want to be very careful about how a "cover record" is defined, because, as you just saw, the consequences can be significant. If the only result is an increased percentage of income from the cover itself, it's not such a big deal—either it's successful and you both make a lot of money, or it's a flop and forgotten. However, if a cover means the publisher gets copyright ownership or an increase on noncover earnings of the song, you must be very tough about what a cover is. Certainly you don't want the publisher's Aunt Esmerelda singing into a tape recorder to be considered a cover. But under many definitions, it would be, because the contract simply says "a recording." (Aunt Esmerelda's recordings are available over the Home Shopping Network, between the cubic zirconia and the porcelain carousels that play "Somewhere My Love.") At a very minimum, you want the recording to be a *commercial* one, and it must be *released* (it's amazing how many people neglect these simple criteria). If possible, you should add that the release has to be on a major record company label, and you should try to require that (a) the recording features a major artist (which you should define as an artist whose last album was gold, platinum, or better), and/or (b) the release itself must achieve some chart position, or else the song comes back to you. As to chart positions, the higher you get, the better—top 5 or 10 is ideal, but even the top 30 or 40 isn't bad. Make sure this is on a national chart such as *Billboard,* and not some schlock local station chart. Ideally it should be a singles chart (which means airplay), but album charts are second best. And it should be on a main pop chart, not country, gospel, etc.

NOW LOOK WHERE YOU ARE!

Here you are, only partway through the book, and you already know enough to answer the final homework assignment I gave after my nine-week music business class at USC Law School. Very impressive! So try your hand at it:

You are a record company and have just been delivered an album by Freddy London, produced by Marvin Lester. Freddy is signed exclusively to Warner/Chappell Music as a songwriter, and he wrote eight of the ten songs on the album. The other two were written by Marvin, who owns his own publishing under the name Marvelous Music.

1. Each time the album is sold, who is entitled to a payment from the record company? (Ignore any recoupment.) Clue: There are *five* parties, but you won't know the last one if you're not on the Expert Track.
2. Freddy makes a promotional video of his single. Who gets paid when the video is played on television?

Answers to quiz

1. Artist; producer; publisher (Warner/Chappell), which includes Freddy's songwriter royalties; publisher (Marvelous Music), which includes Marvin's songwriter royalties; and unions (see page 159).
2. The publisher and writer get public performance monies. (The record company may get a fee from MTV for the right to use all the company's videos, but this fee isn't broken down by video. Also, I never told you that, so you couldn't know.)

If you're on the *Fast Track,*
and if you're in a group,
go to Part IV (chapter 22) on page 309.
If you're on the Fast Track and you're not in a group,
go to Part V (chapter 23) on page 329.
Everyone else, read on . . .

20

Advanced Copyright Concepts

WHO OWNS THE COPYRIGHT?

Copyright ownership is pretty easy to determine if you sit down at the piano and knock out a little ditty by yourself. You, of course, are the owner, since you created it. But we lawyers wouldn't have much to do if it were all that simple, so let me show you how we've managed to fuzz it up over the years.

How About Two People Writing a Song Together?

Suppose you and your cousin Louie sit down and write a brilliant work together. Which one of you owns it?

As you probably guessed, both of you own it. But there's more to it than appears at first glance:

Who Controls the Song? Suppose you want to put it on your next album, and Louie wants to save it until he gets a record deal. Can he stop you?

The Copyright Law, in Section 201(a) of the Copyright Act, spells this out pretty clearly. It says that you and Louie have created a **joint work,** meaning it was created jointly by the efforts of two or more people (keep the puns to yourself). When you have a joint work, either of the authors/owners can deal *nonexclusively* with the *entire* composition, subject to the obligation to pay the other person his or her share of the proceeds. That means you can give all the nonexclusive licenses you want to record companies, film companies, etc., subject to paying Louie for his share of the song. And Louie can do the same. (In practice, there's usually a written agreement which spells out exactly what everyone can do, as we discussed in chapter 19. But now we're talking about what the Copyright Law says, without such an agreement.)

What Do You Own? How about this one: You and Louie sit down together to write a composition, and you write only the music while Louie writes only the lyrics. Suppose you don't like Louie's lyrics and want to take your music and write with somebody else. Can you?

My partner Payson Wolff once told me that creating a joint work is like adding water to a ball of clay and squishing it; it's not so easy to separate the two afterward. My partner Bruce Ramer uses the analogy of scrambling the white and the yolk of the egg together. As you may be starting to guess, the law isn't what you would intuitively think. It says that, even though two people create separate, distinct parts, they each own an interest in the *whole work,* not just their own contribution. Thus Louie owns half the music and half the lyrics, and so do you. So you can't just pick up and leave him. Even if you add new lyrics, he has a percentage of the song.

Does this sound like an absurd result? To some extent, yes; but if you get into dividing up works where the contributions aren't so easily defined as music and lyrics (which is 99% of the time), the alternative is even more impossible. Think, for example, about all the elements that go into making a film. What part is the screenwriter's? The director's? The producer's? The wardrobe designer's? Or what about a song where three people work on the lyrics, while two work on both music and lyrics?

What Makes a Joint Work Joint? By now you're beginning to see that this is more complex than it first appears. Which it is. But we're just getting warm—try this one:

A songwriting team consists of one person who lives in California and writes only music, and another who lives in New York and writes only lyrics. The California writer, totally on her own, writes a piece of music and mails it to her friend in New York. The guy in New York gets it several days later, sits down, and writes the lyrics. Is this a joint work? Did these two people create the composition together?

The law says, to have a joint work, you only need an author who *intends,* at the time of creation, to merge his or her work with someone's else's. In other words, when the musician wrote the music in California, did she intend to have lyrics written for it? That certainly is the case in our example, even though the lyricist never physically got together with the melody writer. (It's almost always a certainty that a lyricist intends to merge the words with music, since he or she probably has little call for poetry readings.) So, to have a joint work, you don't need to be in the same room (or on the same planet), and you don't even have to know each other, as long as there is an intent to merge the work at the time of creation.

If you want to see how this can get carried to the ultimate, get a load of the "Melancholy Baby" case (*Shapiro Bernstein* vs. *Vogel*, 161 F.2nd 406 [1947]). In that case, a guy named Ernie Barnett wrote a song with his wife Maybelle. Ernie wrote the music and Maybelle wrote the lyrics, and they sold the song to a publisher. Well, Maybelle's lyrics were apparently pretty awful (a lot of "moon" and "June," I'll bet), so the publisher tossed them out and had a new set written by a total stranger, George Norton. The result was "Melancholy Baby."

Based on these facts, the court held that "Melancholy Baby" was a "joint work" because, when Ernie wrote it, he had the intent to merge lyrics with it. The fact that the lyrics were ultimately written by someone he never met was irrelevant. And this result also meant the new lyricist held an interest in the *music,* too (although the case didn't deal with that issue). Nice coconuts, eh?

WORKS FOR HIRE

Remember when Teddy Kennedy hired someone to take an exam for him at Harvard? Well, the copyright law is one place where this is perfectly legal. It's done with **works for hire** (technically known as a **work made for hire** in the Copyright Law). A "work for hire" is a situation where you hire someone else to create for you, and if you observe the technical formalities, you actually become the author of the work insofar as the Copyright Law is concerned. And when I say "the author," I really mean *THE author*. It's as if the person you hired doesn't even exist (in the eyes of the Copyright Law), and indeed he or she needn't even be mentioned on the copyright registration form.

I suspect (but I really don't know, and would hate to disillusion myself by researching it) that "works for hire" developed to cover such things as fabric companies that printed copyrighted designs on their cloth, and wanted to be sure that the company (not the dork who actually designed the pattern) was the owner of the copyright. Seems reasonable enough.

Application to the Entertainment Industry

Here's an example of how it works in show biz. Suppose you are Walt Disney Pictures and you hire someone to write the theme for *Snow White* (I picked the example of a motion picture for a particular reason, as you'll see on page 286.) In this situation, Walt Disney Pictures (the corporation) becomes the author of the work, and the person hired to write it disappears. Does this mean the writer won't get his or her name listed as the writer of the song (e.g., on sheet music, in the film, etc.)? Usually not; the real creator customarily gets credit. (But sometimes—for example, with jingles written for radio and television commercials—a creator doesn't.) Also, the amount of compensation paid to the real creator is normally not affected by this type of arrangement—most of the time they're paid exactly the same whether or not the work is "for hire." However, a number of important rights we'll deal with later (on page 288) are drastically different, so whenever you're creating a work for hire, be alert to the consequences.

Technical Definition

A work for hire can be created under the Copyright Law in only one of two ways, which are a bit technical. They are set out in Section 102 of the Copyright Act. (You can skip to the "Duration of Copyright" section on page 286 if technical things bore you. But try it first.)

1. If the work is made by an *employee* within the *scope of employment,* it is a work for hire. An example of this is the fabric designer I mentioned before.

   The test of whether there is "employment" is not the one used for the income tax laws, or in fact for any other type laws. The cases treat it as situations where the employer is actually "directing or supervising" the creation of the work, in a very specific way. (The major case in this area is *Community for Creative Non-Violence* v. *Reid,* 490 U.S. 730 [1989], in which the Supreme Court held that a Vietnam memorial sculpture was not a "work-for-hire" because the people who paid to have the work created did not exercise control over the details of the work, did not supply the tools, had no on-going employment relationship, etc.). Normally (although not always), a songwriter is given quite a bit of latitude in his or her creation. However, if a songwriter is given very specific instructions, and is supervised during the process, he or she might be considered an employee.

2. If not created by an employee within the scope of employment, a work can only be a work for hire if it is: (a) *"commissioned"* (meaning created at the request of someone); (b) created under a *written agreement,* and (c) created *for use in* one of the following:

(a) *A motion picture or other audiovisual work.* This is the most common area where songs are treated as works for hire—musical scores, title songs written for films, etc. Remember, these songs do *not* have to be written by employees. There only needs to be a written agreement saying they are works for hire, and that they are commissioned for use in an audiovisual work. (Note this category does *not* include phonograph records. Great job by the motion picture lobbyists; where were the record lobbyists?)

(b) *A collective work.* A *collective work* is a collection of individual works which, independently, are capable of copyright. Examples are an anthology of short stories; a magazine containing several copyrightable articles; an encyclopedia; etc.

(c) *A compilation.* A *compilation* is a much broader term than *collective work*, although is basically the same thing. The term *compilation* means a work made by compiling a bunch of things, and thus it includes collective works (where the parts are separately copyrightable). However, it also includes works where the compiled materials are not, such as a reference index to the Bible.

(d) *A translation* of a foreign work.

(e) *A supplementary work,* which is a work supplementing another work (clever definitions, these copyright guys, eh?), such as an arrangement of a song, an introduction to a book, etc.

Before we can discuss the dire consequences of something being a work for hire, you need a few more concepts. So, plug it into your memory bank (or put a paperclip on this page if your memory is like mine), and we'll get back to it later.

DURATION OF COPYRIGHT

Remember we said (on page 205) that a copyright is a *limited duration* monopoly? The next logical question is, "How long?"

HISTORY

Prior to 1978, the United States had this bizarre copyright concept, adopted in 1909 and not changed for almost seventy years (the new law was adopted in 1976 but not effective until January 1, 1978, to give those of us who work in this area a year to study it). I tell you about it because (1) it is still relevant for older copyrights, and (2) I had to learn it, so why shouldn't you listen to it?

Anyway, the important thing you need to know is that copyrights used to last for a period of twenty-eight years from publication of the work. (I could spend an entire chapter on what *publication* means and meant, but I'd like you to finish my book awake, so I'll skip it. Basically, it means "distributed to the public.") These copyrights were then renewable for an additional twenty-eight years (total of fifty-six years). (For you purists, I'm aware that some copyrights could be obtained without publication, but none of this stuff is the law anymore, so let's not get carried away with too much detail.) By the way, it used to be the law that, if you forgot to renew, your copyright was gone after twenty-eight years. However, in 1992, Congress passed a law stating that the renewal is now automatic, so there's no loss of copyright if you forget.

So the maximum copyright protection was fifty-six years. If you wanted to sell your copyright, you could sell the full fifty-six years' worth. You were, of course, free to sell much less, but the number of buyers dropped radically. Even if you sold the whole fifty-six years, however, there was one way you could get back the second twenty-eight years. If you signed an agreement transferring all fifty-six years, you automatically got back the second twenty-eight years if you did one little thing during the first twenty-eight years—die. (It's not for everyone, but it's had its fans.) If the author of the work died before the second twenty-eight years started, then the transfer was nullified and the heirs of the author got to renew the second twenty-eight years for their own benefit. If you didn't die, you were stuck with whatever agreement you made when you first sold the work.

Current Law

So much for the old stuff. As to works created after the effective date of the new Copyright Law (January 1, 1978), the duration of copyright is the life of the author plus fifty years. A lot simpler, yes? Well, how about:

1. A work written by two people. Whose life do you use to measure the copyright duration?
2. A work written anonymously or under a phony name (called a "pseudonymous work"). How do you know whose life to check on?

3. Works for hire. Remember, the author is the employer, who could be a corporation. And some of those suckers live forever.

Well, rest comfortably, because all of these have been taken care of. They work like this:

1. In the case of a joint work, the copyright lasts until fifty years after the death of the last survivor. So write all your songs with your five-year-old son.
2. Anonymous (no name) or pseudonymous (phony name) works last the sooner of seventy-five years from publication, or one hundred years from creation. *Creation* means the first time it's fixed in tangible form (written down or recorded). *Publication,* as I said, is a tricky little devil, but for our purposes just take it to mean the distribution of copies to the public.
3. Works for hire. Same as anonymous.

Once the copyright expires, the work goes into the **public domain** (also called **p.d.**), which means anyone can use it for free.

RIGHT OF TERMINATION

One of the best goodies given to authors in the 1976 Copyright Law is the **right of termination.** This concept, together with the concept of measuring copyrights by the life of the author plus some period of time, has existed in other countries for many years. (Heaven forbid we should do anything like the rest of the world, at least until sixty or seventy years later. But we finally caught on to it—and we'll no doubt keep it long after the other territories have abandoned it.)

So putting aside the sarcasm, the termination provisions say that, even if you make a stupid deal, the copyright law will give you a second shot—thirty-five years later. In other words, thirty-five years after a transfer, you can get your copyright back. The exact mechanics get a bit technical, so I've stuck them back on page 294 if you're interested. You can take your time in getting around to it, however, because you can't do anything about it until after the year 2000.

Termination and Works for Hire

Now you know enough to understand the consequences of something being a work for hire (see page 285). With works for hire, there are no termination rights because there has been no transfer—the real author never existed in the eyes of the Copyright Law, which means the one commissioning the creation owns the work as if they created it. Hence there's no transfer, and no transfer to be terminated. And giving up the right to terminate is a serious piece of business, so be aware of the consequences if you create a work for hire.

If you're on the *Advanced Overview* Track
and are in a group, go to
Part IV (chapter 22) on page 309.
If you're on the *Advanced Overview* Track
and you're not in a group, go to
Part V (chapter 23) on page 329.
Experts, keep rollin'.

"FIRST SALE" DOCTRINE

Remember how a copyright owner has the right to control the distribution of his or her work (see page 206)? One reason is that, if this right didn't exist, I could buy unauthorized, pirated copies of a motion picture and freely distribute them to the public. Since I wouldn't be duplicating the picture (my seller presumably did that), if the film company couldn't control the right to distribute copies, it couldn't stop me. Hence the scope of a copyright includes the exclusive right of distribution.

Now suppose I decide to have a garage sale and sell all of my college textbooks (which are copyrighted). Can the various publishers stop me because I'm infringing their right of distribution? Indeed, under the literal terms of the Copyright Law, they could do exactly that. But section 109 carves out an exception. It says the owner of a lawfully made copy of a work can, without the authority of the copyright owner, sell or otherwise dispose of the work. This is known as the **first-sale doctrine** because, once the copyright owner sells a copy of something (after the "first sale"), it can't control further distribution of that particular copy. Note this means I can't duplicate the books, or do anything else that would infringe on their copyrights. But I can sell them. So feel free to have a garage sale without guilt.

This provision also allows stores to sell used CDs, which generated a lot of heat a few years ago because some artists and companies don't like it (since they don't get paid). See page 290 for a discussion of this.

Right to Rent

The first-sale doctrine is the entire basis for the video rental industry. This is because, once a videocassette has been sold to the dealer, he or she is free to sell or rent it, without any further obligations to the film company that owns the copyright in the movie itself.

Record Rental

If this applies to movies, how about records? Can I set up a store and advertise: "Never Buy Another Record! Just come in and rent ours! And we'll even sell you a blank cassette at the same time!" It doesn't take a rocket scientist to figure out people can save lots of money by renting a record (particularly a CD) for $2.00, taking it home and taping it, and returning it to the store the next day. Under the terms of the first-sale doctrine, this was totally legitimate, and indeed beginning to burgeon as an industry. (In fact, it's a big business in Japan.) But you know it couldn't last here.

Enter the Anti-rental Bill of 1984, which states that records can't be rented. End of the record rental industry overnight.

A terrific story goes with this legislation. (I don't know first hand whether it's true, and I'd hate to spoil it by finding out it's not.) Apparently Senator Howard Nielson of Utah was instrumental in seeing the anti-rental legislation through. Walter Yetnikoff, the chairman of CBS Records, grew rather close to Senator Nielson in the process and, when it passed, Walter sent the senator a copy of the album *We Are the World* as a thank you. It was Walter's feeling that the senator truly understood the threat that taping of records presented, and was an industry friend. I'm told Senator Nielson wrote Walter a letter afterward, thanking him profusely for the *We Are the World*, and saying he liked it so much he had duplicated numerous copies and given the cassettes to his staff.

Used CDs

For a while, there was a lot of flap about the fact that record stores are selling used CDs. Garth Brooks, for example, took a public stand against the practice, and a number of record companies (for a short while) attempted to punish retailers that sold used CDs by withdrawing certain marketing goodies. For example, record companies give retailers money for "cooperative advertising" (which means advertising that promotes both the retailer and that company's albums), and the companies were withholding these funds from stores that sold used CDs.

Unlike vinyl discs and tapes, CDs don't deteriorate in any major way. So there's a thriving market for used CDs, which are virtually the same quality as new ones, but much cheaper. However, the record companies, songwriters, and artists are out of joint because they don't get paid for these resales. And there's also an unspoken agenda for this: someone buying a new CD can take it home, tape it and then sell it, in essence, "renting" the record. As we just discussed, the outright renting of records has been prohibited, but the First Sale Doctrine stops anybody from controlling resales.

While this practice was a political hot potato, selling used CDs is perfectly legal—songwriters can't stop it because of the First Sale Doctrine, and the record companies can't stop it because the Sound Recording Copyright (which we'll discuss on page 297) only prohibits unauthorized duplication, not the resale of an authorized copy. Some artist and record company groups have begun rumbling about a change in the law to stop it, or maybe to put a tax on used CDs, like the one on digital tapes (see page 245). But changing the law isn't as simple as you might think. For example, would it be illegal for someone having a garage sale to get rid of their CD collection? As of this writing, the legislative push has no particular momentum, and everybody's gone quiet.

THE COPYRIGHT NOTICE

Let me say a couple of words about the copyright notice. The notice itself is the © followed by the year of copyright (which is the year the work was first fixed in tangible form).

The copyright notice is much less significant under the 1976 Copyright Law than it was under the old law, because the consequences of leaving it off or making a mistake in it are no longer very serious. (Under the old law, it could cost you the entire copyright.) It's not worth getting into all the niceties, but you should know a few things:

1. In music, the copyright notice is significant primarily for printed music. This is because the law doesn't require notice on anything that is not a "visibly perceptible copy." Since you can't "see" a song by looking at a record or tape, there's no need to put a copyright notice on the song.
2. So why do you see copyright notices on albums? Good question! The reasons are:

(a) sometimes the lyrics are printed inside, and since they are "visually perceptible," you need a copyright notice;

(b) there is a copyright in the album cover artwork; and

(c) there is a sound recording copyright Ⓟ notice, which we'll discuss on page 297.

21

Even More Advanced Copyright Concepts

TERMINATION RIGHT MECHANICS

As noted on page 288, the 1976 Copyright Law lets you undo any deal thirty-five years later. For example, if you sell your song to a publisher, you can get it back after thirty-five years by merely sending a notice. Here's how to do it.

You can give a notice of termination no less than two, nor more than ten, years before it is to be effective, and the effective date must fall within five years after the end of the thirty-five-year period. To be more precise, if the grant of the work covers publication, which it almost always does, the right to terminate is effective on the sooner of forty years from the grant, or thirty-five years from publication. This protects you even if the work is never published.

This is easier to understand if we use some actual years. For example, if a copyright was transferred and published in 1980:

Year of Publication	Years in Which Termination Can Be Effective (5 Years After 35 Years from Publication)
1980	**2015 to 2020**
First Year That Notice Can be Sent (10 Years Before First Possible Effective Date)	Last Year That Notice Can Be Sent (2 Years Before Last Possible Effective Date)
2005	**2018**

If you really want to know the details of how this works, take a look at Sections 203 and 304 of the Copyright Act. Since it's not going to be significant until around the year 2000, however, you needn't rush.

Attempts to Avoid Termination

So what have all the publishers done? They've started putting in fancy clauses asking you to assign over this right to terminate, to give it up, to let them have the first chance to buy it, and several other creative solutions that haven't yet come down the pike. However, Uncle Sam anticipated all of these, and the Copyright Law says that nothing you do with the termination rights is valid until you actually have the rights back. The only exception is that you can deal with the guy who has the rights about to be terminated (but no one else) after you've sent the notice, but before you get the rights back. This gives him or her a head start.

EXTENSION RIGHTS

Extension Recapture

What *is* more exciting and relevant today is a little transitional quirk thrown into the law. (This section only applies, however, if you were writing prior to 1978, or are the heir of such a writer. If not, you can skip to the "Sound Recording Copyrights" section on page 297, or read this over for your general education.)

The 1976 Copyright Law says that the fifty-six-year duration of pre-1978 copyrights (remember the twenty-eight plus twenty-eight discussed on page 286) is extended to a period of seventy-five years. In other words, it added nineteen years to the fifty-six years that already existed. More important, however, it gave the author (or his or her heirs) the right to take back these new nineteen years. The recapture procedure is similar to that for termination rights of newer copyrights (the right to terminate after thirty-five years, which we just discussed in the prior section). It's done by a notice given no less than two years, not more than ten years, before the beginning of the nineteen years (i.e., before the end of the fifty-sixth year).

Here's an example: If a song was first published in 1960, the fifty-six years expire in 2016. This means that, beginning in 2006 (ten years before the end of the fifty-six years), and no later than 2014 (two years before), you can give a notice to be effective in 2016. After the effective date of the notice, the new nineteen years added to the copyright (2016–2035) belong to the author, or his or her heirs.

A few years ago, publishers began scurrying around to buy these nineteen-year terms from the authors or their heirs, and it looked like it was going to be a nice business. However, Congress gave the original owners (i.e., the original publishers) a nice perk, which is similar to the termination rights provision. The law says that, before the nineteen years actually come into effect, but after giving a termination notice, the person to whom the original grant was made can make a new deal for the nineteen years. However, no one else can buy the nineteen years until they actually start. Thus, because the original publisher has the ability to buy the rights at least two years before any outsider, it has an enormous advantage in getting them. So, unless the publisher has really been a jerk during the first fifty-six years (which is no small "unless"), it can usually keep the copyrights. And this business dried up.

The Mills Music Case

Another quirk of the termination/extension rights is that the original publisher can continue exploiting *derivative works* (see page 207 for a definition), but it can't create any new works. This derivative work exception is shaping up to be a loophole you can drive a truck through, based on a U.S. Supreme Court case involving the appropriately entitled song "Who's Sorry Now." (If you want to look it up, it's *Mills Music* vs. *Snyder,* 105 SCT 638 [1985].) In this case, the publisher (Mills Music) acquired the rights to "Who's Sorry Now" from Ted Snyder and two other writers. Snyder went to that Great Songbook in the Sky, and in 1978, his heirs exercised their right to terminate the last nineteen years. (So much for my theory that the initial publisher can hang on to the songs.)

After termination, Mills Music argued that all of the *records* it had licensed were derivative works, and therefore it had the right to collect mechanical royalties for sales of these records after termination. As you can imagine, Mr. Snyder's heirs took a contrary view. They felt these rights should come back to them, so they could then license the record companies (and get all the money). The decision flipped back and forth until it came to the U.S. Supreme Court (known to its friends as "the Supremes"). In a closely divided decision (five of the nine justices in favor, four opposing), the Supreme Court found that indeed the records were derivative works, and that the money from them went to Mills Music, the terminated publisher. Mr. Snyder's heirs had the right to money from future recordings, but not the existing ones.

Stay tuned to these extension recapture provisions; as the older copyrights tick on and terminations become more prevalent, there should be a lot of interesting law.

DIGITAL SAMPLES

A digital sampler is a machine capable of taking any guitar sound, drum sound, voice, etc., and making a perfect digital duplication. It can then be played on a keyboard, edited, etc. Unless you've been living in a cave for the last few years, you know that every rapper on the planet samples freely from other people's works. What started out as a minor practice of taking great drum sounds, unusual squeaks and groans (James Brown was and remains a special favorite of the samplers), has turned into a wholesale lifting of rhythm tracks, melodies, etc. For example, M.C. Hammer's "Can't Touch This" was a very close copy of Rick James's "Super Freak."

As with any new practice, everyone started out groping around for what kind of deals to make. In the early days, a lot of sampled records were released before anybody even tried to clear the rights, and the artists and companies often had an attitude along the lines of "If they catch me, I'll make a deal." And when they did catch them, the deals consisted mostly of throwing around a few bucks and buying out the rights.

Can you guess whose rights had to be bought out? The obvious one is the record company owning the sampled recording. But they aren't the only one whose rights you need. The publisher of the sampled musical composition must also be taken care of.

This "catch me if you can" attitude was first litigated in the case of *Grand Upright Music Limited* v. *Warner Brothers Records, Inc.*, 780 F.Supp. 182 (S.D.N.Y. 1991), which involved the rapper Biz Marky sampling Gilbert O'Sullivan's "Alone Again (Naturally)." See if you can guess how the judge ruled in this case by reading the first line of his opinion:

"Thou shalt not steal."

You guessed it—Judge Kevin Thomas Duffy of the New York Federal Court not only slapped the hands of the sampler, but referred the matter to the U.S. Attorney's Office for possible *criminal* prosecution! (As you'll see on page 306, intentional copyright infringement is a criminal offense.) End of the days of casual sampling.

Because of this case, everyone now treats sampling with the utmost care and respect. Record companies won't release a record containing samples without knowing that the samples have been cleared, and you as an artist should want the same thing. Clearing samples is a major pain in the rear end, because any one of these people can cause you to scrap the sample by being difficult. There's nothing in the law that requires anyone to let you use a sample, and thus any record company or publisher is free to make you pull it off your record. And if you're on a tight schedule and/or if it ruins your song to take it out, you won't be a happy camper.

Since there's no compulsory license for samples, you have to make whatever deal the rights owners decide to bless you with. If the usage is minor, and it's a little-known song, you might be able to buy out all of the rights for a flat fee. The range is usually from $1,500 to $5,000 for the record company, and about the same for the publisher. If the usage is more significant and/or the song is well-known, or you happen to hit an ornery rights owner, record companies may still give you a buyout, but the price can go up radically—I've seen costs of $25,000 and more. But publishers rarely give a buyout in these circumstances. Instead, they ask for a piece of the song. The percentage varies with how significant the sample is in the work, and it's usually settled after the publisher listens to the composition and negotiates a deal. If you've lifted an entire melody line, they might insist on 50% of the song; if it's a more normal use, the range is 10% to 20%. Publishers may also ask to coadminister their portion of the composition (see page 272 for discussion of coadministration agreements), and this means they have the right to stop you from granting a particular license. So you often lose control of your own song when you sample.

Even when you get over these hurdles and all the clearances are agreed, the rights granted are often only for phonograph records and promotional videos. If you want more rights, you have to go back to the record company and publishers. They will then be free to charge an additional fee or withhold their permission.

The lesson in all this is that putting a sample in your record is serious business. You may well lose control of your song and your recording when you do it, so think carefully about what it means. A moment of pleasure can mean a lifetime of pain.

SOUND RECORDING COPYRIGHTS

It may surprise you to know that, prior to 1972, the United States had no copyright protection for a sound recording itself. I'm now talking about the *sound recording*, and not the musical composition. Here's what happened:

The Age of the "Lawful Duplicators"

As I said, prior to 1972, nothing in the United States Copyright Law made it illegal to duplicate a master recording (other than the fact that permission was required from the owner of the musical composition, who was almost never the owner of the sound recording.) Thus, to take an easy example, suppose a group made a recording on Elektra Records of "My Country 'Tis of Thee" (or "God Save the Queen," if you're English), which is, of course, a public domain song (see page 288 for what public domain is). Prior to 1972 it was perfectly legal to set up a machine in your garage and begin manufacturing records from that recording without anyone's permission, and more importantly without paying the artist or the record company who invested the money to create the recording. (As a note for you purists, I am of course assuming that the group making the original recording did not create such an unusual arrangement of "My Country 'Tis of Thee" to be copyrightable as a derivative work [we discussed derivative works on page 207]. If this were the case, then the composition would have to be licensed from the publisher. Also, I'm assuming there's no trademark infringement, such as knocking off the Elektra Records name or logo.)

Avoiding the Wrath of Publishers

However, as you can imagine, there wasn't too big a demand for knock-off recordings of public domain songs—people were much more interested in the Beatles, the Rolling Stones, and other best-selling groups of the day. So how did the pirates get around infringing the copyrights in the songs? Since the artist often controlled the publishing and wasn't getting any royalties from the sale of these rip-offs, they certainly wouldn't give the pirates a mechanical license. So the duplicators used our old friend the compulsory copyright license (page 208).

Remember, once a composition has been recorded, the publisher *must* issue a license to anyone else wishing to use it in phonograph records. So the pirates went to the publishers, asked for a mechanical license for their unauthorized duplications and, when they were turned down (which was the case with legitimate publishers), they simply got a compulsory license and proceeded to pay the publisher. Under this guise, and seeking to slip through a loophole in the Copyright Law, the pirates blossomed into a multimillion-dollar industry at the expense of the recording artists and record companies who had invested substantial monies in making the recordings. Many of these sleazebags used names like "Pirate Records," or had a logo with a skull and crossbones, a pirate with a patch and a cutlass in his teeth, etc. Real class. (If you were going to give the music business an enema, this would have been the place.)

Antipiracy Legislation

This smelled like thievery (which it was), and the courts were beginning to stretch to find ways to stop the pirates, usually under state laws. However, it ultimately took an amendment to the Copyright Law to nail the coffin shut. In 1972, Congress enacted a full-fledged, legitimate Copyright Law provision dealing with piracy (which is now Section 114 of the Copyright Act). This prohibits the unauthorized duplication or dubbing of the *sound recording* itself, by creating a copyright in the actual recording. (This is in addition to a separate copyright in the musical composition.) It is imaginatively called a **sound recording copyright,** and is represented by the symbol ℗. Look for it on records in your collection.

Exceptions

Two of the most interesting aspects of this sound recording copyright involve what it did *not* protect. While it's clear you can no longer duplicate records without consent, the sound recording copyright did *not*:

1. Prohibit a "sound-alike" recording, no matter how closely you duplicate the original; or
2. Until recently, give the owner of the copyright any rights to collect public performance monies for playing the *recording* on the radio (as opposed to the publisher and writer of the song, who do get paid for this).

Let's look at these individually:

Sound-Alike. Nothing in the sound recording copyright stops you from hiring a singer to imitate the original artist, or hiring a band that sounds just like the original recording, regardless of how close you come. Of course, you must license the song, and you must disclose that the recording is not the original. If you didn't label your record as an imitation, you would run afoul of various trademark and unfair practices acts which deal with the proper labeling of goods (and thus stop you from defrauding the public into thinking they're getting the original when they're not). These are the same laws that stop you from calling a cereal Grape Nuts if it's not made by Post, even if it has exactly the same ingredients.

Public Performance. Due to recent changes with regard to this rule, public performance now deserves its own section . . .

DIGITAL PERFORMANCE OF MASTERS AND DIGITAL DELIVERY OF MASTERS

Congress recently changed the Copyright Law with something called the **Digital Performance Right and Sound Recordings Act of 1995.** Those folks in Washington sure know how to put a sexy title on something, huh?

The Digital Performance Act did two things that are interesting to the music business:

1. For the first time in U.S. history, it created a right for the *artist* to be paid when records are performed. That's the good news. The bad news is that the right is so narrow that you'll need a pair of tweezers to get any money out of it.
2. The Act extended the compulsory mechanical copyright license (see page 209 for what that is) to include the digital distribution of records. In other words, looking forward to the day when records will be sold by transmission over your telephone lines, or via satellite, and copied directly into your home computer or some other black box, the Act makes sure that the companies selling these transmissions have the right to use the songs in exchange for a compulsory license fee.

Let's look at these areas one at a time:

Public Performance Right for Masters

As we just discussed, the United States has never had a public performance right for *masters* (see above). Quite the contrary, when it passed the antipiracy law in 1972, Congress specifically said that it wasn't creating a right for the artist or record company to be paid when the recordings were played on the radio or TV, or otherwise publicly performed (like at a disco). This was true even though the owner of the *song* is paid for all of these.

Other countries of the world have routinely paid artists and record companies for the performance of their records (see page 185), and they earn substantial amounts of money from it. Because the United States had no such right, these other countries felt no need to pay Americans for overseas performances of their records, under the age-old government theory of "Why should I pay foreigners when I can have more money for my citizens?"

The United States has finally put its toe in the water of master public performance by amending Section 106 of the Copyright Act. Actually, it's only the tip of its little toenail, because the following are the only performances for which recording artists get paid:

1. It must be a *digital public performance*. And what's *digital*? Digital is music made by computers, as opposed to *analog*, which is FM radio, cable TV, and most everything else in use as of this writing. Suffice it to say that digital transmissions are a minuscule portion of the market today.

2. It must be an *audio-only* sound recording that's performed (meaning the artist doesn't get paid for performances of a master in films or TV shows).

3. You only get paid for *subscription transmissions*, which sounds like you have to be reading a magazine while AAMCO works on your car's transmission. Actually, a subscription transmission means the listener pays for the right to hear the station, as opposed to hearing it for free—such as radio in your car, over-the-air television, etc.

So after all those fancy words, artists will only get money from digital radio transmissions of their audio-only records, and then only if the listener pays to get the signal. This may someday be a hot item, shortly after hula hoops return, but today you can make more money opening a soft-drink stand.

Now that I've shown you how meaningless this is, I may as well tell you how people are going to get paid. Basically, two ways:

1. There's a compulsory license, which means that, under certain conditions, the owner of the recording *must* allow its performance for a set fee. (Remember, as we discussed on page 206, that without a compulsory license the copyright owner can prevent someone from using their work.) This license works exactly the same way that the other compulsory licenses work (see page 208).

2. If the transmission does not qualify for a compulsory license, then you get paid whatever you can gouge out of the user.

Compulsory License. How does a broadcaster qualify for a compulsory license? Under the amended Section 114 of the Copyright Act, it has to act like a radio station, as opposed to anything that remotely resembles a transmission for the purpose of the listener's copying it. These provisions distinguish performances from transmissions that are intended to be copied by the user, which someday will be another way to buy records. (Transmissions intended for the user to copy are discussed in the next section.)

The specific requirements to get a compulsory license are:

1. The transmission can't be **interactive** (in other words, it can't be "music on demand" or otherwise allow the user to decide what they want and when they want it)
2. During any three-hour period, there can't be more than two consecutive selections from any one album, or more than three nonconsecutive selections from any one album
3. During any three-hour period, there can't be more than three consecutive selections, or more than four in total, from the same artist or from any box set of recordings
4. The broadcaster can't publish the titles before the transmission happens
5. If the recording has encoded information about the title, artist, etc., that has to be transmitted as well

If the broadcaster qualifies for the compulsory license under the above, it pays statutory license fees. These are set by voluntary industry negotiations, or, if the two sides look like they're going to strangle each other, it's decided by something called the Copyright Royalty Arbitration Panel (I just noticed its initials are "CRAP"). The monies paid are allocated 50% to the record companies, 45% to the featured artist, 2½% to the American Federation of Musicians for nonfeatured musicians, and 2½% to AFTRA for nonfeatured vocalists (see page 75 for who AFM and AFTRA are).

As soon as any of you receive any money based on this public performance, please send me a letter so we can celebrate the occasion. But do it only if your distribution exceeds the price of the postage stamp. I don't expect to hear from any of you for awhile.

Voluntary Licenses. If the performance doesn't fall within the statutory license, then the publisher doesn't have to allow the song to be performed. Since publishers rarely turn their backs on money, this really means they can charge whatever they want. Which is a good thing if you're a publisher.

What kinds of uses fall within this? *Subscription transmissions* (see page 301 for what those are) that don't meet the requirements for a statutory license, such as *interactive transmissions* (meaning you can get specific music you want whenever you want it). Also, every other Tuesday in Tanzania is exempt.

As to voluntary licenses, note that the record company (the owner of the master) holds the rights and makes the deal. So, unlike the compulsory license, the law doesn't require the artist and nonfeatured musicians to be paid anything. This means the record company will keep all the money unless you have a provision in your recording contract that says you get a piece. So it's time to start adding one. (See also page 185 for a discussion of this.)

Digital Pizza Man

The second section of the Digital Performance Act deals with the delivery of music that is intended to be copied by the consumer. This is in Section 115 of the Copyright Act, and it provides a compulsory mechanical license for the right to distribute recordings of nondramatic musical works (see page 210 for what that means) by digital transmission. In other words, a digital transmission intended to be copied requires a mechanical royalty just as if the song had been sold on a CD or cassette. (See page 209 for a discussion of mechanical royalties paid for sales of records.)

Until the end of 1997, the compulsory mechanical license fee will be exactly the same as the fees paid when a cassette or CD is sold (see page 210 for how much that is). Beginning in 1998, all licenses will be set in accordance with an elaborate procedure that is basically identical to the procedure Congress uses for setting the statutory rate for digital public performances (see page 302).

Note that the digital delivery might also be a performance of the master (see the prior section) and of the song recorded on the master (see the new media section on page 376 for a discussion of this).

I realize this section is pretty complex, but remember that it's not going to be very significant for quite a few years to come. That's why I buried it back here in the most advanced section, so only you diehards would plough through it. Good going if you got this far!

REGISTRATION AND DEPOSIT

The Myth

As we discussed on page 206, the myth that you get a copyright by sending something to the Copyright Office is just that—a myth. You get a copyright by fixing the work in tangible form, and nothing more.

The act of registration gives you certain remedies you don't otherwise have, and thus you should always do it if you're going to commercially exploit your work. However, the failure to register doesn't affect the validity of your copyright and, if you're a beginning songwriter, it's probably not worth the money until someone bites.

The old trick of mailing a copy of the work to yourself actually does work. It has nothing to do with giving you a copyright, but it clearly establishes a date on which you had created your work. If you're going to do this, send it by certified mail and don't get excited and open it when it arrives; store it in a safe place, and let a judge open it if someone ever gets cute.

Penalties for Failure to Register

On the other hand, if your work is being commercially recorded (used in a film, commercial, etc.), you should register with the Copyright Office. If you don't, the following penalties apply:

1. You can't collect compulsory license royalties (see page 208).
2. You can't file an infringement action to recover damages or stop someone from using your copyright (see page 306). You can wait and register just before you file the action, but it's a better idea to take care of it as soon as you know there's going to be a recording.
3. If you don't register within five years after first publication, you lose the legal presumption that everything in the registration is valid. This legal mumbo jumbo basically means that if you do register within the five years, a court will assume everything in your registration is correct, and the infringer has the burden of proving it's not. If you don't, you have to prove it.
4. You can't recover attorneys' fees, nor can you get statutory damages (see page 306).

You get the forms you need to register by writing the Copyright Office at:

Information and Publications
    Section LM-455
Copyright Office
Library of Congress
Washington, D.C. 20559

For you techno-whizzes, you can reach them on-line at http://lcweb.loc.gov/copyright.

Deposit

A separate requirement from registration is the obligation to *deposit* copies of your work within three months after publication. If you don't, there is no loss of copyright, but there are penalties and fines. The purpose of this is to keep the Library of Congress overflowing with tons of crap that nobody has ever heard of, and the system works quite well. Under the 1976 Copyright Law, you can deposit either tapes, CDs, or sheet music for songs.

WHAT YOU GET WHEN SOMEONE RIPS OFF YOUR COPYRIGHT

When someone steals your song, they have **infringed** your copyright (meaning they've used it without your permission). What you can get is in many ways peculiar to the copyright (and also trademark) world, and works like this:

1. **You get the fair market value**
   of the use they made. For example, if they rip off your song in a commercial, and the song would be worth $25,000 if they had gotten a license, you can get $25,000.
2. **You can recover the infringer's profits.**
   This is not a common remedy and is extremely valuable. It means that if the sleaze has made a profit using your work, you can recover their profits, which may be more than the fair market value of the usage. (If you pick this remedy, you don't also get fair market value.)
3. **You can get an injunction,**
   which means the court "enjoins" (prohibits the infringer from using) the infringing work. If they continue to use it anyway, they're subject to substantial fines, and sometimes even jail.
4. **You can recover statutory damages,**
   which is a real copyright original. This is used where you can't prove actual damages—for example, your infringer not only was a thief, but also a lousy businessperson who lost money on your rip-off. Or maybe their profits were so well hidden that you couldn't find them. In this case, the court can give you anywhere from $250 to $10,000 for a single infringement (this is per act of infringement, and not the number of copies actually made; for example, putting out 100,000 records with your song on it is still only one act of infringement). The judge can raise this to $50,000 if it's a willful (intentional) infringement.

5. **The court can order the destruction or seizure**
   of any infringing copies. This is also not a common remedy.
6. **If the infringement is willful, there are criminal penalties.**
   An interesting bit of history is that the Marx Brothers stole some
   poor schlub's copyright for a radio show and were convicted of
   criminal copyright infringement.
7. **You can get your court costs**
   and, to a limited extent, your **attorneys' fees.** The latter is unusual, because you normally don't get attorneys' fees when you
   win a lawsuit.

PART IV

Group Issues

22

Groups

If you're a member of a group, everything in this book applies to you. But you also get a whole set of goodies that don't concern individual artists. Let's take a look at them.

GROUP PROVISIONS IN RECORD DEALS

When you're a group, there's a whole section in your record deal that isn't in an individual artist's recording contract. It deals with what happens when the group is no longer a group, or when one individual (a prima donna or the only rational member, depending on the side of the fence where you sit) decides he or she no longer wants to play with the others.

Key Members

First of all, most agreements will say a breach of the record deal by one member of the group is treated as a breach by all members of the group. This, in effect, means that if one of the members refuses to record with the others, the entire group is in breach. This is not such an unreasonable position if we're talking about the lead singer or main songwriter, but it's much less so if we're talking about a percussionist who neither sings, writes, nor knows what city he lives in.

To handle our percussionist friend, we who represent artists gave birth to the concept of a **key member.** Under this system, certain individuals are designated as "key members." If a key member leaves the group or otherwise breaches the agreement, the company can treat the event as a breach by the whole group and exercise its various options (which we'll discuss in a minute). If anyone else does, it can't.

This is something you have to ask for—no company uses a key member concept in its form agreements. Also, as you might imagine, working this out has been known to break up groups, because the people not named as key members tend to get their noses out of joint. Although, as you'll see, it isn't always so great to be a key member.

The Company's Rights to Leaving Members

What can the company do if a member (key or not) leaves the group?

1. All companies provide that, if a member leaves a group, the company has the option to his or her services as a solo artist (and of course as a member of any other group). Even when you have a key member concept, the company may want the right to pick up *any* (even non-key) leaving members. However, I like to argue the company really has no business (or usually interest in) keeping the services of non-key members, such as our percussionist. (This is also how you sell the percussionist on not being a key member—if he decides to leave the group, he can split from the record company and make his own deal, while the key member can't. But if the company insists on the right to pick him up as a soloist even if he's not a key member, it scraps this argument.)
2. The company also gets the option to keep the remaining members as a group (assuming, of course, there's not a total breakup).
3. The company has the option to terminate the remaining members, since the group is no longer the one they signed. Note that this means, if they don't exercise their option for the leaving member, the deal is over. Make sure only a key member's leaving can trigger this right.

Leaving-Member Deals

The terms of a leaving member's solo agreement are spelled out in the group's deal, and are almost always much less favorable than the deal for the group. The record company's position, which is understandable, is that the soloist is an unknown quantity, whereas the group was the reason for making the deal. Success is by no means assured—there are many cases of soloists who have left groups to fall flat on their faces (as well as those who have been more successful than the groups they came from). If the group is important enough, the soloist's royalty may be close to or the same as the group's, but the advance is always substantially less, and the commitment is usually for one album at most (sometimes only demos). As your bargaining power increases, so does your ability to negotiate these clauses, particularly if a member of a group has been emerging as the star, or had an earlier solo career.

TRIVIA QUIZ

Name the lead singers who have had solo careers after leaving the following groups:

1. The Doobie Brothers
2. Creedence Clearwater Revival
3. The Police
4. Traffic
5. The Commodores
6. The Band

Name the groups from which the following soloists came:

1. Don Henley
2. Stephen Stills (*not* Crosby, Stills, Nash & Young)
3. Neil Young (*not* Crosby, Stills, Nash & Young)
4. Eric Clapton
5. Bobby Brown
6. Phil Collins

(Answers on page 325.)

Deficits

Intimately related to all of this is the question of what happens to the group's deficit when a soloist sets out on his or her own (see page 101 for what a deficit is). For example, suppose a group breaks up and is $500,000 unrecouped. The company then picks up one member as a soloist, who sells millions of albums. Can the company take his or her solo royalties to recoup the group's $500,000 deficit? Conversely, if the group was recouped but the soloist is a flop, can the company use the group's royalties to recoup the soloist's deficit?

Many companies, at least in their first contract draft, take the right to do both these things. If you ask, however, they will generally agree that only a pro-rata share of the group's deficit can be charged to the soloist. For example, if there are five members of the group, only one-fifth of the deficit ($100,000 of the $500,000 in the above example) can be carried over to a solo deal. Conversely, if you ask, they'll also agree only to charge the soloist's pro-rata share of *group* royalties with the *soloist's* deficit. The company will sometimes agree not to charge the soloist's share of group royalties with the deficit under the solo agreement, but this takes more bargaining power.

You should be careful to provide that, if the group continues to record without the soloist, no *future* group deficits can affect the soloist's new account, nor should they affect his or her share of group royalties. It's not uncommon for a successful group, after a key member has left, to record several dud albums, which then eat up all the old, successful albums' royalties. If they also eat up the ex-member's royalties on the successful albums, he or she will be, shall we say, perturbed. For example, suppose Harvey leaves the group after making four successful albums. Because the group did well, it is recouped, and Harvey retires to that dream house in West Wilbur, expecting to live on his royalties from future sales of these four albums. The group, without Harvey, then goes into the studio and runs up $400,000 trying to make the next *Sgt. Pepper's Lonely Hearts Club Band,* which sells three hundred copies. If you don't change the form, the company will take Harvey's royalties from the four successful albums and use them to get back the $400,000 it spent on the flop. Harvey will not be pleased.

Most companies will agree not to charge future costs against a person who has left, because the leaving member doesn't participate in the future records' royalties and thus shouldn't bear the costs. But you gotta ask.

INTERNAL GROUP DEALS

Why You Need an Internal Contract

When two plumbers in Pacoima decide to go into business together, they know enough to have a lawyer write them a partnership agreement, or at least they go to the supermarket and buy a printed form. For this reason, it always astonishes me that groups earning tens of millions of dollars sometimes never get around to formalizing their relationship. And, every once in a while, this neglect bites them in the rear end.

The time to make an agreement among yourselves is *now,* when everybody is all friendly and kissy-face. When you're fighting with each other, particularly if there's a lot of money on the table, you may find yourself killing the goose that lays the golden eggs, as well as supporting the Scholarship Fund for Entertainment Lawyers. One of my early experiences as a music lawyer was trying to solve the problems of a major group (that I didn't represent before this problem arose) who had never formalized their relationship. One of the members got pumped up by a relative, who told him he was the real star of the group (even though he didn't sing or write). So he started a fight to stop the others from using the group name, and both sides got so angry they couldn't agree on anything. Because they were set up as a corporation, and were deadlocked on every conceivable issue, we had to have the court appoint a neutral third director to break the tie. The court appointed a tough ex-judge, who had done this for many bitterly fighting corporations. He was to be the tie breaker who would allow the corporation to finally move forward. Well, the judge lasted about three months, saying he had "never seen anything as nasty as this," and disappeared into the sunset leaving behind only a large bill. The upshot was that the litigation lasted over nine years, and cost the parties over $1 million in legal fees. The irony is that the group was killed early in the process, and the fellow who started the fight ended up broke. And all of this could easily have been avoided with a simple agreement and a couple of hours of planning.

So pay attention and take care of it *now*. I know, nobody likes to talk about anything negative (like breakups) when everything is working well. But, believe me, when everything is going well is *exactly* the time to discuss it, because you can do it in a friendly way. It's like insurance—you may never need it, but you'll sure be glad you have it if you do. Find a third party (like a lawyer) to blame for raising the issue, so you don't have take the heat. (I routinely say that I am the jerk insisting on this, so you can be a good guy.)

But enough brotherly advice. On to the practical aspects of what to do.

Corporation Versus Partnership

The major differences between having a partnership and a corporation are the tax planning aspects (which could be a book in itself), the liability limitations, and the fact that corporations are more expensive to set up and run; otherwise, it doesn't make much difference whether you're a corporation or a partnership. By *liability limitations,* I mean that corporations limit what assets someone suing you can grab. In a corporation, they can only get the assets of the corporation. With a partnership, however, they can grab both the partnership's assets *and* the personal assets of *every* partner. Most states now have something called a **Limited Liability Company,** or **LLC**. It is basically a partnership, but it provides the limited liability of a corporation and is becoming the vehicle du jour for many groups.

The only mechanical difference between these entities is that, if you want a partnership, you need a written partnership agreement, and if you want a corporation or LLC, you need both a written shareholders' agreement (meaning an agreement among the shareholders, who are the owners of the corporation or the LLC), and employment agreements between yourselves and the corporation; owners of an LLC are called members.

For purposes of these discussions, I'm going to use partnerships because they're simpler. But all these principles can be built into a corporate or LLC structure if you want.

The Most Important Asset

Can you guess what your most important asset is? Apart from your good looks, charm, and talent, your most important asset is the group name. So, whatever else you do, by all means figure out what to do with your group name if there's a fight. In fact, if you *only* deal with your name in a written agreement, I will be happy (but not ecstatic; to get me there, you have to deal with everything).

You need to think through everything about the group name, such as what happens to it if:

- The lead singer and songwriter leave the group.
- The drummer who doesn't write music or sing leaves the group.
- Three out of five members leave the group to form another group.
- The group breaks up totally and everybody goes back to Waxahachie.

Obviously, there are about ten thousand other possibilities, but all of them can be covered with a few general rules. The means of dealing with the name can be anything you want it to be, but the most common solutions run along these lines:

1. No one can use the name if the group breaks up, regardless of how many of you are still performing together (short of all of you, of course).
2. Any majority of the group members performing together can use the name. For example, if there are seven people in a group that breaks up, any four of them together can use the name.
3. Only the lead singer, Sylvia, can use the name, regardless of who she is performing with.
4. Only George, the songwriter who founded the group and thought of the name, can use the name, regardless of who he is performing with.
5. George and Sylvia can use the name as long as they perform together, but if they don't, no one can use the name.

If one or two people really created the unique sound of the group, I've always thought they should have the right to use the name, because the others alone would not truly represent the group to the public. On the other hand, many groups operate on a "majority rule" principle, regardless of that spirit. Anything you can imagine is okay as long as it has some rational basis and a judge can understand it. Just do *something*.

What happens if you don't do anything? As you can gather from my previous horror story, the law is not very helpful. In fact, there is very little law on the subject (surprising as that sounds). This is because most disputes are settled privately, even though they may start as a lawsuit.

The most likely result is that your name will be treated the same way as any other business partnership asset—meaning *any* of the partners has the nonexclusive right to use it. This conceivably means you could have two or three groups using the same name, and then you're down to the question of which one(s) may be defrauding the public. The argument is that one or more key people are the "essence" of the group, and anyone using the name without them misleads and defrauds the public. If you think this sounds messy and expensive to resolve, you're right. So solve it yourself. *Now!*

Percentages

Now that we've raised the subject of an agreement, the next important thing to decide is everybody's percentages. It may surprise you to learn that there are many bands which, despite laughing, giggling, and grabbing each other's tushies on stage, are in fact owned or controlled by one or two people, and everybody else is merely a hired hand. Being a hired hand doesn't necessarily mean you're on a salary—you can be a hired hand and get both a salary and a percentage of the profits. It does, however, mean you serve at the will and pleasure of the employer, which actually makes for a rather pleasant band atmosphere—somehow the knowledge that they could be out on the street tomorrow keeps people's attitudes a lot healthier than if they think they have life tenure. (Hiring people usually isn't practical for new artists, because you have no money to pay them a salary. So everyone works for a percentage of the future pie.)

Assuming you're all going to be partners, how should the profits be shared? Again, there are no rules, and you can do it any way that makes you happy. The easiest way, of course, is to split things equally—if there are five of you, everyone gets one-fifth, or 20%. This is common in new bands, but it can grow to be a source of irritation if some members work harder or contribute more than others. Another approach I've seen (with a client of mine that was built on a core of two people who were together for a number of years before the others joined) gave these two people bigger percentages than the others. And frankly, even when everyone has been together from the beginning, there may be one or two key members who deserve more than the others.

In addition, nothing says you have to use the same percentage for records that you use for other areas. Sometimes bands split evenly on concert monies (on the theory that everyone is out there sweating together), but have different splits for phonograph records, merchandising, television performances, etc.

Control

Just as ownership of the partnership doesn't need to be equal, neither does *control* of the partnership business decisions. Normally you would vote in proportion to your percentage of profits, but this is certainly not carved in stone. Thus, even if your partnership percentages are equal, one or two key members may control the vote—for example, they may have two votes where everybody else has one. Or it can be set up so that the partnership can't act without one or the other of the key members agreeing, regardless of how many people want to do it. The possibilities are again endless, depending only on your creativity and desires, but they need to be thought out carefully. For example, try not to have an even number of votes, because this allows a **deadlock** (meaning an equally divided vote where nothing can be done). At worst, have a third party like your manager break the tie, but better still, try to have a mechanism to do it inside the group.

Other Issues

Here are the other major issues to deal with in your partnership agreement:

Firing. What kind of vote does it take to fire a member? Majority? Unanimous of everyone else?

Hiring. What kind of vote do you need to take in a new partner, or to hire a lawyer, agent, or manager? Majority? Unanimous? When my son Danny was twelve, we came back from vacation to discover that his band had hired a manager and keyboard player without even asking him. It ultimately broke up the band, and yours could be next.

Quitting. Is everyone free to quit at will? Note this only concerns leaving the other band members. You're not free to quit under your record deal (see page 310), and if you're in the middle of a tour, you're not free to walk out on the concert promoters. However, in other cases, since slavery was abolished in this country, there's no way to force someone to continue working with a group. But it is possible to stop him or her from working as a musical artist after quitting, or to require the member to pay his or her solo earnings to the partnership (meaning the other group members get a piece). These are the real means to enforce such a provision. On the other hand, I've always been in favor of letting people go if they're unhappy, as long as they don't walk out in the middle of a tour.

Contributions. What kind of vote do you need to make partners contribute to the partnership (translation: put in money the group needs) to buy equipment, cover unexpected expenses, etc.?

Incurring Expenses. What kind of vote do you need to approve the group's spending money?

Amendment of Partnership Agreement. What kind of vote does it take to change the terms of the partnership deal? For example, can a majority vote reduce your percentage? Or does it take your consent?

Death or Disability. What happens in the event of your death or disability? The one sure thing is that your partners don't want your surviving spouse or parents voting on partnership matters (not likely they'll get onstage and sing). For this reason, there is normally a "buy-out" (see the next section), and you're treated as if you had quit the partnership or were terminated.

Ex-Partners. What happens after you're terminated as a partner, or after you quit? Do you keep your same percentage level for past activities (almost always "yes")? For future activities (almost always "no")? Do you get bought out of your share of assets of the group (called a **buy-out**), and if so, at what price and over what period of time? Funny you should ask . . .

Buy-Outs

So speaking of buy-outs, here's one used by one of my clients:

Price. The price of the buy-out equals the leaving partner's percentage of all "hard" assets owned by the partnership. "Hard" assets means goods that you can touch and feel (sound equipment, instruments, cash, etc.), as opposed to "intangibles" (such as the group name, recording contracts, television shows, etc.). Thus, if the assets are worth $100,000, and the partner had a 25% interest, his or her value of the assets would be $25,000. This is usually done on a "value" as opposed to "cost" basis, because used equipment is generally worth less than the cost. It can also be done on something called **book value,** which is an accounting concept meaning the "value" on the books of the partnership. Book value is typically the original cost minus some scheduled factor of depreciation that is worked out by your accountant. Of these three methods, book value is likely to be the lowest, although it's possible the real value could be less. Cost is the least accurate measure of anything.

I specifically provide that there is no value given to any intangible rights. First of all, I think they're impossible to value, and secondly, the value may be different after someone leaves the group (for example, if the lead singer/songwriter goes, the group name and record deal may be worthless). Finally, I think the leaving member's contingent payout (discussed in the "Contingent Payout" section below) covers this. On the other hand, not everyone agrees with this approach, and there are certainly cases where a name is worth a lot of money after the group has broken up. For example, The Doors and Led Zeppelin still generate tons of dough from the use of their names in merchandising, and it's not illogical to give an ex-member some reduced piece of materials created after the member has left. (Note that if the band breaks up, as with The Doors and Zeppelin, everyone continues to own their shares of the name.) Despite all that, and despite the fact that it could arguably create an unfair result, I still like my approach better. You can't know in advance what a particular member will really contribute to the value of the name, or how much value will be added after that member leaves. And figuring it out after the fact makes lawyers rich.

Cash Payout. The value of hard assets is paid out over a period of two years, at the rate of 25% each six months. Thus, in our $25,000 example, $6,250 would be paid six months after termination, $6,250 paid twelve months after, and so forth. Because the money is not all paid at once, a leaving partner gets interest (in this deal, 10%) on the unpaid balance.

The reason for structuring a payout over time is to protect the remaining members from having to come up with a big chunk of cash (which they may not have) all at once. It's not uncommon to provide that the terminated partner can look only to the assets of the partnership for his or her buyout payments, which means the other individual partners aren't responsible if the partnership has no money to pay.

Contingent Payout. The leaving member(s) get their continuing percentage from activities of the partnership in which they participated prior to leaving. This means royalties from records on which they played, as well as monies from merchandise using their names or likeness, concerts in which they performed, television programs on which they appeared, etc. (Remember, there are special record contract provisions about leaving members, which may affect their continuing royalties. See page 310.) The leaving member(s) do not get any portion of group earnings from activities after they leave.

Legal Ethics

You should be aware of a common ethical problem groups have. A lawyer that represents a group and draws up a partnership agreement has a built-in **conflict of interest.** A conflict of interest or **conflict** means the lawyer represents two clients whose interests are adverse to each other. (We also discussed conflicts on page 72.) So if a lawyer represents the partnership, he or she cannot take sides and represent any one of you against any other of you. But this is what making a partnership agreement requires, because (unless everything gets divided evenly and goes by simple majority vote) your best interests aren't the same. For example, extra percentages of money or control going to Sylvia must come from the others, whose best interests are to keep them. (A manager, business manager, or agent who counsels you about group matters also has the same conflict.)

This of course happens every day, and all ethical lawyers will advise you of its existence. You can do one of two things:

1. Each member can get independent counsel (which may or may not be affordable) to negotiate the agreement among yourselves. This also takes a long time and can be destructive if anyone decides to be a hero. However, it is the best way to do it.
2. Far more commonly, the lawyer explains all of the issues to you openly, and then lets you decide among yourselves how you want to resolve them. In this case, the lawyer does not represent any of you, but rather just acts as a "secretary," writing down whatever agreement you reach on your own. If you use this

route, your lawyer will ask you to sign a **conflict waiver,** which says he or she has explained the conflict to you and you are going ahead anyway.

WHAT'S IN A NAME?

We talked before (on page 314) about group members' rights in your name. Now let's talk about the rights of people outside the group.

Rights in a Name

A few years back, a band named Green Jellö changed its name to Green Jellÿ to avoid a dispute with the owners of the "Jell-O" trademark. While the group ultimately got terrific publicity from all the flap, having a name that steps on somebody else's toes can be a serious problem. The most common difficulties don't come from naming your band after snack foods, vacuum cleaners, etc., but rather from another group that used the name before you did.

Your group name is protected by a **service mark,** which is similar to a **trademark**—a *trademark* is a name used for goods (like Heinz ketchup, Kleenex, etc.) and a *service mark* is a name used for services (like airlines, dry cleaners, and musical groups). The rule is that you get rights in a mark by having it associated with you in the mind of the public. So if the fans think of you when they hear the group name, it's yours and no one else's. In fact, you can even stop names that are different from yours but are similar enough to confuse the public. For example, there's a famous case from the 1920s where Charlie Chaplin stopped someone from using the name "Charles Aplin," and there's an even more fun case where the Dallas Cowboy Cheerleaders stopped the porno film *Debbie Does Dallas* from calling its star an "X Dallas Cheerleader." (For you research freaks, the case cites are *Chaplin* v. *Amador,* 93 Cal. App. 358 [1928]; and *Dallas Cowboy Cheerleaders, Inc.* v. *Pussycat Cinema, Ltd.,* 604 F.2d 200 [2d Cir. 1979].)

By the way, your association with the group name doesn't have to be nationwide—it can be only in your hometown. Let's take an example: Suppose you live in Tulsa, Oklahoma, and invent the name "Pukeheads." Using this name, you start playing locally in August, 1991, and build up a major buzz and fan base. Then one day in 1994 you walk into the record store and find an album by a group from New York called "Pukeheads." What can you do?

Actually, you may be able to do quite a bit. If you were a Pukehead in Tulsa before the New York guys used the name *in Tulsa* (the date you started using it is key—you have to be first), you can stop them from distributing records in Tulsa. Even if they used the name first in New York, if you were first in Tulsa, that town is yours. (They could, however, stop you from using the name in New York if they used it there first; and if they used it nationally before you, they might even stop you in Tulsa. This gets pretty complicated and depends on the specific facts in each case. But let's assume you own Tulsa.) Since it's impossible for a record company to skip a specific market when it runs a national distribution system, if you own the name in Tulsa, you can effectively block them from using it on records in the U.S. This is a joyful result if you're the band from Tulsa, but nose-dive downer if you're a Pukehead from New York.

Note that your rights come from using the name, *not* from registering it. (Registration means filing a public notice that tells the public you claim a particular name.) When you use a name, the public begins to associate it with you. And if someone else uses the same name, the public could be fooled into thinking it's you, which is a no-no. So your most important rights are from usage, even though you do get some important rights from registering (which we'll discuss on page 323).

Check It Out

So how do you stop from being a New York Pukehead? You have to make sure no one else used the group name before you did, which is a bit of a pain (I'll tell you how in a minute). It's not too serious a problem until you get ready to release records, or at least until you start touring over a broad geographic area. Up to that point, the most trouble you'll likely get is a snippy letter from someone else using the name, and you can usually work it out (see page 322 for how things get worked out). However, changing a name that has built up a local following is not a happy event, and if you really have a roll going, you may want to check out the group name before you have a record deal.

When you get ready to make records, clearing the rights in your name becomes a very serious matter. If someone can stop your company from putting out records (as in our Tulsa example), it could cost them a lot of money. And if it does, the company will turn to you with a hand full of "gimme," asking you to pay for the damage.

After being stung by a few of these situations, most of the record companies check the names of new artists before they put out their records. They use two common sources:

1. *The Billboard International Talent and Touring Directory* has an alphabetical listing of a large number of bands currently touring. You may be able to find it in your local library, or you can order it from Billboard (see page 39 for their address).

2. If they find nothing in the directory, the record companies order a trademark/service mark search to look for registrations (both state and federal) of the group name and anything similar. It currently costs about $250 for a preliminary search, and about another $750 for an in-depth one, which is cheap insurance in the long run. (Yes, it's recoupable from your royalties; see page 101 for what that means.) These searches are conducted by independent search companies and also by lawyers that specialize in trademarks. (If you use an independent firm, it's a good idea to have the report reviewed by a trademark attorney who can advise you whether anything you find might be a problem.) Here's a few:

Trademark Research Corporation, 300 Park Avenue South, New York, NY 10010, (800) 872-6275.

Thomson & Thomson Copyright Group, 500 Victory Road, North Quincy, MA 02171-3145, (800) 692-8833.

Weiss, Dawid, Fross, Zelnick, Lehrman (a law firm), 633 Third Avenue, 14th Flr., New York, NY 10017, (212) 953-9090.

This isn't a 100% foolproof method (for example, there may be a local band like the one in Tulsa that hasn't registered a service mark but has acquired rights in the name by performing), but it's about the best you can do.

If you find a group using your name, or using a name that's similar to yours, you have to deal with it. (If you find a name that's similar, you'll need a legal opinion as to whether or not it's too close—the test is whether the public is likely to confuse the two groups.) Most of the time you can contact the other group and work out a deal. If you find them and discover that they broke up or abandoned the name, they may have lost their rights and you don't even need to make a deal. If they're still using the name, and if they're willing to change it, they'll want to get paid. The most common deal is the payment of a lump sum (usually in the range of $1,500 to a few thousand dollars) in exchange for their drifting into the sunset. However, this is a tricky legal area and you'll need a knowledgeable lawyer to draw up the deal.

If you can't make a deal, then you need to change your name. Sometimes you can keep part of the name by adding something to it, but you need to add something distinctive that clearly separates you from the others. For example, if you were using the name "Silver" and found that it was taken, you might call yourself "Denver Silver." (I always think of that great scene in the movie *Spinal Tap* where they talk about having been called "The Originals," only to find another group had that name, so they called themselves "The New Originals.") But this procedure is tricky, and you'll need legal help.

Registration

At some point in your career you want to file a registration of your service mark. Registration tells the world you're using a particular name, establishes a date on which you are using it, and creates a legal presumption that you own it. (A legal presumption means the other group has the burden of proving you *don't* own it; without the presumption, you have to prove you *do* own it.) Also, in addition to this basket of legal goodies, a registration makes sure that you will show up in any search that somebody else does (see number 2 on page 322). If you're operating only in one state, you're only allowed to register in that state. If you're operating in more than one state, you can (and should) register with the federal government, so that you have a national notice. You can get federal applications by writing to the United States Patent & Trademark Office, 2021 Jefferson Davis Highway, Arlington, VA 22202. You're on your own to find out where to file in each state. Try the governmental listings in your capital city.

Do You Have a Reservation? Since 1989, it has been possible to "reserve" your name before you actually use it. This was a major change from the prior law, which said you could only get rights in a name by using it. You reserve the name by filing something cleverly called "An Intent To Use" federal service-mark application, and all you need is a serious desire to use the name in the not too distant future. If you're the first one to file with your name, then even if someone else uses the name before you do, you can stop them after your registration is issued.

You can turn the "Intent to Use" into a real, live service-mark application by filing evidence that you've actually started using the name. The evidence only needs to be something that shows you've used the name for a performance that was advertised in interstate commerce (meaning across state lines). Things like newspaper ads, posters, promotional materials, etc., all work nicely. If you don't file this evidence within four years, then your application is declared invalid, turns into a frog, and you have to start all over.

As noted above, to get a federal registration, you have to use the name in "interstate commerce." This interstate requirement has been interpreted pretty broadly. For example, it's enough if your performance under the name has been advertised in a newspaper that crosses state lines; if you send a flyer about your performance through the mails to another state; or if you play in a club where out-of-staters like to hang.

After filing your application, it can take a year or more to get the registration. And that's if everything goes smoothly (your tax dollars at work). First, the guys in the federal Patent Office check around to see if someone already has a registered mark that they think is too close to yours. If they do, your application gets bounced, and you can start squabbling with them. If you get past these guys, they will then publish your name in the *U.S. Official Gazette* (so if you haven't made it anywhere else, at least you can happen there). This is so that anybody who reads the *Gazette* (don't you and all your friends?) can object to registering your name because it's too close to theirs.

Once you're registered, you have to continue using the name in order to keep up your rights. In fact, there's a legal presumption that you've abandoned the name if you haven't used it for two years. (A presumption means that in court you have to prove that you didn't abandon it, as opposed to the other guy having to prove you did.) However, if you use a name continuously for five years, you can file something called an "Affidavit Of Incontestability," which is fancy talk for saying that no one else can ever come along and claim they had the name before you did. If you're happening big time, this is a good idea.

Foreign Registration. Many countries of the world have a registration system similar to the United States, but I doubt you could stay awake for a thorough discussion of different territories' intricacies. This is only meaningful when you're having success on an international scale, but at that point you should start registering in foreign places (at least in the major territories). In fact, some countries even have a "first to file" rule, which means that someone could rip off your name, beat you to filing it in that territory, and then stop you from performing there. Since only a moron would rip off the name of a dud group, this is not usually important until you start having some real success. But when you do, you ought to start registering pretty quickly.

Group names are a very complicated legal area, requiring careful analysis of your specific facts. If you have any problems with your name, no matter how small you think they are, you MUST

get a lawyer. Do not ignore the problem—it will only lie there sleeping until you're successful, at which point it will wake up and bite you in the rear-end.

Answers to quiz on page 311:

Groups:
1. The Doobie Brothers—Michael McDonald
2. Creedence Clearwater Revival—John Fogerty
3. The Police—Sting
4. Traffic—Steve Winwood
5. The Commodores—Lionel Richie
6. The Band—Robbie Robertson

Soloists:
1. Don Henley—Eagles
2. Stephen Stills—Buffalo Springfield
3. Neil Young—Buffalo Springfield
4. Eric Clapton—Cream; Derek & the Dominoes
5. Bobby Brown—New Edition
6. Phil Collins—Genesis

PART V

Touring

23

Personal Appearances—Touring

Now let's see what happens when you hit the road to get up close and personal with your fans.

ROLES OF TEAM MEMBERS

Here's what the various players on your team do when you tour:

Personal Manager

As the chief executive officer of your professional team, the personal manager is in charge of the tour. He or she is the one who gets you onto the right tour in the first place; ensures that your agent is making the best possible deals for you (read "hounding the agent on a regular basis"); and once the tour is set up, mechanically makes it happen. He or she has to coordinate:

1. Transportation of people and equipment.
2. Hiring and smooth functioning of crews.
3. Booking hotels.
4. Collecting money on the road.
5. Dealing with and supervising the "promoters" (the people who hire you, rent the hall, advertise the event, etc.; see page 331 for more about promoters).
6. Putting out whatever fires crop up (such as missing equipment, improper advertising, dates that aren't selling well, lapses in security, etc.).

With bigger artists, many of these duties are delegated to a road manager and/or road accountant, but the personal manager is ultimately responsible, and the buck stops with him or her.

Agent

The agent, in conjunction with your manager, books the tour. He or she makes the deals with the promoters (which includes the job of picking promoters that will put on the show professionally and not disappear with your money). At the early stages of your career, they will be pounding promoters to book you. At the later stages of your career, they will be pounded by promoters to book you.

Your agent and personal manager also make the following decisions about your tour:

Itinerary. Your **itinerary** is the route your tour takes and the halls you play in. If you're the opening act for a major tour, setting the itinerary means you show up when you're told. If, however, you're headlining, the itinerary becomes critical. Proper routing can save or lose you a bundle of money. While it may seem obvious, the tour has to be planned so you don't end up going from New York to Oregon to Florida in a four-day period. However, concert halls are not available at all times (due to circuses, hockey games, etc., as well as other rockers), and the juggling act is quite a sight to behold.

Image. How does the tour work with your image? This is twofold:

1. If you're an opening act, is the headliner compatible with your audience? If you're a heavy metal band, for example, you won't want to be the opening act for the Osmond Family Reunion tour.
2. What venues are you playing? It says one thing if you play a brand new 5,000-seat amphitheater in the high-end part of town, and it says something else if you play an older 3,500-capacity hall with no seats, on the poorer side of town.

Skating Through the "Radio Promotion" Jungle. Ever noticed how many radio stations either "present" a concert, or else have concert tie-ins, ticket giveaways, live reports, etc.? That of course never happens by chance; it's always very carefully planned. And apart from just picking the right station, it has to be done in a way that doesn't upset the other stations in the market (who will otherwise promptly drop your record).

When to Put the Tickets on Sale. This is something that can vary from market to market. Some markets will buy tickets way in advance, while others are mainly **walk up** (meaning the bulk of the attendance "walks up" the night of the show and buys the tickets). Also, it's crucial to put tickets on sale the right amount of time before the show—not too late and not too soon—and you have to be careful you're not going on sale the same day as a major tour that's blitzing the market (or maybe they have to be careful of you!).

Pricing of Tickets. Although your first reaction may be to "grab all the gusto you can" by charging the highest ticket prices the market will bear, this decision isn't so black and white. Many managers and agents are squarely within this camp, and their thinking is persuasive— nobody knows how long things will last, make hay while the sun shines, get 'em while you're hot, etc. On the other hand, many respected managers and agents take a different view, feeling a lower-priced ticket draws more people, creates a bigger "hype," makes the show accessible to people who couldn't otherwise afford to go, and in the long run is a better career-building move. Also, some bands intentionally keep a low ticket price because they feel it maintains their commitment to artistry before business. The debate is not only endless, but also related to what sort of audience you appeal to—for example, young kids have more trouble with an expensive ticket than an older audience. And the answer also varies with where you are in your career—if you're an established artist, you needn't worry as much about building for the long term. So feel free to join the debate, because your guess is as good as anybody else's. (We'll discuss more details of ticket pricing on page 336.)

Deposits. Agents are also responsible for collecting **deposits,** which are amounts paid in advance by the promoters. In order to hold you for a particular date, the promoters typically pay 50% of the total price, about thirty days ahead of the performance. It's a way of ensuring that you don't get stiffed (at least completely). So, for example, if your deal is $10,000 for a show, the promoter would pay $5,000 in advance. These deposits are held by the agent and paid to you when you perform the gig.

Promoter

Promoters are the people in each market who hire you for the evening. Promoters are the entrepreneurs who take the full risk of the concert. They can be "local" (meaning they work only in one city or area), regional (several states), national (covering the entire U.S.), or international. They book the hall (which means they owe the rent even if nobody shows up), pay for advertising the concert, and supervise the overall running of the show for maximum efficiency. Promoters actually have a tough time. If they lose, they can lose big, but as acts get more successful they squeeze them and limit the promoter's upside (as discussed below). The result is a friendly game of "hide the pickle" that promoters routinely play in rendering statements of how much has been earned. But I'm getting ahead of myself, because we're going to talk about this later (on page 335).

Business Manager

The business manager is in charge of all financial aspects of the tour. This job begins way before the tour starts by forecasting (a fancy accounting word for predicting the future) what the likely income and expenses are going to be, and about how much you're going to make or lose. If you're a new band, this information lets you go to the record company and beat them up for tour support (see page 157). At all levels, it helps avoid unhappy surprises along the way.

When the tour gets going, all your road personnel (the people that set up the equipment, supervise your crew, etc.) are on payroll, and the business manager is in charge of writing their checks. He or she is also in charge of making sure your performance fees are collected from the promoters (which is physically done by a road manager if you have one), and that all bills (travel, hotels, food, etc.) are paid. And it's their responsibility to make sure the tour doesn't run over budget without an alarm being sounded in advance, while there's still a chance to fix it.

Road Manager

If you have a **road manager** (and if not, your personal manager should be doing the job), he or she will make sure everything runs smoothly for you on the road. This means that the hotel reservations are in fact there, that your airline tickets are where they should be, that the bus is where it's supposed to be, that you are on the bus or plane when you're supposed to be, that only certain groupies get through security, etc. It's the road manager who is responsible for collecting the money due for each show and depositing it in the right place. (As you move up the ladder, you'll have a tour accountant doing the money part of the job.)

PERSONAL APPEARANCE DEALS

Let's start out with a basic truth: You aren't going to make any money in personal appearances until you're a major star. Unless you sell a lot of records, you won't put a lot of tushies on concert seats. So before that time, you'll be touring only to help sell records, which will make you a major star. (There are of course exceptions to this rule. Some artists sell relatively few records, but pack concert halls. Conversely, some artists sell millions of records but can't fill an auditorium. Also, the independent scene has a number of artists who make reasonable livings working a cult circuit on shoestring budgets.)

In the beginning, you lose money on touring. You also get stuck in uncomfortable dressing rooms, with food left over from last night's headliner. And you'll be regularly humiliated, playing to concert audiences who are there to see someone else, still arriving and buying beer while you're performing, talking loudly during your ballads, and chanting the headliner's name if they don't like your show. Did I sugar-coat it too much?

Well, let's look at what the deals are.

NEW ARTISTS

If you're a brand new artist, and you don't have a record deal, you can forget about doing anything other than playing local club dates. If you play only dates in and around the city where you live (meaning you have no travel expenses), and if you can use the local clubs' sound and light facilities, you can make some money from this, create a "buzz," and showcase yourself for record companies. Enough said.

If you're a new artist with a record deal, you don't want to be touring until your record is out. As I said before, the only purpose is to let people know you, so they'll buy your records. And there's no point in their knowing you if you have no records to sell.

The major touring season, not surprisingly, is May through September, primarily the summer months when kids are out of school and can go to concerts every night. Superstars can tour throughout the year, and traditionally new artists toured in the summer months (unless they were opening for a major artist who was touring at some other time). Recently, however, newer bands have taken to hitting the road in the fall, when there is less competition for concertgoers' dollars. This is especially true for college/alternative acts who want college radio blasting while they tour, and who want school to be in session when they get to town.

As a new artist, your choices are to play in clubs (100 to 1,500 people or so) as a headliner, or to be the opening act on a big tour. How you get to be the opening act on a major tour is very political. If your album is only doing so-so, and there are several other groups in your position, then it depends on the political clout of your manager and agent—it's that simple and cold. If you're breaking out in an exceptional way, such as selling a lot of singles or albums, or generating a lot of interest in some other way (like a hot MTV video), you'll have an edge in the political process, but it's still political. The exception is the situation where you're really exploding from the start: In this case, you have a much easier time, and in fact the headliners may want you. (Sometimes a well-known artist goes out on tour and isn't selling tickets very well. To remedy this, they add a hot new opening act that brings people in. But again, this is the exception to the usual order of business.)

Fees

If your record is beginning to make some noise, you can get fees in the range of $250 to $1,500 per night, either from clubs or opening slots. But until you get to that point, your deals look very different. They look like this:

Pre-sells

It may surprise you (but then again it may not) to hear that many clubs now charge for the privilege of playing in them. Thus, rather than give you money to entertain the throngs, these clubs become fancy places to "showcase" your talents and invite industry executives, relatives, etc., to see you perform. The way it's done is the club sells you 125 tickets or so, for about $350 to $500. You can then give away the tickets to key people, or, if you're hot enough, sell them at a markup and make a profit. This practice is known as a **pre-sell,** because the club sells its tickets in advance.

While we're on the subject of pay-to-play, you should know there's a small trend toward major stars requiring opening acts on their tours to pay for the privilege. This has been the practice in Europe for some time, ever since headliners realized the exposure of being on tour was valuable. Accordingly, acts can pay anywhere from $500 to several thousand dollars per night for an opening spot. This hasn't caught hold in the United States, but I've heard rumblings of it recently.

Splits/Guarantees

Some clubs will pay you no front money, but will give you a split of the **gate** (meaning the money charged for admission). The splits run from 20% to 60%, depending on your stature and the number of other acts. For example, if there are three acts, you might divide up 60% of the gate. If your band is the biggest **draw** (meaning you "draw" in the biggest crowds), however, you can ask for a more than equal share. Sometimes you can get up to 100% of the gross after the promoter gets back his or her expenses for the evening (advertising, sound, lights, etc.). This is most common when the promoter is also the club owner and is happy to break even on the door charge just to get thirsty bodies into the seats. As to the accuracy of the club's count, you'll have to rely on the club's reputation or else have Bruno, your 300-pound roadie, stand at the door and count.

If you're really hot locally, and have a following, you might get a minimum guarantee of $100 to $250 or so against your share of the gate. Or you may just take a higher fee, of say $500 to $800 per night (with no share of the gate). (I'm basing the numbers in this section on the club scene in L.A., because it's the one I'm most familiar with. These are also based on a ticket price of $5 to $7. I'm told the basic pattern holds true for most major cities.)

Expenses

The *minimum* cost of putting yourself on the road is the money to rent a van you can use to carry equipment and sleep in, plus three meals a day at McDonald's. And you'd better get along really well with each other, or else expect some violent crimes. The next step up (three or four to a room in cheapie motels, slightly better meals, and perhaps someone to help move the equipment) gets into more expense, as you can readily see. But if you watch it carefully, you can get by cheap enough to play the independent circuit and make a few bucks. If you're headlining larger clubs or doing the opening act on a tour, the minimum cost of putting a four-piece band on the road can run around $10,000 per week, broken down roughly as $1,000 for crew, $2,000 for food and hotels, $2,500 for equipment and personnel costs, and $4,000 for insurance, commissions to managers and agents, equipment repairs, etc. With travel, setup, etc., you can't really do more than five shows per week, and you don't need to be a math genius to see that you're going to lose money doing this. Five nights at even $1,500 per night is only $7,500, which is $2,500 per week less than it costs you to be there. And the longer you stay out the more you're going to lose. So where does this lost money come from? (See page 157 for the answer.)

MIDLEVEL ARTISTS

Let's assume you're now past the new artist level, and are selling 200,000 to 400,000 copies of your albums. You now have the option, in addition to opening for a major artist or playing clubs, of headlining small venues, such as 1,500 to 2,500 seaters.

At this point, you should at least be able to break even, and you may be able to take home a nice profit. If you're playing small venues (1,500 to 2,500 seaters), or if you're going out as an opening act, you should be able to make about $5,000 per night. If you're headlining amphitheaters (meaning venues of about 5,000 seats), you can get $7,500 to $50,000 or more per night, depending on the ticket pricing. Let's elaborate on the ticket pricing: Many artists, for their credibility and/or the fact that nobody will come if they raise their prices, like to keep their tickets cheap (in the range of $10 to $15 per ticket). If this is you, because of the expense of being on the road, you'll break even or make a small profit. However, if you're able and willing to charge $20 to $25 per ticket, you can make a tidy profit. And if you can command a $40 or $50 ticket price, you could get as much as $100,000 per night! Note also that, because your expenses are fixed, the first $10 to $15 per ticket covers them. Thus, almost every dollar of increase (which isn't exactly true because the promoter takes a part, as we'll discuss in more detail in a minute) is profit and goes directly to your bottom line (meaning into your pocket).

At mid-level you can also get into *splits*. (Splits are discussed under superstars, so I won't ruin the surprise. But see that section below if you like ruining surprises.) The only difference is that the guarantees against splits at this level are of course lower than the superstars' (midlevel artist guarantees are in the range of $7,500 to $15,000 per show, or more if you raise your ticket price).

SUPERSTAR TOURING

Now we get into some real fun and money. This is where you make the really big bucks in touring. (And if you pay close attention, I'll tell you on page 342 how to put a lot more of them in your pocket. If you choose not to listen, don't get mad at me when your agent, personal manager, and other team members have more money than you at the end of the tour.)

SPLITS

First let's look at the money you can earn. Here's how the deals work when you're a superstar: Instead of being paid flat fees, you get a **guarantee** against a percentage of the **net profits** of the show. (Your share of net profits is also called a **split,** because you split the profits with the promoter.) The guarantee works exactly the same way as an advance against your record royalties (see page 101); if you don't make any profits, you still keep the guarantee. If you do make profits, the promoter deducts the guarantee and pays the balance to you.

And these numbers are not chopped liver. Major artists in "arenas" (meaning venues of 12,000 to 20,000) get guarantees in the range of $25,000 to $100,000 per night. And major artists can sell multiple nights in the same venue, which can be a substantial savings of costs— you don't have to move the equipment, yourself, or your crew every night, and you can make a better rental rate for the concert hall.

The usual split is 85/15, meaning the artist gets 85% of the net profits of the show, and the promoter gets 15%. Superstars push promoters into 90/10 deals, but it takes a lot of clout.

Here's an example: If a date has gross ticket sales of $250,000 and the promoter's expenses are $150,000, there will be $100,000 in net profits ($250,000 income less $150,000 expenses). 85% of this, or $85,000, is paid to the artist. If the artist got a $60,000 guarantee, this is deducted from the artist's share. Thus, the artist gets an additional $25,000 (the $85,000 share of profits less the $60,000 guarantee):

Gross Ticket Sales	$250,000
Less: Promoter Expenses	– $150,000
Net Profits	$100,000
Times: 85%	× 85%
Artist Share:	$85,000
Less: Guarantee	– $60,000
PAYABLE ON NIGHT OF SHOW	**$25,000**

The sensitivity to ticket pricing, which we covered in the previous section for mid-level artists, is even more dramatic when you get to the superstar level. As we discussed, once you've covered expenses, most of the increase goes directly into your pocket. Accordingly, adult-oriented acts sometimes charge in the range of $75 to $100 per ticket, and occasionally even more. At this level especially when they're playing large venues, the artists can walk away with truckloads of money each night.

Computation of Net Profits

Let's look at some of the finer points in computing **net profits.** Net profits are defined as "gross receipts less the promoter's expenses," and are determined as follows:

Gross Receipts. Gross receipts means gross monies from ticket sales, less selling costs (such as ticket agencies), taxes, and facilities charges. That's pretty straightforward, but your team should go to great lengths to make sure you get an accurate accounting. For example, some of my clients have their tour accountant "count the house" (meaning they actually count the number of seats and people in them) and/or (especially in "festival" dates where there are no seats) stand at the door with "clickers" and count the number of people that come in (in response to which one promoter opened three other entrance doors without telling us). And there are also standard auditing methods such as checking the torn ticket stubs and comparing them to the ticket printer's reports, or looking at the box office books and records.

Expenses. From the gross, the promoter deducts every expense he or she can possibly think of. The major ones are:

1. Advertising. It's obvious when you think about it, but not until then, that the more important an artist you are, the *less* advertising money the promoter has to spend. One or two announcements of a major show usually does it. So watch this expense.
2. Rent for the facility
3. Personnel (box office, cleanup, ushers, ticket takers, doormen, etc.)
4. Rental of equipment (P.A. [public address system], lights, pianos, etc.)
5. Insurance
6. Security
7. Ticket printing
8. Stage crew

9. Limousines for the artist
10. Catering for artist and crew
11. Public-performance license for the music (see page 230 for what this is)
12. Medical

Over the years, as promoters became more and more squeezed (or in some cases more and more greedy), they developed systematic ways of "adding" to the expenses. Crasser promoters have been known simply to create phony invoices for various items. A more sophisticated example might be that the promoter advertises so much in the local newspaper or radio station that they get a "rebate" at the end of the year. In other words, if they spend $100,000 for ads on a radio station, the station gives them back $5,000 at year end. This doesn't show up on each individual invoice, and thus the shows are charged for the full amount.

The interesting part is that everyone knows pretty much what the promoters are doing, and thus there is this little "waltz of the toreadors" while your agent negotiates how much the promoter can steal from you (using much more civilized terms, of course). Because everyone knows what expenses really are, there are accepted amounts of stealing, and it's bad form for (a) the promoter to steal more than is customary, or (b) the artist to "catch" the promoter and not allow the accepted level. So in this bizarre netherland, everyone reaches a happy compromise.

Promoter's Profit as an Expense

Some promoters also ask for a profit to be added as an expense, which has the effect of delaying your split of proceeds until after they get a negotiated amount of money. For example, if the gross from a particular evening is $100,000 and the expenses are $60,000, the net profits would be $40,000 ($100,000–$60,000). If your deal is 85/15, you would get 85% of $40,000, or $34,000. However, if the promoter negotiated for a profit of $10,000 to be added as an expense, the net profits would only be $30,000, because the expenses are now $70,000 (the $60,000 actual expenses plus the promoter's $10,000 profit). Thus, you would only get 85% of $30,000, or $25,500, instead of $34,000. (In other words, you got $8,500 less because you are paying 85% of the $10,000 profit.) As your bargaining power increases, the promoter's ability to add a profit disappears.

Splits Based on Gross

For superstar acts, there has been a trend over the last few years to get a percentage of gross income. (In these deals, the expenses are of course irrelevant.) The range is 65% to 70% of gross, and the artist can get even more when the ticket prices are high. Remember, the expenses are fixed, so that as gross income (i.e., ticket price) goes up, the expenses become a smaller percentage of the gross. Which means the artist can get a bigger and bigger piece of it. For example, if the expenses were $50,000 and the gross was $100,000, the expenses are 50% of the gross. But if the gross was $200,000, the $50,000 expenses would only be 25%. So the higher the ticket price, the bigger the artist's share of gross.

HALL FEES

Over the last few years, agents have become responsible for negotiating **hall fees.** A hall fee is the amount charged by the building for selling merchandise (T-shirts, posters, etc.), and it's a percentage of the gross sales. This is discussed in detail in the next chapter, on page 351.

RIDERS

The actual contracts for each appearance are customarily handled by the agency. At lower levels, they're merely AFM standard printed forms. As you hit midlevel to superstar, they're the same printed forms with an attached **rider** (an addendum that "rides" on another contract). Your attorney (with your manager's and agent's help) puts the rider together for you, and it's the guts of the deal. The contract itself is only one or two pages, spelling out the specific terms (dates, guarantee, hall size, splits, etc.). But riders typically run thirty pages or more.

Here are the major points that should be covered in your rider:

Expenses. If your deal involves splits, the promoter's expenses should be listed separately, with *maximum* amounts for each category. In other words, the rider says you can only be charged for the actual expense, or the maximum in the contract, whichever is *less*. The rider should also spell out your right to verify expenses by examining invoices, checks, etc.

Tickets. The rider should have very strict procedures concerning the tickets, such as printing procedures (requiring the promoter to use a bonded printing house), security for the tickets, how unsold ticket stubs must be retained, etc. The penalty for violating these requirements is customarily that all tickets are treated as if they had been sold at the highest price.

Free tickets. You want to have a certain number of free tickets to each performance for yourself (usually fifty to one hundred), and you want to limit the amount the promoter can give away without your consent (usually twenty-five or so). If you have a tour sponsor, you may have to give and/or sell tickets to them, and the rider must cover this as well. (Remember, most of the revenue lost to free tickets comes out of your pocket, because 85% of the lost ticket money would have been yours.)

Free tickets are usually a minimal item, and not a big deal. However, some artists, in some cities, may not do so well, and the promoter sometimes gives away as many tickets as humanly possible, to make the house look full. This is called "papering the house," and is done very quietly. (If you find a lot of policemen, firemen, city council people, and similar folks boogeying and/or holding their ears in your audience, there's a good chance you've been papered.)

I use an interesting clause that says the promoter's free tickets can't be in the first ten rows. Can you guess why? Answer on page 345.

Billing. You of course want 100% headline billing, and you should have the right to approve the presence and size of anybody else's name in the same advertising, publicity, or sign.

Recording. The rider should have strict prohibitions against recording your performance in any way, either audio and/or visual. A poor-quality (or even worse, good-quality) bootleg tape is a serious rip-off of your professional life. I normally put in extraordinarily tough language, including high six-figure damages for a violation.

Merchandising. Your merchandiser will require you to include specific language giving them the exclusive right to sell merchandise at your concert. (Merchandising is discussed in detail in chapter 24.)

Interviews/Promos. Be sure the promoter can't commit you to any interviews or local sponsors without your consent.

Catering. I have so much fun reading the catering requirements of riders that I've made it a hobby. Many riders have three or more full pages of food and drink that the promoter has to provide for the artist and the crew. They range from relatively mundane foods for the crew to true exotica for the headliner. (I always get a kick out of artists that require whole-grain macrobiotic food, together with six cases of beer and two gallons of tequila.) Here are some of the better items, actually lifted from various riders over the years:

Turkey (white meat only; *never* rolled or pressed)
Gourmet Grade Coffee—no canteen type
Lactaid nonfat milk
Shelled red pistachios
M&Ms, with the brown ones removed

Technical. You need to have very specific technical specifications for your show, such as size of stage, what equipment the promoter must supply, power requirements, exact security needs, dressing room facilities, sound check requests (meaning a time you can come into the actual venue and set the levels of your sound equipment), etc.

Legal. Riders have a legal section regarding cancellation, bad weather, riots, mechanics of payment, etc.

LINING YOUR POCKETS WITH MORE GOLD

And now to my promised method of making you more money. Let me first say a couple of words about money in general.

More Income Versus Cutting Expenses

It's more expensive to put another dollar of income in your pocket than it is to put a dollar of expense savings in your pocket. This may sound a bit weird, so let me explain.

For every dollar of income you make, you have to pay your manager, agent, and perhaps business manager and/or lawyer (if they're on a percentage) out of it. This will leave, for example, only about 65¢ to 70¢ to go into your pocket. On the other hand, for every dollar of expense you save, the whole dollar goes in your pocket because you've already paid the professionals on the money that would have been used to pay the expense. Let's look at an example:

Suppose your tour grosses $1,000,000, and your professional team fees total 35% ($350,000). This means that you have $650,000 after commissions, out of which you must pay $400,000 in expenses. Thus, your net after everything is $250,000 (I'm ignoring income taxes).

Had you earned another $100,000 on the tour, 35% would have gone off the top to your professional team, leaving you $65,000. Since your expenses are already covered, however, the full $65,000 would be in your pocket. Thus your net after everything is $315,000 ($250,000 plus the $65,000). On the other hand, if you didn't earn another $100,000, but instead saved $100,000 in expenses, the picture looks quite different: Instead of deducting $400,000 in expenses, you'd deduct only $300,000, and your net after everything would be $350,000. You thus keep the *full $100,000* by cutting expenses, *which is almost 60 percent more than the $65,000 you would put in your pocket by earning another $100,000.*

Here's a chart:

	Example	EARN $100,000 more income	SAVE $100,000 in expenses
Earnings	$1,000,000	$1,100,000	$1,000,000
Less Commissions (35%)	– $350,000	– $385,000	– $350,000
Subtotal	$650,000	$715,000	$650,000
Less Expenses:	– $400,000	– $400,000	– $300,000
NET	**$250,000**	**$315,000** ($65,000 more in your pocket)	**$350,000** ($100,000 more in your pocket)

And as you add another zero or two to these numbers, they get even more impressive.

What to Do

How do you pull off this minor miracle? It's pretty simple, but you may not like the answer very much: Spend less on yourself on the road.

Here are the biggest areas of abuse:

Salaries. Watch carefully how much you're paying your band and crew, and really think through how many of them you need. This is primarily your manager or tour manager's area of expertise, and you obviously don't want to scrimp on essential personnel. But you don't always need to carry as many people as you think, or pay them as much as they demand. And be extra careful with friends and relatives. Hiring "pals" with little or nothing to do is wasteful and demoralizing to the people who really work.

Stage, Sound, and Lights. Your stage, sound, and lighting systems have to be commensurate with your stature; anything less
cheats your audiences. On the other hand, these expenses can be
enormous and eat up a large chunk of your profits. Remember, your
fans are there to see *you* perform, and if you need an array of trapeze
artists, revolving stages, rocket ships, etc., to keep their attention,
either something is wrong with your show or you're being insecure
and hiding behind the hoopla. (You're better than that—you
wouldn't be where you are if you weren't.) Of course you should do
something innovative and spectacular, but be practical as well.

Travel. You can save a lot by traveling light. This means two things:

1. Almost nothing I know of (except non-income producing real
   estate and owning a restaurant) eats money like chartering (or
   heaven forbid, owning) your own jet. As you reach a certain
   level, it makes economic sense (or at least not a significant difference) to begin chartering planes. But for the most part, flying
   commercial is feasible and substantially less expensive. I know
   it's more inconvenient—the hassles of the public in the airport
   and on the plane, delayed fights, oversleeping and missing
   flights, etc.—but every major celebrity and political figure has at
   one time or another flown commercial, and all survived the
   experience. Remember, it's your own money.
2. Try not to **hub.** Hubbing means you base yourself in a central
   location (say, Dallas-Forth Worth) while you play venues within
   a short flight from that city (all parts of Texas, Oklahoma, and
   Arkansas). When you stay in one place like this, you double your
   mileage—every day you not only fly to the gig, but you have to
   fly back. And most artists like to hub out of expensive cities,
   which increases your hotel/lodging bills.

Catering. Some artists are particularly notorious for having lavish
spreads backstage, much of which is never eaten by them (or even
touched by human hands). Or, worse yet, it's eaten by the
hangers-on that show up to see what they can scam. (I said that just
to make you mad; but it's true.) Because these goodies are supplied
by the promoter as part of your deal, it feels like the promoter is
paying for them. But the truth is that 85% of this expense is yours.
Remember, as you get into the major leagues, you make only a
portion of your money from the guarantee. A nice chunk of it
comes from the profit split, which is usually 85/15 (see page 337

for a description of profit splits). Thus, every dollar spent on food for scavengers is 85¢ less you put in your pocket. So ditch the imported caviar and order in from Burger King. Or at least go in that direction.

Just Watch It. The above is not exhaustive; there are many other ways to cut expenses. I know the road is a hassle and you want to be comfortable. There's nothing wrong with that. But be mindful of your expenses and keep them down. You'll be glad you did when you get home and count your take.

Answer to question on page 341:

Nothing is as much fun as playing your heart out to a packed, standing, screaming audience, only to have a bunch of zombies in three-piece suits sitting in the first ten rows looking at their watches.

Merchandising

PART VI

Merchandising

24

Tour
Merchandising

So now you're famous, and kids can't wait to plaster your face on their backs, front, bedroom walls, etc. And bootleggers can't wait to rip off your name and likeness with illegal merchandise (more about bootleggers later).

So how do you make money from your face? Selling products (posters, T-shirts, bumper stickers, etc.) with your name or likeness on it is called **merchandising,** and there are two basic kinds:

1. **Tour Merchandising.**
   This is the stuff sold at concert venues, for prices you would never pay anywhere else, so you can prove you were there.
2. **Retail Merchandising.**
   This is basically the same stuff (without tour names or dates), but it's sold everywhere *except* concerts, such as in retail stores, by mail order, through fan clubs, etc.

Of the two types, tour merchandise is by far the more significant (assuming, of course, that you're touring; otherwise, it doesn't mean much). While retail merchandising may be more visible, it doesn't create the same intense sales frenzy as concerts do, for the obvious reasons—people are all pumped up by the show, they want a souvenir, etc.

So let's discuss tour merchandising first, and the next chapter will deal with retail.

MERCHANDISERS

Merchandising at concerts (and also at retail) is handled by licensing the right to use your name and likeness to a **merchandiser.** A merchandiser, very much like a record company, manufactures the goods, oversees the sales at your concerts, and pays you a royalty for each sale.

ROYALTIES

The computation of merchandising royalties is substantially easier than record royalties. It's for the most part just a percentage of the **gross sales.** "Gross sales" is a term of art, meaning the selling price to the public, less only taxes (sales tax, Value Added Tax, excise and similar taxes). **Value Added Tax,** or **VAT** to its pals, is something we don't have (yet) in the United States, but is common throughout many other countries of the world. It's a tax on goods at each stage of creation, based on the "value added" at that point. For example, there's a tax on the lumber mill as it cuts down a tree and turns it into lumber (adding value); a tax on the furniture manufacturer when it turns the lumber into furniture (more value added); a tax when the upholsterer does its thing, etc. The tax gets bigger and bigger at each stage, but through a system of crediting back (which I have never had any need to fully understand, so I don't) each guy gets a credit for the tax paid by the previous guy. But it pumps up the price to the consumer.

The range of royalties, for sales at concerts in the United States and Canada, is generally 26% to 40% of gross sales. There are higher deals for superstars, and sometimes a split of profits with the merchandiser. It's not uncommon to escalate your royalties based on sales, which can either be on a per-night basis, or a cumulative basis for the entire tour. This is a good thing to remember if you're getting stuck with a low royalty.

Foreign royalties run somewhere around 80% of the U.S. rate, but if your royalty is lower in the United States, you can try for the same foreign royalty. However, you're probably going to end up around 80%.

The programs sold at concerts are usually based on a percentage of net profits, regardless of how everything else is calculated. This is because the merchandisers finally figured out they weren't making much (or any) money on programs, but were paying the artists a lot of royalties for them. (Programs are expensive—they have to be assembled, set up for printing, have artwork designed, etc. Thus the profit split evolved, and it's now the norm.)

Artists of major status will sometimes have **designer goods,** such as an expensive (fifty dollars plus) sweatshirt. Because a designer is paid a fee (or royalty) on these goods, your royalty is negotiated separately and is lower.

HALL FEES

Over the last few years, as artists have pushed royalties higher, the merchandisers have sought to limit the **hall fees.** We touched briefly on hall fees in the last chapter (on page 340), but now let's take a more detailed look.

Your merchandiser doesn't actually hire people to sell product in each of the venues. Instead, they make a deal with the hall to supply the personnel, displays, etc. The merchandiser pulls up its truck early in the day, "checks in" a certain quantity of merchandise to the hall personnel, and at the end of the evening gets back the unsold merchandise plus cash for what's been sold or otherwise disappeared. From the money that's turned over, the venue keeps a percentage, and this is the "hall fee." It covers the cost of hiring the people who actually sell and the venue's profit. (By the way, not all the venues actually supply the merchandise personnel themselves. There are a couple of companies that contract with venues to supply these people, pay the hall a percentage, and keep the difference as profit.)

A standard hall fee is 35% to 40% of the gross monies collected for the merchandise, and superstars can knock it down to about 32% (or even lower in rare instances). So if you sold $10,000 of merchandise, the hall would keep 35% to 40% ($3,500 to $4,000) and pay the balance to the merchandiser. (These are U.S. numbers; you can sometimes get lower fees in foreign markets.)

The royalties paid by merchandisers to the artist are based on gross *before* deducting hall fees. So, historically, the hall fees never affected the artist. However, as artists demanded higher and higher merchandising royalties, the merchandisers finally had their profits squeezed so tightly that they began making artists deliver hall fees below a certain percentage. So today's deals almost always set a limit on the hall fees, and if you go over it, the excess comes out of your royalties. For example, a merchandise deal might say that you have a royalty of 32% and that the hall fee cannot exceed 35%. Under this deal, if your hall fee for a particular date was 40% (i.e., 5% more than the allowed 35%), the extra 5% would come out of your royalty, and instead of 32% you would only get 27%. By the way, unless you ask, you won't get any part of the savings for beating up the hall fees *below* the maximum level. If you do ask, you can usually get a percentage (50% to 75%) of the savings. In the above example, if you got 50% of the hall savings below 35%, and if you pushed the hall fee down to 30% (i.e., you saved 5% below the 35% maximum), your royalty would increase from 32% to 34.5% (the 32% royalty plus 2.5% for 50% of the 5% hall fee reduction). Your argument to win this point is that, if you don't share in the decrease, you don't have any incentive to do it.

As noted in the prior chapter, hall fees are negotiated by the agent (at the same time they make the overall deal for the guarantee, splits, etc.). Ironically, the agent doesn't get paid for this—the agent's commission is based on the earnings of the artist only from the performance, and not from merchandising. So the agent is in the position of negotiating a part of the deal that gives him or her no benefit. However, their incentive goes way up when the artist glares daggers at them, and so they have gotten quite good at muscling down the hall percentages.

Another deal that's becoming more common is simply to pay the artist a combined royalty/hall fee percentage of, say, 65% to 70%. Under a 65% deal, for example, if the hall fee was 30%, the artist would get a 35% royalty; if the hall fee was 40%, the artist would get 25%; etc. This means that the artist gets 100% of the hall fee savings, as well as 100% of the burden for higher fees.

ADVANCES

As you learned from record and publishing deals, where there are royalties, there are advances. And merchandising is just such a place. The advances are based on, and paid over the course of, a tour. For example, if your merchandising advance is $250,000, you might get $50,000 when you sign the deal, $100,000 one-third of the way through the tour, and the balance two-thirds of the way through. As your bargaining power goes up, you get more of the advance sooner.

When you get an advance, the merchandisers require you to perform for a minimum number of people, and at a minimum number of shows and/or cities (this is discussed in detail in page 354). They also want the tour to start within a reasonable period after signing (say ninety days), or else they have the right to get out of the deal and/or charge you interest on any advances you got. And if they decide to get out, they want back the money they gave you on signing plus interest. (There are other things that trigger paybacks, which we'll discuss on page 354.)

The size of the advance is a projection of your gross sales times your royalty rate. It can run from nothing to $10,000 or $20,000 for a baby act, to over $1,000,000 for a superstar. It will also vary with the size of the tour—the more bodies you play in front of, the more merchandise you can sell.

TERM

The term of most merchandising agreements is one year, or until the advance is recouped, whichever is *longer* (note this means the deal could go on forever). Also, the contract generally says that, if the term ends in the middle of a tour, they have the right to finish the tour even if the year is up and you're recouped. When you're negotiating, try to get the right to repay the advance and terminate the deal after the one year, so that you don't find yourself with a perpetual merchandiser. For example, if you have a one-year term with an extension until recoupment, and at the end of the year you have recouped all but $10,000 of a $200,000 advance, it means you've done pretty well over the tour. However, if you don't have the right to repay, the term would continue until you recoup. Thus, the merchandiser would get your next tour (which might be a year later) automatically and for no advance. If you have the right to repay, however, you can write them a check for $10,000 (which would be more than covered by the advance you get for your next tour), and move on. Or more commonly, you rattle your saber by threatening to repay the advance, which brings the merchandiser to the negotiating table and gets it to pay you an additional advance and make a new deal. (Note this payback right can only be good for you. If the unrecouped amount is very large, it means something is seriously wrong and you won't leave because no one else wants you; if it's a small amount, you don't want to lock them into the next tour. And for this reason, it's also getting harder to come by.)

ADVANCE REPAYMENT

Unlike record deals, tour merchandise contracts require repayment of the advance, generally with interest, in the event of certain contingencies:

- The tour doesn't start on time. This was discussed above.
- You're disabled or otherwise unable to perform all or part of the tour. This is based on the same theory as the tour not starting on time, and also protects them from your delaying for years until you recover and maybe aren't so popular.
- You don't meet a **performance minimum** (which is discussed in the next section). This means you agreed to play before a certain number of people and fell short. Most companies want back the

entire advance if you fall short, but you should try to get a pro-rata formula based on how many people you actually played for. For example, if you agreed to play before 200,000 people, but only played before 100,000, you would only want to pay back one-half (100,000/200,000) of the advance. Also, the merchandiser may only be willing to prorate if you hit a certain percentage of your performance guarantee. In other words, if you only played for 10% of the people, they may not be willing to give you any credit whatsoever. A typical compromise is that you must hit 50% to 90% (depending on bargaining power) of the performance minimum before you get the benefit of prorating the advance. For example, if you agreed to perform before 200,000 people and you had to hit 50% before you could prorate your advance repayment, you would need to perform before at least 100,000. If you didn't, then you would have to pay back the entire unrecouped balance. If you did, then you'd only have to pay back the unrecouped balance, not to exceed 50% of the advance (because you played to 50% of the people). If you played to 150,000 people (which is 75% of the 200,000), you'd only have to pay back 25% of the advance.

When you negotiate all of these, it is *absolutely imperative* to make sure you don't have to pay back any more than your unrecouped balance. For example, if you only hit half your performance criteria and owe back half the advance, but you're recouped, you shouldn't owe the merchandiser anything—the company shouldn't have the right to get its money back more than once. However, I have yet to see a form that gives this to you if you don't ask.

PERFORMANCE MINIMUM

The requirement to perform before a minimum number of people (the **performance minimum**) is not nearly as simple as it sounds, and indeed over recent years it has gotten pretty complex. Let's first look at why it's important.

How successful you are in selling merchandise is calculated in terms of **per head** amounts, meaning the average amount spent by each person who attends a concert. For example, if 10,000 people attend a show, and your merchandising gross revenue is $30,000, you did $3.00 per head. Doing $3.00 to $5.00 per head is a reasonable average at this writing for adult-oriented groups, such as Elton John, Billy Joel, etc. Rock 'n' roll bands, heavy metal groups, and strong alternative bands (read "fanatic kids attend their concerts and spend a lot of money") tend to do around $6.00 to $9.00 per head. Major events (like the Lollapalooza tour) and a few megastars (like U2, The Eagles, Pink Floyd) can do $8.00 to $10.00 per head, and sometimes even more. That gets to be serious money when 16,000-plus attend each show.

Because this is how merchandisers measure sales, you can see why they want you to guarantee how many heads will pass before their merchandising stands (called a **performance guarantee**). It doesn't mean much for you to do $12.00 per head if only ten people show up. Thus, merchandising deals require a minimum number of people to attend your shows.

So, figuring out how many people attended your shows (to meet your performance criteria) should be pretty simple—just count heads, right? *Wrong.*

Paid Attendees. First, the only people who count are those who *paid* to see your show. The theory is that people who get freebies are lousy merchandise buyers, so they're excluded from the count.

Adjustments. Second, there are usually two important adjustments to the paid attendee number:

1. **Stadium shows**
   (meaning venues of roughly 20,000 plus) are treated differently, because the per-head amounts tend to be lower at these shows. This is logical; since there are so many people, they can't all be die-hard fans. Also, magnify this effect if there are a number of headlining acts (like at a festival), because many people came only to see another artist. Thus, stadium per-head figures are usually distorted (meaning lower).

   The most common adjustment is to reduce the number of stadium paid attendees to a negotiated number (like one person counts only as one-half or two-thirds of a paid attendee). I prefer, however, tying the reduction to the per-head figures at the stadium show over the average per-head figures at other shows, which may mean no adjustment. This is easy to understand with an example: Assume that, throughout your tour, you're averaging $3.00 per head in merchandising. Then assume you have two stadium shows, where you average $2.00 per head. If 30,000 people attended each stadium show, for purposes of your performance criteria, ⅔ of them (the $2.00 per head stadium figure over the $3.00 per head average), or 20,000, count toward your performance minimum.

2. Foreign

The second adjustment is for performances outside of the United States and Canada. This is again either a negotiated fraction (one-half, two-thirds, etc.), or else a reduction based on the per-head figures in the territory involved versus the United States per-head figures. For example, if, in the United States, your merchandising average is $2.00 per head, but in England your average is only $1.00 per head, then each person in England would count as one-half ($1.00/$2.00) of a paid attendee for purposes of meeting your requirement. Accordingly, for example, a show for 5,000 people in England would count as 2,500 against your performance requirement.

If you're a major international act, you can negotiate specific attendance figures for each territory (e.g., you agree to play for 50,000 people in Germany), and then there is none of this adjusting (except for stadium shows). This is really just saying the same thing in different words: A 25,000-person requirement that counts people as one-half each is the same as agreeing to play for 50,000 people.

EXCLUSIVITY

Tour merchandise deals require some exclusivity, which is normally a statement that you can't sell your merchandise within twenty miles of a concert site, within forty-eight hours prior to the show. Be sure you exclude retail sales from this (you might find yourself in breach of both your concert and your retail sales agreements if you don't), and you should also exclude any record company promotions (such as a T-shirt or poster giveaway to promote your album). If you have a tour sponsor or have done a commercial, and they have the right to give away or sell merchandise, you have to deal with this specifically in your merchandising agreement—and your merchandiser isn't going to like it very much. So be extremely careful in giving these rights to a commercial sponsor. The usual compromise is to limit the amount of merchandise the sponsor can give away within a few days before the concert, which is in both your and the merchandiser's interest. (If the sponsor gives all your fans a T-shirt just before the show, your concert sales won't be so hot.)

CREATIVE CONTROL

You should have the right to approve the design, artwork, photos, drawings, layout, etc., used in all merchandise, as well as the quality of the good themselves. If you have a federally registered service mark for your name, you need to approve the quality in order to preserve your service mark's legal status. (As we discussed on page 320, a **service mark** is like a trademark; it's your group's or individual professional name.) Even if you haven't registered your service mark, however, you should still insist on approving quality for purposes of maintaining your claims in the name, as well as keeping your image up.

SELL-OFF RIGHTS

At the end of the term, the merchandiser wants the right to sell off any remaining merchandise. This is usually for a period of six months, and they should have no right to *manufacture,* only to *sell* whatever is on hand. They will ask for the right to sell it through wholesale (meaning retail) outlets, since there won't be any concerts. You get a royalty for these sales, which is the same as if they were sold under a retail deal (see the discussion of retail royalties on page 359).

Here are some other things to ask for, which are very similar to the sell-off rights under print music deals which we discussed on page 237:

1. The right to sell off must be totally nonexclusive, so you can have another merchandiser in place.
2. The merchandiser can't **stockpile** goods. This means it can't manufacture a ton of goods right before the end, so that the company has a lot of leftovers to sell. You should get language that restricts manufacturing to "only such quantity of goods as is necessary to meet reasonably anticipated sales requirements."
3. Merchandisers can't have **distress** sales, meaning they can't sell your goods at low prices just to get rid of them. (This practice is also called **dumping**.) Otherwise, you'll be adorning a lot of Kmart shoppers and swap-meet fans. It also perturbs your new merchandiser, who is trying to sell your stuff at full price.
4. You should have the right to purchase the merchandise at the end of the term. And if you buy it, the merchandiser has no sell-off rights at all. (If you don't, the merchandiser gets a six-month sell-off period, and at the end of that you should have a

second right to purchase the leftovers.) *Never* take the *obligation* to repurchase; if they can't sell this crap, why would you think you can? But always take the *option*—if you're successful your next merchandiser may want it.

5. At the end of the sell-off period, they have to destroy anything you don't buy.

BOOTLEGGERS

Merchandisers want the right, and you should encourage them, to chase **bootleggers.** Bootleggers (as the name implies from its original usage during Prohibition, where bootleggers sold illegal booze) are people who, without any authority, manufacture merchandise with your name and/or likeness on it, and sell it outside the venues. Legitimate merchandisers are always inside the facility; bootleggers are the guys who hit you on the street approaching the building. (One of their better tricks is to hire college students for $100 or so per night, so the vendors look wholesome, clean-cut, and somewhat innocent, while the manufacturers stay out of sight.) Not only are these people costing you money because you don't get paid for the merchandise, but their goods are usually of inferior quality. And guess who gets the complaint letters when some Schenectady fan's T-shirt shrinks to fit her Barbie doll?

The legitimate merchandisers have been relatively successful in dealing with these pieces of slime, and have indeed discovered that in many cases they are large, sophisticated operations (one even owned its own T-shirt factory). Through means I'm not free to tell you, the merchandisers have been able to track the bootleggers down, and they then get the courts to stop them. Thus, over the last few years, at least in the United States, this practice has decreased. (The laws abroad aren't always so hospitable.) The merchandisers will ask you to pay part of the money to chase the pirates, but if you have some clout, they'll front it and have you bear a percentage out of either the recovery and/or your other royalties.

25

Retail Merchandising

This category covers the various ways of selling merchandise besides at concerts—retail stores (poster shops, etc.), through mail order, fan clubs, etc.

The retail merchandiser acts not only as a manufacturer/distributor (as you would expect), but also as a middleman between you and other merchandisers. Since there are numerous small companies that specialize in particular areas (posters, buttons, belt buckles, condoms, stickers, patches, trading cards, etc.), it's better to license some of these rights to an expert. Also, it's not economical for the merchandisers to engage in all these areas, since they're not great profit centers compared to clothing. Thus, your retail merchandiser will **sublicense** these smaller rights (meaning license out the rights to someone else). When merchandisers do this, they keep a percentage of the license income, ranging generally from 20% to 30%. In other words, they make a deal with a bumper-sticker company to manufacture and sell bumper stickers with your name, and they pay you 70% to 80% of the royalties and advances they get from the sticker company. In exchange for their percentage, they negotiate and sign the license agreement, and afterward "police" it (read: "make sure you get paid"). Because entering into a number of these licensing agreements yourself is best described as a "pain in the butt for small money," paying this percentage is usually worth it. As you move further into the superstar realm, you may want to make some of these deals directly, but only as the numbers begin to get pretty big.

ROYALTIES

The royalties merchandisers pay you when they manufacture the goods themselves (as well as the royalties they get when they license someone else to manufacture) are generally in the following range (for the United States):

1. **Sales through retail stores:** 10% to 20% of the wholesale price. This includes T-shirts, sweatshirts, hats, posters, buttons, cards, bumper stickers, belt buckles, etc.
2. **Mail-order sales:** 25% of the price charged. This is higher because they are, in this case, the actual retailers selling directly to the public, and there is no distributor taking a profit in the middle. Thus, they get more for the goods than when they sell them to a wholesaler.

Retail royalties have taken a recent jump, thanks to one particularly rebel company that has offered very high deals and forced a lot of the marketplace to follow. That's why the above numbers are substantially higher than the historical 10% to 15% of wholesale that merchandisers like to pay.

Foreign royalties are roughly 80% of the U.S. rates.

OTHER DEAL POINTS

When you make a retail merchandise deal, many of the considerations are exactly the same as tour merchandising deals, such as:

1. Approval of the merchandise items
2. Approval of your likeness
3. Approval of the designs and layout
4. Restrictions on sell-off rights
5. Right to purchase merchandise at the end

In addition, there are a couple of points peculiar to retail:

Approval of Sublicenses. You want the right to approve all agreements they make with sublicensees concerning your product.

Cross-Collateralization. If your retail agreement is with the same company that has your tour merchandise, you have to deal with whether the advance under the tour agreement is cross-collateralized with the retail deal (and vice versa). (For a discussion of cross-collateralization, see page 104.) Cross-collateralization is *never* good for you; allow it only if they offer you a humongous amount of money that you can't get any other way.

If you're on the *Fast Track* and
You're interested in Classical Music, go to chapter 26 on page 365.
You hate Classical and like Multi-Media, On-Line, and Cyberspace, go to chapter 27 on page 371.
Both of those sound boring, saunter over to Film Music in chapter 28 on page 383.
If you answered "None of the Above," *Fast Track* to the Conclusion on page 421.

CAUTION

Before you tackle the rest of the book, be sure you have a pretty good understanding of record and publishing basics in chapters 7, 8, 15, 16, and 18. If you skipped ahead and don't already know this stuff, I suggest you go back. Even if you're reading straight through, you might want to review these chapters quickly. The areas we're about to discuss are a bit complex, so be sure you have a solid grasp of the basics before attempting them.

PART VII

Classical Music

26

Classical Music

I shall now tap my baton on the music stand to politely engage your attention, as we move into the world of classical music. Please do not applaud between movements, and speak only in hushed tones for the duration of this chapter.

The principles of royalty, advance, etc. are the same for classical as for rock and all other kinds of music. However, several areas differ radically, and here they are:

TERM AND PRODUCT

Because classical artists don't generally compose the material they record, and because their recordings are in essence "live performances," they can make records much faster and more often than pop artists. Also, since the compositions already exist, the recordings can be planned very far in advance, which is not generally possible in the pop world. So for both of these reasons, it is typical for classical artists to record between one to three albums per year, and it is also typical for the company to commit to recording for a period of four to five years on a firm basis.

As the classical world creeps toward pop, some companies have started to introduce the concept of options in their deals. These options are both as to the number of years under the recording agreement (see page 119), and as to the number of albums per year (see page 116). For example, the company might commit to a three year term, with a two year option, and during each year they would commit to one album firm, with the right to ask for another one or two albums per year.

ROYALTIES

The economics of classical music are quite different because the market is so much smaller and the costs of recording can be quite large.

For example, the cost of recording with a full orchestra can run $150,000 to $400,000, and typical album sales are in the 5,000 to 10,000 unit range *worldwide* (the sales levels that we've been using for pop artists are only for the United States). In fact, a "big seller" is 50,000 or more worldwide. (A major exception to all of this is an "event driven" album, meaning a recording of a famous show. An example is the Three Tenors album [with Pavarotti, Domingo, and Carrera], which was recorded at Dodger Stadium and I understand sold over 1,000,000 copies.)

In light of the sales levels, you won't be surprised to hear that royalties in the classical world are much lower. The good news, however, is that you're paid on every record sold, meaning the company eats all of the recording costs. In other words, the only thing recouped is the advance you put in your pocket. This is a radical difference from the pop world, where the company will recoup anything it can get its hands on (see page 103 for a discussion of this).

How much lower are the royalties? A typical deal is in the range of 7.5% to 10% of SRLP (pop music royalty ranges are on page 109). Classical artist's royalties aren't "all-in" (see page 110), which means you aren't responsible for a producer, and so you get to keep all of the royalties (though you often have to share them, as noted in the next paragraph).

In classical, unlike pop, the albums are often amalgamations of several different artists, so the royalties are spread around. Important guest soloists get a royalty, and so do major conductors and very successful orchestras. In fact, it's sometimes difficult to tell whose album it is. For example, is an album on which Leonard Wheezebottom, violin virtuoso, performs with the Tarzana Symphony (Axl Rose conducting), a Rose, Tarzana, or Wheezebottom album?

As in the case of joint recordings on the pop side (see page 174 for what those are), the royalties are allocated in an agreed manner amongst the participants. While there's no hard and fast rule, a principal soloist might get 4% to 5% of SRLP, a conductor 1% to 2%, a guest soloist 2% to 3%, and a well-known orchestra 1% to 2%.

ADVANCES

As noted above, a typical classical release sells far less units than a typical pop release (or at least less than what the pop company hopes to sell). So because of this, advances are much smaller, typically in the range of $5,000 to $10,000 per album. If an artist has "marquee" value, meaning that his name is recognizable (e.g., Yo-Yo Ma, Luciano Pavarotti, John Williams, etc.), his advance is generally from $15,000 to $50,000.

The size of an advance also depends on:

1. The extent to which you participate in the recording. If you're only guesting, for example, your advance will be lower than if you're the principal soloist.
2. The type of work being recorded. If you're the principal piano soloist on a recording, for example, you'll get a lower advance for an orchestral recording (which is expensive) than you will for a recording of piano solo works (where they just set up a microphone and drop a few bucks in your brandy snifter).
3. And lastly, your advance depends on that common denominator of all business: Clout and leverage.

MECHANICAL ROYALTIES

Much of classical music is in the public domain, which means that no mechanical royalties are paid for the music (see page 288 for a discussion of public domain, and page 219 for a discussion of mechanical royalties). However, some of the compositions may be more recent, or even contemporary, and thus mechanical royalties have to be paid to the publishers of these works. Also, *arrangements* of public domain works are copyrightable if they have enough originality, and mechanical royalties have to be paid for the arrangement.

When mechanical royalties are paid, there is often a reduction of your royalty. You are usually charged about half of the burden, although this is negotiable, and it's not always as simple as I've just stated. For example, it's sometimes a reduction of your royalty rate, which at the end of the day, results in your eating about half of the mechanicals.

If you're on the *Fast Track*, and you're interested in Multi-Media, On-Line, and Cyberspace, go to chapter 27 on page 371.
If you're interested in Film Music, go to chapter 28 on page 383.
Otherwise, *Fast Track* to the Conclusion on page 421.

PART VIII

Music in Multi-Media, On-Line, and Other Adventures in Cyberspace

27

Music in Multi-Media, On-Line, and Other Adventures in Cyberspace

The good news about music in multi-media is that it's so new that the law and industry customs haven't hardened into stone. So those of us who have been in the music business for years don't have any more expertise than you do. Also, wildcat entrepreneurs have a lot of opportunities because the big players haven't taken over the landscape. So there'll be a lot of action here in the coming years.

Now for the bad news. So far, multi-media hasn't been very profitable because the industry is so small. But it's growing at a massive pace, and we're in for some profound changes.

WHAT'S GOING ON TODAY?

The two major areas of music in multi-media today are **CD-ROMs** and **On-Line Services**.

CD-ROM means "Compact Disc—Read Only Memory" which is a fancy way to say that you can play it but you can't record on it. CD-ROMs look just like the music CDs you buy, but when you put them in your computer, they display visual material, such as graphics, pictures, text, and videos. (Enhanced CDs are also a form of CD-ROMs, but they are treated more like records, as discussed on page 172. This section deals with full-blown CD-ROMs.)

On-line services means anything that can connect your computer to the outside world, such as the Internet or one of the commercial services (Prodigy, CompuServe, America On-Line, etc.). If you don't know the basics of how to get on-line and surf around, there are a lot of good books on the subject that can walk you through the process.

Also, the commercial services would be delighted to send you free software and teach you how to use it, so that you can sign up and pay them a lot of money.

Let's look at these two areas one at a time:

CD-ROMS

CD-ROMs have been successful in the game area (like Myst and Seventh Guest), as well as in the encyclopedia/archive type (like *Encyclopaedia Britannica, Guinness Book of Records,* and *Cinemania,* which is Microsoft's listing of films, clips, and information). Celebrity-driven CD-ROMs, such as the ones that featured Prince and Bob Dylan, have met with limited success.

Clear the Decks

In order to put out a CD-ROM, you need to **clear** the rights, which means getting permission to use whatever materials you want to include. The process of clearing multi-media rights is almost as enjoyable as having your teeth drilled, as it involves making lots of itty bitty deals for small amounts of money, where the other guy has no reason to move quickly because he doesn't make much.

Here's what needs clearing:

1. **Musical clearances**: CD-ROM clearances are very much like those for records, meaning that the owners of materials usually want a royalty every time the CD-ROM is sold. We'll discuss the details of these royalties in the next section.

2. **Non-musical clearances**: This includes photos, text, data base, film clips, inflatable squeaky toys, etc., and also some weird things like the right of publicity and privacy and "moral rights" for some countries outside the United States (see page 266 for a discussion of moral rights). Also, the unions have a say in all of this, because when you take existing recordings from one medium to another you are putting musicians out of work (since you don't have to hire them again). Accordingly, the unions want something called re-use payment. (Re-use payments are discussed in the film section, on page 390.)

The Economics of CD-ROM Deals

There are two different kinds of deals for CD-ROMs: a **whole package deal** and a **piece-meal deal** (these aren't industry terms; I just made them up). A *whole package* means that the CD-ROM company makes a single deal with all the rights holders in a bundle. An example would be a CD-ROM that features one artist, where the company contracts with the artist and his or her record company for all of the rights to the recordings, publishing, likeness of the artist, etc. The royalties on these deals run somewhere in the range of 10% to 20% of wholesale, with the norm being in the 10% to 15% range. (At the time of this writing, wholesale is approximately $21.00 to $26.00, for a suggested retail of $39.95 to $49.95. The companies haven't yet figured out how to charge packaging deductions, so don't tell them.) Sometimes the royalty escalates with sales, although the escalation points are low by record standards because these titles sell a lot less copies. For example, a deal might be a 10% royalty up to 25,000 units, 15% from 25,000 to 50,000, and 20% over 50,000.

Some of the CD-ROM deals are done with a 50/50 profit split instead of a royalty. This is very similar to a profit split on record deals (see page 198), where the CD-ROM company first gets back all of the costs and expenses from gross revenues, and then the rights providers and the company split the profits on a 50/50 basis.

Assuming that the CD-ROM company is unable to do "one-stop shopping," they have to run around and acquire rights from a lot of different places. This is what I call a *piece-meal deal*. It's also what I call a *major pain in the butt*, because it means making lots of deals with a bunch of people. And who are these people? Why, the owners of the:

1. Master recordings
2. Songs
3. Videos
4. Still photos
5. Reviews, liner notes and other text material
6. Whatever other junk you include

The payment for small stuff (like reviews) is usually done on a **buy-out** basis, meaning there's no royalty (just a flat fee and an "hasta la vista"). The fees generally range around $250 to $1,000.

People who own songs and recordings are not nearly so accommodating, and so either the buy-outs are more expensive, or more commonly the owners want a royalty. The amount paid for masters and songs is usually about the same, and there are no hard and fast rules. If the publisher gives a buy-out, which is increasingly rare, it will be in the area of $500 to $5,000 plus (depending on the length of use and the importance of the material). Also, if there are only a few songs played in full, it will be more expensive for each song than if there are little snippets of a lot of songs. When there's a royalty, a "snippet" type use would get about 1¢ to 5¢ per song (plus another 1¢ to 5¢ for the master), usually with a guaranteed minimum of 10,000 units. If the CD-ROM is music driven (meaning the music is an essential element, like a Bob Dylan or Peter Gabriel project), then it goes up to the range of 8¢ to 15¢ per unit, again with a 10,000 unit minimum.

Sometimes the royalty is based on a percentage of the wholesale price (5% to 10%), which is divided amongst the songs on the basis of playing time, often with a guaranteed minimum of 10¢ to 15¢ per song. So, for example, if you had a two minute use of your song and there was twenty minutes total of music, you would get 10% of the total royalty, but not less than 12¢. One recent deal I saw paid the music 50% of the royalty paid for all of the rights (in that case, 10% of wholesale), because the essence of the product was music.

These grants of rights are usually for a limited time (about three to five years), and they may also be limited to the United States or other designated territories. The licenses are also nonexclusive, which means that the owner is free to grant the same rights to any other CD-ROM company. However, in the case where the CD-ROM is a capsule of one artist's career, the company will want some exclusivity to prevent anyone granting rights to a competitive CD-ROM that features the same artist's career.

Another aspect of these licenses is that they limit the **platforms**. A *platform* means the type of medium in which the product may be sold. A CD-ROM is one platform, and on-line usage is another. There is usually an argument whether the company is granted rights to license the product in future technologies, such as DVD (see page 179 for what that is). The answers depend on bargaining power.

Because of all the above complications, a lot of CD-ROM companies have simply thrown up their hands and taken the position that they should create their own music. So they hire someone to write the music for a fee (generally from $10,000 to $50,000), and the company then owns it and doesn't have to pay any royalties or clear any music rights. Recently, the creators of this music have become more sophisticated, and many of them want to share in uses of the music outside the CD-ROM.

ON-LINE SERVICES

The current services are:

1. **Web sites**, which have information available for reading and **downloading** (meaning copying onto your personal computer),

such as publicity materials, photos of artists, tour schedules, sound samples (usually less than 30 seconds, which at the time of this writing take 2 to 5 minutes to load onto your computer). Most of the record companies have web sites, as do a lot of the major artists (many artists have more than one, some of which are unauthorized).

2. **Chat rooms**, where you can connect with a bunch of other people interested in the same subject and communicate back and forth through your keyboards. Chat room communications are in *real time*, which means the messages you send are received by the other people almost instantly. There are a number of music chat lines around, where fans can trade information and gossip. There's also an "insiders" industry chat line, the location of which is pretty well guarded, and in fact I've never seen it. I'm told that record company executives go in there under phony names and trash each other.

3. A **bulletin board**, which is a place to read electronic messages, and also a place where you can leave messages for other people to read. Most major music groups have bulletin boards devoted to them.

4. **On-line audio services**, which are basically "radio stations" on the Internet, and which use a software that plays music in *real time* (as noted above, that means you get it almost at the same instant they're sending it). As of this writing, the sound quality is nowhere near CDs.

There are also services like virtual record stores, meaning you can electronically browse through their catalog and then order the records via credit card. The records are mailed to you within a few days.

On-line music deals today are basically considered promotional, meaning two things:

1. The uses are primarily to "promote" the artist involved, by encouraging people to buy their records, see their concerts, etc.; and

2. No one's figured out how to make any money with it yet.

People who run "legitimate" on-line services get licenses from the owners of the materials. Since most rights owners view this as promotional (meaning it's not a profit-making enterprise in itself, but it helps promote the artist by providing information to fans), they license small bits of material for free. At the time of this writing, you can normally get a usage of thirty seconds or less without charge because people believe it will sell records. On the other hand, a lot of web sites are run by fans who decided to set up their own shop and can't be bothered with some new-fangled concept like getting the rights to do it.

The Current Laws of the Electronic Frontier

The law in the on-line area is quite new and trying mightily to adapt itself. Any time you have a concept created in 1909 being applied to technology that wasn't even conceived, you create a healthy fund to put lawyers' children through college. The problem is that these uses aren't quite records, aren't quite radio, aren't quite television, or maybe they're all of them. Certainly everyone who has the ability to collect money for anything is going to stand in line with the age-old expression "Where's my piece?" For example, the music publishers want to treat on-line usages as performances, meaning they want to be paid the same way they're paid when songs are played on the radio. The publishers also want to treat the fact that someone might download material as a sale of a record, which would trigger a mechanical royalty (see page 303 for a discussion of a recent amendment to the copyright law that deals with this).

So far, the law has protected the rights holders pretty well. In one famous case, *Playboy* sued an outfit that was putting up centerfolds and allowing people to download them for free. *Playboy* whipped them resoundingly in court, based on an infringement of *Playboy*'s copyright (making these pictures available violated *Playboy*'s right to distribute and to display the pictures; see page 206 for what all that means), as well as a violation of *Playboy*'s trademark (see page 320), and two other legal theories. For your lawyers, the theories were (a) unfair competition and passing off, by not attributing ownership of the photos to *Playboy,* and (b) the decision that these activities weren't a "fair use." The case is *Playboy Enterprises v. Frena,* 839 F. Supp. 1552 (1993).

The major on-line case in the music area, which was settled under a confidential arrangement, is pretty interesting. The National Music Publishers Association (a group of publishers) sued CompuServe (an on-line services provider) because of their MIDI Forum. MIDI stands for "Musical Instrument Digital Interface," which is a high-falootin' way of hooking your keyboard up to a computer. What happened was that on-line subscribers were making MIDI arrangements of copyrighted songs and posting them on a bulletin board provided by

CompuServe. Other folks then downloaded the arrangements, and many of these new people changed the songs and reposted them on the bulletin board.

The publishers argued that all this copying was a violation of their copyrights, which it certainly was. The really interesting issue, however, was whether or not CompuServe was responsible for it. Under the law, if someone writes a newspaper article that infringes a copyright, a newsstand that merely sells the paper isn't guilty of copyright infringement, even though the writer and newspaper publisher are. This is because the publisher and writer have control of the content, while the newsstand doesn't. CompuServe argued that they were only a "newsstand," and the music publishers argued that CompuServe had the ability to control what went into their computers and were thus responsible. Since CompuServe is neither a newspaper publisher nor a newsstand, the issue was a new one. And because the case was settled secretly, we'll have to wait to find out the answer.

Another issue concerns whether on-line services need performing rights licenses. In other words, are they "broadcasters," like a TV or radio station. The argument is that each time the materials are sent over the wires, it's arguably a "performance" (see page 230 for a discussion of performance rights). This is by no means an easy question. An electronic transmission isn't a "performance" in the traditional sense, because it isn't being played in a form to which you could listen. (Actually, you could listen, but it's a stream of electronic information that sounds like a parakeet in a blender.) Once the information is received, however, it can then be played back in the normal fashion. So maybe it was "performed." Also, these transmissions are arguably the sale of a record, triggering a mechanical royalty (see pages 219 and 303), because the person downloading it now has a copy, just as if they had bought the record. Confusing? Welcome to Cyberspace.

WHERE DO WE GO FROM HERE?

At the time of this writing, it's not practical to download music very quickly. (Notice I say "at the time of this writing" because it may have changed before I finish typing this.) A few years ago, Aerosmith did a promotion where they allowed a new single to be downloaded. For a record that was approximately two and one-half minutes in length, it took anywhere from 45 minutes to one and one-half hours to download the copy (depending on your modem speed). However, modems are getting faster, compression technologies are getting better, and it won't be long before music can be downloaded in high-quality real time, meaning that you can record it as fast as you can play it. And I'm sure it won't be long after that before music can be downloaded even faster than it can be played, in a burst of digital joy.

My techie friends tell me it will be quite a while before we get "music on demand," meaning you could simply dial up your favorite record and copy it instead of going to the store to buy it. Although it's inevitable that records will be sold this way in the future, I don't think it will ever replace record stores because there's too much "experience" and "vibe" in going into a store. On the other hand, it will forever change the way business is done. Shall we count the ways? Here are two:

1. On the economic side, record companies will no longer have the costs of manufacturing, distribution, freight, etc., and so their profit margin on these kinds of sales will be spectacular.

2. Because you don't have to fund the costs listed in #1, anybody can become a record company and start putting out their music. Thus, we'll have a generation of artists who get their records directly to fans, without having a record company executive as a gatekeeper. I think this will lead to stronger bargaining power for artists, because they may wait and sign with a record company after they're already successful. That of course will radically shift bargaining power and change the entire face of the business. For example, I'm guessing we'll see shorter term deals and bigger advances. Won't that be fun!

The dark side of digital transmission becoming faster and easier is the problem of someone buying a CD, copying the information, and then spreading it around to all their friends or, worse yet, putting it on the Internet so that anyone who wants it can copy it for free. Even though I think the courts will hold that it's an infringement to duplicate someone's copyrighted work this way, policing every Internet site is impossible. For every one you stomp out, three more pop up somewhere else. And whose law governs? If the infringing site is in a country with no copyright laws, is there a problem if I copy it over the Internet? And if so, what court has jurisdiction? Nobody knows.

For all these reasons, I think the solution must come from technology and not from the courts. In other words, there's a need for an encryption (scrambling) system that will technologically prevent anyone's copying of a CD. Otherwise, the ability of artists to profit from their work will be seriously eroded.

Just like a new country that's setting up its borders and having skirmishes with its neighbors, Cyberspace frontiers are still taking form. There will be a lot of action, and it will intensify as the money gets bigger. It will also be a lot of fun. Keep your arms and legs inside the car, and hold on to your hats, sunglasses, and small children.

If you're on the *Fast Track*, and you're interested in Film Music, go to chapter 28 on page 383. Otherwise, *Fast Track* to the Conclusion on page 421. All others, boogie on.

PART IX

Motion Picture Music

28

Overview of Motion Picture Music

Congratulations again! You are now in graduate school. To understand music in films, you need a complete knowledge of the music business (records, copyrights, and publishing), as well as a knowledge of the film business. I couldn't have put this chapter earlier in the book, because you wouldn't have been ready for it. But now you are, so let's go.

INTRODUCTION

I have seen music screw up more motion pictures than bad directors. This is because music is a stepchild in movies. It's a small item compared to the budget of the film, and as you'll see, music in films is quite complicated. It is normally left to the last minute, at which point there's a massive panic and very little time to get it together properly. Often this is for good cause—it may not be possible to record the music until the studio knows exactly what the picture looks like—but many times it's simply a matter of neglect. As music supervisors become more important in the industry (more about who they are later), this seems to be changing (a little). However, there are always panicked emergencies, no matter what.

ONE SONG—FIVE DEALS

One of the main difficulties is that film people, by and large, don't fully understand music (not that they should—their expertise is in making films). And it doesn't help that film music is complicated. For example, for every song going into a film, there are always deals to be made with three, and up to five, entities:

1. The performer (singer/instrumental)
2. The songwriter
3. The record producer
4. The record company to whom the performer is exclusively signed
5. The record company putting out the soundtrack album

If any of the above balls drop to the ground while you're juggling, or if any of the rights under one agreement don't match those required by another, the song may have to be trashed. And film producers on a tight delivery schedule with a multimillion-dollar film at stake don't like to be told a song is holding up their picture (would you?).

For all these reasons, the music supervisors/business affairs/lawyers/studio executives in charge of film music have extraordinarily difficult jobs. If they deliver the music and pull off minor miracles by balancing all the competing interests, it was expected and they're lucky to get a thanks. However, if something goes wrong and the film producer can't use a song, they're the villains. Wanna sign up?

All in all, if I were going to sum up clearing music for films, I'd describe it (as we say in Texas) as being like a one-legged man in an ass-kicking contest. But it's fun and satisfying when it works, and so, if you're strong of heart, come along and I'll show you this side of the business.

THE RIGHTS INVOLVED

Film music rights fall into two categories:

Acquisition of rights *for* the picture. These are deals to put music in the film, meaning deals with:

1. Performing artists
2. Songwriters, composers, publishers
3. Record producers
4. Record companies (both for using existing masters in the film, and clearing the right to put new recordings of their artists on a soundtrack album)

Licenses of rights *from* the picture company to others. Once the film company acquires the rights, these are the deals to let other people use them:

1. A deal with a record company to release a soundtrack album
2. Licensing film clips for music videos
3. Possibly a publishing administration deal

Category 1 will be our focus, since it's the main area that will concern you. But I want to give you a feel for the second area as well, so it's sprinkled through the discussion, and dealt with in depth in chapter 34.

29

Performer Deals

OVERVIEW

The deal for an artist to perform music in a film consists of two distinct parts. One is for the artist to perform in the picture itself (which is pretty simple and straightforward), and the other is to use the performance on a soundtrack album and/or single (which can be horrendous).

PERFORMANCE IN THE FILM (NO RECORD RIGHTS)

The deal for an artist to perform a song in a picture is usually for a flat fee. No muss, no fuss, no complications. Since no phonograph records are involved, there's no need to deal with the artist's record company. (Technically, home video devices of the film could require the record company's consent, because these devices are treated as "records" under most deals. See the discussion of this on page 151. Also, under many deals the company won't let the artist violate the re-recording restriction, as we discussed on page 148.)

Fees

The artist's fee can range anywhere from union scale (see page 103 for what that is) up to $100,000 plus for a major artist. The norm is about $5,000 to $10,000 for a minor artist, escalating to perhaps $15,000 to $25,000 for a midlevel artist. Superstars tend to be in the $50,000 to $75,000 range, with some occasionally going higher if the film company is hot for them and the star is playing hard to get. Title songs (i.e., songs played over the opening or closing credits) usually pay better than background music.

All-in Deals

Some artists prefer to negotiate an all-in type deal with the film company. For example, for a total of $75,000, they will record and deliver a completed track. The artist in this case pays the recording costs out of the $75,000, and keeps the difference as a fee. Unless the fee is extraordinarily high, and the artist produces himself or herself for records, I generally don't like to do this. Directors are fussy about what goes into their films, and you don't want to be in the position of having to re-record it several times at your expense. Also, if the artist is not the producer of the recording, you have to pay a producer's fee to someone else, which can be an unknown quantity. I much prefer just having the artist show up, sing, and leave.

Credit

The other major negotiating point is credit. Unless you have the title song (which I'll talk about in a minute), you won't have much to say about credit. Just make sure your credit is no less prominent than any other artist's, both as to size and placement in the film. In reality, this means you'll be included in the **crawl,** which are the credits resembling an eye chart that roll by at the end of the film after everyone's left the theater. (Everyone except me, that is, because I always stay to see who did the music. And half the time I can't read it because it goes by too fast.)

If you do the title song, you can sometimes negotiate a credit in the **main titles** (where the director, writer, and stars are credited). Whether or not you get main-title placement, a title song performer should be able to get a **single card** (meaning no other credit is on the screen at the same time as yours) or at least a card shared only with the songwriter. You should also ask for your credit to be the same size as the first star's, director's, writer's, and producer's credit.

RECORD RIGHTS TO FILM PERFORMANCES

When we move into phonograph records, things get much more complicated. First of all, before you even start negotiating, *you must clear the deal with your record company.* In case you didn't hear me, let me say it again: *Before you start negotiating, you must clear the deal with your record company.* Failure to do so is the cause of the biggest disasters in film music. And don't think you're immune because you're a big name—it happened to Michael Jackson on the *E.T.* album, and CBS Records actually went to court and stopped MCA Records from distributing the record until they made a deal. Record companies take it very seriously if you don't follow this rule, because they see it as a violation of their exclusive rights to your recording services. And they're right.

Today, the major film companies have been stung enough to make sure the artist's record company has blessed the deal. But minor and independent film companies may not be so careful, and in the rush of the moment, any one of us is likely to forget. Also, there can sometimes be missed signals and miscommunications. For example, a manager might think he's cleared the rights with the record company, and indeed he has (sort of). He may have discussed it with the company, and the company said it "sounds okay." However, the record company people meant their approval was subject to working out a deal to compensate them, while the manager genuinely believed they had approved without qualification. So the moral is: Have the film company talk directly to the record company.

Of course, if you can build an exclusion for soundtrack albums into your record deal at the outset (see page 150), you don't have to worry about this. But much of the time you can't. And even if you have an exclusion, you may not want to use it for this film. (If the company agrees you can do a particular soundtrack, you might want to save the exclusion for a time when they don't.) Or you may have already used the exclusion—exclusions usually allow only one cut every year or so, which you may have done, and there may be a second film you want to take. Or the film company may require more rights (like singles) than your exclusion allows. So be sure everyone knows what everyone else is doing.

Assuming you get your record company to go along, you must now negotiate a deal to use your recording on the soundtrack album. There are six aspects to this:

1. What's your royalty?
2. Does your record company get a piece of your royalty?
3. What can your record company recoup against your royalty?
4. What can the company distributing the soundtrack album recoup against your royalty?
5. Exactly what phonograph record rights does the film company get?
6. Who is responsible for what in connection with music videos?

Let's take these in order:

Royalty

Artists' royalties on soundtrack albums generally hover in the range of 10% to 13%, all-in (i.e., including the producer), and if you're a new artist, you may even get less. If you're midlevel and up, this is lower than you would get in the marketplace (because the film company takes part of the royalties).

If there are a number of artists on the album, at about the same level, the 10% to 13% is about right. However, if you're the only star on the record (such as a situation where the other cuts on the album are minor artists or underscore ["underscore" is defined on page 398], or where you're the superstar among midlevel artists), you should definitely get more because the other cuts bear substantially lower royalties. In these cases, I think you're justified in asking for a much higher royalty, say in the 16% to 18% range. The companies will kick and scream, but if you have enough clout you can pull it off.

Your Company's Rights

Record companies want to collect all the royalties you get from soundtrack albums and singles. How much of it they get to keep is subject to negotiation between you and them. It can range anywhere from zero (for a really major superstar) to 50%, which is the norm. The record company justifies keeping 50% of the royalties as a cost of waiving your exclusivity and allowing your recording to be released on somebody else's label. They treat the part they don't keep (the other 50%) as royalties under your deal. This means they use your 50% to recoup your deficit, if any, or if you're recouped, they pay it to you on your next accounting statement. In fact, even if they agree to keep nothing, they'll use your royalties for recoupment. You may be able to get half or all of your share paid to you even if you're unrecouped; the ability to do this varies directly with your bargaining power. (By the way, if your record company happens to be distributing the soundtrack album, you should ask for 100% of the royalty, because you're not being released from any exclusivity. Usually this is agreeable, but you gotta ask.)

Your record company will want to be a party to your deal with the film company. And in fact the film company will want this as well—that way they're sure that you've cleared the rights involved.

Recoupment

Unlike record deals, where everything is recoupable, in films you can often knock out a good portion (or even all) of the costs. Let's look at them individually:

Recording Costs. You can sometimes make all or a portion of the recording costs nonrecoupable. The way to do this is to argue that the costs of recording are really costs of the film, which they would incur even if there were no album, and thus it's not fair to charge them against record royalties. If you're a superstar, you can pull it off; if you're not, you will end up with anywhere from 25% to 100% of the costs being recoupable.

Artist's Performance Fee. Another question is whether any of your fee to perform in the film is recoupable from your royalties. Again, you can take the position that this is a fee to perform in the film, not on records, and so they shouldn't recoup it. If you have some bargaining power, you can pull this off; otherwise, a part of it may be recoupable. (As a negotiating ploy, if you want to increase your fee and are getting nowhere, try making a portion of the increase recoupable. But use this as a last resort.)

Conversion Costs. As good as all this news sounds, however, there are other costs recouped against you under film deals that aren't chargeable under record deals (because they don't exist). These are known as **conversion costs,** a name I take credit for inventing. (I'm really a pretty modest guy, but every once in a while something gets the better of me.) Conversion costs are the costs of converting a film recording to a recording which can be used in a phonograph record. For example, the recording for the film might only be thirty seconds, but the record company needs a full three-minute version for the album. The conversion costs are the costs to do this, and include those costs you would expect, such a remixing, editing, overdubbing additional instruments (called "sweetening"), and sometimes even totally re-recording the composition. But they also include something you haven't seen before, called:

Re-use Fees. Whenever you use a recording made for one medium (in this case, a motion picture) in another (in this case, records), the union charges you a fee. These fees are called **re-use fees** or **new-use fees** because they are charges to "re-use" an existing recording in a different way (a "new use"). (Re-use fees are also payable when you go the other way around—taking a recording made for records and using it in a film—and in other situations like going from television to records, records to television, records to commercials, etc.) The reasoning is that, when you use an existing recording, you don't have to hire the musicians you would have needed to re-record the composition. Since you're putting union members out of work, the union allows you to do this only if you pay them an amount listed on a schedule (which is close to union scale for the missed sessions).

The amount of re-use fees payable for a particular recording is directly proportionate to the number of musicians on the track. Thus, a three-piece band is cheap, and the Los Angeles Philharmonic Orchestra is not. Indeed, for a fully instrumental, orchestral soundtrack album, the re-use fees can run $90,000 or more.

Conversion costs nowadays are almost always recoupable from your royalties. If you're a major superstar and want to squeeze, you may be able to make 50% to 100% of them nonrecoupable. But it's getting tougher all the time.

What Rights Are Granted

If you can help it, you don't want to give the film company any more than the right to use your master in the film, on the soundtrack album, and on a single. This means you're excluding things such as K-Tel-type licenses, licenses for commercials, licenses for other films, etc. You and your record company should control these other rights. Unless you have very little bargaining power and are up against an obnoxious film company, none of this should be a serious problem (although the usual form contract gives them all rights unless you change it). The only difficulty you may have is that some film companies want the right to use your recording in sequels, remakes, etc. You'll probably have to give this up, but I've sometimes been able either to resist it or get an additional fee.

Use on Artist's Own Record. One nice goodie you can sometimes get is the right to use the recording on your own records. If the film company allows this, they'll say you can't put it on your record for a period of somewhere between six months (if you've really got clout) to two years, with the norm being around nine to twelve months. This period before you can release is called a **hold-back.** The time period may start at release of the picture, release of the soundtrack album, or release of your recording as a single. Whatever you do, though, be sure the date someday arrives. For example, if you measure your period from release of the soundtrack album, and the album is never released, you could never use it. If you ask, the film company will usually agree to a specific date after which you can use it no matter what.

The hold-back effectively means the soundtrack recording will end up on a Greatest Hits album, because it's going to be stale by the time they let you use it (especially if it's released as a single in conjunction with the film). And that's not a coincidence; the film company wants people buying the soundtrack album (not your record) to get the song. Sometimes, however, your record company wants you to put the cut on your own album at the same time as the soundtrack album is out (no hold-back). The film company (and especially the record company with the soundtrack album) won't like this at all. But if you're important enough, and it's the only way they can get you, they may go along.

The film company may ask for a piece of your royalty if you use it on your record, and my general response to this is to tell them to stuff it. So far, they've all stuffed it.

Re-recording Restriction. Just like your record deal, soundtrack deals include a re-recording restriction (see page 148). The period is generally five years, but the date can be from recording, from release of the picture, or release of an album or single. If the date is measured from anything except the date of recording, be sure the restriction period someday expires.

Singles. Another major point of contention is the question of who can put out a single with your performances on it. (We touched on this on page 150.) This is a delicate issue. Record companies don't like the idea of some other company releasing your single. The argument is that it dilutes their exclusivity, and this is true. But one of their secret fears (and I may get clobbered for telling you this) is: They despise the idea that another record company might have a bigger hit with you than they've had. Apart from the embarrassing publicity, it begins to give you the idea that you might be better off elsewhere.

On the other hand, your record company (because it doesn't have the soundtrack album) has nowhere near the economic incentive to push your single as does the other company. Remember, singles make little (if any) money for the record company (and it's shrinking daily), but they do help sell a lot of albums. So your record company is in the funny position of promoting a single (on which it can't make any money) to sell somebody else's album (for which it makes little or nothing while someone else makes a lot of money). Still, the company does have a long-range investment in you, and a hit single at the right time can do wonders for your career, even if you're between albums.

Historically, the company with the artist's exclusive agreement never parted with single rights. However, in recent years there is a slight trend to the contrary. As singles sell less and less, some companies have come to the conclusion that it may not be such a big deal for somebody else to put them out and pay all the marketing and promotion costs. But this varies from company to company, and it's always decided on a case by case basis.

Music Videos

If there is going to be a music video, and there always is if your song is a single, the record and film company usually share the cost of it 50/50. The film company customarily supplies footage from the film (at no cost) to be included in the video.

In the beginning, film companies turned these videos into long previews of the movies. This worked terrifically until MTV and the other broadcasters figured out they were giving away free advertising time for the film, at which point the practice came to an abrupt halt. Now the videos are allowed to have only limited footage from the film, and otherwise must consist of visual performances of the artist or other materials.

When the film company supplies footage, they need some control over the exploitation of the video. This is because improper usage can trigger union problems, both in terms of needing consent and requiring payments. As long as the video is shown in close proximity to release of the film (including television release, home video release, etc.) there should be no union problems; it's considered a promotion of the film. If, however, it's exploited at other times, the film unions may require payment to use footage with their members in it (actors, musicians, singers, etc.), and the film company may also need the consent of union members performing in the clip.

The record company will want to recoup some portion of the video costs from your royalties. Remember, we said that in normal record deals, 50% of the video costs are recoupable (see page 180). In this case, however, the record company is only paying 50% of the costs, and thus there is a strong argument that none of it should be recoupable. The outcome will depend on your bargaining power.

30

Film Songwriter Deals

TERMINOLOGY

Let's now look at film songwriter deals. By songwriter deals, I mean deals for *songs* (both music and lyrics, or sometimes instrumental only) written for the film, as opposed to what's known as the **score** or **underscore,** which is the background music used underneath dialogue, action, etc. (We'll deal with underscore in chapter 31.) Also, this chapter deals with *creating* a song for the film, as opposed to licensing an existing song (not written for the film). (Licensing existing songs is covered on page 412.)

DEAL POINTS

The payment for writing a film song is a fee plus songwriter royalties. If you're a songwriter of sufficient stature, you may be able to keep a piece of the publishing as well.

Fees

The range of fees is anywhere from zero—for someone who just wants to make performance monies (see page 233, dealing with the fact that songs in films can earn substantial performance monies in foreign territories, as well as on television here)—to $40,000 plus for established writers. There are occasionally deals even higher in the stratosphere, but they're rare; the vast majority fall in the range of $5,000 to $25,000, with most in the $7,500 to $15,000 range. Whether or not the writer gets a part of the publishing also affects the size of the fee. (By the way, the film company will never obligate itself to use a song. The most it will do is agree to pay the fee, which is known as **pay or play** because it can either use you [play] or pay you to go away. Pay-or-play provisions in record deals were discussed on page 116.)

Step Deals

Songwriter deals are sometimes done on a **step** basis, meaning the deal is done over a series of "steps." The steps are:

1. The writer writes the song and gives the company an informal demo recording for a small amount of money.
2. If the film company doesn't like it, the company either passes or goes to step two, which requires the writer to rewrite the song for a small additional fee (or maybe no more money). If the company then likes it, it's a firm deal; if not, the deal is off.
3. Once the film company people are happy, it goes forward on a prenegotiated deal to use the song. At this point, the deal is the same as the songwriter deals we just discussed, although I like to ask for more money because we've covered their downside.

All of this is a fancy way of saying the writer does it **on spec** (meaning "on speculation"; i.e., he or she writes the song without a commitment from the film company to pay a full fee for it). The deal may be completely on spec, meaning a film company pays nothing or perhaps a few hundred dollars for the cost of a demo. Or the film company may pay a smaller fee ($1,000 to $5,000) for writing the song, and then have the option to go forward if it likes it (by paying a full fee).

If you're a major songwriter, you shouldn't do anything on spec, because you don't want to spend your time working on a project that may pay you less than your normal fee. Also, rejection is not good for your self-image unless you get your full fee. (It isn't great even then, but at least you didn't totally waste your time.)

If you have to take a step deal, at least try to get some guaranteed money for your trouble, such as $1,000 to $2,500. (Major songwriters can sometimes get up to half their normal fee guaranteed in spec deals.) You should also provide that, if they don't go forward, you get the rights to your song back. The film company will want its money back for this, but you can usually resist it by saying the money was for the right to purchase the song if the company went forward, and it chose not to. A compromise is to give the company part of the money back, or better yet, only give back part of the money (or all if you have to) when you use the song (which means that if it's never used, you don't owe anything).

Buy-Outs

The fee to write the song is a **buy-out,** meaning it "buys out" all usages of the song in any media (including home video, television, etc.), as you would expect. What you might not expect is that it also normally buys out usages in sequels, remakes, television series, and "any other film produced by this producer or studio." When I represent a writer of sufficient stature, I always try to get a separately negotiated, arms-length fee for any usages other than in the original film. A compromise is that it can be used in this film plus sequels and remakes, and perhaps even a television series based on the movie, but anything else requires a fee. This is not an easy point to get; it requires a lot of muscle.

Royalties

The songwriter royalties for films look exactly like those in the normal songwriter deals we discussed on page 252 (e.g., 6¢ for sheet music; 10% wholesale for folios; 50% of all other earnings). However, you can usually do a bit better on the sheet music. Instead of the customary 5¢ or 6¢, you can get 8¢ to 12¢ for major songwriters. Whoopee.

Publishing

Until the last several years, writers got no share of publishing on film songs. Now, with clout, you can get from 25% to 50% of the publishing income, but the film company will want to keep the copyright ownership and the exclusive administration rights. (See page 277 for a discussion of administration.) You may be able to keep control of certain types of synch licenses (such as commercials), just like in any other songwriter deal (see page 266), but this again takes muscle. At a minimum, try for consultation rights on commercials, which means they have to discuss proposed usages with you even though they can make the final decision alone.

If you have sufficient bargaining power, you may be able to administer your own share of publishing. But even in this event, the film company keeps control of synchronization licenses (because they don't want you to license the song to some other film), and it also keeps ownership of the copyright. And if you can't get this, try to get paid directly by the record company and performing rights society.

Credit

The other provision negotiated in a songwriter deal is credit. Normally, unless you write the title song, you get a credit in the "crawl" (see page 387). If this is the case, there's not much to say except that your credit shouldn't be any less prominent than anyone else's. If you write the title song, however, you may be able to get credit on a single card (meaning no one else's is on the screen at the same time), or a card shared only with the artist performing the song. Possibly you can get your card in the main titles (meaning those listing the stars, director, etc.) and, if so, you should ask for the size to be no less than that of the first star, writer, director, or producer.

Unless you're the performer as well as the writer, you don't usually get a single card—at best, you share credit with the performer, in a form such as "Title song performed by *X,* written by *Y.*" If you are *really* a major writer, you may be able to get credit in paid ads for the film, but this is extraordinarily hard to come by. A compromise for superstar writers is to get credit in full-page ads in New York and Los Angeles only (which is great, unless your mother lives in Des Moines). You may also be able to get credit in full-page *trade* ads (meaning entertainment industry ads, such as *Variety, Hollywood Reporter,* etc.), so at least other people in the industry know what you did.

31

Composer Agreements

Composers are the guys and gals who write the **underscore.** Underscore, also called **score,** is the music underneath the dialogue, action, transitions, etc., that you're not supposed to notice but that enhances the mood of the story. If you've ever seen a film without music, you know how stark and empty it feels. A good underscore can radically increase the impact of a movie, just as a bad one can make a movie feel weird and cheap. (For an example of a bad underscore, rent any porno movie at your local video store.)

DEAL POINTS

Deals for composers are similar to those for songwriters, except that a composer almost never gets any share of the publishing. The fee for writing and conducting a major studio theatrical motion picture underscore ranges anywhere from a low of $50,000 to a high of $500,000 plus for the superstars. The normal range is from $125,000 to $300,000. These amounts are just the fees; the film company pays the recording costs on top. Independent companies pay less, and often do "package" deals, as we'll discuss on page 403.

Most of the issues we discussed in chapter 30 concerning songwriters are also relevant to composers. But here are additional points to cover in composer deals:

Delivery Date. The delivery date of the score is a critical point of negotiation. You would expect the fuss to be over your having to deliver by a set date, but surprisingly this isn't the case. In fact, form composer deals don't even have a set date unless you insist on one. For years, the studios simply had a phrase that said the composer would start and finish whenever the film company decided they wanted him or her to do so. This resulted in composers sometimes being tied up on a film for years at a time, all for a relatively minor fee. As the composers got more sophisticated, they began negotiating periods of time within which the film company could use their services, and if the company wanted them longer, it would have to pay additional amounts. Typically, these terms run somewhere in the range of ten to twelve weeks, if the companies will give any term at all. Some companies still refuse, especially at the higher prices.

Exclusivity. Composer deals used to be exclusive throughout the term (meaning you can't do anything else during that time), but now are more commonly **first priority,** which means you can take other work as long as you don't short-change this film while doing it. In fact, some are even **nonexclusive** (which means you can do anything else you want, as long as you perform on time). However, even the most liberal deals require the composer to be exclusive from **spotting** through recording. *Spotting* means there has been a final cut of the film, and the composer and director have sat down and determined precisely which "spots" need music, and the precise length of each piece of music needed (measured in tenths of seconds). (I was surprised to learn that a change of even one second in a scene may require a total rewrite of the music for that scene. This is because a well-written score moves precisely with the action on screen, and even a slight variance throws everything off. It's like a marching band doing an extra half-step between beats.)

Payment Schedule. Normally composers get their fees in either thirds or fourths. If it's in thirds, you will usually get one-third upon spotting, one-third upon commencement of recording, and one-third upon completion of services. If you're paid in fourths, expect one-fourth upon spotting, one-fourth on commencement of recording, one-fourth on completion of recording, and the balance on completion of services. Completion of recording is almost always the same as completion of services, but occasionally you have to stick around and help with dubbing the recording into the picture, editing for the soundtrack album, sweeping the floor, etc.

Orchestrations. It may surprise you to know that many composers don't have the ability to write musical parts for each instrument in their orchestras. (Indeed, some composers don't even read music, although this is rare. These guys are known in the trade as "hummers.") Most of us think of composers as John Williams, who is obviously a premiere orchestral conductor and arranger, and who understands the subtleties of every instrument. However, many composers are musicians who write only the melody line for the underscore. This melody line is then given to an **orchestrator,** who is someone that takes the melody and writes out the parts for the trumpets, oboes, clarinets, violins, etc. Next time you see a film, look for the orchestrator's credit buried among the assistants, makeup people, grips, and gaffers (whatever they are).

Orchestrators are not just used by composers incapable of writing their own instrumental parts. Quite the contrary, virtually all composers use orchestrators, if for no other reason than to save the time and/or tedium of mechanically doing it themselves. Often, however, classically trained composers sketch out the parts pretty thoroughly, and the orchestrator then becomes more of a copyist. (By the way, I know of one situation where a composer, under extreme time pressure to finish a film before its release date, hired three orchestrators at the same time to crank out the parts.)

The orchestrator is of course paid for his or her services, usually at union scale. Scale for orchestrators varies with the size of the orchestra and number of pages of music. As a rough guideline, at the time of this writing, the price for *simple* orchestrations is roughly $400 per minute of music (e.g., 30 minutes is $12,000), while complex orchestrations can exceed $30,000 for a film.

It's an important aspect of negotiation whether or not your composer's fee includes orchestrations. Even if the film company knows you aren't capable of doing this job, you may be responsible for paying the orchestrator out of your fee. Conversely, you may be perfectly capable of doing orchestrations but (a) your time doesn't permit it, or (b) you want to do the orchestrations only if you're paid additional money to do so. If the film company agrees your composer's fee doesn't include orchestrations, you have to negotiate how much the company will pay for them. Usually it's the actual cost, with a cap on both (1) the amount "per page" (meaning what can be paid for each page of orchestrated parts) and (2) the total orchestration fees. For example, your composer's fee might be $100,000, plus the cost of orchestrations at union scale, provided the total for orchestrations can't exceed $10,000. (If it does, you pay.) If you don't raise this issue, the film company will include orchestrations as a part of your fee.

Record Royalties. A film composer, being a songwriter and not a performer, doesn't automatically get record royalties. These royalties are paid for two distinct services, which may (but may not) be performed by the composer: (a) conducting the orchestra; and/or (b) producing the recordings.

Conducting Royalties. As to conducting, the composer becomes (in a sense) a recording artist when he or she leads the orchestra. The customary range of these royalties is 5% to 8% of retail, pro-rated on the number of cuts (see page 173 for a discussion of pro-ration) and further pro-rated for royalty artists on any particular cut (see page 174 for a discussion of joint recordings). However, if you don't conduct the orchestra, or if you conduct for the film but the selection is re-recorded by someone else for the record, you won't get any record royalties.

Producing Royalties. If you produce the recordings (see page 133 for what producing is), you can get 2% to 3% of retail. (Note this is independent of conducting royalties; you can produce even if you don't conduct, or vice versa.) Like other producer royalties, at many studios these can be retroactive to record one after recoupment (see page 134 for a discussion of retroactivity). You can usually insist on producing the underscore for records, but composers have had singularly bad luck imposing themselves as producers of *songs*. This is because artists may simply refuse to work with them. The best you can do is say that the film company must use you as the producer of all songs if the artist and record company approve. Sounds great, eh? Unfortunately, it's almost meaningless, because most artists don't want a film composer producing them. (If a composer is a producer of note in his own right, that is of course a different story. For example, Mark Knopfler [of Dire Straits] composed the music for the film *The Princess Bride,* and he would be welcomed as a producer by any artist.)

Floors. Major composers can sometimes get a "floor," meaning that if you do absolutely nothing on the record, you still get a royalty, usually 2% to 3% of retail. This point is relatively easy to get when the album is mostly underscore, but it gets difficult to impossible if you're working on a "music" picture, consisting of a number of pop songs, such as *The Bodyguard, Beverly Hills Cop, Dirty Dancing, Top Gun,* etc. The reason is obvious—the company must pay royalties to a lot of expensive outside artists, and there's no assurance how many score selections you will have on the album (if any) or what part of the royalties will be left over for the composer.

Recoupment. With composers, the record company normally re-coups the kitchen sink—meaning all recording costs and all conversion costs. (Conversion costs are discussed on page 390.) With more bargaining power, you can make part or all of the recording costs nonrecoupable, but you'll still be charged with conversion costs.

Credit.

- *Credit in the Film.* Composers normally get main title, single-card credit. (See page 387 for a discussion of film credits.)
- *Paid Ads.* Major composers can usually get credit in paid ads. (See page 397 about paid ads.)
- *Soundtrack Album Credit.* Composer credit on soundtrack albums is a hot issue. As we discussed, the composer isn't really an "artist"—he or she only wrote the music, and maybe conducted it or produced the record. Thus, it isn't a foregone conclusion that the composer will get credit on the soundtrack album. So you gotta ask.

    You should ideally try to get credit on the front cover, but the film company will argue (correctly) that it doesn't control this—it's up to the soundtrack album record company. So you'll probably end up with a commitment for the film company to use its "reasonable efforts" to get you front-cover credit.

    Whether you get front-cover credit also depends on the nature of the album. If it's a compilation of songs by major artists, you're not likely to get credit on the front cover—bluntly, your name won't sell as many records as the names of the artists. However, if it's purely a score album, with only your music, front-cover credit shouldn't be too difficult. If you do get it, insist on tying your credit to the size of the title of the film (100% or 50% of the title size, for example).

    You should always insist (and the film company should have no trouble agreeing) that you get credit on the back cover of the album.

Travel Expenses. It's not uncommon for composers to have to travel (for example, to England, Ireland, Germany, or Canada, where it may be cheaper to record). In this case, you should negotiate for reimbursement of your expenses. On a high-class, big-budget picture, this should be first-class travel, plus something in the neighborhood of $2,000 to $2,500 per week to pay for your hotel and meals. Expect slightly less if you're not going to an expensive city. For low-budget flicks, you'll get Greyhound tickets and Motel 6 vouchers.

    If you're going to a foreign country, it's important to get your expense money in the local currency, as you don't want to be in the business of speculating whether the dollar is going to be worth more or less than the peso. For example, suppose your London hotel room costs £100 per night, which at the time of your deal is $150. If your deal is $150 per night in dollars, and if the dollar drops against the pound so that your $150 only equals £90, you're in trouble. The room is £100, but you only get £90 for your $150. So you'll be coming up £10 short. But if instead your deal says you get £100, you're covered.

PACKAGE DEALS

There is a trend in recent years for some composers to do **package** deals, especially for television composers. A "package" is very much like a "fund" in record deals (see page 111 for a discussion of funds). In other words, the composer agrees to deliver a completed score for a set fee, and the fee includes both the compensation for the composer's services and the costs of the score. Not surprisingly, most package deals are done by composers who create "electronic" scores. By this I mean a small number of musicians (sometimes only the composer) create the music on a synthesizer (which of course these days can sound like the Academy of St. Martin in the Field).

Package Prices

The range of payment for packages can be anywhere from $50,000 for a low-budget film up to $900,000 plus for a mainstream feature. At the high end, there is a recent trend for major composers to take their standard fee (see page 398 for the range), plus an additional $100,000 to $150,000 or so to deliver a packaged electronic score. In these deals, there may also be a budget for nonelectronic score (like an orchestra) in addition to the package price. At the other end of the scale, I've seen starving composers do low-budget film scores for a $5,000 to $10,000 package price. In this case I always try to keep the publishing, and sometimes I can keep the soundtrack album as well. At the very least, you should get a nice chunk of the income from publishing and records, since you're taking so little up front.

Exclusions

If you're going to make a package deal, you have to worry about exactly what's in the package. Most contracts just require you to deliver "all music," and the trick becomes negotiating what *isn't* going to be included. This turns out not to be such an easy question, and by the courtesy of my friend Michael Gorfaine (one of the most experienced film music agents in the business), I bring you the following list of exclusions:

Licensing of Outside Music (i.e., songs not written by the composer). Since most contracts say you must provide "all music," I've seen film companies license an expensive outside tune and expect the composer to pay for it. You can't control the costs of outside songs (indeed, one license could eat half your package fee), so *never* agree to this.

Re-use Fees. (See page 390 for a discussion of these babies.) Not your problem.

Re-scoring. This is one of the most important and trickiest areas. The concept is to save your rear end in situations where the director tells you he wants bands of angels accompanying his scene, which you record and deliver, only to have him decide later he really meant heavy metal. In other words, if the film people require you to re-record for reasons totally beyond your control (as opposed to your screwup), it should be on them.

Lyricist Expenses. If the producer wants to hire a lyricist to write words to your music, it should be on his or her nickel.

Vocalist Expenses. As with lyricists, if the company wants somebody to croon your newly created song, the company should pay.

Music Editor Fees. The music editor's fee should be a film cost, not a package cost. A **music editor** is to film music what a film editor is to film. In other words, this is the technical person responsible for getting all the music in the right places. He or she will create the **spotting notes** (which are detailed notes, down to a tenth of a second, as to where music goes), help with any technical difficulties, edit music to fit a scene if the film has been cut, etc.

Mag Stock and Transfer Costs. **Mag stock** is the actual soundtrack imprinted on the film, and **transfer costs** are the costs of transferring the music from audiotape to the film. The purpose of this exclusion is to clarify that you only have to deliver a standard audiotape, and that the cost of putting this taped music into the film is a motion picture, and not a package, cost.

Pre-records. This is music recorded before shooting, to be lip-synched or danced to in the film. (We'll discuss this further on page 414.) Include the cost of pre-records only if it's specifically negotiated up front.

Payroll Service. This is a service that handles all the mechanics of hiring and paying musicians, which is more complicated than it sounds. Both unions and the federal government require the employer (you) to file forms, and you have to pay union pension and welfare contributions, employer payroll tax deposits, etc. All in all, these chores fall under the category of "pain in the rear," and so the payroll services developed. For a fee, they'll gladly take over your burdens. Who pays their fee is the question.

Sidelining. This is a situation where a musician either gets on camera and pretends to perform, or actually performs. Film companies have been known to charge the cost of this against the package, which again is a matter of negotiation if it's applicable.

Excess Musicians. It's a great idea to limit the number of musicians you can be required to supply. For a package, this is usually small—in the range of four or five at the most. The limit gives you ammunition to ask for more money if the director has a sudden attack of orchestra-itis.

Any of the above exclusions may be included in your package if it's negotiated up front and you budget for it. But be sure they're only in there when you expect them, or you may be paying the film company for the privilege of using your music.

TELEVISION COMPOSERS

Television composers live in a different world from the film composers. The time to compose and deliver is shorter because, as I'm sure you know, television programs are knocked out like pancakes right before they go on the air. Also, the budgets to produce TV shows are substantially lower than those for motion pictures, and so the music budgets (being a piece of this smaller pie) get squashed down along with everything else. Thus, the composer's fees and the money available for recording costs are much less than for theatrical films. The good news is that, even though the fees are low, the performance monies generated by television programs can be substantial—much more than for films—because programs may be shown over and over, forever. And remember (from page 230) that you get performance monies each time your music is played on television. (By the way, when I say shown "forever," I really mean "forever." My kids watch some of the same shows I did when I was a kid, although they think the old Superman half-hours are stupid. I loved them.)

Background Score

Because of the short time frame and lower budgets, television music is tailor-made for electronic score packagers (the folks who get an all-in amount that includes both their fee and the recording costs, as we discussed on page 403). And in fact, most television deals are packages. Typical package fees (which include recording costs) are around $5,000 to $7,500 for a half-hour television episode, $10,000 to $17,500 for a one-hour program, and $20,000 to $45,000 for a two-hour movie of the week.

If the deal is done on a fee basis (meaning the television production company pays the recording costs and the composer gets a separate fee), look for about $1,500 to $4,500 for half-hours, $3,500 to $5,750 for one-hours, and $17,000 to $35,000 for two-hour movies. Often, but not always, orchestration fees (see page 399 for what those are) are on top of these fees, and if so, the orchestration costs are capped, generally between $2,000 and $5,000. Orchestrations are always included in package fees.

If you want to give somebody a good chuckle, just ask the TV people if you can have a piece of the publishing. In the television industry, the producer's commandment to hold on to publishing is not just carved in stone, it's tattooed across their foreheads.

The other deal points to raise are the payment schedule (usually 50% on commencement of services and 50% on completion), songwriter and record royalties which are the same as motion picture composers' (see page 396 and page 401), and credit (you want main title, separate card, which you can usually get for two-hour movies, but you'll probably have to settle for end-title crawl on half-hours and one-hours; see page 387 for what all this means).

TV Themes

Composers sometimes write just the main title theme for a television show. Fees for this can be around $30,000 for very well-known writers, and about $10,000 to $20,000 for lesser-knowns. If the song has lyrics, the fee is split with the lyricist. And don't forget the huge performance monies that may come rolling in.

Sometimes TV themes are done as a package, meaning that the amount includes both the fee and the recording costs (we discussed this concept on page 403). In this case, a typical price is in the range of $15,000 to $30,000, sometimes up to $100,000-plus for a superstar.

If you're a big name or firmly established composer, themes are the one place you can sometimes get a piece of the publishing. If you do, it's 25% to 50% max, and all the considerations that apply to splitting publishing on songs apply (see page 270).

If you're on the *Advanced Overview Track*,
go to the conclusion, on page 421.
Experts: Onward . . .

32

Licensing Existing Recordings and Existing Songs for Motion Pictures

This chapter deals with licensing existing records and songs (records and songs not created for the film). Unless you're a record or film company, you'll only be involved in these deals as a secondary player. By "secondary player," I mean you're not directly involved in the deal—the primary players are your record company and the film company, who make a deal with each other. The money is paid to your record company, who promptly pockets half and treats the balance as artist royalties under your deal. If your record company agreement says they need your consent to license records for a film (see page 160), they'll call up and ask for your consent. If the record company doesn't need your consent, they may not even call you, although most will as a courtesy. (By the way, even if you don't have the right to consent in your record deal, but you wrote the song and control the publishing, you can block the deal—remember, the right to use the master recording is only the right to use the physical recording itself. The record company can't give the film company the right to use the musical composition [they don't have these rights], and so the film company has to contact both the record company *and* the publisher to get a full set of rights. Thus, if you're the publisher, you have the right to control the deal through the side door even if you don't have it through the front door. Another good reason to keep control of your publishing.)

Because you'll be asked to consent to these deals, and because you share in the income, you should know how they work. Let's take a look.

MASTER LICENSES

The record company–film company master license deal consists of three main elements:

- How much is the fee to synchronize the master in the film?
- If the master is also going on a soundtrack album, what's the royalty?
- Who pays the re-use fees? (For an explanation of re-use fees, see page 390.)

Let's examine each in order:

Master License Fees

The fee varies directly with how important the song is in its own right (was it a number-one single, or an obscure album cut?), and how it's used in the film (is it in the background on a radio for ten seconds, so that you need a radar detector to even know it's in the film, or is it played in its entirety, with action on screen following the lyrics, so that it takes on a dramatic content and moves the story forward?). Obviously, there are all shades of variations in between these, and sometimes it's just a question of how much the producer has fallen in love with this particular cut.

Theatrical Films. For theatrical motion pictures, the range is anywhere from a low of $5,000 to a high of $150,000 for a well-known song. For a title song that is also the title of the film it can go as high as $150,000 to $200,000 or more. The most common range, however, is from about $10,000 on the low end to about $40,000 on the high end (unless it's a title track, in which case it can run to perhaps $75,000). These fees also include a buyout of all rights to use the recording in any media, such as theaters, television, home video, etc. Although the publisher of a musical composition may receive additional compensation for these other usages (see page 412), it's not customary for the owner of the master recording to do so.

Television Programs. For television licenses (meaning the license is to use the recording in a television program, as opposed to a theatrical film), the fees are substantially lower and usually broken into a bundle of rights. The fees again vary with how it's used and the importance of the song. For the right to broadcast the program on **free** (as opposed to **pay** or **basic cable**) television, fees can run from as little as $500 to as high as perhaps $7,500 for full usages in an important movie of the week. The normal range is about $1,500 to $2,500, and sometimes more for featured songs. **Free television,** as you might guess, is over-the-air broadcast TV that you can receive free. **Basic cable** means stations you get free when you're a cable subscriber (like CNN, WTBS, MTV, etc.); they have commercials and are advertiser supported. **Pay television** is a service for which you pay a separate monthly fee, such as HBO, Showtime, etc.

The production entity will want an option to exercise the following rights in addition to free television (the amounts quoted are not hard and fast rules):

1. Foreign theatrical. Movies shown on television in our country are often released in theaters outside the United States. This triggers an additional payment of about $5,000 to $10,000, depending on the use. Note this could be more than the original fee.
2. Home video. If the television program is ever released in home video, there's an additional payment of about $3,500 to $6,500.
3. Pay television. If the program turns up on pay television, the company pays about the same as the original fee.
4. Basic cable. About the same as the original fee.

At first glance this looks like the record company is getting more money for television (with multiple fees) than for theatrical films (where there is only one fee). But in fact the television production entities save money. First of all, the numbers are smaller to begin with. Secondly, instead of paying a large price for a total buyout, they're paying a small price for only the rights they know they'll need, and merely taking an option for the rest. Thus, they only have to pay for what they use.

Royalties

If the deal also grants record rights, the range of royalties is typically 11% to 13% of retail, pro rata (see page 173 for what *pro-rata* means). Again, if your master is the key master in the album (meaning, for example, it's the only song in an album of underscore, or it's the only hit in an album of otherwise minor artists or obscure songs), then your royalty should be higher. You can usually get a **favored nations** treatment for the master (meaning no one gets a higher royalty), at least insofar as other *existing* masters are concerned. (The film company usually wants the right to pay more royalties on recordings created for the film.)

Also, if you have an important master, you can sometimes get a **floor**, meaning that no matter how many tracks on the album, the royalty will be no less than $\frac{1}{10}$ of the total royalty (or $\frac{1}{11}$ or $\frac{1}{12}$, depending on your negotiating power). For example, if you had a 10% royalty and a floor of $\frac{1}{10}$, you'd get 1% on the album even if there were 14 masters. Without the floor, you'd get $\frac{1}{14}$ of 10%, or .07%. Usually the floor is merely stated as a royalty rate, such as "10% pro-rata, with a 1% non-pro-rata floor."

Recoupment. Since there are no recording costs, the only things that can be recoupable are the union re-use fees (see page 390), and this too is negotiable. The fee paid to use the recording in the film or television program should *not* be recoupable under any circumstances.

Other Master License Deal Points

The other deal points are about consent: the AFM (American Federation of Musicians) and you.

AFM Consent. There is an obscure rule in the AFM labor agreement that requires not only the payment of re-use fees, but also the *consent* of the AFM to put existing masters in a motion picture or television program. The theory is that the union won't put musicians out of work (i.e., by not requiring a new recording session) unless it's such a unique master that a new recording won't do justice to the film. An example would be a Buddy Holly master, which obviously can't be duplicated, since Buddy Holly isn't available. In actual practice, however, I've never seen the union object to any licensing—in fact, this rule is almost always ignored and no one even asks. If you do ask, their consent is a rubber stamp.

Should You Consent? Remember, the above is the deal between your record company and the film company, and you're not directly involved. But once the deal gets underway, the record company will call up your manager and ask if you'll consent to the use of your master in a particular film. How do you evaluate this?

On the financial side, you should review the deal and decide if you think it's fair. The above criteria should give you a pretty good feeling for it. If that sounds OK, then proceed to the next step, which is just as important as checking the financial terms, but often overlooked: You should find out precisely what's going on in the film when your song is being played. I have avoided a number of disasters with this simple question. For example, I once found that a film company wanted to use a recording of one of my clients during a scene in which a number of kids were shooting drugs. Or perhaps it's a graphic sexual sequence (which, depending on your image, could be a plus). Remember, it's your music and your career, so be careful about the creative aspects.

LICENSING EXISTING MUSICAL COMPOSITIONS FOR FILMS

As we discussed above, the money paid to use a master recording goes to your record company. This means two things:

1. Right off the top, they get half of it.
2. If you're unrecouped, you never see the other half.

Not at all an appetizing proposition. But remember the film also needs a synchronization license for the *song* in the master. So if you wrote the song and own the publishing, they now need to make a deal directly with you, and this side of the equation looks entirely different: You keep all the money. No minor distinction.

Fees

Licenses for the song look very much like licenses for the master recordings, and indeed the fees are often similar. Thus, the range of fees for the master recordings set forth on page 409 can be used for the songs as well.

However, it's not always a good idea to just blindly license your song for the same price the record company quoted for the master. For one thing, the record company may have other masters in the motion picture, or may have other deals with this film company at the same time. Thus, the film company may be getting a "package" price, as to which you are only a small part. (This is not to suggest there's anything illegitimate about this practice, but it does mean you should do your own evaluation before accepting their figures.) Or it may be the composition is a very important one, but the master recording involved might not be (especially if the artist isn't you). In any event, make your own quote, independent of the record company, and ignore the film company's whining that your song is costing more than they're paying for the master. I've been known to say, when the film company complains the package price for the master/publishing is too high, that they should go back and reduce the price of the master. For a nice guy, I can be pretty cold at times.

Home Video

If you can avoid a home video buyout, and instead opt for an advance against a royalty, by all means do so. This is becoming increasingly harder to get, as more and more film companies are simply refusing. However, if they're hot enough for your song, you can sometimes get a **rolling fee** instead of a royalty. (Not all companies will do this— many will just pass on your song.) A rolling fee is a sort of disguised royalty that allows the film company to save face, and it works like this:

The film company prepays you for the right to use your song in *x* home video units (say 250,000). At such time as sales exceed 250,000, they pay you for another 50,000 units. If sales exceed 300,000, you get a fee for the next 50,000, and so forth. As you can see, this arrangement is really a royalty—in fact, it's better than a royalty, because you get paid on units not yet sold. However, it appeals to the film companies that use it because they don't have to call it a royalty.

A few film companies will actually give you a royalty, which hovers in the range (for U.S. sales) of 4% of wholesale, prorated on the playing time of the music in the film. Foreign royalties are handled by the local mechanical rights societies in each territory (see page 239).

FILM MUSIC QUIZ

You are the representative of an independent film company, which is producing a teenage motion picture. The music supervisor called Capitol Records and got a license to use the Beatles recording "She Loves You" in the film, for a payment of $10,000. The license is fully signed, the money has been paid to Capitol, and the master is recorded in the film.

Assuming you're now aware of everything that has been done with respect to this situation, are there any problems in going forward and distributing the film? If so, what?

Answer to quiz:

They haven't licensed the *song* for the film, only the recording. Thus they can't use the track until they make a deal with the publisher. (See page 238 if you want a refresher.)

33

Music Supervisors

Music supervisors are a relatively new breed of individual that didn't exist until about 1980. Now they're in widespread use, and are always hired for a film that has music as a major element.

ROLE

The music supervisor's job, as the title implies, is to coordinate all the music for a picture. He or she first sits down with the producer and director to work out the types of music needed, ideally before production. If the film is either a musical or relies heavily on music (such as a dance film), the music supervisor *must* be involved in advance. This is because songs performed on camera must be **pre-recorded,** meaning they're made in a recording studio before commencement of photography of the film (and merely lip-synched or danced to on film). As you can imagine, it's difficult to dance to a song not yet recorded.

Actually, I was once involved in a situation where the opposite happened. A dance scene had been shot to a specific composition, but after the film was finished, the writer of the song refused to make a deal with the film company, and the song had to be scrapped. A client of mine then wrote a new song for the dance sequence (obviously having to match the beat precisely), which ended up being a number-one hit.

After meeting with the director and producer, the music supervisor comes up with suggestions for artists, composers, songwriters, etc., for the film. The director and producer make the final decisions, and the supervisor then oversees the whole process of making it happen. He or she contacts the creative people, arranges for meetings with the film personnel, negotiates and structures the deals (or oversees the negotiation and structuring, depending on the supervisor and the film company), and supervises the recording sessions.

Done properly, being a music supervisor is one of the most difficult jobs on the planet earth. You start out with a number of strikes against you. First of all, other than pre-recorded music (which we discussed above, and which is a tiny minority), most of the music can't be finalized until the film is complete. (See page 399 for why.) The studio has millions of dollars riding on the fact that a film must be released on a specific date, and music is at best considered a minor element in the overall production, even if it's a central element in the film. (The cost of a *major* music budget is maybe $1,500,000, while most major studio films are $30 million to $35 million, not to mention multi-millions for advertising and marketing. And a more typical music budget is about $500,000 to $800,000. Moreover, most studio executives [with a few outstanding exceptions] do not understand music nearly as well as they understand films (which is why they're film executives instead of music executives). This can make it very difficult to conclude a deal—the executives think the prices and rights demanded by the music people are outrageous (which they often are), and they have no patience for the complexity of a bunch of little deals. Remember, each piece of music in a film can represent five deals (see page 383 for what they are), and because music comes in last, complicated deals have to be made under enormous time pressure, which increases the likelihood of mistakes geometrically. It is the music supervisor's job to keep all these diverse, competing interests satisfied, and to ensure a happy ending.

Now that I've painted this bleak picture, let me say that good music supervisors are worth their weight in gold. They call on their relationships to get favors and smooth out difficult situations, thereby putting music into pictures that couldn't be there any other way. Music supervisors are in a sense "marriage brokers." They creatively marry music and films, which is no easy process, as well as marry the two industries on a business level (which is even more difficult). For this reason, the top ones are paid handsomely.

FEES AND ROYALTIES

By handsomely, I mean that the upper-level music supervisors get fees of $100,000 to $200,000 per picture (sometimes even more), and the majority fall in the range of $75,000 to $125,000. The top supervisors also have royalties on the soundtrack album, usually in the range of 1% to 2% of retail. A recent major supervisor deal I did was a $150,000 fee, with a royalty of 1% retail, escalating to 2% of retail for U.S. sales over 500,000 albums.

34

Soundtrack Album Deals

As an artist, you have nothing to do with soundtrack album deals—not even consent or consultation (other than, as we discussed, the fact that the deals can't be made without your record company's clearance). Soundtrack album deals are made between the film company and a record company to put out the album, and in a sense are "none of your business." However, they affect the types of deals you can make with the film company, and so you should know about them.

Once the film company has acquired the bundle of rights we discussed in chapters 28 through 32, they turn them over to a record company to put out a soundtrack album. There are two broadly defined types of soundtrack albums—*score albums* and *song albums*—and the type you're dealing with radically impacts the deal.

SCORE ALBUMS

A score album is an album wholly of underscore (i.e., with no songs), usually because there is only underscore in the film. Unless there is something extraordinary about the score (for example, if the composer is a star in his or her own right as a recording artist, or if the film looks like it's going to be huge), the soundtrack album deal is relatively modest. The reason is simple—underscore albums usually don't sell very well (15,000 to 30,000 copies or so). Many record companies aren't interested in this product at all, and will only put out a score album if someone forces them. (For example, a film company owned by the same parent company as the record company may force them to take an album just to satisfy the ego of a film producer or star.) Assuming someone is interested, the deal for pure score albums is usually an advance equal to the re-use fees, and sometimes there is no advance at all (which means the film company has to pay the re-use fees). (For a discussion of re-use fees, see page 390.) The royalty on these albums also tends to be lower than for the song albums, usually in the range of 16% to 18% of retail.

SONG ALBUMS

At the other end of the spectrum is an album of songs by major artists, particularly songs that (a) are completed before the soundtrack album deal (so the record company can hear them), and (b) sound like hits. For these albums, the price escalates dramatically. In fact, some soundtrack albums, if they're extraordinarily hot, can command advances of $750,000 or more. More commonly, the advances are in the range of $250,000 to $400,000, or perhaps as high as $500,000 if the record company is frothing at the mouth and there's a bidding war going on. (These prices include re-use fees.) The royalty on song albums is also higher, usually in the range of 18% of retail, and sometimes with escalations to 19% and 20% at sales levels of, say, 1 million and 2 million albums (U.S.).

Often, however, these deals are made before the music is actually in existence. Depending on what everyone believes the music will be, and to a large degree depending on the reputation of the film producer (and the producer's prior history with soundtrack albums), the advances can still be quite high. In these situations, the record company may require a certain number of "gold" or "platinum" artists be included on the album, and the advance may vary depending on this. Here's a deal one of my film company clients made for a major "hot" film:

The advance for the album was $350,000, including re-use. If there was a platinum artist on the album and the company got the right to put out a single of that artist (see page 392 for a discussion of singles in soundtrack deals), the advance increased by $75,000. If there were additional platinum artists, with single rights, it increased by an additional $50,000 for each one. If there was a gold artist with single rights, the advance increased by $25,000 per gold artist. In no event could the total advance exceed $600,000 (including re-use).

NONFINANCIAL ISSUES

There are other issues which are of major concern in these deals:

Release Timing

The record has to be released in coordination with the film. The film company wants maximum promotion for its film, and the record company wants maximum promotion for its record, all from the cross-advertising and cross-marketing of the film and album, radio play of the record, etc. Thus, both sides are extraordinarily touchy about delivery and release dates. Both the film company and the record company want a single out approximately six weeks ahead of the film, and they want the album released about two to four weeks ahead. This allows the single and album to gather steam by the time the film is out. The major reason for blowing this ideal timing is usually the film company not having the recordings ready, or not having the film artwork ready, or some combination thereof. However, the record company may have problems getting records manufactured and released for reasons unrelated to the film, such as a number of their major artists delivering albums about the same time as the soundtrack album. Accordingly, the release date and balancing these competing interests are all part of the negotiation.

Film Release

The record company wants a guaranteed release of the film. They argue (quite rightly) that their album isn't worth much without a film to go with it. Film companies are very reluctant to do this, since they never give it to any of their actors, producers, directors, etc. For some film companies, it's an absolute no-no. For others, they'll work out some compromise, such as a minimum number of theaters.

Who Owns the Masters?

There are obviously two choices: the film company or the record company. The film company argues that it paid for them, and thus it should own them. The record company argues that the advance it pays under the soundtrack album deal pays for the masters, and thus the record company should own them. The record companies are particularly touchy when the master is recorded by one of their exclusive artists; they can't stand the idea of someone else owning that recording.

The actual ownership is not as important as who controls what rights, but for many companies it's a "religious issue." There is no reason why there can't be some split ownership—the film company owns the recordings for the film and other nonrecord rights, while the record company owns them for phonograph records—which I've done on occasion. On the other hand, many record companies insist on owning the masters and licensing them back to the filmmaker, while film companies insist on owning them and licensing them to the record company. Compromises run all over the map, but most often the record company owns the masters and licenses them back to the film company.

To me, the real issue in all of this is who controls the masters outside the area of the film, the soundtrack album, and singles. This covers such things as synchronization rights (for other films, television programs, commercials, etc.), and usages on phonograph records (other than the soundtrack album and singles), like K-Tel repackages, the artist's albums, etc. Both sides have legitimate arguments, and the answer is just one of bargaining power. However, regardless of who ends up with the ownership and control, most film companies will insist (and most record companies will agree) that the film company has ultimate control over licensing the masters for usage in other films, television programs, etc. The record companies are sensitive to the fact that these usages could dilute the film company's right to have the song identified exclusively with their movie.

Related to the issue of control is the question of who gets the money from usages outside the film and records. If the record company ends up with the rights, then the monies are split between it and the film company (or credited to the film company's account if unrecouped). If the film company keeps the rights, then it usually keeps the money (but not always).

Videos

Who makes the videos and how are the costs recouped? Is the film company supplying footage without additional charge? Will the film company pay for part of the videos?

Credit

What type of credit will the record company have in the film? Will it be in film ads as well as on screen? What credit will the film company get on the records and in record company ads?

Advertising

Will either company guarantee advertising of the album and/or the film?

Marketing

Will the film company pay any money for marketing, promotion, etc.? Will the record company?

Conclusion

This concludes the informational portion of our program.

Congratulations! Whichever track you took through the book, you now have a better overview of the music business than 98% of your colleagues (or at least 97.63%). Despite my informal style of writing, the material in this book is very compact, and there's a lot of information. So you've learned much more than you may think. In fact, you now have everything you need to go as far as your music and drive will take you, without being pillaged and plundered along the way (or at least you can only get zapped with your eyes open).

To get the most from this book, keep it handy as a reference. It was important for you to read it through as a solid framework on which to build, but it will be even more valuable as you apply it to specific situations in your life. When you get involved in a particular deal, look up that section and read it again. Seeing it for the second time, you'll pick up things you might have missed before. And they'll be far more meaningful to you in practice than they were in theory. It's like reading a book on flying when you're home in bed, and then reading it again just before you pilot an airplane. Now you're ready for takeoff, so—

Go get 'em!

Index

About the Author

DONALD S. PASSMAN is a Phi Beta Kappa graduate of the University of Texas, and a cum laude graduate of Harvard Law School. He lives in Los Angeles with his wife and four children, and practices law with the firm of Gang, Tyre, Ramer, and Brown, Inc.

After initially practicing tax law, Don has specialized in the music business intensively for over twenty years. His clients include major entertainers, publishers, record companies, songwriters, industry executives, film companies, managers, producers, and other participants in the music industry. Don is listed in *The Best Lawyers in America*, and has lectured extensively on the subject of the music industry, including teaching a course at the University of Southern California Law School's Advanced Professional Program, and lecturing for the UCLA Entertainment Law Symposium, Harvard Law School, the American Bar Association, the Practicing Law Institute, the USC Entertainment Law Institute, and the Los Angeles Copyright Society.

Don's hobbies include real estate investment, guitar, five-string banjo, weight-lifting, chess, ham radio, magic, dog training, and karate. He is a licensed real estate broker, a magician member of The Magic Castle, a dog obedience trainer with degrees in the United States and Mexico, and the highest possible amateur radio licensee (Amateur Extra), all because he is a bit weird and enjoys taking tests.

Don has also been active in community and charitable activities, including acting as president of the Music Industry Division, and sitting on the national board of The City of Hope; as a Trustee of the Artists' Rights Foundation; as vice-president for the Center for Early Education; and as a Federation Chief in the YMCA Indian Guides Program (presiding over three hundred father and child Indian braves and princesses).

He is currently writing a fiction book, which you are all required to buy.